CW01261196

NETWORKS OF EMPIRE

Kerry Ward argues that the Dutch East India Company empire manifested itself through multiple networks that amalgamated spatially and over time into an imperial web whose sovereignty was effectively created and maintained but always partial and contingent. *Networks of Empire* proposes that early modern empires consisted of durable networks of trade, administration, settlement, legality, and migration whose regional circuits and territorially and institutionally based nodes of regulatory power operated not only on land and sea but discursively as well. Rights of sovereignty were granted to the Company by the States General in the United Provinces. Company directors in Europe administered the exercise of sovereignty by Company servants in its chartered domain. The empire developed in dynamic response to challenges waged by individuals and other sovereign entities operating within the Indian Ocean grid. By closely examining the Dutch East India Company's network of forced migration, this book explains how empires are constituted through the creation, management, contestation, devolution, and reconstruction of these multiple and intersecting fields of partial sovereignty.

Dr. Kerry Ward is currently Associate Professor of World History at Rice University. She has a PhD from the University of Michigan, an MA from the University of Cape Town, and a BA from the University of Adelaide. She has published in the fields of comparative slavery and forced migration, comparative imperialism and colonialism, Indian Ocean history, South African and Southeast Asian history, historical memory, and public history in South Africa.

STUDIES IN COMPARATIVE WORLD HISTORY

Editors

Michael Adas, *Rutgers University*

Philip D. Curtin, *The Johns Hopkins University*

Other Books in the Series

Michael Adas, *Prophets of Rebellion: Millenarian Protest Movements Against the European Colonial Order* (1979)

Philip D. Curtin, *Cross-Cultural Trade in World History* (1984)

Leo Spitzer, *Lives in Between: Assimilation and Marginality in Austria, Brazil, and West Africa, 1780–1945* (1989)

Philip D. Curtin, *The Rise and Fall of the Plantation Complex: Essays in Atlantic History* (1990; second edition, 1998)

John Thornton, *Africa and Africans in the Making of the Atlantic World, 1400–1800* (1992; second edition, 1998)

Marshall G. S. Hodgson and Edmund Burke III (eds.), *Rethinking World History* (1993)

David Northrup, *Indentured Labor in the Age of Imperialism, 1834–1922* (1995)

Lauren Benton, *Law and Colonial Cultures: Legal Regimes in World History, 1400–1900* (2002)

Victor Lieberman, *Strange Parallels: Southeast Asia in Global Context, c. 800–1830, vol. 1: Integration on the Mainland* (2003)

Networks of Empire

Forced Migration in the Dutch East India Company

KERRY WARD

Rice University

CAMBRIDGE
UNIVERSITY PRESS

CAMBRIDGE UNIVERSITY PRESS
Cambridge, New York, Melbourne, Madrid, Cape Town, Singapore, São Paulo, Delhi

Cambridge University Press
32 Avenue of the Americas, New York, NY 10013-2473, USA

www.cambridge.org
Information on this title: www.cambridge.org/9780521885867

© Kerry Ward 2009

This publication is in copyright. Subject to statutory exception
and to the provisions of relevant collective licensing agreements,
no reproduction of any part may take place without the written
permission of Cambridge University Press.

First published 2009

Printed in the United States of America

A catalog record for this publication is available from the British Library.

Library of Congress Cataloging in Publication Data
Ward, Kerry.
Networks of empire : forced migration in the Dutch East India Company / Kerry Ward.
p. cm. – (Studies in comparative world history)
Includes bibliographical references (p.   ) and index.
ISBN 978-0-521-88586-7
1. Nederlandsche Oost–Indische Compagnie – History.   2. Forced migration – History.
I. Title.   II. Series.
HF483.E6W37   2008
325–dc22   2007046372

ISBN 978-0-521-88586-7 hardback
ISBN 978-0-521-74599-4 African edition paperback

Cambridge University Press has no responsibility for the persistence or
accuracy of URLs for external or third-party Internet Web sites referred to
in this publication and does not guarantee that any content on such Web
sites is, or will remain, accurate or appropriate. Information regarding
prices, travel timetables, and other factual information given in this work
are correct at the time of first printing, but Cambridge University Press
does not guarantee the accuracy of such information thereafter.

In memory of my parents, Jack and Molly Ward, and my godmother, Janis Erica Evans

Contents

List of Maps		*page* xi
Acknowledgments		xiii
1	Networks of Empire and Imperial Sovereignty	1
2	The Evolution of Governance and Forced Migration	49
3	Crime and Punishment in Batavia, circa 1730 to 1750	85
4	The Cape Cauldron: Strategic Site in Transoceanic Imperial Networks	127
5	Company and Court Politics in Java: Islam and Exile at the Cape	179
6	Forced Migration and Cape Colonial Society	239
7	Disintegrating Imperial Networks	283
Bibliography		309
Index		331

List of Maps

1.	VOC Shipping Networks.	*page* xvi
2.	VOC Nodes in the Indian Ocean.	48
3.	VOC Batavia & the Indies Archipelago c. 1750.	84
4.	The Cape Cauldron.	126
5.	Shaykh Yusuf's Indian Ocean Network.	178
6.	The Cape Colony c. 1798.	238

Acknowledgments

Writing a book about networks has helped me to keep in mind that conducting research and writing a book is not always a solitary pursuit. I am eternally grateful for the generosity of family, friends, and colleagues who have accompanied me in this long journey around the Dutch East India Company empire.

Research funding for this book and for the dissertation it was based on came from a number of sources. The University of Michigan International Institute, History Department, Rackham Graduate School, Center for the Education of Women, and Center for Afroamerican and African Studies provided doctoral funding. I was also awarded an International Doctoral Research Fellowship from the Social Science Research Council and a Bernadotte E. Schmitt Grant from the American Historical Association. The William Fehr Collection granted me a museum internship at the Castle of Good Hope. At Rice University, support from the Jon and Paula Mosle Research Award and the History Department helped me turn the dissertation into a book. Any errors in this book are mine alone.

My mentors at the University of Michigan, David William Cohen, Julia Adams, Fred Cooper, and Vic Lieberman, have continued to support my intellectual growth, and I have appreciated continuing conversations with them. Anthony Reid was always encouraging during my time at Australian National University. The World History Association has provided a stimulating forum for thinking globally; thanks especially to Jerry Bentley, Pat Manning, and Anand Yang for comments on my written work. The members of the Houston Area African Studies Group created exciting opportunities for sharing ideas. At Rice, I am indebted to Eva Haverkamp, Moramay Lopez-Alonzo, and Allison Sneider for reading draft chapters of this book. Thanks also to Lauren Benton at NYU, Clifton Crais at Emory, and Peter Dear at Cornell for inviting me to present work to their graduate seminars, and to Eric Tagliacozzo for giving me the opportunity to participate in the Cornell SEAP speaker program.

Colleagues and friends at the University of Cape Town and the University of the Western Cape have been amicable comrades over the years. Particular thanks to those who have commented on my work, including Antonia Malan, Susan Newton-King, Nigel Penn, Gerald Groenewald, Robert Shell, Sandy Rowaldt Shell, Shamil Jeppie, Premesh Lalou, Candy Malherbe, Ciraj Rassool, and Leslie Witz. Lalou Meltzer at Iziko Museums has always shared her creative spark and helped me to think of other avenues for intellectual production. Christopher Saunders and Pam Allen have been wonderful friends and supporters since my undergraduate days.

I am fortunate to have an intersecting network of collegial friendships, including Robert Ross, Steven Pierce, Wayne Dooling, Ruth Watson, Lisa Lindsay, Aims McGuinness, Anu Rao, Lynn Thomas, Dias Pradadimara, Kirsten McKenzie, Clare Anderson, Mike Charney, Atsuko Nano, Henk Niemeijer, Jan-Bart Gewald, Markus Vink, and Jim Ward. Jim Armstrong is still a guiding light to the VOC. Eric Tagliacozzo has been a great mate. Ned Alpers, Gwyn Campbell, and Michael Pearson have generously included me in fascinating discussions about the Indian Ocean. I have probably left a few people off this list, but it is a result of memory lapse and not disregard.

Special thanks are due to the two anonymous reviewers of my manuscript. Their keenness pointed me in the right direction for revisions. I'm very fortunate to have worked with Eric Crahan at Cambridge University Press, who has been a supportive and patient editor. Thanks to Anoop Chaturvedi and Sweety Singh for making this a better book. Eva Garza from the Rice University GIS Data Center kindly spent weeks with me drawing maps. Many librarians and archivists in Cape Town, The Hague, Leiden, and Jakarta have helped in the course of my research. The Cape Archives also gave me permission to reproduce the cover image. For Chapter 4 of this book, I have used material from my chapter "'Tavern of the Seas?' The Cape of Good Hope as an Oceanic Crossroads during the Seventeenth and Eighteenth Centuries," in Jerry Bentley, Renate Bridenthal, and Kären Wigen, eds., *Seascapes: Maritime Histories, Littoral Cultures, and Transoceanic Exchanges*. Honolulu: University of Hawaii Press, 2007.

Martha Chaiklin, Gretchen Elsner-Sommer, Eva Haverkamp, Sheryl McCurdy, Laura Mitchell, Alison Paulin, Allison Sneider, Menuk Sudarsih, Mary Louise Totton, and Merran Welsh have been true struggle sisters. Greg Maddox, Kairn Klieman, Ussama Makdisi, and Elora Shehabuddin continue to make Houston a good place to live.

My family in Australia has always cheered me on and welcomed me home with open arms. I'm especially grateful to my girl-cousins who keep my ties to Oz strong with their love and middle-of-the-night conversations across multiple time zones. Norman Etherington first sparked my curiosity about South Africa. Patricia Sumerling and Robert Martin have been constant in their confidence and companionship. Rosemary and Bob Barker have warmly welcomed me into my new Houston family.

Without Nigel Worden's friendship and inspiration this book would not have been started, let alone finished. Pamela Scully and Clifton Crais lured me to the United States, shared their home and family life with me, and have shown by example how to be a great historian and to live life to the full.

Special thanks go to Colleen O'Neal, who has engaged enthusiastically, energetically, and with incredible insight to this book from the very beginning, when we were graduate students together discussing our research ideas, through to the very end with her contribution in the last few months as editor, mentor, and collaborator in revising and seeing this book to its completion. Colleen got exactly what I wanted to say and helped me say it clearly, concisely, and with conceptual precision. This book would be much the poorer without her contribution.

My final thanks are for my husband, Mack Smith, who now knows more about the Dutch East India Company than he ever dreamed possible and has wholeheartedly read and commented on multiple drafts of this book and proofread the final product. He knows how much his support and encouragement have meant to me. We are both looking forward to exploring new horizons together.

I have dedicated this book to my parents, Jack and Molly Ward, who always let me travel my own path and had unshakable faith that I would find my way in the end. I dearly wish they were alive to see this book come to fruition and to celebrate, but they will always be with me in life's journey.

VOC Shipping Networks

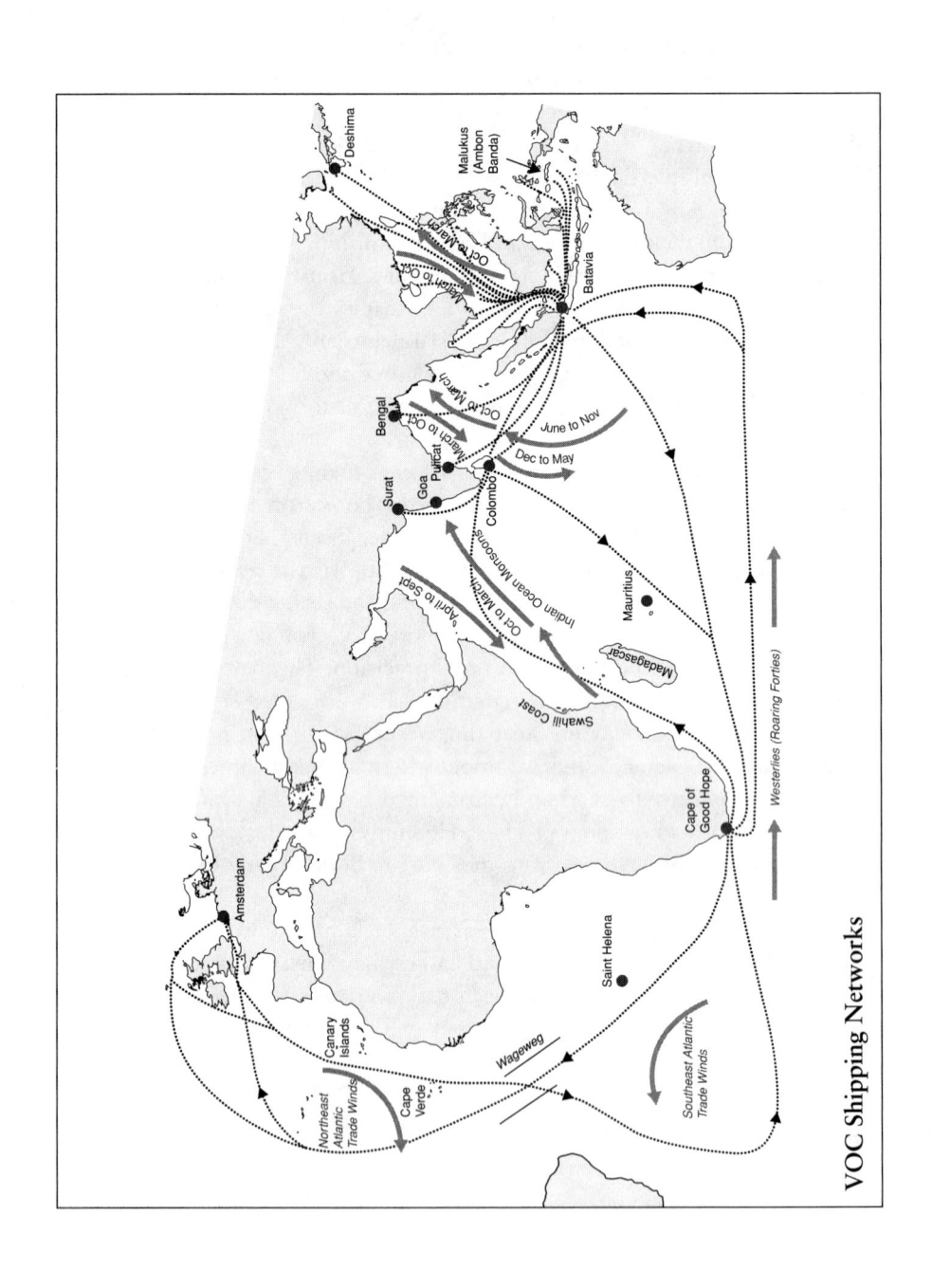

I

Networks of Empire and Imperial Sovereignty

In the Cape Town spring of 1997 one of the twentieth century's greatest heroes and liberators, Nelson Mandela, Nobel Peace Prize winner and the first democratically elected president of South Africa, met with one of the century's greatest tyrants and dictators, General Suharto, President of Indonesia, who came to power after a bloody coup that ushered in over three decades of authoritarian military rule. One official event in Suharto's South African visit involved the two elderly presidents trudging up a steep path of foot-worn stone steps, entourages in tow, leading to an austere white-washed and green-domed shrine where both men paid homage to a shared national hero. Today a plaque on an outside wall of the structure marks the day they stood together on that windy hill overlooking the Cape coast at the tomb of a Muslim saint known locally as Shaykh Yusuf of Makassar, who was exiled from Java by the Dutch East India Company (*Verenigde Oostindische Compagnie* – VOC) and died at the Cape of Good Hope in 1699. Through Shaykh Yusuf, Mandela and Suharto implicitly acknowledged a common colonial past in the VOC empire.[1] Shaykh Yusuf had already been claimed by Mandela to be a forefather of the liberation struggle in South Africa. Suharto had also declared Shaykh

---

[1] The Dutch East India Company, *Verenigde Oostindische Compagnie* (VOC), is correctly translated as the United East India Company. However, the common English usage is the Dutch East India Company, which is used in this book interchangeably with the "Company" and the "VOC." The United Provinces of the Netherlands is referred to as either the United Provinces or the Netherlands. Holland is used to refer specifically to the province, not the whole country. Dutch refers to the Dutch language, the people who originated in the Netherlands, and people in the VOC empire of Dutch descent (unless otherwise specified.) European is the more general term for people from Europe, of European descent, and the ascribed legal category.

Yusuf Tajul Khalwati a National Hero of the Republic of Indonesia.[2] Although the commemoration in 1997 was staged as a public relations exercise that punctuated the more immediately pressing bilateral negotiations taking place between the two leaders and their governments, their coming together through a relatively obscure historical figure brought to the fore the complexities of historical interpretations that forge their respective national pasts.

Almost ten years later, at a lavish formal banquet in the Indonesian State Palace in Jakarta, South Africa's second president, Thabo Mbeki, addressed these same historical links in a toast to the first directly elected president of the Republic of Indonesia, Dr. Susilo Bambang Yudhoyono. The construction of the Istana Negara (state palace), located on Jalan Merdeka (Freedom Road), began in the last years of the VOC and was eventually taken over by the Dutch colonial state as the governor general's official residence. This symbolic bastion of the colonial past no doubt threw the burden of the present into sharp relief that evening. Like Suharto's visit to South Africa, Mbeki's visit to Indonesia marked a first in diplomatic relations between the two nations and was evidence of a political transformation that had taken place within and between both countries. On this occasion President Mbeki chose first to honor Autshumao, a Khoekhoe leader and South Africa's "earliest freedom fighter" who was taken on board an English ship from the Cape to Java in the 1630s and returned only to be later imprisoned on Robben Island by the Dutch after they invaded the Cape in 1652. Having established that indigenous African resistance to European colonialism predated Shaykh Yusuf's exile as a "freedom fighter who fought against Dutch colonialism," Mbeki stressed the role of "unsung heroines and heroes" of the past who were "transported as human cargo to the Cape to serve as slaves to the colonists" and became "builders of our new nation." He further affirmed that the local community in South Africa had built the shrine visited by Mandela and Suharto to honor "Shaykh Yusuf and others who were brought to South Africa against their will" and declared that the site was being designated a national monument.[3]

---

[2] *Cape Times* and other press sources, November 21, 1997. See also *Impact International* 24(6), 1994, p. 10, for Mandela's speech regarding Shaykh Yusuf as a liberation struggle fighter. For a report of Suharto's declaration of Syekh (Shaykh) Yusuf Tajul Khalwati as a national hero see *Kompas* (Jakarta), November 10, 1995.

[3] Thabo Mbeki, "Reply by the President of South Africa, Thabo Mbeki, to the Toast Remarks by His Excellency, the President of the Republic of Indonesia, Dr Susilo Bambang Yudhoyono, at the State Banquet, Istana Negara, Jakarta," April 19, 2005, http://www.info.gov.za/speeches/2005/05042008451004.htm.

Successive presidents of the independent modern nations of South Africa and Indonesia continue to invoke seventeenth-century links between the two regions as a shared history of forced migration and the struggle against European colonialism that created a common heritage of community. Although these speeches serve contemporary political interests and potential alliances, they do indeed represent a reinterpretation of an historical narrative of the nation in both South Africa and Indonesia. For South Africa, nation building requires a history of inclusion in the struggle against oppression and dispossession of the majority. Indigenous resistance and forced migration are paired processes of a colonial past that are considered direct precursors to the struggle against apartheid. For Indonesia, historical links across the Indian Ocean to South Africa exist in a broader continuum of cultural expansion and migration that began in the first era of the great transoceanic voyages of the Malay seafarers, nearly a millennium before Shaykh Yusuf arrived at the Cape in 1694. Yet even within this longer trajectory of ocean crossing, the importance of a shared Islamic heritage is of much greater significance to Indonesia as the most populous Muslim nation in the world. Shaykh Yusuf was already a scholar of renown in seventeenth-century Indian Ocean Islamic networks and therein lies his significance for Indonesians.

Although Shaykh Yusuf is revered as a common national hero exiled for his beliefs and struggle against the VOC, the history of forced migration in the form of slavery, which was widespread in indigenous Southeast Asian societies as well as European colonies in the early modern period, is not emphasized as formative of the Indonesian nation. Neither South African nor Indonesian narratives of Shaykh Yusuf as a national hero highlight his having gone into exile accompanied not only by numerous members of his family and followers but also by his slaves. In South Africa this acknowledgment would dilute the force of his struggle against Dutch colonialism; in Indonesia it would not be considered relevant because debt slavery was an ancient and ubiquitous indigenous social practice only later adapted and adopted as chattel slavery by the Dutch in the evolution of their empire.

In both cases the presidents of South Africa, Mandela and Mbeki, and of Indonesia, Suharto and Yudhoyono, were well aware of their roles in creating new historical narratives that attempt to build unity among the diverse class, religious and ethnic groups of their respective nations. Colonial histories and hagiographies in both South Africa and Indonesia pronounced the Dutch East India Company period the origin of the modern nation and the bringing of European civilization to backward indigenous peoples. This narrative was reinforced in South Africa under apartheid while simultaneously being abandoned after World War Two in independent Indonesia. Although their historical trajectories of colonialism diverged after the end of the Dutch East India Company period in the closing years of the eighteenth century, both countries have borders created as a legacy of their colonial past and have sought to maintain their territorial boundaries in the transition to independence and democracy. As modern states, South Africa and Indonesia have grappled with ethnic, religious, and regional tensions that have threatened their territorial integrity. The apartheid regime that ruled South Africa from 1948 to 1994 partially implemented its white supremacist ideology of "separate development" that divided the country into racially based invented "homelands" that would eventually be granted independence and leave no black South Africans with claims to citizenship in the Republic of South Africa. The end of apartheid was accompanied by a reorganization of provincial boundaries that reintegrated the former homelands into larger regional political entities.

Indonesian nationalists under Sukarno declared independence in 1945 after the end of the Japanese occupation during World War Two. Since then, the Republic of Indonesia has met repeated challenges from within by regional religious and ethnic movements. These movements claim the right to secede from the Republic to become independent nations. The challenges have ranged from the successful independence struggle in East Timor, which was invaded and incorporated into Indonesia in 1975, to the persistent civil war waged in Aceh province. The port-polity of Aceh was formed as a Muslim sultanate on the north coast of Sumatra around 1500 and fiercely defended its autonomy from external domination. When the VOC entered the Southeast Asian arena it compared the Sultan of Aceh, Iskander Muda (1607–36), to a young Alexander the Great.[4] The modern independence struggle was brought to a halt only by the force of nature after the region was devastated by the 2004 Indian Ocean tsunami. The official national motto of the Republic of Indonesia, "unity in diversity," has been an ideal yet to be fully realized. Under vastly different circumstances both Indonesia and South Africa have sought to implement this vision of a unified nation and continue to do so.

[4] Successive Dutch colonial regimes attempted to subdue Aceh. This was finally achieved by brutal military occupation by 1910 – only three decades before the Dutch colonial state would itself collapse instantly under invasion from the Japanese. Although Aceh was also a center for Indonesian nationalism, there remained powerful forces in the region who demanded autonomy if not outright independence from the Republic. Anthony Reid, *An Indonesian Frontier: Acehnese and Other Histories of Sumatra*. Leiden: KITLV Press, 2005, pp. 5–20.

It is therefore not so surprising that Shaykh Yusuf, a seventeenth-century exile who embodied the principles of cross-cultural and inter-regional community building through his role as a religious leader in the early colonial periods of both Indonesia and South Africa, has come to the forefront as an important historical figure in contemporary nation-building narratives. Less explicitly acknowledged within this emerging narrative is a shared past through the Dutch East India Company as an imperial entity that claimed sovereignty over parts of the Indonesian archipelago and the Cape of Good Hope for nearly two hundred years before its demise at the end of the eighteenth century. During this period, the Dutch East India Company created networks across the Indian Ocean that brought partial territorial and legal sovereignties into a single imperial web. As an empire, the Company did not seek primarily to become a colonizer, and its territorial ambitions differed substantially among the various sites where it operated.

This book seeks to explain what constituted the Dutch East India Company as an empire by examining the networks through which its sovereignty was exercised. It focuses particularly on the networks of free and forced migration to begin to explain how the Company developed and coalesced as a system or web of networks. From this perspective, Shaykh Yusuf emerges as a person engaged in these networks against his will, first as a political prisoner and later as an exile of the Company. The network of imperial power included the categorization of people as slaves, convicts and political prisoners. These legal categories of bondage intersected with, but were not constituted by, the network of forced migration comprised of the slave trade, penal transportation and political exile. Despite having been banished to multiple and far-flung Company controlled sites, Shaykh Yusuf managed to circumvent VOC efforts to neutralize his influence. As a scholar, teacher, and political leader of renown in Islamic networks of worship, writing and pilgrimage across the Indian Ocean, Shaykh Yusuf's capture and exile by the Company in Batavia, then Colombo (Ceylon) and finally the Cape, enhanced rather than diminished his reputation. As a result he was able to extend the reach of autonomous Islamic networks to the southern tip of Africa.

By concentrating on the circuit of forced migration connecting the Cape and Batavia, the Company's imperial headquarters on the island of Java, one can begin to envisage how other circuits of forced migration operated and, over time, coalesced into a network that constituted an important dimension of VOC sovereignty. Shaykh Yusuf's story is just one of many examples of how the VOC network of forced migration intersected in dynamic relation with indigenous Indian Ocean cultural and religious networks to produce unexpected consequences for the Company. Attending to the dynamic interaction of VOC, European and indigenous networks in the Indian Ocean therefore enables one to consider Shaykh Yusuf and other captives in their contemporary context in an early modern world and highlight their capacity for agency and influence. In this world, the Dutch East India Company was but one of the European merchant companies interjecting itself into a regional grid of ancient and vibrant cultural, religious, and trading networks that had long eluded domination by any one merchant enterprise, polity or empire.

Defining Imperial Networks

This book argues that the Dutch East India Company empire manifested itself through cultural, legal, administrative, transportation, territorial, military and exchange networks that amalgamated spatially and over time into an imperial web whose sovereignty was effectively created and maintained but always partial and contingent. It advances the view that early modern empires were comprised of the material manifestations of lands and peoples conquered, and that these durable networks, with regional circuits and sub-circuits, and territorially and institutionally based nodes of regulatory power, operated not only on land and sea but discursively as well. It further advances the view that these components of imperial sovereignty were constituted through negotiations between the Company's governing body in the metropole and the people who managed its forts, factories, settlements, and colonies established in its charter domain. VOC imperial sovereignty also developed in dynamic response to challenges waged by individuals and other sovereign entities operating within the same geographic grid, mainly in the Indian Ocean, but extending to the South China Sea as well. By closely examining one imperial network, forced migration, *Networks of Empire* seeks to explain how the Dutch East India Company constituted its entire empire through the creation and management of these multiple and intersecting fields of partial sovereignty. It follows the Company's subjects of bondage across multiple continents and examines their lives with respect to the dynamic evolution of imperial sovereignty in the Indian Ocean region during the seventeenth and eighteenth centuries.

The traditional historiography of empire has been dominated by the temporal and spatial oppositional binaries of "rise and fall," "expansion and decline," and, more recently, "center and periphery" and "metropole and colony." Most of these analyses privilege the imperial center, or metropole, as the driving force of the rise or expansion of empire. Accordingly, histories written from this perspective focus primarily on power as it flows from an imperial core to a colonial periphery at the level of the management and governance of its trading colonies and, conversely, on the products of extraction and trade as they flow back from the settled colony to the imperial center.[5]

The postcolonial critiques of the 1980s, however, reset the analysis to focus on the colonies and to thereby view colonized subjects as active participants in the colonial project. This reversal left the center-periphery model intact as it created new subjects of analysis that included the construction of identities of difference through a colonial discourse of race, class and gender. In discarding a single privileged vision of empire emanating from the European center, these scholars demonstrated that both metropole and colony were formed through their mutual encounters.[6]

In its second stage, the "new imperial history" of the 1990s sought ways to conceptualize empire as a more dynamic configuration of metropole and colony that could be studied from within a single analytical framework. Fred Cooper and Ann Stoler in particular proposed abandoning the binary formulation of metropole and colony and working instead towards a conceptualization of the temporal and modular elements of imperial sovereignty without losing sight of the articulation of local and global patterns of social transformation.[7] Their critiques of the presuppositions of colonial historiography have left historians with a daunting analytical challenge for the reconceptualization of the complexities of empire.

The concept of a network has proven useful in applying these insights to explain the multiple dimensions, partialities and instabilities of empires

---

[5] Edward Gibbon's *The History of The Decline and Fall of the Roman Empire* published between 1776 and 1789 inspired the title variation of "Rise and Fall," both of which have been used by subsequent generations of historians. For a recent example of center and peripheries see Jack P. Greene, *Peripheries and Center: Constitutional Development in the Extended Polities of the British Empire and the United States, 1607–1788*. Athens: University of Georgia Press, 1986.

[6] See for example collected editions including Nicholas Dirks, ed., *Colonialism and Culture*. Ann Arbor: University of Michigan Press, 1992; Frederick Cooper and Ann Laura Stoler, eds., *Tensions of Empire: Colonial Cultures in a Bourgeois World*. Berkeley, Los Angeles, and London: University of California Press, 1997; Catherine Hall, ed., *Cultures of Empire, a Reader: Colonizers in Britain and the Empire in the Nineteenth and Twentieth Centuries*. Manchester: Manchester University Press, 2000; Antoinette Burton, ed., *After the Imperial Turn: Thinking with and through the Nation*. Durham, NC: Duke University Press, 2003.

[7] Ann Laura Stoler and Frederick Cooper, "Between Metropole and Colony: Rethinking a Research Agenda," in Cooper and Stoler, eds., *Tensions of Empire*, p. 4.

that cannot be adequately defined with reference either to their metropolitan "centers" or their colonial "peripheries." Alan Lester has been most successful to date in employing this concept through what he terms 'geographies of connection' in his analysis of Britain and South Africa in the context of the global reach of the British empire. He argues that "colonial and metropolitan sites were connected most obviously through material flows of capital, commodities and labour.... By the late eighteenth century, British material culture was already located within intensively developed circuits connecting Western Europe, Africa, Asia, and South America.... The nodal points holding this expanded imperial web and its extra-imperial trading partners together were ports and the means of transmission between them, ships... However, colonial and metropolitan sites were articulated discursively as well as materially and through the same kinds of network infrastructure that serviced global commerce."[8] Lester's reconceptualization of an empire through its networks recognizes the multiplicity of imperial connections as it paradoxically narrows the analytical lens to create a more fully realized view of a particular dimension of the constantly changing and unstable imperial web.[9] Examining the constitution of empire through its networks has led to further studies that refocus attention from the European metropole to imperial centers in African, Asian and South American colonies. Thomas Metcalf portrays India as "a nodal point from which peoples, ideas, goods, and institutions – everything that enables empire to exist – radiated outward."[10] India, in other words, had its own peripheries in the Indian Ocean.

These studies of imperial networks have imposed specific constraints to achieve narrative coherence for this dynamic, multilayered and complex topic. Metcalf limits chronological periodization to examine multiple networks across the broad spatial range of the Indian Ocean, or the "British Lake" as this oceanic region became known in English during the nineteenth century.[11] Lester focuses on "geographies of connection" between two regions of empire, the British metropole based in London and its South African colony, to analyze the contingent material and discursive networks of empire.[12] The metaphor of network successfully transcends the meta-geographies that Martin Lewis and Kären Wigen argue have

---

[8] Alan Lester, *Imperial Networks: Creating Identities in Nineteenth-Century South Africa and Britain*. London and New York: Routledge, 2001, p. 6.
[9] Ibid., p. 13.
[10] Thomas R. Metcalf, *Imperial Connections: India in the Indian Ocean Arena, 1860–1920*. Berkeley, Los Angeles, London: University of California Press, 2007, p. 1.
[11] Ibid., p. 9.   [12] Lester, *Imperial Networks*.

shaped modern perceptions of the world into continents, nation-states and binary global divisions of East and West.[13] Using the framework of "imperial careering" as form of biography that takes us more deeply into the operation of empire, Lambert and Lester have brought together a variety of narratives about individual colonial professionals who in many cases were highly mobile within their respective imperial networks.[14] Of course, while biographical writing allows for an exploration of the nuances of individual lives, it is an analytical form that is by definition temporally constrained by the span of a lifetime. Studying empire through biography therefore limits a consideration of the evolution of imperial sovereignty over an extended period of time.

Networks of Empire expands upon these prior insights by alternating between spatial and temporal levels of analysis to present a history of the Dutch East India Company's (VOC) empire from its inception in 1602 to its disintegration in 1799 across the entirety of its geographical domain of the Indian Ocean region. It does so without losing sight of the lives of individuals who were constrained by, also helped determine the limits of, imperial sovereignty. To render its movement from the imperial to the individual level of analysis more intelligible, *Networks of Empire* further develops the analytical framework of the imperial network.

In this book, an empire is comprised of an intersecting set of networks that, when considered as a whole, constitute a sovereign totality or imperial web that can be studied in both its temporal and its spatial manifestations. The Dutch East India Company was created as a merchant company through its charter granted by the States-General of the United Provinces in 1602 and disbanded through bankruptcy in 1799 when its remaining networks were taken over by the emergent Dutch state. The Company's empire evolved through the assumption and expression of sovereignty granted by the partial rights of independent governance in its charter domain east of the Cape of Good Hope and through the Straits of Magellan. The States-General awarded the Company exclusive rights in this geographical grid to create and impose laws, establish forts, factories and settlements, exercise monopolies of trade, sign treaties and wage

---

[13] Martin W. Lewis and Kären E. Wigen, *The Myth of Continents. A Critique of Metageographies*. Berkeley, Los Angeles, and London: University of California Press, 1997.

[14] David Lambert and Alan Lester, "Introduction: Imperial Spaces, Imperial Subjects," in David Lambert and Alan Lester, eds., *Colonial Lives Across the British Empire: Imperial Careering in the Long Nineteenth Century*. Cambridge: Cambridge University Press, 2006, pp. 21–24.

conflicts with foreign nations, and inflict capital punishment on individuals under its jurisdiction. These sovereign rights were limited because ultimate power resided in the United Provinces of the Netherlands to the extent that the repercussions of wars in Europe were also played out in the Company's charter domain. This was particularly relevant in the wars against the Iberian states and in the series of Anglo-Dutch wars that provided a legal basis for VOC conquest of European nodes and networks in the Indian Ocean grid.

Conceptualizing empire as the totality of networks within a chartered domain allows for a macroexamination of shifting patterns of connection, dissolution, and reconnection within and among domains of imperial activity and, when historical sources provide, for a microexamination of the lived lives of people who populate the imperial field of action. This approach differs from J. R. and William H. McNeill's characterization of world history as "the human web." Because they are dealing with the whole of human history, the McNeills envisage a process of ever-increasing density of webs as sets of connections linking people in patterns of cooperation and competition that characterize human progress. They use the now familiar metaphor of the world-wide web to define successive historical contexts leading up to our contemporary globalized cosmopolitan present.[15] At a "bird's-eye view" this image of human history is compelling. However, defining imperial formations requires a closer examination of the way in which networks are created, strengthened, broken, reconnected, and sometimes dismantled entirely. Moreover, the interchangeability of networks and nodes within an imperial web, as described in this book, does not necessarily imply increasing density over time.

As conceived within this study, an empire consists of multiple material networks including those of bureaucracy, correspondence, trade, transportation, and migration, as well as discursive networks of law, administration, information, diplomacy, and culture. These independent yet intersecting networks exist simultaneously as paths of circulation for people, goods, and information and in a more condensed capacity as nodal regulatory points most often located in regional centers where power and authority generally tended to originate. These nodes not only include ships, factories, forts, settlements, urban centers, colonies and their frontier zones, but also certain charismatic individuals like Shaykh Yusuf. The VOC settlement at the Cape of Good Hope, for example, was

---

[15] J. R. McNeill and William H. McNeill, *The Human Web: A Bird's Eye View of World History*. New York: W. W. Norton and Company, 2003.

established in 1652 as a refreshment post for shipping networks traversing the Atlantic and Indian Oceans between the United Provinces and various sites in Asia. The Cape did not inevitably evolve from refreshment post to colony. The decision to extend territorial sovereignty was made in the 1670s, and the commitment to develop a permanent settlement was not made by the Company until the early eighteenth century. In allowing the settlement and migration of colonists to the Cape, the Company created the conditions whereby successive generations of colonists became increasingly localized in their identities and loyalties and finally presented a challenge to Company sovereignty. The Cape of Good Hope was unique in this trajectory because no other VOC node became a full-scale settler colony.

Networks of Empire places the VOC network of forced migration onto a larger regional grid of migration that included the East African slave trade, and it focuses specifically on the circuit of forced migration running between the imperial nodes of Batavia and the Cape of Good Hope. As an imperial node in the Company's empire, the Cape of Good Hope intersected with and evolved from particular circuits of other imperial networks with which it engaged. A circuit is thus conceptualized as a partial segment of a network, without which the network would likely continue, though perhaps in an altered or diminished state. The VOC network of forced migration included the slave trade, penal transportation, and political banishment of people legally categorized respectively as slaves, convicts and exiles. However, individuals so categorized in this spectrum of bondage did not necessarily experience forced migration if they were never transported forcibly to another location for the period of their incarceration. The Cape of Good Hope also had its own localized sub-circuit of forced migration that linked it to other imperial nodes including Robben Island and, for a limited time, Mauritius and Madagascar. Though located in the same geographical region of the Indian Ocean grid, these sub-circuits did not necessarily intersect with the Batavia–Cape circuit.

To recapitulate, the VOC network of forced migration was based on an extension of Dutch sovereignty that constituted an imperial domain in which the Company could impose its laws to run its business and turn a profit. Forced migration was legitimated by the Dutch East India Company's governing body in the United Provinces and was subsequently developed through a comprehensive legal system in its settlement nodes, in particular Batavia, that enabled the Company to rationalize the forcible movement of people after formally assigning them an identity as a prisoner, convict, or slave within an overall registration and identification program of everyone whom the Company determined fell within its legal purview. The VOC network of forced migration was based in one part on a legal conceptualization of the Company as a sovereign entity; in another on the laws and regulations that assigned legal identities and enforced decrees of punishment; in yet another on the material resources needed to transport, house, maintain, and supervise legally identified slaves and transgressors to other nodal points and hinterlands within the empire; and, finally, on the effects forced migration had on recipient nodes within this VOC network. The Company's legal and forced migration networks were not identical or uniformly developed, nor were they necessarily linked across time and space. When one examines the fragmentation, interaction, and overlapping of these networks, one comes closer to understanding the modular nature of the VOC empire and the dynamics of historical change within its sovereign realm.

The legal identities imposed upon every individual within the Company empire determined their position in society and consequently imposed constraints and opportunities upon their actions, though one's legal identity could and did change over time and place. For example, a free burgher could commit a crime in Cape Town be arrested, tried, and sentenced to penal transportation, and thereby become a convict for a specific amount of time on Robben Island before returning home to resume his prior legal identity as a burgher. A slave born in Bali who was forcibly migrated to Batavia through a circuit of the slave trade might be manumitted and thereby become a free person. Conversely, a free person from an indigenous polity might be captured and transported through part of an indigenous slave trade and subsequently sold to the Company or one of its subjects and thereby become a slave. A prince banished as a political exile might be returned to his homeland, and, in ending his banishment, resume his previous royal status.

These and other such hypothetical examples of a process of forced migration intersected with preexisting practices of bondage in the VOC empire, which when considered in contemporary context, help elucidate the dynamics of the movement of people in the Company empire. These hypothetical individuals would have had legal identities that were necessarily overlaid by other identities including gender, ethnicity, and religion that also determined their propensity for being forcibly migrated. Moreover, ethnic identities were not stable between different sites, even within the legal system of the Company. It is in the examination of the complexities of historical reality and the lives lived by real individuals like Shaykh Yusuf and his family, followers, and slaves that the network of forced migration in the Dutch East India Company begins to take shape, and it is through these historical details that this book makes a more general contribution to the study of empire.

Every Company ship and settlement had in common the fact that without people, there was no Company. Labor, from the high and mighty governor-general to the lowliest Company slave, made the Company work, fight, trade, and profit. That is why examining the peopling of empire gets to the heart of the enterprise, and this includes factors like motivation and volition. As David Eltis suggests, "[t]he distinction between free and coerced migration hinges on who makes the decision to leave, the migrant or some other individual."[16]

Bringing free and forced migration into the same analytical framework, however, moves beyond questions of volition into definitions of legal identity. Every early modern European empire had its own unique network of imperial migration that moved people within the circuits and nodes of homeland, shipping fleets, settlements, and colonies. Timothy Coates shows how the first Portuguese empire from the sixteenth century onward, the *Estado da India*, with its imperial capital at Goa on the west coast of the Indian subcontinent, used "criminals, sinners, orphans, and prostitutes as colonizers" around its transoceanic realm through the network of forced migration, its judicial system, and its Overseas Council.[17] Likewise, England and France in the early modern period had their own specific networks of free and forced migration, including their massive African slave trade that populated their colonies in the Americas and the Caribbean. In the long nineteenth century, over 150,000 British convicts found themselves unwilling colonists in distant Australia.[18] The evolution of the Company empire through its legal network also laid the basis of its network of forced migration linking Batavia and the Cape and ultimately its right to rule over its subjects.

---

[16] David Eltis, "Introduction: Migration and Agency in Global History," in David Eltis, ed., *Coerced and Free Migration: Global Perspectives*. Stanford, CA: Stanford University Press, 2002, p. 6.
[17] Timothy J. Coates, *Convicts and Orphans: Forced and State-Sponsored Colonizers in the Portuguese Empire, 1550–1755*. Stanford, CA: Stanford University Press, 2001.
[18] Stanley Engerman, ed., *Terms of Labor: Slavery, Serfdom, and Free Labor*. Stanford, CA: Stanford University Press, 1999; Stephen Nicholas, ed., *Convict Workers: Reinterpreting Australia's Past*. Cambridge: Cambridge University Press, 1988; Ian Duffield and James Bradley, eds., *Representing Convicts: New Perspectives on Convict Forced Labour Migration*. London: Leicester University Press, 1997; Clare Anderson, *Convicts in the Indian Ocean: Transportation from South Asia to Mauritius, 1851–53*. Houndsmill, Hamps. and London: Macmillan Press and New York: St Martin's Press, 2000.

The connections between the Company's networks and its territorial nodes changed over time and generations. In many cases, challenges to one or more of its networks laid the groundwork for the dissolution of the empire itself. This is particularly evident in the Dutch East India Company imperial node at the Cape of Good Hope where, over generations, the interests of the Company increasingly conflicted with those subjects who developed primary identification with their colonial homeland at the expense of loyalty to their merchant rulers. Initially, the Cape spawned a colonial society completely dependent on and embedded in the Company networks. Over time, the initial motive for settlement, to provide food and supplies for passing ships, was such a success that it generated protests from Cape-based settlers and traders. The Company's restrictive commercial monopolies designed to maximize its own profits clashed with the interests of these free colonists by denying them access to the agricultural and commercial markets created by its transportation network.

Company subjects and officials had access, albeit illegal, to the indigenous trading networks that linked its settlements to the spice-producing archipelago of the Moluccas and to the trading networks that intersected with and formed part of the vast Chinese trading network of the entire eastern region. Despite all their attempts, the Company was never successful in completely monopolizing, diverting, or destroying indigenous and regional trading in the area. Nor was it successful in eliminating illegal trading and profiteering in these Asian networks by its own subjects and officials, as the criminal records of the Company and this book will attest. The point is that the networks of the VOC empire intersected with other sovereign networks in unique ways according to the specificities of individual settlements and colonies within their regional contexts such that in the various arenas of intersection within a particular network Company sovereignty was neither equivalently expressed nor uniformly enforceable.

Split Sovereignties in the Evolution of the VOC Empire

Analyzing the Dutch East India Company as an imperial web raises questions about the nature of state and empire in the early modern period. The Company's empire lasted from 1602 until 1799 and was a particular manifestation of the split sovereignty of the United Provinces of the Netherlands. State formation in the United Provinces, as Julia Adams argues, was characterized by patrimonial rule that segmented sovereignty through the granting of political and economic privileges to corporate groups. These corporate groups were often constituted from familial networks that were locally and civically based but able to transcend the local in the form of chartered mercantile companies.[19]

Although the Dutch East India Company was only one part of these patrimonial networks that comprised governance in the United Provinces, it also constituted an empire in its own right. Under its founding charter, issued in 1602 by the States-General of the United Provinces, the Company was delegated sovereignty over the trade and territory east of the Cape of Good Hope and through the Straits of Magellan. The Dutch East India Company mirrored the split sovereignty of the United Provinces in its own bureaucratic organization, being composed of provincially based chambers. As Adams argues, "these bodies were controlled by members of a hereditary patriaciate – a merchant-regent elite."[20] At the same time, the VOC was an imperial entity that possessed and governed territory within its own realm. It was, significantly, an empire within a state that preceded the transformation of the United Provinces into a unitary state under the Batavian Republic in 1795 in the aftermath of the French Revolution. The Dutch East India Company networks therefore contributed to the complexity of the structures of sovereignty as they emerged in early modern Europe.

The legal network of the Dutch East India Company empire, while based in the laws of the United Provinces, operated separately from the exercise of law in the Netherlands. The rule of law in the empire authorized the control of people and products in settlements and colonies across a vast imperial realm spreading from the Cape of Good Hope on the southernmost tip of Africa to Deshima Island, an extension of Nagasaki, in Japan. It also included the maritime realm of ships in the Atlantic and Indian Oceans and surrounding seas. The application of imperial law by the Company within this realm was not universally accepted and did not go unchallenged by those whom it attempted to incorporate and control. As an empire, the Company did not have the ability to enforce its laws equally throughout its settlements. The exercise of sovereignty was negotiated and contingent on relations between the Company and

---

[19] Julia Adams, *The Familial State: Ruling Families and Merchant Capitalism in Early Modern Europe*. Ithaca, NY: Cornell University Press, 2005, pp. 13–38.

[20] Julia Adams, "Principals and Agents, Colonialists and Company Men: The Decay of Colonial Control in the Dutch East Indies," *American Sociological Review*, 61, February 1996, p. 15.

the indigenous states and polities in which the Company nodes were located.

The Company's empire was not a homogenous colonial realm, but a series of negotiated networks both on land and on sea. Its ships could be described as seaborne colonies where the exercise of Company authority was absolute. Territorially, the Company's empire centered on coastal forts, factories, and differently sized urban settlements with varying degrees of incorporation of their hinterlands and surrounding seas. The extension of Company sovereignty was therefore negotiated as a diplomatic, legal, and territorial relationship. Company authority on board its ships was a constant, although this too was occasionally challenged by mutiny. It was the extension of territorial sovereignty in particular Company settlements, however, that constituted the historical transition from a merchant enterprise to a corporate-based colonial empire. This process of sovereign expansion began early in the Company's history, though not all Company settlements became territorially based colonies. Some, like the Company post on Deshima Island in Japan, remained isolated trading posts dependent entirely on the indigenous host state. The exercise of Company sovereignty in these locations was therefore extremely limited. In places where the primary network of empire was the commercial exchange that constituted Company trade, the issue of sovereignty was not significant.

The focus of this book is the circuit between two of the major Company colonies, Batavia and the Cape of Good Hope, both of which developed permanent settler populations that, to differing degrees, challenged the Company's right to govern. These examples attest that the Company's empire was in a constant state of negotiated relations with its own subjects. Adams explores how the connections between patrimonial principals operated within metropolitan and colonial arenas. She demonstrates how the agents of these principals could subvert the interests of their patrons by pursuing other avenues of gain in the colonies. However, the Dutch East India Company empire can also be examined from the perspective of the tensions produced by the fragmentary nature of the empire's geographical realm comprised of the nodes of imperial capitals, regional centers, main colonies, and temporary settlements.

The Company colonial government, located in the port city of Batavia on the island of Java, acted as an imperial headquarters that within some networks competed with the authority of the Company's ruling body based in Europe, the *Heren XVII* (Seventeen Gentlemen). Within the legal realm, the governor-general and the Council of the Indies in

Batavia, who together constituted the High Government, were the highest authority. While authority lay with the Seventeen Gentlemen in the United Provinces, they rarely intervened in individual legal cases. Major settlements also exercised their own right to pass laws and ordinances pertaining to their specific local situations. The codification of Company law was an iterative process that was negotiated and amended in a legal network that extended from Batavia, as the source of laws applicable throughout the empire, to Company authorities based in other colonies who were legislating for local conditions. The Company's Court of Justice in Batavia was the highest court in the empire, operating as the appellate court as well as the superior court. In matters of criminal law there was no recourse to courts in the United Provinces. In civil cases the situation was more complex and depended on whether the people involved were Dutch citizens and had recourse to their rights as subjects of the United Provinces that could be used to challenge the authority of Company courts.[21]

Defining Legal Identities

European powers in the early modern period did not create their imperial legal systems in a global legal vacuum. Wherever they encountered other polities and made claims to colonial rule it was necessary to negotiate cross-cultural concepts of legality and the rule of law. Lauren Benton argues that "contests over cultural and religious boundaries and their representations in law become struggles over the nature and structure of political authority." Her study of colonial legal regimes demonstrates how these jurisdictional struggles shaped not only the nature of empire but also broader patterns that underpin the modern global order. "Global legal regimes – defined for our purposes as *patterns of structuring multiple legal authorities* – provided a global institutional order even in the absence of cross-national authorities and before the formal recognition of international law" [original emphasis].[22] Empires were foundational in creating a global international order, but imperial legal systems were not homogenous or uniformly enforced, even within the networks and nodes of a single empire. Local circumstances shaped how imperial law

[21] For a fascinating civil case regarding a marital dispute and divorce that was negotiated between both husband and wife claiming recourse to courts in both Batavia and the Netherlands, see Leonard Blussé, *Bitter Bonds: A Colonial Divorce Drama of the Seventeenth Century*. Princeton, NJ: Markus Wiener Publishers, 2002.
[22] Lauren Benton, *Law and Colonial Cultures: Legal Regimes in World History, 1400–1900*. Cambridge: Cambridge University Press, 2002, pp. 2–3.

was adapted and applied. This can be clearly demonstrated in the Dutch East India Company's empire where forms of legal pluralism depended upon the legal orientation of local polities the Company encountered. For example, the Company's recognition and incorporation of elements of Javanese legal constructs in Batavia were more complex and enduring than the Company's adoption and adaptation of Khoekhoe law at the Cape, which after 1672 it did not officially recognize at all.[23]

Establishing the rule of law was a major preoccupation of the Company rulers. The Company's legal system therefore constituted a primary network within and outside the VOC empire: internally through the application of civil and criminal law to its subjects and externally through treaties and international law negotiated with indigenous rulers. These aspects of the Company legal system in turn helped shape an evolving network of forced migration comprised of the slave trade, penal transportation, and political exile. The VOC archives attest that the Company was preoccupied with controlling its populace and that it sought this control by assigning everyone in its realm to a category that defined his or her legal and to a great extent social status. However, people in different categories were not incorporated into the rule of law equally as subjects and as a result identity categories comprised a spectral rather than a binary relationship. For example, one of the major categories within Company law differentiated between free and slave and another between Christian and heathen. These categories were not mutually exclusive or racially based, with a few crucial exceptions. Europeans could not legally be slaves or heathens. The punishment for apostasy by a European was death, unless the individual so condemned had been forced to convert to Islam as a prisoner of war and was willing to repent and reconvert to Christianity. These primary categories had implications for the individual concerned in the application of Company law, administered according to status.

Individuals were first categorized according to their position and status within the Company's empire. The majority of Company servants were sailors, soldiers, artisans, and administrators. Ranks were strictly hierarchical all the way to the pinnacle of power in the Company, the governor-general who presided over Batavia Castle. Theoretically, all Europeans who engaged themselves as servants (employees) of the Company did so

---

[23] For an analysis of the American frontier zones of legality, see Eliga Gould, "Zones of Law, Zones of Violence: The Legal Geography of the British Atlantic c.1772," *William and Mary Quarterly*, 60, July 2003, pp. 471–510.

out of their own free will, but the system of *zielverkoopers* (soul sellers) that recruited servants for the Company through a form of debt-bondage was rife in the Netherlands. Free Asians could also be employed by the Company in various capacities on land and sea throughout the empire. This was particularly the case in Java where there were large numbers of Asian mercenaries under contract to the Company. All Company servants were subject to multiyear labor contracts signed and solemnized by a legal oath. As previously mentioned, the Company owned its own slaves who were categorized as Company assets. Additionally, the Company hired free laborers and privately owned slaves whenever extra labor was necessary. The overwhelming majority of the Company servants were men, for very few women were direct employees of the Company. However, female Company slaves were not uncommon, as is evident by the population of the Company Slave Lodge at the Cape where some but certainly not all women slaves notoriously were coerced or agreed to work "unofficially" as prostitutes for the Company servants, civilians, and sojourning men.

The second major category of people under Company jurisdiction, and particularly important at the Cape of Good Hope, were the so-called free burghers. Initially, these were Company servants granted permission to engage in trades or farming for the profit of the Company. Over generations they provided the basis of the settler populations throughout the Company settlements, although a steady flow of Company servants applied for release from their labor contracts to become free laborers. When burgher status was no longer automatic, these released laborers were known as *knechten* (sing. *knecht*) or overseers. At the Cape, they were mostly employed as slave managers on farms but could eventually rise in status to become burghers. Freed Company servants were also supplemented by direct migration of European civilians under the sponsorship of the Company. Despite the hopes of the early Company empire builders like Jan Pieterszoon Coen that colonization would be based on large-scale free migration from the Netherlands, this policy was not supported by the governing body of the Company and never materialized over time. The natural growth of the burgher population came largely through the initial assimilation of indigenous women into the European population by marriage and through the children produced by these unions. Officially, European status was also synonymous with Christian identity. The burgher populations of the Company settlements were legally subjects of the Company and were not free to move about the empire at will. There was very little movement between imperial settlements by whole burgher families, though the strategic marriage of a daughter to a high-ranking

Company official elsewhere was considered a desirable match and an extension of family influence and an increase in access to resources.[24] Many of these burgher families maintained links with their extended families in their home countries over generations as they settled permanently in their newfound homelands. It took considerable financial resources to move back to Europe and live comfortably. Not all Company nodes had a self-reproducing burgher population; in this sense the colony at the Cape was unique in the extension of territorial sovereignty through settler expansion in the rural hinterlands and more distant frontier zones.

Theoretically, the Company could sentence a free burgher to forcible reenlistment as a punishment for a crime. Although this option was rarely exercised, it was deeply resented by the burgher population. So was criminal punishment in the form of banishment for serious infractions of the moral, religious, or legal codes of the Company settlements. Burghers could be banished to other Company settlements or the fatherland. Banishment to the fatherland was basically expulsion from the Company realm without the option to return. This form of banishment of burghers was rarely implemented and fell short of the severity of penal transportation whereby a person subject to Company law became recategorized as a criminal and was transported elsewhere in the realm.

In the circuit of forced migration from Batavia to the Cape, people banished were mainly categorized as either *bandieten* (convicts) or *bannelingen* (exiles). These categories overrode other official or self-imposed identities in terms of treatment under the law and by definition included the circumscribing of individual rights under the terms of punishment and/or banishment. Moreover, the social distinctions between convicts and exiles were unintentionally blurred in Company practice and procedures. Documentation on individual prisoners was sometimes lost in transit, causing confusion at the Cape about the status of a particular prisoner. In these cases, the Cape authorities tended to criminalize the exile until they received evidence to the contrary. This did not prevent people from resisting these imposed categories or the punishments that accompanied their status, and the most common form of resistance was escape. Nor did it stop people from using the Company's network of banishment for their own ends, particularly in the spread of Islam to the Cape and the circulation of religious knowledge that was antithetical to the Company's mandated religious beliefs.

---

[24] Jean Gelman Taylor, *The Social World of Batavia: European and Eurasian in Dutch Asia*. Madison: University of Wisconsin Press, 1983.

The most important element in the network of forced migration was a legal slave trade that operated in combination with a legal network that created laws of slavery for the purpose of utilizing slave labor in the Company's empire. The Company's slave laws, based on Roman laws of slavery, operated according to basic shared principles across the empire but differed in detail according to local context. One of these shared basic principles was that it was illegal to enslave the indigenous population. At the Cape of Good Hope, it was therefore illegal to enslave the indigenous Khoesan, but enslaving other Africans from outside the region or buying African slaves from elsewhere was allowed and indeed encouraged. In the Indies archipelago, it was illegal to enslave the Javanese, but it was legal to buy and sell indigenous people already enslaved or to enslave indigenes from areas outside Company jurisdiction.

Slavery in the Netherlands had not been common since medieval times and was rare compared with slavery in sixteenth-century Portugal and Spain.[25] Slaves brought to the United Provinces were in theory automatically emancipated, but Dutch citizens returning from the colonies sometimes brought their slaves with them. The practice was widespread enough to warrant several edicts against it, including one in 1776 stating slaves were to be emancipated after one year's residence.[26] The Synod of Dort in 1618 laid down principles of conversion to Christianity in relation to Dutch slavery in all the colonial realms, resolving that conversion to Christianity by a slave did not automatically lead to freedom.[27] The Dutch East India Company was itself engaged directly in multiple networks of the Indian Ocean slave trade. However, it was the other Dutch imperial enterprise, the West India Company, that profited from the extensive African slave trade that fuelled the Atlantic system.[28] There was very little exchange between these Dutch merchant companies who squabbled initially over areas of jurisdiction under their charters and during their entire existences did not engage in significant mutual trade. The VOC engaged in slave trading solely for its own labor needs and those of

---

[25] Robin Blackburn, *The Making of New World Slavery: From the Baroque to the Modern, 1492–1800*. New York: Verso Books, 1997, p. 34; P. C. Emmer, *The Dutch Slave Trade 1500–1800*, trans. Chris Emery. New York and Oxford: Berghahn Books, 2006, p. 13.
[26] Karel Schoeman, *Early Slavery at the Cape of Good Hope, 1652–1717*. Pretoria: Protea Book House, 2007, p. 38.
[27] Robert C.-H. Shell, *Children of Bondage: A Social History of the Slave Society at the Cape of Good Hope, 1652–1838*. Johannesburg: Witwatersrand University Press, 1994, pp. 330–370.
[28] See Emmer, *Dutch Slave Trade*.

its settlers and subjects. Although the slave trade was not a major source of revenue, it was significant, for the VOC was a corporate slave owner in its own right. The Company engaged in trading slaves as commodities across its realm and also imposed penal transportation upon slaves as punishment for legal transgressions.

All slaves, all Company servants regardless of racial classification, and all Europeans fell under the jurisdiction of Company law. Jurisdiction over other categories of people depended upon local contexts and these differed widely across the Company's nodes and networks. For example, the subtleties of recognizing regional ethnicities like Balinese, Bugis, or Butonese that existed in Batavian ethnic categorization were not applied with the same degree of specificity at the Cape, where ethnic categories in convict registers were generalized as *Indiaanen*, meaning "Asian." The Company devised a system that differed across imperial nodes, in civil and criminal law, and in which laws applied in each case. Indigenous people living within Company jurisdiction were incorporated differently depending upon the negotiated relationship with surrounding indigenous polities. It was in the realm of criminal law that the Company attempted to maximize its power, because monopolizing the definition of criminality allowed it to discipline people who transgressed and thereby threatened its interests.

The punishment of penal transportation could be administered to anyone in the Company realm regardless of category and status. It was, however, extremely rare for high-ranking European Company servants or civilians to be convicted or punished in this fashion. The exception proved the rule, as was the case in the arrest at the Cape and repatriation to Batavia Castle of the ex-Governor-General Adriaan Valckenier who was returning home to the Netherlands in 1742 to retire after his role in the infamous 1741 massacre of the Chinese population of Batavia. The Seventeen Gentlemen sought to impose their punishment upon the Company's senior imperial official before he reached the Netherlands and was beyond the reach of the Company's criminal legal system. He died instead, imprisoned in Batavia castle before his trial. This case was, of course, exceptional. Penal transportation was by far more commonly the punishment for low-ranking Company servants, indigenes and Chinese people under Company jurisdiction, and slaves.

The third major element in the network of forced migration, exile, was created in the arena of external relations conducted between the Company, representatives of rival European powers, and indigenous polities. The Company used political and religious exile as an effective tool of diplomacy. It is significant that the emergence of what later became known as public international law in Europe during the course of the seventeenth century was largely forged in the web of Indian Ocean imperial networks of trade and diplomacy. The relationship between the Dutch East India Company and indigenous states and polities was encoded into the legal network of empire, and the diplomatic memory of the Company was embodied in the written treaties and official reports of political negotiations and formal court politics in which Company officials participated, though not always on terms of their own making. Batavia engaged in diplomatic relations with indigenous polities on terms that reinforced its role as imperial capital at the expense of control by the central Company authorities in Europe. Protocols of diplomacy reproduced elements of the court culture of indigenous Javanese polities in Batavia and became part of the exercise and display of political power. The exercise of political power in the external relations of the Company included not only drastic measures like the conduct of war but also more individualized relationships like the banishment of high-ranking enemies, or the enemies of allies as prisoners of state, like Shaykh Yusuf. The Company also banished many "rebels" who resisted political incorporation into the VOC imperial realm. The difference between prisoner of state and rebel was one of legal jurisdiction. Once the VOC claimed partial sovereignty over a particular area it could enforce laws that demanded acquiescence if not loyalty to Company rule. Further resistance, even by indigenes, could be tried as rebellion. The ability of the Company, and particularly Batavia, to utilize the extent of its geographical realm for exile was a political advantage in its external relations that buttressed the extension of imperial rule on the island of Java.[29]

The Company's monopoly in categorizing legal identity as part of its strategy of rule, enforced and promulgated through its knowledge network, was crucial in determining how the official circulation of this information affected individuals. The multiple forms of intelligence that circulated as correspondence and official reports among Company headquarters in Europe, Batavia, and other Company regulatory nodes constituted a major bureaucratic and administrative enterprise. This is not to suggest

---

[29] Exile in this book is defined, consistent with contemporary usage, as involuntary banishment. Although modern usage of exile implies some element of volition, this is not the case in the Company era – except to the extent that exile was sometimes an alternative to execution, and that most people hoped it was a temporary state, then it could be said to be partly voluntary.

that the VOC was a model of bureaucratic efficiency as record taking and keeping was often quite lax in different nodes and networks of empire. As Adrien Delmas points out, the writing and circulating of daily registers in some VOC nodes was a powerful discursive network of imperial knowledge that served to reinforce the Company as an empire.[30] The physical circulation of legal papers, case notes, and correspondence via shipping and transportation was essential in the implementation of imperial law.[31] Yet even this process was challenged by indigenous claims to status. The families of exiles also regularly wrote to the governor-general or regional Company governing officials imploring or demanding their release. This form of correspondence challenged the Company's categorization of individuals as prisoners by using diplomatic means to renegotiate their status and freedom.

Other networks of knowledge in the Indian Ocean arena intersected with Company's in ways that went beyond the ability of the Dutch to manage and control. In particular, the Islamic networks that linked various Indian Ocean pilgrimage routes to developing Islam in archipelagic polities in the early modern era were clearly important circuits of knowledge, religion, and culture in the region. They intersected with the Company's network of forced migration through the transfer of slaves, convicts, and political and religious prisoners who practiced or were converted to Islam at their sites of banishment or sale. The circulation of Islamic knowledge along this network of forced migration was especially feared by Company officials at the Cape, and indeed appears to have been far more extensive than has previously been recognized by historians. It involved using a much greater range of Islamic texts and talismans than just reciting and transcribing of the Qur'an from memory, which is a pious act attributed to more than one of the exiles. Some high-ranking exiles were experts in religious and other literatures. Shaykh Yusuf, among others, was the author of religious texts in wide circulation in Islamic networks of the Indian Ocean. Some of these exiles returning to their homelands would have transmitted knowledge about the practise of Islam at the Cape to their respective religious communities in Java and the Indonesian archipelago. The implication here is that Islamic knowledge

---

[30] For an anlaysis of the epistolary nature of the Dutch East India Company, see Adrien Delmas, "The Role of Writing in the First Steps of the Colony: A Short Enquiry into the *Journal of van Riebeeck*, 1652–1662," in Nigel Worden, ed., *Contingent Lives: Social Identities and Material Cultures in the VOC World*. Rondebosch: Historical Studies Department, University of Cape Town, 2007, pp. 500–511.

[31] Delmas, "Role of Writing."

did not flow in one direction and Islam at the Cape was not as isolated as has been presumed.

Historiographies of Empire and Nation

The history of free and forced migration within the Company empire has not been a major focus of studies on the Dutch East India Company. Nevertheless, writing the history of the Company has undergone a renaissance inspired by the 2002 quatro-centenary of the Company's founding. This in itself was an interesting catalyst for reflecting on the role the Company played in the historiographies of its ex-colonies and metropolitan centers. A flurry of publications, academic conferences, museum exhibitions, historical reenactments, and public celebrations in the Netherlands, and to a lesser extent in the major ex-colonies of South Africa and Indonesia, reinvigorated the field by including more contemporary perspectives on the Dutch colonial past. Like all historical commemorations of foundational moments in national pasts, the commemoration of the Dutch East India Company did not go by without protest by those people whose historical loyalties and associations lay with the victims of invasion and colonialism rather than with the victors. Celebrations in Holland tried for the most part to adopt a more inclusive view of the early colonial past, or at least to present a more neutral vision by celebrating the origins of modern consumerism through displays of the commodities that constituted the major items of trade first sought and produced by the Company.[32]

This is in stark contrast to the official South African commemoration of the tercentenary of the Dutch East India Company's settlement at the Cape in 1952. Coming four years after the Nationalist Party victory that ushered in the apartheid era, the 1952 commemoration celebrated bringing European civilization and Christianity to darkest Africa. Leslie Witz and Ciraj Rassool argue that this commemoration was a symbolic enactment of apartheid, and the protests it generated were a response to this interpretation. Part of this commemorative performance was the reenactment of the arrival of Shaykh Yusuf as a royal exile in 1694, who in the 1952 version was greeted civilly in person by the governor of the Cape, Simon van der Stel. This historical fantasy sought to place the Cape Malays within the racial hierarchy of apartheid as having brought

---

[32] See, for example, Els M. Jacobs, *Merchant in Asia: The Trade of the Dutch East India Company during the Eighteenth Century*. Leiden: CNWS Publications, 2006; Leonard Blussé, "Four Hundred Years On: The Public Commemoration of the Founding of the VOC in 2002," *Itinerario*, XXVII(1), 2003, pp. 79–92.

their own brand of civilization, Islam and artisanal skills, to the founding of modern South Africa. Slavery, forced migration, and exile were not explicitly addressed as part of this nationalist commemoration.

The trajectory of South African and Indonesian historiography diverged after the generation of historians who recovered the histories of indigenous states within both regions as part of the renegotiation of the meaning of nationalist histories. In South Africa, a major preoccupation of historians has been analyzing the emergence of racially based capitalism and the social and cultural origins of apartheid. The VOC era has been completely reoriented by revisionist historians in the post-1980s era to explore the dynamics of the settler slave society at the Cape. Nigel Worden's examination of the rural slave economy at the Cape, Robert Ross's analysis of slavery and resistance in the Company era, and Robert Shell's quantitative analysis of slavery and his examination of patriarchy in Cape slavery have been foundational studies for subsequent work in this field.[33]

The comparative framework in which Cape slavery has been analyzed has centered on other settler slave societies in the Atlantic world. Only recently has there has been an attempt to compare slavery at the Cape during the Dutch East India Company era with slavery in the rest of the Company empire. Karel Schoeman's book on early Cape slavery examines part of the broader imperial framework by exploring the slave trades from Batavia and Madagascar to the colony.[34] The lacunae in VOC slavery studies are partly a result of the weakness of the historiography of slavery in the Netherlands East Indies and in Southeast Asian history generally. Unlike the Dutch West India Company histories, where slavery and the slave trade in the Atlantic are major focuses, the Dutch Indian Ocean slave trade has been the subject of not a single monograph.[35] Markus Vink has written one of the first articles analyzing overall patterns of the Dutch slave trade in the Indian Ocean.[36] The last monograph

---

[33] Nigel Worden, *Slavery in Dutch South Africa*. Cambridge: Cambridge University Press, 1985; Robert Ross, *Cape of Torments: Slavery and Resistance in South Africa*. London: Routledge and Kegan Paul, 1983; Shell, *Children of Bondage*; Richard Elphick and Hermann Giliomee, eds., *The Shaping of South African Society, 1652–1840*. 2nd ed. Cape Town: Maskew Miller Longman, 1989.

[34] Schoeman, *Early Slavery at the Cape*.

[35] Johannes M. Postma, *The Dutch in the Atlantic Slave Trade, 1600–1815*. New York: Cambridge University Press, 1990.

[36] Markus Vink, "'The World's Oldest Trade': Dutch Slavery and Slave Trade in the Indian Ocean in the Seventeenth Century," *Journal of World History*, 14(2), 2003, pp. 131–177.

devoted to study of slavery in the entire Indonesian archipelago was Kalff's book on the subject written in 1920.[37] Anthony Reid's edited collection on slavery and bondage in Southeast Asia remains the only volume on the issue that specifically addresses the Company era and also integrates indigenous understandings of bondage with the VOC's practice of slavery.[38] In the context of the history of Batavia, the examination of slavery is more extensive.[39] For example, Hendrik Niemeijer's history of Batavia analyzes slaves and bondspeople in the context of colonial society.[40]

Nor has forced migration in the early colonial period in Indonesia been a major issue in Indonesian historiography. This is interesting considering that the abolition of slavery in the Dutch East Indies occurred only in 1860, and even after this date indigenous slavery in the form of debt-bondage was much more difficult to eradicate. One comparative study that integrates the Atlantic and Indian Ocean spheres is focused on the abolition of slavery in these different contexts.[41] Moreover, a study of the longer trajectory of forced migration in Indonesia encompassing forced labor and penal transportation in both the colonial and postindependence regimes, as well as contemporary human trafficking, awaits further research.

The fracturing of South African and Indonesian historiographies partly followed the trajectory of national histories but was also partly a result of the ordering of the colonial archives.[42] The main repositories for the Dutch East India Company archives are divided between the national archives of the respective ex-colonies and the central holdings of the metropole situated in the *Nationaal Archief* (National Archive) in The

---

[37] S. Kalff, *De Slavernij in Oost-Indie*. Barn: Hollandia-drukkerij, 1920; Heather Sutherland, "The Historiography of Slavery in Indonesia," unpublished paper, Kuala Lumpur, 1980.

[38] Anthony Reid, ed., *Slavery, Bondage and Dependency in Southeast Asia*. St. Lucia: University of Queensland Press, 1983; Bruno Lasker, *Human Bondage in Southeast Asia*. Chapel Hill: University of North Carolina Press, 1950.

[39] See for example F. W. de Haan, *Oud Batavia*. 3 vols. Batavia: G. Kolff & Co., 1922.

[40] Hendrik Niemeijer, *Batavia: Een koloniale samenleving in de 17de eeuw*. Amsterdam: Uitgeverij Balans, 2005.

[41] Gert Oostindie, *Fifty Years Later. Antislavery, Capitalism and Modernity in the Dutch Orbit*. Leiden: KITLV Press, 1995.

[42] For the examination of the nature and structure of the colonial archives in South Africa see, Carolyn Hamilton, Verne Harris, and Graeme Reid, eds., *Refiguring the Archive*. Cape Town: David Philip; Dordrecht: Kluwer Academic Publishers, 2002.

Hague.[43] Both the Cape Town Archives Repository in Cape Town and the *Arsip Nasional Republik Indonesia* (National Archive of the Republic of Indonesia) in Jakarta contain collections of archival sources that are not entirely reproduced in the Dutch National Archive.[44] More extensive research on the connections between Batavia and the Cape requires movement among three continents. Projects of this kind are extremely expensive to fund, particularly from South Africa or Indonesia, because of currency exchange rates and limited access to research funding.[45] The Dutch National Archive has begun a new initiative in digitalizing parts of the colonial archives of South Africa, Sri Lanka, and Indonesia (and other sites) for collection in The Hague and redistribution among the various archival sites through Web-based databases and collections.[46] These archival and logistical matters have had, and still have, implications for the possibilities of writing comparative or connective histories of the Dutch East India Company empire. The Dutch East India Company looks a very different entity depending on which archival collection one is investigating. In particular, the Cape loses its preeminent position in the records of the Company's empire once one leaves the Cape archives. Issues of the circulation of knowledge through imperial networks are therefore not only historical considerations in the Dutch East India Company but are also deeply embedded in the ordering of archival sources.[47]

---

[43] M. A. P. Meilinks-Roelofsz, Remco Raben, and H. Spijkerman, eds., *De archieven van de Verenigde Oostindische Compagnie (1602–1795)*. Algemeen Rijksarchief, Eerste Afdeeling. 's-Gravenhage: Sdu Uitgeverij Koninginnegracht, 1992. The published inventory and guide of the VOC archive holdings in Dutch National Arichives is over 550 pages long.

[44] The State Archives in South Africa have been reorganized and renamed the National Archives and Record Service. The Provincial Archives and Records Service of the Western Cape is now known as the Cape Town Archives Repository.

[45] Before the end of apartheid, South African researchers were ineligible for visas or research permission in the Republic of Indonesia.

[46] The project TANAP: "Towards a New Age of Partnership" is funded by the Dutch Government and is organized by the National Archive and Leiden University. The project aims to train local historians and archivists to manage the collections in their home countries (http://www.tanap.net).

[47] See, for example, Raben, "Batavia and Colombo: The Ethnic and Spatial Order of Two Colonial Cities," Unpublished PhD dissertation, University of Leiden, 1996; James Armstrong, "The Chinese at the Cape in the Dutch East India Company Period," unpublished paper presented to the UNESCO Slave Route Project Conference, Cape Town, 1997; Nigel Worden, "Cape Town and Port Louis in the Eighteenth Century," in Gwyn Campbell, ed., *The Indian Ocean Rim: Southern Africa and Regional Co-operation*. London: Routledge-Curzon, 2003.

This book addresses the aforementioned issues by creating a connective history of the Dutch East India Company empire that attempts to keep Batavia and the Cape in the same analytical field, while simultaneously acknowledging that the unsettledness of the relationship was an intrinsic and self-conscious part of the empire itself. Decentering the metropole, in this case the Seventeen Gentlemen and the Company administration in the United Provinces, and instead concentrating on the networks between colonies within the imperial web undermines the binary concept of metropole and colony.

Migration and the Peopling of Empire

In recognizing the significant and highly visible population of unfree Europeans in the form of transported convicts, who sometimes compared themselves with slaves, this study also suggests a reconsideration of the correspondence of race and the status of freedom and bondage and of how these statuses were destabilized over time and space within the VOC imperial web.[48] Convicts and to a lesser extent exiles sent to the Cape provided cheap labor for the Dutch East India Company within its nodes and networks of empire. Convicts were used exclusively by Company officials and on its public works and, unlike slaves, had no book value for the profit-conscious VOC. Forced migration in the form of penal servitude was entirely self-contained within the colonial circuits of the imperial web because penal transportation from the United Provinces to the VOC empire did not take place. However, Dutch courts, like the Court of Holland, had the right to banish people from their own provinces, forcing convicted criminals into exile from the regions of Holland, Zeeland, Friesland, and Utrecht. This was a common punishment meted out by the courts, and banished individuals had few options for sustaining themselves.[49] For a man, to be recruited into the Dutch East India Company would have been an alternative to exile in a foreign Dutch or European territory. Although the Dutch courts could not sentence criminals to penal transportation to the Company territories, the sentence of banishment may well have had the same effect in many cases.

---

[48] Gerrit Schutte, "Between Amsterdam and Batavia: Cape Society and the Calvinist Church under the Dutch East India Company," *Kronos*, 25, 1998–99, p. 47.

[49] A. H. Huussen, "De rechtspraak in strafaken voor het Hof van Holland in het eerste kwart van de achittiende eeuw," *Holland: Regionaal-historischtijdschrift*, VIII(3), 1976, p. 132.

Conversely, European convicts of the Dutch East India Company were regularly banished from the imperial realm to the "fatherland," although they could not be sentenced to hard labor or further punishment upon their return to the United Provinces. Clare Anderson's work on convict transportation in the British East India Company empire from South Asia to Mauritius in the first half of the nineteenth century contributes to the argument that convict labor was a far more important source of labor for imperial powers than has been generally recognized, especially after the official end of the slave trade and the beginning of large-scale indentured servitude.[50]

This circuit was one of several in the British network of forced migration in the Indian Ocean. Around the turn of the nineteenth century and before the end of the slave trade and slavery, Indian convicts were also sentenced to labor in recently formed Straits Settlements and Bengkulen in Southeast Asia where, as Anand Yang points out, "they lived and labored alongside the East India Company's other major coerced labor group, African slaves, who had been brought primarily from Madagascar."[51] The scholarship of convict transportation in the British empire has been dominated by studies of the early period of transportation to the American colonies and the subsequent founding of penal colonies in Australia. Anderson and Yang show that even this one circuit of the forced migration network in the British Empire was far more complex than penal transportation to Australia. Forced migration in the form of convict transportation, exile, and the slave trade by the British in the Indian Ocean constitutes another European imperial network worthy of further research.[52]

This study of the network of forced migration within the Dutch East India Company empire contributes to flourishing debates on convict transportation that explore the movement of people on a global scale in the early modern era throughout the nineteenth century. Engaging with forced migration and the categorization of people as a form of imperial discipline and control challenges Michel Foucault's assertion that these processes were always embedded in the emergence of the modern nation-state and not earlier in the early and premodern eras.[53]

---

[50] Anderson, *Convicts in the Indian Ocean*.
[51] Anand Yang, "Indian Convict Workers in Southeast Asia in the Late Eighteenth and Early Nineteenth Centuries," *Journal of World History*, 14(2), 2003, p. 184.
[52] Anderson, *Convicts in the Indian Ocean*; Coates, *Convicts and Orphans*; Ruth Pike, *Penal Servitude in Early Modern Spain*. Madison: University of Wisconsin Press, 1983.
[53] Michel Foucault, *Discipline and Punish: The Birth of the Prison*. Trans. Alan Sheridan. New York: Vintage Books, 1987.

The Dutch East India Company was created for the purpose of making money in long-distance trade between Asia and Europe. Like all other merchant trading companies operating in the Indian Ocean grid of the early modern period, the VOC originally sought to use cultural and economic information to buy cheap in Asia and sell dear in the markets of Western Europe. The opportunities and costs of Indian Ocean and Asian trading networks soon forced the VOC into inter-Asian trade. The VOC was first and foremost designed to turn a profit for its shareholders, and this was the core of its imperial ideology. In this regard, as a purely capitalist enterprise its performance was patchy at best and declined precipitously after the mid-eighteenth century. Yet, as the economic vagaries of the early twenty-first century have taught us, a company's bankruptcy could mean ruin for its average stockholder and employee but does not preclude the accumulation of massive wealth for the inner managerial and investor circle.

In a more complicated way, this was the fate of the VOC. Over almost two centuries of its existence, the VOC had accumulated not only stockholders and employees, assets and liabilities, but was also transformed from a merchant enterprise into an empire. In the process, as the cost of maintaining this empire overtook profits, the Company elite sought to protect their families' and patrons' personal wealth at the expense of other creditors, including the Dutch state.[54] Territorial acquisitions that laid the basis for the development of imperial nodes were made reluctantly and always for the purpose of profit. Inevitably, the process of territorial settlement took on a life of its own and eventually became a demanding source of expenditure and financial debt that, when combined with the decreasing profitability of trade and continued war in Europe, undermined its access to markets, increased the vulnerability of Company settlements and ships, and contributed to the Company's eventual demise.

Empires are built on the blood, sweat, tears, and desires of people. This might seem too obvious to point out, but many histories of empire are devoid of the lives of ordinary individuals. The process of peopling an empire lies at the heart of this enterprise and, in that sense, this book is a social and cultural history of the peopling of the Dutch East India Company empire. It is fundamentally concerned with what people did and thought in relation to, and as part of, the Company's empire. The migration of nearly one million people from Europe traveling in the

---

[54] Femme S. Gaastra, *The Dutch East India Company: Expansion and Decline*. Zutphen Walburg Pers, 2003, pp. 166–167.

transportation network of over 4,700 ships fitted out for the journey from the United Provinces during the nearly two hundred years of the Company's existence is only part of this story. A closer examination of the Dutch East India Company's major imperial nodes reveals that Europeans were a minority population as compared to free and enslaved indigenous peoples, and that in archipelagic Southeast Asia, Chinese traders, laborers, and sailors were also fundamentally important to the Company's maintenance of its trading nodes and networks.

Although this book focuses on the circuit of forced migration running between the imperial capital of Batavia and the Cape of Good Hope, it also acknowledges migration circuits that included the spice-producing region of Makassar, the archipelagos of the Moluccas, and Colombo, the major Company town in a string of coastal settlements on the island of Ceylon (modern Sri Lanka). Each of these major nodes and their territorial and oceanic hinterlands were bound in a migration network that constituted the peopling of the VOC empire through free and forced migration and the more limited circuit of free Europeans migrating to and from the seaports of the Netherlands. This multidimensional process of people moving across time and place determined by the evolution of VOC sovereignty accounts for the permanent, temporary, and transient residency of people in particular territories, whether or not they moved among nodes as the empire developed. It also takes into consideration, particularly in the age of sail, the literally floating population who spent most of their lives at sea but still lived within nautical networks of navigation, transportation, and trade that were the lifelines of the early modern empires.

The "hidden history" of these networks as examined by Peter Linebaugh and Marcus Rediker in the Atlantic World has parallels in the Indian Ocean world that have not yet been thoroughly explored.[55] Nigel Worden's research on sailors ashore at the Cape attests to a distinct "sailor culture" in the VOC.[56] And as Emma Christopher suggests for the Atlantic Ocean, the ethnicity and status of sailors and slaves on board slave vessels were not starkly demarcated as the categories of crew and cargo suggest.[57] The same observation holds true for VOC ships. In its

---

[55] Peter Linebaugh and Marcus Rediker, *The Many Headed Hydra: Sailors, Slaves, Commoners, and the Hidden History of the Revolutionary Atlantic*. Boston, MA: Beacon Press, 2000, p. 47.

[56] Nigel Worden, "Sailors Ashore: Seafarer Experience and Identity in Mid-18th Century Cape Town," in Worden, ed., *Contingent Lives*, pp. 589–601.

[57] Emma Christopher, *Slave Ship Sailors and Their Captive Cargoes, 1730–1807*. New York: Cambridge University Press, 2006.

crudest form, historical studies of colonial migration have been split along the lines of race and have equated race with freedom or slavery. These newer perspectives offer insight into the process by which free and forced migrants move and settle along imperial networks and within imperial nodes and thereby contribute to the peopling of empires.

Imperial migration first developed from the maritime migrations of sailors, soldiers, and merchants to fledgling trading posts. Some of these outposts remained limited in function to trading and entailed less complex patterns of migration than would later develop in the imperial centers. Other outposts and settlements were abandoned or conquered and were thereby separated from a particular imperial web without causing it to collapse. The trading posts that did evolve into permanent settlements required more varied functions to be performed by the maritime populations, merchants, administrators, artisans, food producers, and laborers, and this inevitably led to more complex interactions with indigenous populations. Relationships between settlers and indigenous populations often involved engagement with forms of free and forced labor, including in the early modern period, slavery and the slave trade. Over time, free and forced migrations to some parts of an empire led to the development of settler societies whose creole population became self-sustaining and decreased the need for in-migration to maintain and reproduce the colonial labor force. Each of these processes operated in dynamic unison to constitute the entirety of the VOC imperial network of migration. Early modern European merchant voyages and the empires they spawned from the fifteenth century onward involved, to a significant extent, monitoring the people engaged in these trading networks. In the first instance, the manning of ships with sailors, soldiers, and merchants comprised the foundation of imperial migration from the metropole to the trading post. It was a highly gendered process and in this sense the sea-borne population of early modern European empires from the fifteenth century until the end of the eighteenth century was overwhelmingly male.

The massive scale of the Dutch East India Company migration from Europe gives some perspective of both the size of this ostensibly sojourning male population and the multiplicity of networks that were created within the Company's ships and settlements. As Company servants, sailors and soldiers constituted their own mobile communities with links to port towns throughout the maritime world. Artisans were another major group of European employees of the Company; thousands were employed throughout Asia. As essential skilled and semiskilled labor, they tended to remain in the settlements and colonies to which they had been assigned, at least for the duration of their five-year contracts.[58] The total recruitment figure of nearly one million people from Europe during the entire Company period from 1602 to 1799 does not take into account the exceedingly high proportion of deaths at sea and on land, but it still gives an indication of the density of sailing community networks. Moreover, these figures do not include tens of thousands of locally engaged Asian and Chinese sailors who sailed the inter-Asian and Indian Ocean maritime networks of the Company's empire.[59]

Although the provisioning of supplies, storage of cargo, and boarding of sailors and passengers on VOC ships sailing from the United Provinces were closely monitored, many Dutch East India Company fleets sailed from Europe with one or two women illegally masquerading as men in their crews. Captains were obliged to give details in the ship's logs about the discovery of these women sailors, who were inevitably taken on as passengers once their gender had been determined. In the close quarters below decks, it is not surprising that women were eventually "uncovered," although one wonders what social and sexual strategies they used to avoid (or perhaps to hasten) being brought before the captain. Still, these exceptional women proved the rule that while sailors and soldiers could be of any ethnicity, they had to be heterosexual males. The punishment for the discovery of homosexual activity was the execution of both guilty parties usually by tying the men together and throwing them overboard to drown in each other's arms.[60] Shipboard discipline was harsh and meted out with speed and determination. These strict laws of behavior and deference to authority were designed to ensure the smooth running of the isolated world of the vessel as a society in miniature. Given the number of attempted and successful mutinies aboard

---

[58] Opper suggests that previous residence and preexisting networks of trade and transportation linked to the major towns that constituted the core of the Company's seven chambers influenced recruitment patterns. Edward Opper, "Dutch East India Company Artisans in the Early Eighteenth Century," unpublished PhD dissertation, Indiana University, 1975, pp. 16–48.

[59] Femme Gaastra, *De geschiedenis van de VOC*, 2nd ed. Zutphen: Walburg Pers, 1991; Meilink-Roelofsz, Raben and Spikerman eds., *Archieven van de VOC*; Frank Lequin, *Het personeel van de Verenigde Oost-Indische Compagnie in Azië in de achttiende eeuw, meet in het bijzonder in de vesting Bengalen*. Leiden: Rijksuniversiteit Leiden, 1982.

[60] For examples of the analysis of homosexuality in the context of the VOC see Susan Newton-King, "For the Love of Adam: Two Sodomy Trials at the Cape of Good Hope," *Kronos*, 28, 2002, pp. 21–42, and Theo van der Meer, "Sodomy and Homosexuality in an Early Modern World: Simultaneity and Disparity," in Worden, ed., *Contingent Lives*, pp. 428–436.

merchant vessels of all European origins it is not surprising that shipboard justice was swiftly applied. It was from this social and legal context that the territorial nodes of empire took their initial codes of conduct. This maritime justice system also provided the foundation of criminal law for the Dutch East India Company.

The Company was only one of many merchant companies seeking a route to the fabled "spice islands" and an inroad into profitable trading networks with and among Asian societies. As mentioned previously, the network of migration as outlined for the VOC in this book could be multiplied many times over, each in a unique formulation according to the particular constitution of the imperial merchant enterprise being examined. Perhaps the most productive comparison with the Dutch East India Company is that of the Portuguese empire that the VOC partially displaced in the Indian Ocean grid during the Iberian wars.

Portuguese merchants under the ultimate authority of the crown had, since the late fifteenth century, been fanning across the world's oceans in search of riches. Although the history of Iberian involvement with the societies of the Americas is well known, the Portuguese empire is rarely examined as a global network of free and forced migration. Studies of Portuguese imperialism tend to separate along oceanic lines, cutting off the Atlantic from the Indian Ocean parts of the realm, and, in the strictest sense, this separation does not allow for an accurate view of the Portuguese imperial world. The Portuguese empire in the Indian Ocean had a separate basis of administrative authority in the *Estado da India*, ruled by the viceroy of Goa at its imperial base in India. From Goa, the *Estado da India* directed the expansionist policies of the Portuguese and allied traders in Asia, starting at the beginning of the sixteenth century. The other two viceroys were located in Peru and Mexico and operated in the Americas and the Atlantic world. The American colonies were peopled partly by slaves from Africa, and the Portuguese empire in that region was intimately engaged with the African slave trade along the length of the West African and central African coast. The Portuguese empire was complicated in its legal networks by the dual authority of the Crown and church. The Portuguese imperial ideology did not separate secular and spiritual realms, and its empire was supposed to be a manifestation of God's work on earth. This ideology had implications for the way the legal system operated within its imperial web by binding the nodes of empire closely to the core of authority in the European-based Crown and church.

This relationship was fundamentally different in the Dutch East India Company empire, having emerged from a more tolerant culture of religious difference and secular political authority in the United Provinces. The officers of the Reformed Church in the Dutch East India Company were company servants who had no recourse to a higher religious authority that might challenge the moral basis of Company policy at the level of imperial rule. Moreover, the Company was practically indifferent to proselytizing; its imperial ideology remained faithful to mammon rather than to the will of God, as interpreted by the Dutch Reformed Church.

Within its more integrated networks of authority, free and forced migration between Portugal and its colonies, and within its overseas realm, the Portuguese empire did not divide neatly between the Atlantic and Indian Oceans. The imperial migration network of the Portuguese was fundamentally global in its reach. Timothy Coates traces penal transportation along circuits from Portugal to the colonies and between the colonies themselves, including the state-sponsored migration of orphans from Portugal, and the exile of reformed prostitutes sent to all major nodes of its empire.[61] Significant numbers of women circulated as nominally unfree migrants in these networks of the Portuguese empire. Their participation in migration networks from the homeland and among the colonies in both the Atlantic and Indian Oceans shaped the development of Portuguese colonial societies by increasing the proportion of European-born women distributed as marriage partners by imperial and church authorities.

In these respects, migration in the Dutch East India Company empire differed significantly from migration in the Portuguese and British empires. The Dutch East India Company was not a direct functionary of the state and was not tied to the criminal legal systems of the United Provinces or the religious authority of the Reformed Church. Nor did it entice or encourage forced migration from the metropole to its colonies. On the other hand, the Portuguese Crown and Catholic Church were the highest powers in the Portuguese empire, and these close ties enabled the Portuguese state to impose gendered forced migration from its territory on the Iberian Peninsula to the colonies.

A similar pattern emerged in Britain, although with the intercession of Parliament instead of the church as the legal authority mandating forced migration to the colonies. Particularly in the establishment of the North American colonies, the intersection of free and forced migration from Britain served both economic and political ends. From their beginnings

[61] Coates, *Convicts and Orphans*.

as merchant trading ventures, the merchant companies sought settlers to people their territorial and trading enterprises in North America. Voluntary migration of men and women to the American English settlements in the seventeenth century was insufficient to develop profitable colonies. So began the system of indentured servitude whereby willing migrants from Britain contractually bound themselves to masters who "purchased" them in the colonies for a fixed period at what were in theory binding conditions of employment and wages but in practice often deteriorated into a form of debt-slavery.

Alongside this ambiguously free migration network, most American colonies also accepted British convicts who were transported to penal servitude by the English courts. The boundary between convicts and political prisoners was particularly blurry in the case of Irish exiles. Convicts were transported across the Atlantic and sold to masters for a fee to work at hard labor for the duration of their sentences. In both indentured and penal servitude, individuals often did not live to see their eventual freedom. Both systems of bound labor were open to abuse, although historians of colonial America have argued that the earlier generations of indentured servants prior to the eighteenth century had far more chance of upward social mobility, if they survived, than did later generations of servants entering what were by then highly socially stratified and well-established colonies. There was also a gendered element to this form of servitude, with women servants in the earlier generations often able to marry up the social ladder because of the shortage of marriage partners for the overwhelmingly male population.[62] The demands for labor in the American colonies and the inadequacy of free and forced migration strategies from Europe led, at the end of the seventeenth century, to a new form of forced migration of slaves from Africa.

In the Netherlands, there was no centralized political structure with the authority and legal system to institute penal transportation. The United Provinces was unusual among early modern European states because it did not actively seek to rid itself of its own criminal elements by sending them overseas to colonies. It is perhaps no coincidence that the United Provinces, and particularly urban centers like Amsterdam, were at the forefront of the development of modern prisons founded on the principle

---

[62] See for example, Peter Wilson Coldham, *Emigrants in Chains: A Social History of Forced Emigration to the Americas of Felons, Destitute Children, Political and Religious Non-Conformists, Vagabonds, Beggars and Other Undesirables, 1607–1776*. Surrey: Genealogical Publishing Company, 1992.

of the redeeming nature of labor. The Dutch preferred to punish and attempt to reform their criminal elements at home, and their strictly gendered Houses of Correction became the toast of reformers all over Europe and a tourist attraction in Amsterdam.[63] However, major cities and towns still used older patterns of internal exile to rid localities of their undesirable elements. Yet there existed no centralized religious authority in the United Provinces like the Catholic Church that sought to parallel or supersede the legal or disciplinary structures of the regionally based secular courts.

Penal transportation emanating from the United Provinces was not used to people the Dutch East India Company empire, in part because the States-General granted the Company the right to create its own legal system and punish offenders under its charter and the further right to develop an imperial system of forced migration through the elaboration of Company law, including capital punishment. Furthermore, the government of the United Provinces did not have a legal mechanism for imposing penal transportation or exile to the Company's empire as a punishment for criminals sentenced by Dutch courts. These legal reasons precluded the systematic penal transportation or forced political exile of men, women, and children from United Provinces to the Company's colonies and settlements.

One group of migrant refugees was, however, produced from the expulsion of the Protestant Huguenots from Catholic France who fled to the United Provinces and other Protestant states after Louis XIV revoked the Edict of Nantes in 1685. By this time, the Dutch East India Company node at the Cape had evolved into a port town with an agriculturally productive and rapidly expanding hinterland. The Company recruited 156 Huguenot refugees directly from Holland to settle in the Cape. These migrants were not scattered throughout the Company's empire but constituted instead a single strand of European migration in the Company's network that was carefully controlled geographically.[64] No other migration of religious or political exiles equivalent to the Huguenots took place in the Dutch East India Company empire. Other free migrations of potential settlers occurred on a more limited basis.

---

[63] Simon Schama, *The Embarrassment of Riches: An Interpretation of Dutch Culture in the Golden Age*. New York: Vintage Books, 1997. pp. 14–24.

[64] Huguenots were also recruited by the Dutch West India Company to settle in the recently conquered colony of Brazil. Although the Dutch interregnum in Brazil was brief, and migration between WIC and VOC colonies rare, the WIC had its own imperial network centered on South America and the Caribbean; Cornelis Goslinga, *A Short History of the Netherlands Antilles and Surinam*. The Hague: M. Nijhoff, 1979.

Between 1685 and 1705, the Company provided free passage to men and women who agreed to settle at the Cape. The policy was not particularly successful in attracting agricultural settlers to Africa. Many of the new immigrants preferred to stay in town and become part of the service industry provisioning ships and providing for sailors and soldiers ashore. The dominant pattern for creating a settler population was to allow Company servants at the Cape to apply for release from their contracts and become free burghers. This meant that they were no longer Company servants at the beck and call of a Company that could send them anywhere in the empire without their consent. However, this did not mean that burghers were free to roam at will. Their movements were carefully monitored although almost impossible to completely restrict. This was the process whereby colonial settlers at the Cape of Good Hope became embedded in the land they would come to identify with as "Afrikaners" by the end of the eighteenth century.[65] In other places, like the Banda archipelago, Dutch colonial plantation owners developed their own settler identities as *Perkeniers* (planters) as they established a monopoly on nutmeg plantations in the region after the violent conquest and depopulation of these tiny islands by the VOC in the 1620s. Outside the main settlement areas of Java, there were no other major settler societies that emerged in the VOC era although many of the other settlements and colonies had a minor colonial settler presence.

European empires in the early modern period generally had to solve to the problem of how to provide a viable population of traders and settlers by encouraging them to form stable families that would cement their commitment to the locality. Various imperial and merchant enterprises had grappled with this problem, and the Dutch East India Company devised its own solution. At first, the Seventeen Gentlemen were reluctant to acknowledge the permanent existence of a settler population within their overseas enterprise and therefore stymied attempts by VOC governors to create and stabilize a ruling European class. Official disapproval in the Netherlands of the practice of keeping concubines also initially hampered the full recognition of an emerging creole population within the major settlements that evolved inevitably as a result of male Company servants who, in most cases, were not permitted to have their wives and children

---

[65] Susan Newton-King, *Masters and Servants on the Cape Eastern Frontier, 1760–1803*. Cambridge: Cambridge University Press, 1999; Nigel Penn, *The Forgotten Frontier: Colonist and Khoikhoi on the Cape's Northern Frontier in the 18th Century*. Athens: Ohio University Press, 2005; Laura J. Mitchell, *Belongings: Property, Family and Identity in Colonial South Africa: An Exploration of Frontiers 1725–c1830*. New York: Columbia University Press, 2008.

emigrate from Europe, sought sexual and marital partners from among the local populations where they lived. The few attempts to emulate the Portuguese strategy of bringing Dutch orphan girls or poor women to the Indies were sporadic and not at all successful. The European population in the Company's empire expanded instead by incorporating indigenous women into stable family structures through conversion and marriage, unions that changed their legal status and their children's, into European. Company settlements were, for the most part, colonial slave societies and the sexual exploitation of slave women by their masters and other men was widespread.

Slave masters had the additional option of recognizing and legitimating their slave progeny and to manumit and marry their slave women, under condition of their conversion to Christianity and learning some smattering of Dutch language, which thereby assured their children a superior place in colonial society as legal Europeans. Indeed, the Company in Batavia engaged in the slave trade of indigenous women expressly for the purpose of providing brides for their lower ranking servants, and it also controlled the formalization of these relationships. Over generations, this created a "Eurasian" colonial population that was the basis of Dutch settler society in Asia. This trend for lower-level Company servants contrasts with the practices of the Company's elite servants, whose wives and concubines were more often brought out directly from Europe or who circulated within imperial networks to create what became a Dutch Creole elite with ties to all Company nodes. As Jean Gelman Taylor has demonstrated through genealogical records, whereas the Company elite generally sent their sons "home" to Europe for an education, their girls remained behind in the colonies to be raised as suitable marriage partners for their class. It was through Creole women and marriage alliances that the Company elite cemented their ties to each other.[66] Eurasian and slave women provided the basis of the lower classes of the colonial settler population throughout the Company's empire because the incorporation of their children into the category "European" enabled their continued reproduction as a dominant group.

The final component of the Company's imperial migration network in terms of forced labor was the slave population. Slaves were drawn from the indigenous slave trade in networks of the Indian Ocean grid and incorporated into the Company's empire through its network of forced

---

[66] Jean Gelman Taylor, *The Social World of Batavia: European and Eurasian in Dutch Asia*. Madison: University of Wisconsin Press, 1983, pp. 1–52.

migration. The multiethnic slave population of all Company settlements attests to the complexity of this network that also intersected with other networks of European slave trade in the region. As has already become clear, the slave population cannot be easily separated out from other people in the imperial migration network. Slaves were subject to forced migration through the slave trade, the migration of their owner's household and through being convicted for crimes. Slaves were not exempt from penal transportation, although slave owners had to agree to the punishment or pay fines and costs in lieu of sentencing.

No historian has yet tackled writing a book that analyzes slavery and the slave trade in the Company's empire, and regional historiographies of slavery are uneven. It is beyond the scope of this book to elaborate on slavery as a form of forced migration except where it affects other forms of forced migration, like penal transportation. Focusing on the variations of bondage in Batavia and the Cape of Good Hope is one way of illuminating the imperial dynamics of forced migration by tracing movements of people across the Dutch East India Company empire.

Organization of this Book

The concept of a network has multiple meanings and has been put, accordingly, to multiple tasks in writing this history of forced migration in the Dutch East India Company empire. In one sense, considering sovereignty as having been constituted along various intersecting networks opens out to a coherent vocabulary (i.e. circuits, sub-circuits, nodes, webs and grids) through which to envision the multidimensional histories that might be better rendered on a three-dimensional grid on which time, space, and their points of contact are in constant flux. As a visual organizing principle, the network helps compensate for the limited capacity of the written word and two-dimensional map to represent dynamic and complex historical processes over an extended period of time. Thus the maps in this book, while essential for marking the density and reach of the Dutch East India Company's imperial web in the Indian Ocean grid, are better interpreted suggestively rather than literally. In another sense, a network is a structuring mechanism that is especially well suited for moving analytically among multiple layers of sovereignty and identifying important nodes of intersection among them. The network is employed in this sense as a conceptual framework for unifying macro- and micro-levels of analysis.

In yet another sense, a network is more literally the path taken by a specific form of relational power in early modern empires, for example law, trade, or material circumstances, like shipping. In tracing the density and reach of a particular network within a particular imperial web, one becomes privy to the waxing and waning of specific vectors of imperial sovereignty as well as to the unique character of early modern empires and their interactions with indigenous polities. In a final sense, a network is a credible representation of sovereignty as it was consolidated and contested "on the ground." Here, tracing the lives of imperial subjects along a single network as it intersects with others in salient circuits and nodes helps the historian to construct a coherent and meaningful narrative from fragmentary evidence. While VOC subjects did not speak or write in terms of networks, it appears that many understood in practice how forced migration, legality and trade operated as discrete vectors of imperial power, often to their detriment.

For example, Cape settlers in the eighteenth century protested against specific aspects of forced migration, banishment, and penal transportation and not, initially, against the Dutch East India Company empire as a whole. They used the Company's hierarchy to press their claims for access to trade networks through specific channels of legal and communication networks and not through others. Likewise, Shaykh Yusuf's family in Makassar used similar channels to lobby for his return from the Cape, although they were not successful during his lifetime. So too did British and Dutch colonial rulers negotiate at the end of the VOC era and the beginning of the British era at the Cape of Good Hope the retention and elimination of specific circuits of forced migration.

In developing the concept, lexicon, and analysis of the imperial network, this book demonstrates, not only the vigor of the network concept but also its fit to the material at hand; the constitution and operation of imperial sovereignty in the early modern era. The analysis and articulation of networks in this book are, however, contingent and bear further scrutiny against the historical record. Nevertheless, the network remains a promising concept for opening new ways of thinking about empire, particularly considering the piecemeal and disconnected nature of archival evidence. In short, the full exploratory power of the imperial network has yet to be tapped in writing world history. *Networks of Empire* is offered as one way to begin doing so through the examination of the network of forced migration in the Dutch East India Company empire.

Chapter 2, "The Evolution of Governance and Forced Migration," takes a wide-angle perspective of the Dutch East India Company through an examination of its charter to argue that the opportunities of partial sovereignty granted by the States-General of the United Provinces outweighed the constraints. This broad sweep through the chronological and regional activities of the Company enables VOC specialists and non-specialists alike to envisage the extension of imperial sovereignty through the Company's imperial nodes and networks in its charter domain. The creation of the Company's institutions of bureaucracy and governance was based on the corresponding evolution of its legal system. As Batavia became a major urban center and the imperial capital, founding its civic institutions went hand-in-hand with passing laws to accommodate the increasing complexity of governance. The 1642 codification of Company law in the Statutes of Batavia and articulation of the principles of jurisprudence became a template for the rule of law and the conduct of diplomacy throughout the empire. The Statutes provided guidelines for law and governance but were not necessarily directly referred to for legal decisions in Company nodes. Often local circumstances determined the relative application of Company and indigenous law. When possible, the Company asserted jurisdiction, particularly in criminal law, over its own subjects and also over other people living in its settlements.

The focus of this book is the peopling of empire. Accordingly, this chapter ends with a discussion of the implications of governance for the Company's own personnel and for slaves, two of the major sources of labor in the empire. The high incidence of illness amongst Company servants meant that the proportion of these men condemned as criminals to hard labor and/or penal transportation was higher than the raw figures suggest. Although slaves were more difficult to enumerate, they clearly formed the largest portion of bonded labor in Company settlements and a significant source of Company labor. The VOC engaged in a complex slave trade network in the Indian Ocean arena and instituted a form of corporate slave ownership foreign to indigenous slave practices.

With Chapter 3, the focus narrows to a closer examination of these processes in the imperial capital, Batavia, and to a more limited period of time, between 1730 and 1750. As the city grew, Company and civil authorities enumerated the population and assigned people to distinct ethnic and religious categories. These ascribed identities had implications for an individual's legal status and, consequently, his or her potential treatment in court. This chapter explains the events surrounding the 1740 massacre of Batavia's urban Chinese population through the Company's criminal records and examines the conduct of the city's courts immediately before and in the aftermath of this event. The Company's criminal records offer a glimpse of the social world of the city's underclasses and shows that the Company was vigilant in punishing its own servants for crimes, particularly desertion, the crime most commonly committed by slaves. Furthermore, the sentence of penal transportation was implemented for a whole range of crimes. This chapter follows the lives of individuals who, in committing these transgressions, were incorporated into the Company's network of forced migration.

The network of forced migration is traced along a particular circuit that extended to the Company's emerging settlement at the Cape of Good Hope in southern Africa. Chapter 4, "The Cape Cauldron," considers the history of the Cape as a familiar refreshment stop for European ships traveling to Asia before the Dutch East India Company established a post on the littoral of Table Bay. Sites along the southern African coast had previously been investigated for potential Portuguese and English settlement by dumping prisoners ashore, but these forays failed to prompt further settlement. European travelers had also long visited Robben Island during their attempts to obtain fresh food and water. Because it could be secured as a defensive post and used to isolate prisoners, Robben Island was fundamental to the success of the Dutch settlement.

Company officials at the Cape struggled to stabilize the fledgling settlement by ensuring the compliance of their own subordinates while they pondered the problem of generating sufficient labor to produce food for ships in port. From the outset, forced migration was an important element in the supply of labor for the Cape. The perspective of Company officials reflected their early understanding of the ability of the imperial network of forced migration to supply the Cape with convict and slave labor. For a brief moment, the Cape's first commander fantasized about enslaving the indigenous population and sending them to the slave market in Batavia so he could confiscate their cattle and gain stable control of the region. This suggestion was not seriously considered. Within decades of its founding, the Company was sending slaves, convicts and exiles to the Cape, despite the latter two being considered an undesirable source of labor in the settlement.

The Company also sought to conduct its relations with indigenous Khoekhoe polities through the principles of VOC law. Initially, the Khoekhoe people remained under the jurisdiction of their own laws, but after the Company induced Khoekhoe leaders to sign treaties ceding the Cape to Company sovereignty, they became increasingly subject to Company law. To alleviate a continuing labor shortage and provide the colony with a direct supply of slaves, the Cape also developed its own intermittent sub-circuit of forced migration through slave trading in the southwest Indian Ocean.

The extension of the Company's network of forced migration to the Cape through political exile from the eastern Indian Ocean region, particularly through Batavia and Colombo, had unforeseen consequences for the Company empire. Chapter 5 tracks the experiences of people caught in the Company's circuit of exile to the Cape. By focusing on individuals, this chapter demonstrates how the Company's use of exile as a political strategy drew the Cape into Javanese and Makassarese politics and into VOC diplomatic relations with Asian powers. It also suggests that the presence of some of these exiles at the Cape, including Shaykh Yusuf, was crucial to the transmission of Islam through Muslim exiles and slaves developing shared practices of their faith. Political exile revealed the limitations of Company sovereignty wherein, to a certain extent, the Company found it could control people physically, but not the spread of their ideas, beliefs, and practices it might wish to contain. The use of forced migration, particularly political exile, linked the Cape to cosmopolitan Indian Ocean Islamic networks of communication, religion, and pilgrimage. The focus on political exiles here reveals only one of many ways Company networks intersected with and were altered by various preexisting and developing indigenous networks in the Indian Ocean.

By the early eighteenth century, the Cape had evolved into a small settler colony based primarily on slave labor and had become both a crucial node in the Company's transportation network as a provisioning stop for transoceanic shipping and a hospital for seafarers. Chapter 6 argues that the Cape's position in the transportation network simultaneously facilitated forced migration through the slave trade, penal transportation, and political exile. The slave trade was conducted through formal Company and informal private avenues. Penal transportation and political exile were exclusively under VOC control, and these practices were increasingly resented, not only by local Company officials, but also by local settlers. As subjects of imperial law, settlers were vulnerable to banishment in the circuits of penal transportation and this angered them. The Company's use of Asian exiles as *caffers*, executioner's assistants who also had policing duties that included powers of arrest and chastisement of free burghers, angered them further and exposed the double-edged nature of forced migration. The presence of convicts and exiles in positions of authority disrupted emerging social and racial hierarchies in Cape colonial society and provided an additional source of tension in Company-colonist relations that led some settlers to challenge Company governance. This chapter examines individual and group acts of resistance by people who sought to maximize their own autonomy and sometimes regain their freedom. Thus did forced migration support the extension of Company sovereignty in some nodes, like Batavia and Colombo, and present a challenge to the rule of law in others, like the Cape of Good Hope.

The circuit of forced migration between Batavia and the Cape was not dismantled until the end of Company rule. Chapter 7, "Disintegrating Imperial Networks" shows how this particular imperial circuit continued to incite protest among an increasingly localized settler population whose loyalties had, over generations, shifted from the Company to their adopted homeland. Political protests by the settlers sought to challenge Company rule at the Cape, initially through appeals about corrupt local officials made to the governing hierarchy within the Company, the High Government in Batavia and the Seventeen Gentlemen in the Netherlands. By the latter decades of the eighteenth century, appeals were made directly to the States-General against Company rule itself. As an indicator of their failed allegiance, the local population in Cape Town did little to resist the British when they invaded the Cape in 1795.

The transfer of the Cape took nearly twenty years and involved a serious of transitional British and Dutch governments from 1795 until British sovereignty was formally recognized through treaty in 1814. During this period, the British integrated the Cape into its own imperial networks but maintained continuity in the rule of law, except in the frontier regions. Tracing the process of transformation whereby the Cape went from being a Dutch to a British colony is a particularly good way to observe how networks constitute partial imperial sovereignty. For example, the Company's network of forced migration to the Cape went from being primarily focused on the Indian Ocean slave trade, penal transportation, and political exile from Batavia and Colombo, to being primarily focused on the British *anti-slave* trade network in the Indian Ocean and on a minor and irregular circuit of penal transportation to Britain's Australian colonies.

Taken together, these chapters present a cross section of the network of forced migration in the Company's empire by focusing on the circuit from Batavia to the Cape that included slavery, penal transportation, and political exile. They present a detailed portrait of the partial and complex sovereignties of this early modern Dutch commercial empire. They suggest that understanding the legacy of VOC imperial rule is fundamental to comprehending the creation of nations as diverse as South Africa and

Indonesia and how these societies interpret their histories in the present. *Networks of Empire* brings these national histories into a single analytical framework and links their long-term trajectories of nation-building to their histories of empire, while expanding our understanding of a global past.

VOC Nodes in the Indian Ocean

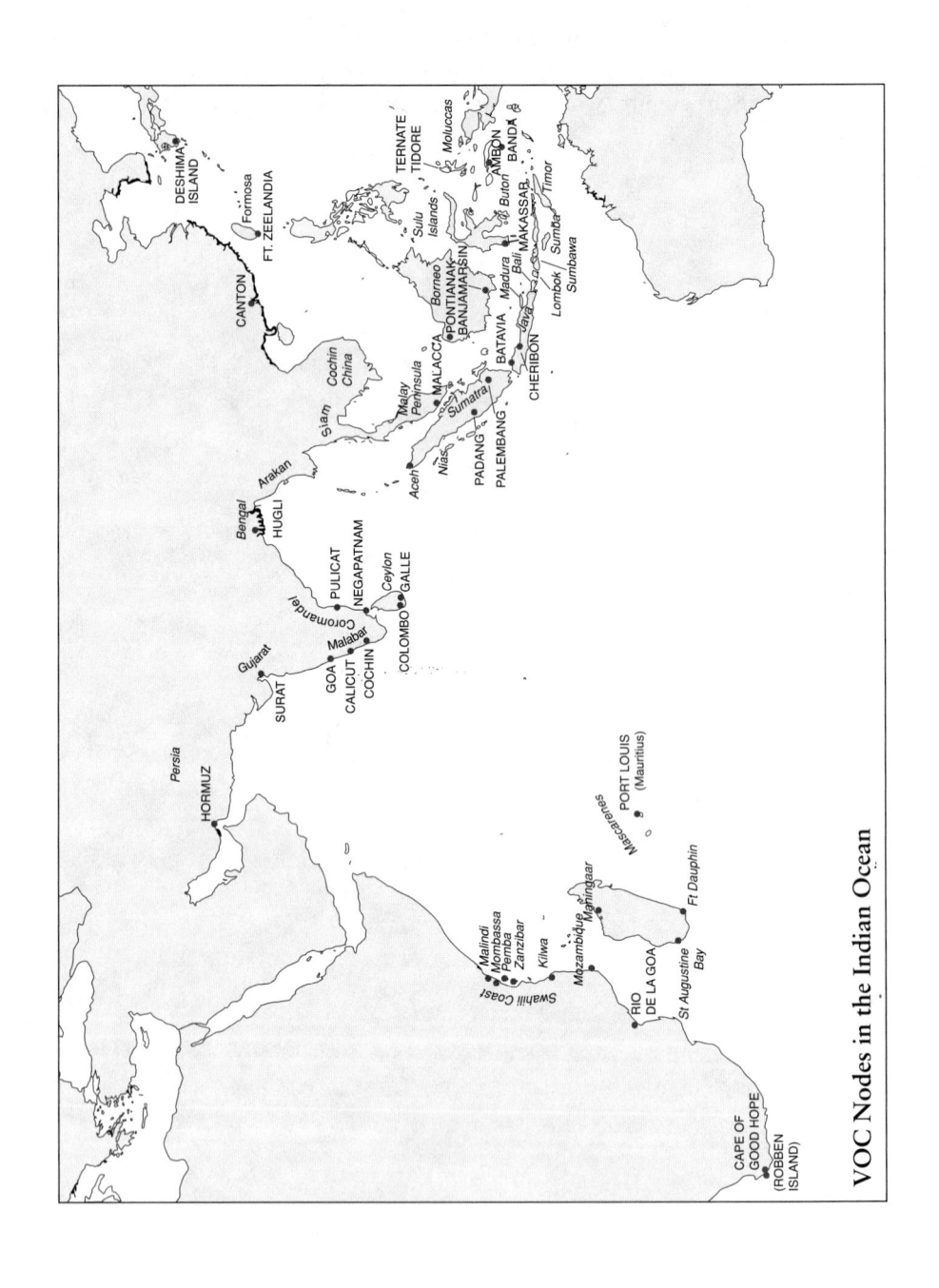

2

The Evolution of Governance and Forced Migration

Six Amsterdam ships set sail from the Texel roadstead in 1602 with a full crew carrying, along with provisions and armaments, the authority of the newly sealed Charter endorsing the sovereign rights of the Dutch East India Company and its first fleet. The States-General, as the highest ruling body of the United Provinces, had granted the charter on March 20, 1602, and, while it did not literally provide ballast to keep the ships from floundering, it did become the legal cornerstone for VOC operations on the coastal fringes of the Indian Ocean.[1] The Dutch East India Company was undoubtedly first, foremost, and forever preoccupied with trade and profit. Nevertheless, its charter contained the legal conditions of possibility for its transformation from trading company to empire by allowing the enactment of laws to maintain order and discipline within the Company's own ships and settlements and by defining the principles for the Company's engagement with foreign powers, including terms of trade, diplomacy, and conquest. Although not anticipated by the States-General in 1602, the Dutch East India Company created in situ and over time, economic, political, social, legal, and administrative networks through which its partial sovereignties coalesced into an imperial web that spanned a large part of the Company's *octrooigebied* (charter domain) east of the Cape of Good Hope and through the Straits of Magellan. This empire lasted until the end of 1799, by which time the British East India Company had substantially usurped and reconfigured the Company's colonial domain, and the VOC itself was nationalized by the new Dutch Republic.

Initially, the Dutch East India Company fleets were the "world in miniature" of the Company's seaborne trade. Depending upon local conditions,

---

[1] Femme S. Gaastra, *The Dutch East India Company: Expansion and Decline*. Zutphen, Netherlands: Walburg Pers, 2003.

the Company might restrict its activities in its first trading sites to factories, forts, and trading posts or it might attempt more broadly to secure a monopoly on trade through conquest. Where trade intensified and conquest succeeded, some of these limited territorial footholds expanded into more densely populated and securely settled nodes along the Company's evolving trading network. Increasing population and commercial activity in turn necessitated a corresponding expansion in Company sovereignty and administrative oversight over the population living in its territorial domain, if control of its labor force was to be achieved and production and trade stabilized to maximize profits.

The number of Company ships and employees over two centuries of operations is impressive. Over 4,700 ships were fitted out by the VOC to transport almost one million people from Europe to Asia. At its height around 1750, the Company enumerated over thirty-five thousand people employed throughout its domain.[2] These numbers do not accurately portray the size of its empire because they omit indigenous people employed by the Company, Company and personal slaves, and free people of various legal categories living within its realm. The Dutch East India Company was a massive enterprise by any standards, at its widest reach extending from the Cape of Good Hope on the southern tip Africa to Deshima Island adjoining Nagasaki on the East China Sea.

The management of people over such a far-flung empire was essential to the extension and operation of VOC maritime trade and to the orderly growth and management of the diverse populations who inhabited its settlement nodes. The Company devised a legal system to facilitate its trading interests through diplomatic relations with foreign powers and to control whom it determined resided under Company jurisdiction through its internal decrees. The system was developed in Batavia and extended across the Company's Indian Ocean domain through a robust communication network. The Company's legal and communication networks enabled the subsequent creation of its network of forced migration, through which political and population dynamics could be controlled on land and on sea across an expanding imperial web.

Controlling Company servants and European civilian subjects proved to be difficult enough, but the Company also had to contend with indigenous and migrant Asian populations within its boundaries. The VOC ensured discipline and secured labor by passing criminal laws that sentenced

---

[2] Ibid., pp. 80–88.

transgressors to punishment that included penal transportation to and among its various settlement nodes. Most importantly, the VOC developed its own slave code in a departure from the Dutch tradition of eschewing slavery and thereby secured a more dependable labor force by regulating engagement in regional slave networks and passing laws that governed people defined as slaves.

The parameters of forced migration were thus defined a priori by the jurisdictional reach of the VOC legal system and were comprised of the slave trade, penal transportation, and political banishment, each with its respective category of legally assigned identity: slave, convict, exile. Alliances and hostilities with foreign powers also generated prisoners of state and prisoners of war, each of whom were subject to exile under the VOC legal system. Banishment was used to control individuals perceived as a menace to Company interests and was applied in multiple forms throughout the empire.

The VOC Charter

The Dutch East India Company's charter was issued by the States-General in 1602 and inscribed both the possibilities and the limitations of sovereignty that became its basis of empire. Drawing upon the political structures of the United Provinces set in place in 1579 under the Union of Utrecht, and based upon strong links among patrimonial elites, a similar town-based corporate structure was negotiated for the unification of trade under the VOC, with Amsterdam being the dominant chamber.[3] In examining the early modern European state systems, Julia Adams argues that they were

patrimonial states in the making, not fully constituted sovereign entities, as the concept of a strong state implies. These nascent systems of rule were marked by

---

[3] The States-General was comprised of civic and regional chambers. The VOC was similarly divided into six chambers: Amsterdam, Zeeland, Delft, Rotterdam, Hoorn, and Enkhuizen. Sixty to seventy nominated Company directors from each chamber (also major stockholders) nominated the seventeen members of governing directorate. Under the original charter, the States-General chose the first Seventeen Gentlemen, but thereafter they were nominated internally within the Company. The directorate was designed to prevent dominance by the Amsterdam Chamber, which had eight representatives.

Ball claims that after 1640 the *Haags Besoignes*, the Company's permanent directorate in The Hague, chaired by the Chief Advocate, was the real power in the VOC. It conducted daily administration, while the Seventeen Gentlemen and the chambers met bi-annually to "rubber stamp" the permanent directorate's decisions. John Ball, *Indonesian Legal History*. Sydney: Oughtershaw Press, 1982, pp. 2–3; Gaastra, *Dutch East India Company*.

a segmentation or parcelization of sovereign power among the ruler (or rulers) and corporate elites. The patrimonial ruler ruled... by relying on self-governing corporations charged with key economic and political obligations, such as estates and guilds, chartered companies, and so on, which were charged with the tasks of formulating and enforcing collectively binding decisions on the people and activities under their jurisdiction. Corporate elites derived economic resources, representation, and symbolic legitimacy in return.[4]

The configuration of patrimonial regent elites in the estatist Netherlands, with their wealth being increasingly generated by the colonial trade in bulk luxury goods, ensured that the interests of the VOC would be protected by the States-General.[5] The overlapping patrimonial networks of the States-General and the VOC also meant that men from merchant elite families were leaders of both bodies.[6] The States-General retained supreme sovereignty in its own name under the VOC charter. They did not, however, exercise these powers until the Company began to weaken in the late eighteenth century, at which time they took measures to establish administrative control that did not succeed in reversing the Company's financial decline. For all intents and purposes, the States-General protected the monopoly of the VOC from its inception until its final dissolution and did not effectively interfere directly in the empire.[7] It is not surprising then that the VOC was able to don an important vestment of sovereignty by minting its own currency and circulating it as one of the many trading currencies in Asia.[8] The right to create its own money

---

[4] Julia Adams, "Trading States, Trading Places: The Role of Patrimonialism in Early Modern Dutch Development," *Comparative Studies in Society and History*, 36 (2), 1994, p. 326.

[5] Julia Adams, *The Familial State: Ruling Families and Merchant Capitalism in Early Modern Europe*. Ithaca, NY: Cornell University Press, 2005, chapters 2 and 3, pp. 38–105.

[6] Janice E. Thomson, *Mercenaries, Pirates, and Sovereigns: State-Building and Extraterritorial Violence in Early Modern Europe*. Princeton, NJ: Princeton University Press, 1994, pp. 1–20. Thomson argues that sovereignty is the international institution that empowers states vis-à-vis people and organizes global politics, including war. "Mercantile companies were, as a rule, granted full sovereign powers," p. 35.

[7] Ball argues that the Republic's civic rivalry was reproduced in the earlier period of the *voor-compagnies* and subsequently replicated in the Company charter and its structures. The first thirty-three articles of the Charter focused on formalizing the relations between the six chambers, while only thirteen articles detailed the concessions granted by the States-General. Ball, *Indonesian Legal History*, pp. 1–2.

[8] H. R. Hahlo and E. Kahn, *The South African Legal System and Its Background*. Cape Town: Juta, 1968, p. 535. Leonard Blussé provides an interesting account of the relationship between Company coinage and the Chinese leaden *pici* coins used on Java. The VOC manipulated its stocks of lead, eventually minting these in Batavia, to stimulate trade in Java in favor of the Batavia market. Blussé further notes that attempts by Batavia in the 1640s to mint copper coins were rejected by the Seventeen Gentlemen because the

was not granted under the charter and the VOC had therefore violated the limits of sovereignty set forth by the States-General, but nothing was done to stop this practice.

Recent studies have recognized that European colonialism was created through the development of legal systems that supported the maintenance of power by the colonizers and their local allies. However, studies of colonial law have tended to assume that European jurisprudence was brought to the colonies as a preexisting legal system upon which various amendments were made to conform to local conditions. As Martin Chanock has succinctly observed, "The law was the cutting edge of colonialism, an instrument of power of an alien state and part of the process of coercion."[9] Indeed, public international law in the United Provinces developed partly through the creation of the VOC legal network in which it was used in support of a forced migration system that included corporate slavery. The imperatives and interests of state formation in the United Provinces were thus deeply imbricated with those of the VOC empire.[10]

Under its founding charter, the VOC was entitled to pass and enforce its own laws, including the right to wage war against foreign powers and impose the death penalty within its charter domain. The VOC could not declare war on another European power operating in the Indian Ocean. Yet the wars the United Provinces fought in Europe resulted in these animosities applying to its merchant enterprises where limited retaliatory action could be taken. This relationship, for example, provided the VOC with the authority to conquer Portuguese imperial nodes when the United Provinces were at war with Portugal. It also made the Company vulnerable to attack, particularly when the United Provinces were at war with the English and, by extension, their East India Company. The legal documents contained within the VOC archive are immense in volume and reflect these complexities of imperial sovereignty as well as confirm that the "rule of law" was a major preoccupation of the Company within its empire. Company officials documented all sorts of legal matters in civil,

---

States-General did not grant the Company permission to mint currency. Nevertheless, by the eighteenth century VOC copper coins were in common usage. Leonard Blussé, *Strange Company: Chinese Settlers, Mestizo Women and the Dutch in VOC Batavia*. Dordrecht-Holland: Foris Publications, 1986, pp. 35–48.

[9] For example, M. B. Hooker, *A Concise Legal History of South-East Asia*. Oxford: Clarendon Press, 1978; Martin Chanock, *Law, Custom and Social Order: The Colonial Experience in Malawi and Zimbabwe*. Cambridge, UK: Cambridge University Press, 1985, p. 4.

[10] Julia Adams, "The Familial State: Elite family practices and state-making in the early modern Netherlands," *Theory and Society*, 23(4), August 1994, pp. 505–539.

criminal, and international law, and wrote about the operation of these laws in both principle and practice.

The checks and balances contained in the VOC charter to keep its operations subservient to the States-General were not systematically or consistently applied. At first, this had the effect of strengthening VOC sovereignty, although it did not forestall the Company's eventual collapse. For example, attempts by the States-General to examine the VOC accounts at the end of the first ten years of the charter were thwarted by the Seventeen Gentlemen. Thereafter, the Seventeen Gentlemen managed to shield its accounts from the States-General overseers who were not able to conduct an external audit of VOC finances until they appropriated some of its administrative functions prior to the Company's bankruptcy at the end of the eighteenth century. The secrecy with which the Company guarded its financial records extended to all manner of documentation.[11] Moreover, as Company directors, the Seventeen Gentlemen were exempt from the control of their shareholders, who were prohibited from speculating on Company stock and protected by the States-General from having lawsuits brought against them in the courts of the Republic.[12] The incremental development of VOC sovereignty through its legal and administrative networks therefore had the secondary effect of diminishing the authority of the States-General and, likewise, its capacity to oversee the Company's Indian Ocean domain.

In return for its patronage, both intended and unintended, the VOC paid the States-General handsomely periodic to renew its charter, share prizes, and grant payments to the state upon request. Throughout the VOC era, which spanned the period from the emergence of the United Provinces as the most powerful economy in Europe to its eventual eclipse, the Dutch Republic was plagued by war and continual battles to ensure its own survival as a sovereign entity. Although the Republic's economy was remarkably diversified, without stimulation by VOC revenues, the Dutch Golden Age would not have shone quite so brightly.

The eventual devolution of the split sovereignty constituting the United Provinces occurred in the wake of the French Revolution and coincided with revocation of the VOC charter at the end of the eighteenth century when the Company dissolved through bankruptcy. With the birth of the Batavian Republic in 1795, a new concept of sovereignty was embraced

---

[11] Clive Day, *The Policy and Administration of the Dutch in Java*. New York: Macmillan and Co., 1904, p. 86.
[12] Day, *Policy and Administration*, p. 87.

in the Netherlands, one that incorporated the remains of VOC imperial power, as embodied in its remaining nodes and networks, directly into the emergent Dutch state.[13]

From Company Charter to Company Empire

The interpretation of the VOC as reluctantly or accidentally making the shift from "merchant to prince" has been the daily fare of Dutch colonial history for generations.[14] Sovereignty in this interpretation rests squarely on the shoulders of the princely ambitions of the "men on the spot," including the founding father of Batavia, Jan Pieterszoon Coen.[15] These histories emphasize the "center" of empire based in Batavia extending through parts of Java and radiating outward. A more powerful explanatory model conceptualizes the VOC empire as developing instead through the extension of various networks, circuits, and nodes that did not always focus on territorial acquisition, and were in some cases transitory. The extension of VOC shipping and trading networks was motivated by profit. If potential opportunities for trade were apparent, the Company would

---

[13] Adams argues that the Company was delegated sovereign rights but remained dependent on the state in the above matters, and that although supreme authority was vested in the States-General, the colonies were left in the hands of the chartered companies. Adams, "Trading States, Trading Places," p. 332. Dianne Lewis is therefore incorrect in stating that "[t]he Netherlands government did not reserve any rights to regulate or control the VOC's activities." Dianne Lewis, *Jan Compagnie in the Straits of Malacca 1641–1795*. Athens, Ohio: University Center for International Studies, 1995, p. 13. Ball outlines the legal submission of the Company to the States-General but argues that "rights of sovereignty which the VOC obtained were acquired almost imperceptibly as each acquisition would, at the time, have been considered merely as a means of increasing its trading profits." Ball, *Indonesian Legal History*, pp. 4–5.

See Hahlo and Kahn, *South African Legal System*, chapters 14–16. The political and economic predominance of Holland meant that the laws of the VOC would most closely resemble that province. See G. G. Visagie, *Regspleging en Reg aan die Kaap van 1652–1806*. Cape Town: Juta, 1969, p. 21.

The close familial ties between the provincial regents and the VOC elite, coinciding with the emergence of the Netherlands as a global economic power in the seventeenth century, sponsored the development of public international law through the patronage of some of the greatest legal thinkers of the age, including Hugo Grotius. Charles S. Edwards, *Hugo Grotius The Miracle of Holland: A Study in Political and Legal Thought*. Chicago: Nelson-Hall, 1981. Martine van Ittersum calls Grotius "an unyielding VOC apologist," p. 488. Martine Julia van Ittersum, *Profit and Principle: Hugo Grotius, Natural Rights Theories and the Rise of Dutch Power in the East Indies (1595–1615)*. London: Brill, 2006.

[14] See, for example, J. J. van Klaveren, *The Dutch Colonial System in the East Indies*. The Hague: Martinus Nijhoff, 1953, p. 53.

[15] Van Klaveren, *Dutch Colonial System*, pp. 24–25.

endorse its agents to negotiate establishing a node in the form of a factory or fort. The form of the node determined the extent of administration, communication, and legal networks that were subsequently extended to the site.

Where a VOC node was weak, if it consisted only, for example, of a factory in a foreign polity, the extension of other networks beyond production and trade was sparse and, correspondingly, Company sovereignty was limited. In which case, the legal network was restricted to the chain of command within the Company at that site and applied mainly to Company personnel. Conversely, where trading nodes developed into complex settlements or colonies, the density of Company networks increased together with the administrative and legal institutions of government that underpinned its sovereignty and control over people. While the network of forced migration may or may not have been part of establishing Company nodes, this differential process accounts for the incremental development of imperial sovereignty that resulted in the modular construction of empire.

The density of networks linking Batavia to other Company nodes also increased and decreased according to their particular circumstances. For example, the main circuit of penal transportation and political exile operated along shipping routes linking Batavia to the major colonies, including the Cape, where the Company's internal territorial control was most secure. The extension of Company sovereignty and territorial occupation at the Cape, however, created a localized settler population who increasingly identified with their African homeland. Correspondingly, these settlers agitated against both convicts and political exiles coming to their colony and demanded that this particular circuit of forced migration be discontinued. They also simultaneously demanded direct access to the East African slave trade for their own benefit and profit.[16] Placing Batavia's interests at the analytical center of this issue provides only a partial understanding of the effects of forced migration at the Cape and fails to account for the broader context of the Cape as an important node in its own right whose security, from the Company's perspective and that of its settlers, was in jeopardy of being lost. The Batavia-to-Cape circuit of forced migration became over generations an increasing source of

---

[16] Andre du Toit and Hermann Giliomee, *Afrikaner Political Thought: Analysis and Documents, Volume One: 1780–1850*. Cape Town: David Philip, 1983, pp. 1–9; Schutte, "Company and Colonists at the Cape, 1652–1795," in Elphick and Giliomee, *Shaping of South African Society*, pp. 283–323; James Armstrong and Nigel Worden, "The Slaves, 1652–1834," in Elphick and Giliomee, *Shaping of South African Society*, pp. 118–119.

tension between Batavia Company officials and Cape Company officials and their settler population, as interests at the Cape in maintaining social order diverged from interests in Batavia of securing labor and discipline for the capital.

The VOC became not only a "state within a state," to quote Charles Boxer's famous phrase but also an "empire within a state" that preceded the transformation of the Dutch Republic into an imperial power in its own right. Although the Seventeen Gentlemen, comprised of elected officials from each of the Company's six chambers, were the supreme governing body of the Company and controlled both the composition of the fleet and commercial policy, the legal and administrative networks that created authority within the VOC empire were split along several of its imperial circuits. Ultimate political authority in the Company was split between the Seventeen Gentlemen in the United Provinces and the High Government in Batavia, which was composed of the governor-general and the Council of the Indies (*Raad van Indië*). The Seventeen Gentlemen controlled the appointment of the governor-general and councilors but this decision was often a ratification of recommendations from Batavia.

As the Company's empire diversified, so did a number of its intersecting and often competing circuits of trade, information, and political authority. Because of the time and distance involved in exchanging orders between the United Provinces and Batavia, governance emanated largely from the High Government, despite the Seventeen Gentlemen being theoretically the apex of authority. This trend of authority moving away from the Seventeen Gentlemen was reinforced during the course of the seventeenth century as its directors and executive officials were less likely to have had direct experience in Asia. Meanwhile, the corresponding trend of the governors-general and the Company elite being more likely to be born or married into elite family networks in its colonies meant that, practically, they began to exercise more influence in the Asian imperial web than the Seventeen Gentlemen. In principle, Batavia had power over all other Company nodes because it was the seat of the High Government. In practice, the exercise of Batavia's power was modified by a number of factors, including distance, which created regional circuits of authority within the empire as the Company continued to extend its realm.

Shifting Fortunes of Trade Networks and Territorial Nodes

In the first twenty years of the Company's existence, the diversity of expanding and contracting networks and nodes in the evolving empire was already apparent. The rapid consolidation of its imperial outposts necessitated a further evolution of Company's administrative and legal networks. Already by the 1620s, the Seventeen Gentlemen recognized three categories of Company claims in its settlements: rule by conquest where the VOC exercised direct territorial sovereignty, like the Banda islands and Batavia; authority and trade by monopoly contracts, as was the case in Ambon and Ternate; and trade by treaties with Asian rulers that the Company negotiated with its allies. This latter arrangement could lead to the development of a profitable but limited node like the factory on Deshima in Nagasaki, or to a temporary node as in Pegu, Burma, which lasted only from 1635 to 1645 before being dismantled because it had not generated sufficient profit.[17] The 1650 General Orders from the Seventeen Gentlemen formalized this system of claims into a corresponding political hierarchy under the overall rule of the governor-general and the Council of the Indies in Batavia.

Titles denoting responsibilities of governance were apportioned by size, complexity, and importance of the settlement. By the late seventeenth century, Governors headed settlements in which the Company exercised full or partial territorial sovereignty. These included Ambon, Banda, the Moluccas, Coromandel, Ceylon, Malacca, the Cape of Good Hope, Java's north coast, and Makassar. The major Company nodes had the largest garrison presence, were regional headquarters of administration, and in the case of Batavia, Banda, and the Cape, primary sites for burgher settlement. In other words, they were fully fledged colonies heading regional circuits that included other Company sites of lesser status and/or permanence. Directors headed the next level of Company settlements that included Bengal and Surat. A Commander ruled trading posts in Malabar and the west coast of Sumatra and a Resident controlled Company interests in Cheribon, Banjamarsin, and Palembang. Where the Company exercised minimal control over the conditions of trade, as in Japan, the principal officer of the trading post was an *Opperhoofd* (factory head).[18] These categories of leadership did not emerge all at once, but rather as Company governance evolved over time. Thus the evolution of the VOC empire was dependent primarily on the extension of the trading network that subsequently required more complex forms of settlement and administration.

Before the organization of the VOC, Dutch traders used long established indigenous Indian Ocean shipping and trading routes that followed

---

[17] Gaastra, *Dutch East India Company*, p. 53.
[18] Gaastra, "The Organization of the VOC," pp. 24–25.

the monsoon winds. They navigated the coasts of the Indian subcontinent along these routes extending trade while seeking access to the spice market. The holy grail of trade was the precious spicery of the Moluccas in the eastern Indies archipelago. The VOC pursued its desire for monopolies through conquest and negotiated trade, which in turn depended upon having trading goods from India to exchange for these valuable commodities. In 1612, seven years before Batavia was established, the famous navigator Hendrik Bouwer, who later rose to governor-general, observed: "The Coromandel Coast is the left arm of the Moluccas, because we have noticed that without the textiles of Coromandel, commerce is dead in the Moluccas."[19] Inter-Asian trade was therefore an essential part of the evolution of the VOC trading network. The trading circuits in the Indian Ocean and South China Sea intersected at the vital transoceanic crossroads on the Straits of Malacca. Prior to its conquest by the Portuguese in 1511, the Sultanate of Malacca had been the greatest trading entrepôt in the whole region for over a century. When the VOC established Batavia along the Straits of Malacca, it sought to emulate Malacca's former glory as the center of transoceanic trade. The VOC conquered Malacca in 1642, securing Batavia's claim for predominance in the region. The Governor of Malacca, Cornelis van Quaalbergen, wrote in his report to his successor in 1684 that the port city was not being maintained because of "fear that... Malacca would be made too great in prejudice of Batavia."[20]

Dutch East India Company networks extending to the Indian subcontinent were an essential part of developing inter-Asian trade. Market based regional sub-circuits that linked minor VOC settlements in the western Indian Ocean did not depend for their existence on the acquisition and maintenance of a territorial base. One such circuit was centered on the Company node in Surat that connected the western Indian Ocean trade network to minor VOC trading posts and circuits in the Red Sea. For a time, Surat emerged as an important site for the Company because it was the gateway of Indian trade to Persia, Mocha, and the centers of

---

[19] Quoted in George Winius and Markus Vink, *The Merchant-Warrior Pacified: The VOC (The Dutch East India Company) and Its Changing Political Economy in India*. Delhi, India: Oxford University Press, 1994, p. 13. Hendrik Brouwer developed the "roaring forties" navigational route that utilized strong winds and substantially accelerated sailing times between the Cape and Java.

[20] Cornelis van Quaalbergen, quoted in J. E. Hoffman, "Early Policies in the Malacca Jurisdiction of the United East India Company: The Malay Peninsula and Netherlands East Indies Attachment," *Journal of Southeast Asian Studies* (hereafter, *JSEAS*), 3(1), March 1972, p. 4. See also Lewis, *Jan Compagnie*. Lewis argues that by the 1670s Batavia's rise had resulted in the decline of trade in Malacca. p. 25.

the Mughal empire. In return for trading privileges, Mughal authorities insisted that VOC ships convoy Indian ships to the Red Sea to protect them from pirates.[21] In this way, the VOC and other European companies became intertwined with indigenous Indian Ocean trading networks. Despite their best efforts, however, no one polity or company was able to secure sustainable monopolies of trade and shipping.

The VOC began to cut its losses from costly military engagement in the Red Sea circuit as early as the 1620s because trading profits did not offset the expenses in this region.[22] Their post in Persia was marginal and practically outside the orbit of Batavia's political control, by virtue of its direct trade and correspondence links with Europe. Nevertheless, it was part of the Company's legal network with authority centered in Batavia.[23] George Winius and Markus Vink argue that VOC networks in this region and other sub-circuits in South Asia were "emporialist" rather than "imperialist." They contend that Company's partial sovereignty "signifies rather that markets – emporia – were the targets of European seaborne entities and not territory *per se*."[24] This book argues that the appearance and disappearance of VOC nodes in this region demonstrates the modularity of the nodes and networks that made up its imperial web.

Ceylon was another major center and crossroads for indigenous trade, religious, and cultural networks, as well as the source of the valuable spice, cinnamon. The Portuguese had established trading posts along the coast and the VOC entered into a military alliance with the indigenous Kandyan kingdom to oust the Portuguese from the region. Conquering the Portuguese was costly and required decades of hostilities.

The first governor of Ceylon, the ambitious Rijkloff van Goens Sr., had visions of establishing a rival imperial headquarters in Colombo and

---

[21] Om Prakash, *The Dutch East India Company and the Economy of Bengal 1630–1720*, Princeton, NJ: Princeton University Press, 1985. p. 259; Winius and Vink, *Merchant-Warrior Pacified*, p. 65.
[22] Gaastra, *Dutch East India Company*, pp. 50–52.
[23] Winius and Vink do not consider the VOC in South Asia a part of an empire, although their description of VOC activity supports my argument regarding the nature of the networks of empire, viz., "... there never actually was a Dutch 'empire' in India, but rather some nearly unrelated Dutch operations which were in reality departments of an enterprise centred in Java and ultimately in Amsterdam ... any study of the region should include the Persian Gulf factories as well as India itself, in the light of the existence of a symbiotic relationship and interlacing framework between them and the VOC Indian operations." Winius and Vink, *Merchant-Warrior Pacified*, pp. 1–2.
[24] Winius and Vink, *Merchant-Warrior Pacified*, p. 5.

rendezvous node for the Company's Asian shipping network at Galle that would bypass Batavia completely. Competition between high-ranking officials governing both Ceylon and Batavia intensified as they vied for political prominence and mastery over regional networks that if won would result in greater chances for garnering personal profit. Rijkloff van Goens Jr., who also later became governor of Ceylon had similar imperial ambitions to challenge Batavia as the Company headquarters and main node for the VOC shipping fleets. In 1670, Governor van Goens Jr., protested to the Seventeen Gentlemen that "the city of Batavia is almost jealous of the good fortune of Ceylon."[25] While Malacca's glory did indeed fade under Company rule, Colombo was the center of a regional circuit in the Indian Ocean and remained an important political and trading node in the Company's realm.

In the end, familial rivals among the elite in Batavia asserted political influence at the level of the Seventeen Gentlemen to bring about Van Goens' downfall. He was eventually forced to resign, as was his father who was governor-general in 1680. This competition for regional dominance demonstrates that the network of correspondence that linked the Seventeen Gentlemen to the imperial nodes was not used solely as a neutral conduit of official Company business. It could also be used to further individual interests, for as in this case, personal rivalries in the VOC determined the course of individual careers but not the extension of networks of trade and communication or the fate of a particular imperial node. Ultimately, Ceylon, with its capital in Colombo, emerged as the second most important colony in the Company after Batavia. Colombo also became the regional headquarters for the whole Indian Ocean circuit of South Asia. Thus the evolution of VOC regional circuits and their mutual reinforcement did not necessarily develop through a political vision shared by Company officials of the major governing centers.

To secure Company claims in Ceylon, the VOC initiated several invasions of the Malabar coast which were also aimed at increased pepper trade, and on the Coromandel and Bengal coasts, important indigenous regions of textile production. The extension of Company networks in these regions was initially aimed at intra-Asian trade, but during the eighteenth century the volume of trade from this region increased in Europe as markets for printed cottons and raw silks expanded.[26] On the Indian

---

[25] Rijklof van Goens quoted in Hoffman, "Early Policies in the Malacca Jurisdiction," p. 4.
[26] Prakash, *The Dutch East India Company and the Economy of Bengal 1630–1720.*

subcontinent, European trading companies tried to secure trading monopolies with local rulers who had their own political ambitions in the region and played one European company off against another. The VOC's attempts to establish monopoly trade sometimes failed, however, when it did not fulfill the terms of its treaties with indigenous rulers. The Zamorin of Malabar invited the English to set up a factory in Calicut in 1664 after the Dutch had reneged on the treaty conditions they had negotiated with him.[27]

By virtue of its geographical location in the Indies archipelago, the imperial capital at Batavia exercised closest political authority over Company nodes in the neighboring islands and peninsulas. The formal extension of territorial sovereignty during the Company era was concentrated in the Indies archipelagic arena, particularly in Batavia's inland and coastal hinterlands on the island of Java, and in the Moluccas. The VOC imperial capital was also the focal node for the East Asian trading circuit extending from Malacca to China and Japan.

Dutch East India Company fortunes in Formosa (Taiwan) were short-lived because the Company could not secure its settlement against the more powerful claims of neighboring China. This VOC colony lasted only thirty-eight years, from 1624 to 1662. Whereas the Company settlement faded away in Mauritius for lack of profitability, its success in developing sugar production based on Chinese labor in Formosa, paradoxically, sowed the seeds of its own destruction. Tonio Andrade calls this VOC node an example of "co-colonization" based on Chinese labor that succeeded only insofar as the Chinese and Japanese states chose not to exert their regional power in controlling the island. The Company recruited Chinese settlers from the mainland who lived under VOC rule and developed land into farms and sugar plantations that remained tax free for four years. The VOC also played Chinese interests against those of indigenous Formosans to achieve their own ends. This policy created tensions and resulted in a Chinese uprising in 1652 that was suppressed by the small Company garrison and backed up by a much larger contingent of Formosan soldiers. Ten years later, Zeelandia, the main VOC fort, was conquered by the Xiamen-based warlord Zheng Chenggong who had secured the loyalty of most of the Company's Chinese settlers, thereby ending VOC rule on the island.[28]

---

[27] Winius and Vink, *Merchant-Warrior Pacified*, pp. 35–39.
[28] Tonio Andrade, *How Taiwan Became Chinese: Dutch Spanish and Han Colonization in the Seventeenth Century*. New York: Columbia University Press, 2006.

These events corresponded chronologically with the VOC decision to establish a trading post at the Cape of Good Hope in 1652. While geographically distant from the main Company colonies in Batavia and Ceylon, the Cape was the primary refreshment post for all Company shipping plying the oceans between Europe and Asia. Jan van Riebeeck, the first head of the Company settlement at the Cape of Good Hope, held the rank of chief merchant with the title of Commander. By 1690, as elaborated in Chapter 4, the Cape had evolved into a permanent colony. Its first governor, Simon van der Stel, was a member of the Company's familial elite. One year after assuming office, he was also promoted to Councillor-Extraordinary of the Indies, a rank given only to governors of the most important Company colonies: Ceylon, Coromandel, the Moluccas, Makassar, and Java.[29]

In contrast, VOC claims to Mauritius, the Indian Ocean island and notorious pirate haven, devolved until it was finally abandoned. Company ships visited Mauritius from the late sixteenth century, and it was formally occupied in 1638, primarily to circumvent other European claims. The island, a source of valuable woods, was also utilized as a regional slave trading post under its second commander, Adrien van der Stel, whose son Simon was born there in 1639. The VOC settlement in Mauritius became a subordinate node of the Cape sub-circuit after its strategic and commercial value had diminished. Although Mauritius was a refreshment stop on the old navigational route to Asia after the adoption of the "roaring forties" or Brouwer route in the 1630s, Company fleets increasingly bypassed the island in their transportation network. The VOC settlement on Mauritius finally became more costly than it was worth, and the Supreme Government ordered Company subjects to pack up and move to the Cape or Batavia in 1710. Soon thereafter, the French claimed the island and developed a settler colony with sugar plantations worked by slave labor. It remained a part of the French imperial web until the early nineteenth century when British anti-slave trade networks in the Indian Ocean precipitated its invasion and incorporation into the British empire.[30] The fate of Mauritius demonstrates the sometimes unstable and contingent status of marginal nodes in networks of empire. The island was integrated into three successive empires (Dutch, French, and English)

---

[29] Schutte, "Company and Colonists," pp. 295–296.
[30] Dan Sleigh, *Islands: A Novel*. Trans. André Brink. London: Secker and Warburg, 2004; Megan Vaughan, *Creating the Creole Island: Slavery in Eighteenth-Century Mauritius*. Durham, NC: Duke University Press, 2005, pp. 1–33.

in the eighteenth and early nineteenth centuries. Mauritius's role as a refreshment post was supplanted by the Cape under VOC governance, and the Company post on the island became part of the Cape's regional sub-circuit of forced migration as a transit point for the slave trade and a settlement used by the Cape for penal transportation.

Communication and Administration in the VOC

The VOC empire was created and maintained partially by its ability to utilize knowledge networks in the form of laws and ordinances, correspondence, minutes of meetings, reports, criminal and civil legal records, personnel registers, accounts, inventories, drawings, and maps, all generated by its vast bureaucratic machinery.[31] Economic power was developed from trade networks intersecting with Company territorial nodes and shipping fleets, supported and sustained by the use of military technology.[32] The Company's trade network was underpinned by gathering intelligence about commodities and markets.[33] Although information did not flow freely between Company nodes, the intelligence network that filtered to Batavia and the Seventeen Gentlemen sustained the unity of the imperial web.

Through the most sophisticated secular bureaucracy ever organized in Europe, the VOC linked these numerous forts, factories, settlements, and colonies into a disparate unity woven together through several networks of empire. The Seventeen Gentlemen backed Batavia's role as an imperial capital, but not all the circuits of knowledge passed through Batavia Castle. Although the record keeping practices of the Company far

---

[31] Outside the United Provinces, Company administration was headed by the High Government who appointed members to the Council of Justice as the high court of the VOC and had ultimate authority over the twenty-six *subordinate buiten comptoiren* (outer settlements) including the Cape. In Batavia, the High Government devolved administrative functions into various committees including the Council and Court of Aldermen. Gaastra, *History of the VOC*. The Seventeen Gentlemen had difficulty keeping track of the VOC bureaucracy and commissioned Pieter van Dam to write a Company overview in 1705. Pieter van Dam, *Beschrijvinge van de Oostindische Compagnie*. 7 vols. F. W. Stapel and C. W. Th van Boetzelaer, eds., s'Gravenhage: Rijks gescheidenkundige publicatien, grote series nos. 63, 68, 74, 76, 83, 87, 96, 1927–1954.

[32] See J. R. Bruijn, F. S. Gaastra, and I. Schoffer, *Dutch-Asiatic Shipping in the 17th and 18th Centuries*. 3 vols. Den Haag: Rijks geschiedenkundige publicatien, grote serie, nos. 165–167, 1979 and 1987.

[33] For the financial records of the VOC see the above publications and J. P. de Korte, *De jaarlijke financiele verantwoording in de Verenigde Oostindische Compagnie*. Leiden: Het Nederlandsch Economisch-Historisch Archief, no. 17, 1984.

outstretched the capacity of any other merchant company or state in Europe during the early modern era, the distribution of this knowledge was fractured throughout its empire. The Seventeen Gentlemen and the High Government in Batavia were sometimes at loggerheads over the desirability of extending trade and correspondence networks directly from other Company posts and Europe. For example, because the Cape of Good Hope was the refreshment stop for all outbound and return fleets, direct contact with Europe was both practical and logical.[34] Although Batavia was not able to prevent the multiplication of direct circuits between Europe and some of the Company posts, the governor-general and Council did have other circuits of empire clearly under its command, particularly in the Indies archipelago.

The Cape of Good Hope was a relative economic backwater to these major colonies, although it was of great strategic importance. A constant complaint made by Cape governors was that Batavia was taking advantage of its position by sending them too many political prisoners and convicts and thereby endangering their security. The frustration of one of the Cape governors, Maurice Pasques, Marquis de Chavonnes, is apparent in this letter to the Seventeen Gentlemen in 1715: "Regarding the convicts sent annually from Batavia, Ceylon, and other places, we wish to state that we are being swamped with the rascals."[35] Numerous petitions from the Cape authorities to both Batavia and the Seventeen Gentlemen went unheeded, or were ignored in practice. This is not surprising given the position of the Cape within the Company empire. Using the Cape as part of its network of exile was to the advantage of both Batavia and, to a lesser extent, Ceylon, and posed little direct threat to the Cape while protecting the interests of these major colonies. From the very earliest days of the Cape colony, at least some members of its expensive garrison were

---

[34] The correspondence network linked to the Seventeen Gentlemen included an overland circuit via Hormuz that serviced Company nodes in Persia and South Asia as well as the sea route that serviced the Cape. Both by-passed the communication circuit centered on Batavia. See P. A. Leupe, "Letter Transport Overland to the Indies by the East India Company in the Seventeenth Century," in M. A. P. Meilink-Roelofsz, M. E. van Opstall, and G. J. Schutte, *Dutch Authors on Asian History*. Dordrect-Holland: Foris Publications, 1988, pp. 77–90. Pauline Milone claims that the wealth of documentation on Batavia between 1619 and 1815 compared with the relative scarcity between 1815 and 1949 influenced the way she was able to write a history of the city in favor of the VOC period. Pauline Milone, "'Queen City of the East': The Metamorphosis of a Colonial Capital," unpublished PhD dissertation, University of California, Berkeley, 1966, p. 104.

[35] CA: LM, vol. 31. Letter despatched from the Cape to Amsterdam, March 30, 1715.

also occupied in guarding convicts and exiles sent there to be imprisoned by orders from Batavia and Colombo.

In outlining these administrative systems it is tempting to envisage a well-oiled smoothly operating enterprise, but this was hardly the case. Disjunctures within knowledge circuits in the VOC provided individuals with avenues of opportunity to pursue their own interests, or merely existed as blind spots in the administrative network. When one examines the gaps of imperial knowledge created by VOC administrative practices, these fault lines within and between imperial nodes and networks become more apparent. Embedded in these disjunctures are indications of the instability of imperial VOC imperial power. As will be discussed in Chapter 4, free burghers at the Cape of Good Hope in 1705 brought charges against the governor, Willem Adriaan van der Stel, by writing protests directly to Batavia and the Seventeen Gentlemen, deliberately bypassing the Cape administration.

Most personnel issues were not pressing from the perspective of The Hague or Amsterdam. From the perspective of the colonies, however, exercising strategic control over people within Company nodes was crucial to maintaining the rule of law. From the VOC headquarters in Batavia, imperial power included the gradual extension of territorial governance, particularly in Java. Batavia focused its interventions most directly in the Indies archipelago, where its territorial inroads and political and military alliances were most intense, but rarely intervened in local legal decisions that were not directly related to its own interests. Localized knowledge of politics and trade within the respective colonies was filtered through official correspondence and was partial at best. Moreover, as the eighteenth century progressed and the Company's trade network and financial position weakened, so did these lines of communication.

Structures of Government and Law in the VOC

The first VOC factories, forts, and colonies were stabilized through the development of the Company's foundational structures of governance established between 1602 and 1642. These years encompassed the arrival of the first VOC fleet, which aimed its trading activity at the Moluccas, but was based initially in the coastal Sultanate of Banten in Java. These first four decades encompassed the arrival of first fleet; followed by mixed results in establishing trade contracts for spices in the Moluccas, the subsequent shift of VOC trading headquarters from Banten to the invasion and founding of Batavia on the island of Java in 1619; the conquest of the nutmeg-producing islands of Banda and unsuccessful struggles to impose monopolies of trade in cloves from the indigenous polities of Ambon; and the first codification of VOC law under the Statutes of Batavia in 1642.[36]

Initially, the center of authority of the VOC in the Indies was the Admiral of the most recent fleet to arrive there, who carried with him the latest instructions from the Seventeen Gentlemen and presided over trade and the discipline of VOC personnel on land and sea. Banten proved to be unsuitable for the Company's fleet and headquarters because the Dutch remained in a subservient position, along with other European traders, in this powerful port polity. When the VOC decided to move its activities from Banten, they conquered the nearby minor port town of Jayakarta and renamed the settlement Batavia in 1619. This town grew quickly into a city that became the center of VOC government, the rendezvous point for fleets, and symbolic imperial capital known among Europeans as the "Queen of the East."[37] During the VOC era, decision making within the Company was not only relegated to Batavia Castle, it depended also on local contingencies that maximized opportunities for trade.

Jan Pieterszoon Coen recognized the element of force that this might necessitate when he wrote to the Seventeen Gentlemen in 1614: "Your Honors should know by experience that trade in Asia must be driven and maintained under the protection and favor of Your Honors' own weapons, and that the weapons must be paid for by the profits from the trade; so we cannot carry on trade without war nor war without trade."[38] The VOC was constantly under military pressure from various indigenous Indian Ocean polities who challenged the Dutch presence in their midst,

---

[36] Of the forty-eight subject categories in the Statutes of Batavia, twenty-nine deal directly with the administration of justice, the organization of the military, security measures for Batavia, the detection and punishment of crimes, and slavery. Most of these twenty-nine categories set out descriptions of office; chain of command; definitions of jurisdiction; security measures for the militia and guards; judicial procedures, including those of arrest, sentencing, and execution; the definition of particular crimes and their punishment, including drunkenness, desertion, and piracy; wages and conditions of employment of the more minor positions; the days and times at which administrative and judicial bodies were obliged to convene; and finally, the oaths of office. G. C. Klerk de Rues, "Geschichtlicher Überblick der Administrativen, Rechtlichen und Finanziellen Entwicklung der Niederlandisch-Ostindischen Compagnie," *Verhandelingen van het Bataviaasch Genootschap van Kunsten en Wetenschappen*, vol. 47, 3. Batavia: Albrecht en Rusche, 'sHage: Martinus Nijhoff, 1894, pp. 140–141.

[37] Milone, "Queen City of the East."

[38] Quoted by Boxer, *The Dutch Seaborne Empire, 1600–1800*, p. 107.

as well as rival European trading enterprises. From its inception, the VOC also intervened in local politics to provide military assistance to a real or potential ally, gaining in return a treaty that ensured payment of tribute and granted monopoly trade. This was an expensive way to do business, and income, in many settlements, did not exceed expenditure.

Coen's statement foreshadowed the conquest of the port town of Jayakarta, a minor vassal of Banten. The town was razed and renamed Batavia to invoke the mythical Germanic tribe, which legend had was the origin of the Dutch people. Coen had intervened militarily without the explicit permission of the Seventeen Gentlemen and was reluctant to the point of implicit refusal to enforce their orders to cooperate with the English in the region. The best interests of the Company were often perceived differently by officials in Asia and the Seventeen Gentlemen, who acted in accord with the European political policy of the States-General. As Batavia evolved into the Company headquarters, the governor-general and the Council of the Indies as the High Government exercised *de facto* independence because of the time and distance involved in awaiting instructions from the Gentlemen Seventeen in Europe. The gap in correspondence for writing a letter and receiving a reply between Amsterdam and Batavia could be two and a half years. This meant that the evolution of VOC law in Batavia took place through the passing of various decrees (*plakaaten*) and resolutions (*resoluties*) that became in many cases foregone conclusions by the time the Seventeen Gentlemen were asked to consider the situation and had delivered definitive decisions back to Batavia, although ratifications were not always forthcoming.[39]

In his study of the seventeenth-century judiciary, Jacobus la Bree posits that the granting of the VOC charter was succeeded by three periods of increasing centralization, culminating in 1620 under the governor-generalship of Jan Pieterszoon Coen when the administration of justice in Batavia had achieved its final form.[40] In 1620, Governor-General Coen

---

[39] Taylor, *Social World of Batavia*, pp. 3–33. Taylor traces the shift from the hereditary Indies elite of the Company era to a new European-born colonial elite by the mid-nineteenth century.

[40] Originally, the administration of justice was organized within the governing structures. The Company Charter had no provisions for a separation of powers. The appointment of the first governor-general in 1610 was supposed to have unified the administration of justice under the governor-general and council in Banten. However, time and distance between Company nodes meant that local officials acted independently. It was not until 1617 that these local Company councils were expressly granted jurisdiction in civil and criminal cases, ratifying the existing practice. La Bree, *Rechterlijke Organisatie*, pp. 13–26.

devised the separation of government and judicial structures.[41] A Bailiff (*Baljuw*) administered justice within the city walls. After 1651, a *Landdrost* (local administrator/bailiff) was empowered with maintaining peace and order in the outer environs of the city. After 1655, the Bailiff and *Landdrost* were assisted by both European and indigenous district supervisors (*Wijkmeesters*).[42] A Council of Aldermen was created to handle judicial powers, local government, and policing within the environs of Batavia through the Court of Aldermen.[43] Residents of Batavia and its environs who were not Company servants were tried by the Court of Aldermen, under the ultimate control of the High Government. A Council of Justice had its original base in the Batavia fortress, making explicit the link between the castle and the center of power of the Company. It held jurisdiction where no other Company court applied and was the appellate court for all the other Company posts in the VOC empire. Serious crimes committed on board Company ships were also tried by the Council of Justice. The governor-general and the Council of Justice had to approve the imposition of the death sentence and also had the power of pardon.[44] The prosecutor in the Court of Alderman was the Bailiff

---

[41] "Ordinances and Instructions, concluded by the Governor-General and Council of the Indies, on the 16th of June 1625, regarding the college of aldermen; bailiff and other officers of justice; order of procedure in criminal cases; procedures of arrest; abandoned estates; settlement of debts; slaves; orphan chamber; additional items regarding justice; police; and succession." This ordinance confirmed that the judges were to refer in the first instance to the laws of Holland and Westvriesland, and the cities of Holland. J. K. de Jonge, *De Opkomst van het Nederlandsch Gezag in Oost-Indie. Versameling van onuitgegeven stukken uit het Oud-Koloniaal Archief.* Vol 5. 'sGravenhage: Martinus Nijhoff; Amsterdam: Frederick Muller, 1870. pp. 57–84.

[42] Ball, *Indonesian Legal History*, pp. 17–24.

[43] In 1623 the VOC gave Chinese Batavians representation on the College of Aldermen in recognition of their economic importance. After 1666 the Chinese community was represented by a Captain, or ward-master. City administration structures did not expand with the increase of Chinese immigrants to the outer districts after 1680. Blussé argues that this lack of political and administrative structure, combined with the deteriorating authority of the Chinese captain, created conditions for the 1740 massacre of the Chinese population in Batavia. Blussé, *Strange Company*, especially Chapter 5, "Chinese Batavia 1619–1740," pp. 73–96.

[44] The Council of Justice had jurisdiction over all criminal and civil cases concerning VOC soldiers and servants and all crimes against the Company. Its President and nine members (under the Statutes of Batavia) were appointed by, and in effect subservient to, the High Government. The Seventeen Gentlemen attempted to make the court independent of the Batavian officials by directly appointing judges. After 1625 private notaries, advocates, and attorneys were allowed to represent individuals in Batavia. Several estate chambers were established, including the Orphans Chamber (1624); the Non-Christian Estate Chamber (1640); and a council to administer the estates of VOC servants (1648). In 1625 a Commission of Matrimonial and Petty Causes was founded to adjudicate marriages

and the *Fiscal* fulfilled this role in the Council of Justice. The *Fiscal* was also the police chief with an executioner under his command. The organization of governance therefore evolved somewhat gradually in the initial period as Batavia grew in size and complexity as an urban port city. These institutions and laws were created through necessity rather than grand planning.

Judicial administration in other Company settlements was developed on an *ad hoc* basis according to need and with a more simplified structure than in Batavia. In minor outposts, justice was imposed according to the Company's chain of command. In colonies with a proportionally large European settler population like the Cape, burghers were represented in legal institutions, but under the control of the Company. The Council of Justice in Batavia exercised ultimate jurisdiction over the city and its environs, with outposts on Java sometimes forwarding capital cases to Batavia for trial. Capital cases were tried on site at the Cape, where the numerous death sentences imposed by the local Council of Justice were expedited with a haste and frequency that horrified many visitors who wrote about their travels.[45] The legal oversight of Batavia over all Company nodes and networks was, however, partial at best.

The Statutes of Batavia and the Principles of Jurisprudence

The impetus for the codification of VOC law was to bring some order to the numerous ordinances and decrees that had been issued as needed by the Seventeen Gentlemen, the governor-general, and the Council of the Indies. The Company's legal records do not make explicit the extent to which VOC officials in the colonies outside the Indies archipelago actually used the Statutes of Batavia as a working legal code. At the

---

in Batavia's multireligious and slave-owning society. Ball, *Indonesian Legal History*, pp. 19–27.

The Advocate-Fiscal acted as public prosecutor and the head of police. In 1660 the office of Water-Fiscal was established to police the Batavia roadstead and prosecute both VOC servants and civilians for illegal trade. The Seventeen Gentlemen created the office of "Independent Fiscal" in 1689 to detect and prosecute corruption in Company settlements. Gaastra argues that this initiative failed by 1719 precisely because corruption was so endemic in the Company at all levels that it was impossible to eradicate. F. S. Gaastra, "The Independent Fiscaals of the VOC, 1689–1719," in Centre for the History of European Expansion, Rijksuniversiteit Leiden, *All of One Company: The VOC in Biographical Perspective*. Utrecht: Hes, 1986, pp. 92–107.

[45] See, for example, the impressions of the Swedish naturalist, Anders Sparrman, quoted in Victor de Kock, *Those in Bondage: An Account of the Life of the Slave at the Cape in the Days of the Dutch East India Company*. Pretoria: Union Booksellers, 1963, p. 165.

Cape, the Statutes of Batavia were rarely quoted in legal decisions and in the issuing of local decrees.[46] Legal cases brought at the Cape were not overseen by Batavia unless forwarded there by Company officials, or when Cape burghers chose the route of challenging the decision of the Council of Justice, a process both costly and time consuming. The right to appeal to the Council of Justice was open to those who could avail themselves of the privilege or were desperate enough to escape sentences imposed locally. Nevertheless, one part of the Company's legal network and the application of justice was the imposition of exile and penal transportation as a form of punishment. Batavia consistently sent prisoners to the Cape, Colombo, Banda, and Ambon. Colombo also had its own circuit of penal transportation that included the Cape. The Cape, in turn, intermittently banished convicts to its own sub-circuit in Rio de la Goa or Mauritius. It also banished prisoners to Batavia, but the main flow of prisoners was in the opposite direction.

In establishing judicial administration, the VOC had to deal with several principles of jurisprudence that went above and beyond the existing laws of the Netherlands. The main question raised by the Company was which law was to be applied and who was to fall within its jurisdiction. Two principles governed this issue, the "Concordancy Principle" and the "Conflict of Laws" theory. The Company developed the Concordancy Principle to determine which law had predominance and it set up the following hierarchy of application. First, specific laws passed by the VOC pertaining to local circumstances took predominance in deciding any legal matter. Second, the laws and customs of the United Provinces were to be applied. This was no easy matter to define, as the legal system of the United Provinces was itself evolving alongside that of the VOC. Third, the most common recourse given the above, was that the laws of Holland and its cities would apply. The Concordancy Principle thus provided Company courts with the guidance they sought in the application of internal law.[47]

The Company developed the Conflict of Laws theory, or private international law, to deal with the plurality of laws applying in the imperial web. Again, a hierarchical interpretation determined the choice of law,

---

[46] Thanks to James Armstrong for pointing this out to me, and providing a list of the legal decisions at the Cape that referred to the Statutes of Batavia.
[47] Ball, *Indonesian Legal History*, pp. 28–31. Hilton Basil Fine, "The Administration of Criminal Justice at the Cape of Good Hope 1795–1828," unpublished PhD thesis, University of Cape Town, 1991, p. 441.

jurisdiction, and enforcement in cases concerning people who ordinarily came under different legal codes.[48] Remco Raben makes the point that this plural structure was not a Dutch invention, but rather that the Company adapted local Asian social and economic practices in order to do business in the region. He argues that

> [t]he plural structure offered a practical solution to the Dutch authorities, who refrained from interference with the indigenous population. The Company was neither able nor willing to impose its legal system on the Asian population and left complicated issues such as civil jurisdiction to indigenous political leaders.[49]

Raben stresses the "practical" and contingent nature of Company administration.[50] Certainly, it is a gross exaggeration but tempting, nonetheless, to read into the VOC archives a master plan of administrative and judicial efficiency. The VOC sought to reconcile its actions to the principles of its legal system. In doing so, it created a legal justification for incorporating every person living within the Company's territorial jurisdiction into the orbit of its laws, whether they were Company servants, European civilians, Eurasians, indigenes, or other foreigners. The Company, however, exercised direct territorial sovereignty in very few of its imperial nodes because the local circumstances of each settlement differed to the extent that indigenous authority structures were in place and successfully exerted their power.

In Batavia, all VOC European servants of whatever nationality were subject to Company law, as were all European free burghers and foreign Europeans.[51] Mestizos, including the Portuguese-speaking Christian *Mardijkers* who were descendents of manumitted slaves, were also subject to Company law. The Eurasian children of European men and Asian women were considered European if they were recognized by their fathers. This was not always the case if Eurasian children were under the control of the Company orphanages.[52] Less obvious was the jurisdiction over Chinese, indigenous Javanese, and other Asian ethnic groups. The

---

[48] Hooker, *Concise Legal History*, p. 187; A. Schiller, "Conflict of Laws in Indonesia," *The Far Eastern Quarterly*, 2(1), November 1942, pp. 31–47.
[49] Remco Raben, "Batavia and Colombo: The Ethnic and Spatial Order of Two Colonial Cities." Unpublished PhD dissertation. University of Leiden, 1996, p. 197.
[50] Ibid., pp. 197–233.
[51] Stapel points out that the English residents in Batavia were under VOC jurisdiction. F. W. Stapel, "Bijdragen tot de Geschiedenis der Rechtspraak bij de Vereenigde Oostindische Compagnie 1," *Bijdragen tot de Taal-, Land-en Volkenkunde van Nederlandsch-Indië* (hereafter *BKI*), 89, 1932, p. 52.
[52] La Bree, *Rechterlijke Organisatie*, pp. 94–95.

Chinese residents of Batavia were considered a special category because of their crucial position as traders and laborers in the city, falling under the jurisdiction of VOC law, except for minor and civil cases, where they had their own representatives.[53]

One of the crucial differences between Company and Dutch law concerned slavery. From the earliest days of settlement in the Indies, the VOC participated in indigenous Southeast Asian social and labor practices by procuring slaves for its own labor force through indigenous slave trading networks.[54] Company personnel and European civilians also bought slaves for their own private use and many profited personally from a private trade in slaves. However, the Company practice differed from Southeast Asian forms of slavery because it was the first institutional owner of slaves in the region.[55] These slaves were the property of the VOC itself and were listed among its financial assets. Slave labor was absolutely essential to the Company, not only in the Indies but in the main colonies as well. The Cape of Good Hope has rightly been called a slave society during the Company period because the economy relied to such a great extent on slave labor.[56]

Slaves were deemed necessary and procured by the Company in part because the labor compelled from indirectly coercing indigenes into colonial service and hiring wage laborers was not sufficient to sustain the development of the urban centers of Batavia, Colombo, and the Cape. The Company tried as far as possible to regulate the slave trade within its territories in the same way it attempted to control the entire network of free and forced migration. In the sense that the slave trade, penal transportation, and exile within the VOC empire all constituted forms of involuntary bondage they are comparable forms of forced migration. However, one must bear in mind the different scales of these forms of forced migration and the proportion of the colonial population that was constituted by these bonded people.

---

[53] This pattern seems to have persevered even after the massacre of two thirds of the Chinese population in 1740. Although the inner city Chinese population never recovered its previous levels, the Chinese population outside the city walls matched previous levels within a decade. Raben, "Batavia and Colombo," Appendix 3: Censuses Batavia, Inner City and Ommelanden, 1673–1797, pp. 305–332.

[54] F. de Haan, *Oud Batavia*, vol. 1. Batavia: G. Kolff & Co., 1922, pp. 451–462.

[55] James Fox, "'For Good and Sufficient Reasons': An Examination of Early Dutch East India Company Ordinances on Slaves and Slavery," in Anthony Reid, *Slavery, Bondage and Dependency in Southeast Asia*. St Lucia: University of Queensland Press, 1985, pp. 248–249.

[56] Ross, *Cape of Torments*; Worden, *Slavery in Dutch South Africa*; Armstrong and Worden, "The Slaves," pp. 109–183; Robert Shell, *Children of Bondage*.

Slaves were incomparably more significant as a source of labor than convicts or exiles. However, in the major Company colonies the simultaneous presence of slaves, convicts, and exiles blurred the spectrum of bondage facilitated by the forced migration network. The day-to-day treatment of these bonded people was in many cases similar; indeed slaves in Cape Town who lived independently and paid their masters a premium from their earnings exercised more daily and personal freedom than European convicts. All slaves in Company territories, no matter their country of origin or religion, were subject to the jurisdiction of Company laws for whatever crimes were committed by or against them. Moreover, slaves could be sentenced to penal transportation while Europeans who were transported as convicts often lived lives that were indistinguishable from local slaves. Of course, the main legal distinction was that VOC law created chattel slaves whereas convicts were rarely sentenced to punishment "for life." Penal transportation and political exile involved various forms of personal restrictions ranging from being free to support oneself to being riveted in chains and incarcerated. The slave trade created and facilitated the movement of people legally defined as slaves.

Company Law and Indigenous Law

More than any other area of jurisprudence the relationship between VOC law and *adat* (civil and customary laws of Indies societies) depended upon local circumstances. Although the principle of the superiority of Company law remained intact, the application of *adat* depended upon each locality and the political relationships the Company had established with local rulers. As the Company extended its sovereignty or partial jurisdiction over previously independent polities, arrangements were made by treaty or conquest or both concerning the application of the conflict of laws principle and the creation of structures of legality in each territory.[57]

The VOC did not encounter a legal blank slate when its servants and settlers began trading with and living among the indigenous societies of

---

[57] The literature on the administration of justice in the Netherlands-Indies is extensive. For one of the classic studies, see F. W. de Haan, *Priangan: De Preanger-Regenschappen onder het Nederlandsch Bestuur tot 1811*. 4 vols. Batavia: G. Kolff & Co.; 'sGravenhage: Martinus Nijhoff, 1910. For a more recent see Mason C. Hoadley, *Selective Judicial Competence: The Cirebon-Priangan Legal Administration, 1680–1792*. Ithaca, NY: Cornell University Southeast Asia Program, 1994.

Asia and Africa. A range of negotiated relationships between the Company and indigenous polities emerged that was first based on regulating trade. Given that the VOC was primarily engaged in trade and that it was by no means always able to determine the terms of this trade, Company officials initially complied with the provisions for foreign traders established by indigenous polities in the regions where they had a trading presence, often in the form of a factory or a warehouse. The Company's construction of a fort in any particular site signaled an assertion of self-governance and the possibility of permanent settlement. As such, this first step was often resisted by local polities. Outright military conquest whereby the Company assumed direct sovereignty was at the other end of a continuum of relationships between the Company and indigenous polities. The extent to which the Company incorporated, adapted, or ignored local laws in crafting their own legal network was not uniform and cannot be generalized across the empire except in terms of general principles.

The extension of the Company's territorial sovereignty began with the conquest of Portuguese fortresses and settlements in Asia, the first being in the Moluccas on the clove-producing island of Ambon in 1605. Two years later the Company built its own first fortress in the nutmeg archipelago of Banda on the island of Neira in an attempt to enforce a monopoly of trade in that valuable aromatic spice. Nassau Castle was an ominous sign for the indigenous inhabitants of the islands. Over the next fifteen years, the VOC used its own soldiers and Asian mercenaries to defeat the loose alliance of Bandanese polities that made up the archipelago; executed their leaders, the *orang kaya* (headmen); exiled much of the Bandanese population; and introduced slave labor from other parts of the archipelago to work on Dutch-controlled plantations. The first VOC settler colony was thus established through conquest and forced migration. The Company's attempt to eliminate competition from rival Portuguese and English traders and disrupt local trade networks to impose monopolies prompted its first territorial conquests in the Moluccas and Java. Having established sovereignty over these territories by right of conquest and occupation, the VOC was faced with having to create the rule of law in evolving colonial societies where Europeans were always in the minority of the population. Raben quotes Company sources contemplating the situation in Batavia that stated bluntly:

[we] have to be constantly on our guard against attacks from both inside and outside and secure ourselves against it; which shall be done by fortifying our city

well and by stationing a fair-sized garrison in closed redoubts, and by punishing all brutalities severely, as that is what these Indian nations are accustomed to and that is how they wish to be governed.[58]

It is beyond the scope of this book to outline the variety and complexity of customary law systems encountered by the VOC, as it was indeed beyond the scope of the Company itself.[59] The Company's encounter with indigenous law was an historical process, an accumulation of partial knowledge, and a practical incorporation of local practices that developed within the extension of Company control over territory throughout its empire. Ultimately, it was beyond the power of the Company to completely control the indigenous populations in its realm. The legal system constructed by the VOC was rather more haphazard than systematic. Company officials manifested their "colonial anxiety," Raben contends, partly through a "registration mania" that categorized people in an attempt to establish control over their expanding empire.[60] As Heather Sutherland points out, Company efforts to enumerate and define people's legal identities were not entirely successful as individuals resisted or subverted this form of categorization.[61] The Company's distinction between the administration of civil and criminal law did not result in the complete separation of these spheres, nor could the Company completely control how this legal system was accessed by individuals.[62]

The legal system evolved throughout the Company period and was particularly complex in its negotiation with indigenous law in Batavia and Java. In an attempt to overcome local legal variations in Java, Governor-General Jacob Mossel (1750 to 1761) proposed the codification of Javanese law in preparation for establishing Company administrative bodies in West Java during the 1750s. The incorporation of territory in the Cirebon-Priangan region significantly extended imperial sovereignty inland in this region of Java.[63] In these core territories, even the partial and regionally diverse structures of Company and indigenous administration

---

[58] Raben, "Batavia and Colombo," p. 198, quoting the *Generale Missiven* dated December 9, 1637.
[59] H. W. J. Sonius, "Introduction," in J. F. Holleman, *Van Vollenhoven on Indonesian Adat Law: Selections from Het Adatrecht van Nederlandsch-Indië* (vol. 1, 1918; vol. 2, 1931). The Hague: Martinus Nijhoff, 1981, pp. 33–58.
[60] Raben, "Batavia and Colombo," pp. 77–237.
[61] Heather Sutherland, "Perfoming Personas: Identity in VOC Makassar," in Worden, *Contingent Lives*, pp. 345–370.
[62] Raben, "Batavia and Colombo," p. 216.
[63] Hoadley, *Selective Judicial Competence*, p. 143.

in the various nodes under VOC jurisdiction had the effect of consolidating Batavia as the capital through its legal structures and network.

Company Personnel: Incapacitation and Incarceration

During the first years of its existence, Company sovereignty was defined by its fleets and applied only to its own personnel. These fleets were comprised of ships belonging to each of the six chambers of the Company. Sailors assigned to these ships and soldiers were likewise contracted to the individual chambers that together constituted the Company as a whole. The VOC administrators and ship's captains kept meticulous records of every ship, including its name and class or type, chamber of origin, dates of journeys and places visited during voyages, the number and categories of people onboard, the number of deaths (and very occasionally, births), cargoes, equipage, and whatever unusual events or disasters befell the voyage. As the complexity and density of the Company's nodes and networks increased, the Seventeen Gentlemen ordered a standardization of record keeping including a yearly survey of the entire personnel employed in the charter domain.

From 1686, the Company's annual General Land and Sea Muster Rolls provided a record of every contracted person serving in the Company by name, hometown, rank during previous year, rate of pay, wages owed, first year of service, rank upon initial entry, VOC chamber of service, and, when necessary, date of death. This personnel system summarized data from ship's pay ledgers and the rolls of qualified civilian and military employees based on land. It was a massive feat of administration and accounting that required every Company servant, regardless of rank, to personally update their information at their local pay office on a prescribed date according to where they were stationed.[64] A similar system was put in place for locally engaged employees of the Company. Even with a large margin of error, the bureaucracy involved in keeping these records was impressive by today's standards and was unprecedented for an early modern enterprise. A host of scribes were the ink-stained conduit through whom this information passed from pen to paper in multiple copies – up to six – one for each VOC chamber in the United Provinces. The mechanics of producing these records were likewise meticulously recorded down to the orders for every single piece of paper, according to specific quantities

---

[64] B. J. Slot, M. C. J. C. van Hoof, and F. Lequin, "Notes on the Use of the VOC Archives,"' in Meilink-Roelofsz, Raben, and Spikerman, *De archieven van de VOC*, pp. 47–70.

and sizes, for each of the Company offices. Pieces of paper were easier to keep track of, however, than people, and the Company constantly struggled to control its personnel. Desertion was an endemic problem in most settlements.

It was upon this information that all Company servants were paid their miserly salaries. Company employees meanwhile used every ounce of their ingenuity to profit from their situation, more often than not at the expense of their employer. Thus there was an inherent economic tension within the Dutch East India Company. The Company was founded to generate licit profits based on establishing trade, preferably monopoly trade, through the negotiation of treaties with indigenous polities. Under certain circumstances, treaties also provided for the payment of tribute or the granting of territorial sovereignty to the Company. The people who created and sustained these trade and diplomacy networks had little or no stake in maximizing shareholder dividends. It was often in the interests of Company servants to generate illicit profits garnered from opportunities created through these same imperial networks. Correspondingly, there was an inherent social tension in the Company between disciplining people within its realm to ensure the smooth running of business and those very same people trying to maximize their freedom to pursue their own self-interests. The Company tried to resolve these tensions by creating a legal system that would help maintain peaceful order and productivity. It did so partly by imposing social, religious, and ethnic categories that in turn determined one's legal identity and consequently the punishments that could be imposed for transgressions against Company law.

Keeping accurate personnel records required reports from each Company factory, fort, settlement, and colony. The Land Muster Rolls for the mid-to-late eighteenth century show the fluctuation in Company personnel across the empire and reflect where Company control was waxing and waning. Every roll was therefore different, and the returns for the island of Java alone reflect just how complex these networks of record-keeping and Company sites were. For example, the small outpost of Lampong Toulang Bouwang in western Java, with a Company population of about forty, was only intermittently surveyed.[65] The same applies for Bandjermassing on the west coast of Borneo (Kalimantan), a polity with close ties to eastern Java.[66]

---

[65] NA: 5189-5198, 1741-1750; 5208, 1760.
[66] NA: 5181-5182, 1733-1734; 5196-5197, 1748-1749; 1203, 1755; 5208, 1760; 5213, 1765; 5228, 1780; 5233, 1785.

What clearly emerges from the Muster Rolls is that the major concentrations of Company servants were in Batavia, which always had the largest population, averaging approximately 5,000 for the period 1720 to 1780; other sites included Ceylon, 2,700; the northeast coast of Java, 1,750; the Cape of Good Hope, 1,280; Mallabar, 1,100; Maccassar, 1,070; Ambon, 1,000; Banda, 950; Ternate, 860; and Coromandel, 780. These averages give some idea of proportion, but there are exceptional fluctuations in Company personnel in certain sites. The Mallabar coastal region, for example, underwent more than a ten-fold increase between 1720 and 1730 (from 129 to 1,535). The number of Company servants at the Cape doubled from 800 to 1,687 over the whole period from 1720 to 1780. Meanwhile Batavia's Company population dropped from a high of 6,306 in 1750 to 3,283 in 1780. These numbers suggest the extent and density of networks in each of these Company nodes. Significant fluctuations indicate several possibilities including an increase or decrease in Company activity, a shift in economic or military presence, or perhaps a greater or lesser commitment by the Company to a particular place in the imperial web.[67]

Another pattern in the Muster Rolls with serious implications for the labor capacity of imperial nodes is the illness rate in each settlement. The numbers of deaths were not recorded in the Muster Rolls, but a high rate of illness suggests some correlation with mortality. In the major settlements, the rate of sickness among Company personnel hovered between approximately 1 and 5 percent, with the exception of the Cape and Batavia, where the figures were closer to 10 percent. Given that the Cape and Batavia were major transit nodes for Company fleets and that both towns had a hospital as one of their primary institutions, it is not surprising they had the largest proportion of incapacitated Company personnel. However, Batavia's highest sickness rate was in 1770 when it included a quarter of Company personnel in the town.

This increase in morbidity reflected a shift in the city's environment as malaria became endemic and the Company was no longer investing in urban maintenance. The Muster Roll figures do not accurately reflect the situation at each post as it is likely that every post had a fluctuating and, in the tropics, seasonal, proportion of ill Company servants. Moreover, not all sites enumerated their sick personnel, presumably because these numbers were not significant to its operation. The incapacitation of

---

[67] NA: 5168, 1720; 5178, 1730; 5188, 1740; 5198, 1750; 5208, 1760; 5218, 1770; 5228, 1780; 5238, 1790.

Company servants meant that their labor was not available. Furthermore, they were not only costing money for their treatment and convalescence but also requiring additional labor for their care and supervision, whether in a hospital or in barracks and residences. It is in this light that the numbers of convicts need to be analyzed, as they potentially comprised a higher proportion of the labor available to the Company than first appears in the Muster Rolls.[68]

For the purpose of this study, it is the inconsistent enumeration of those Company servants categorized as prisoners that is important. Between 1720 and 1780 the average total number of Company servants in Batavia was approximately five thousand. Around four hundred of these employees were serving on the islands of Edam and Onrust in the Batavia bay area. These islands were ship repair and timber processing sites, but they were also sites for the incarceration of different categories of prisoners. These prisoners were not always enumerated in the Muster Rolls as they do not correspond with the numbers of people being sentenced to punishment in the criminal records. Consistent annual listings of at least some prisoners occurred in Batavia, Ceylon, Banda, Ambon, and the Cape of Good Hope. Other settlements only intermittently listed prisoners as part of their enumeration of Company personnel. Batavia, Ambon, Banda, and the Cape all list secondary sites of incarceration in their personnel inventories. These were smaller islands from the main settlement where prisoners could be further isolated. Ambon used the island of Buru or forced labor in the indigo works, Banda kept the tiny atoll of Rosengain as a secondary prison, and the Cape of Good Hope had the well-known prison on Robben Island. According to the Muster Rolls, the Cape had the largest proportion of Company convicts of any site in the empire. Batavia's imprisonment rate hovered around 1 percent whereas the Cape's fluctuated between approximately 5 and 10 percent. Although the Muster Rolls do not indicate where these prisoners originated, the Batavia criminal records show that penal transportation, even if it was within the Indies archipelago, was a common judicial punishment. The prevalence of prisoners enumerated at any particular site suggests that this category of Company servant was significant. When compared with an average sickness rate of around 10 percent of all Company servants, the incarcerated population was actually a higher proportion of able-bodied Company servants than the raw figures suggest.[69] Considering that labor shortages

---

[68] Ibid.   [69] Ibid.

were endemic in the Company, even these small figures are significant because of the added burden of supervising convicts sentenced to hard labor. Penal transportation was therefore both a benefit and a liability for the Company. Nevertheless, it was consistently used as a method of control within the empire, particularly from Batavia and Colombo where penal transportation was directed towards particular nodes like the Cape of Good Hope.

Slave Trades in the Indian Ocean and VOC Slavery

Apart from its own servants, slaves were by far the most important category of people in the Company's empire. The VOC engaged in various indigenous Indian Ocean slave trades and practices of slavery. Over time it developed the most extensive slave trade network in the Indian Ocean that encompassed all of its territories from the Cape of Good Hope in the west to the Moluccas in the east. Yet unlike its smaller and more limited counterpart, the Dutch West India Company, which operated in the Atlantic slave system, the Dutch East India Company did not derive its main source of revenue from its trade in slaves. Its slave trade was used instead as a major source of labor both for the Company, its servants and settlers, as well as indigenous residents in many Company nodes. Moreover, individuals profited from their personal small-scale slave trade, particularly if they had access to the Company's transportation network in which to sell their slaves at sites where they could obtain higher prices.

The VOC was the first political entity to introduce a form of slavery whereby slaves were purchased or born as Company property, devoid of the directly personal, religious, and/or judicial connections that characterized indigenous forms of bondage in the Indian Ocean. The Company's ownership of slaves therefore introduced a change in the social dimension of slavery and the lived experience of being a slave at the intersection of colonial and indigenous slave networks of the Indian Ocean grid. The VOC purchased slaves for its own labor force or captured them from enemies and supplemented this form of bonded labor with judicial punishments that included forced labor in chains for convicted slaves, the penalization of slaves in lieu of their masters, and the forced confiscation of slaves from individuals in Company jurisdictions. The VOC purchased its slaves and those to be sold to individuals at the intersection of its own slave trade and the various complex slave trade networks in the Indian Ocean and South China Sea.

Forms of bondage in the Company were further complicated by the ad hoc evolution of Company ordinances that controlled forced migration. In 1717, a Company ordinance governing prisoners of war decreed that "prisoners of the enemy shall be used as slaves on galleys and in other servile labor without respect for quality or condition, either spiritual or worldly."[70] These *kettinggangers* (chain gangers) were both European and indigenous, Christian and "heathen" and included Company servants who had escaped the death penalty. The network of forced migration and the legal forms of slavery and bondage instituted by the Company had general features that were consistent across the empire with regional variations to accommodate local conditions.

The complexities of the Company's slave trade networks are beyond the scope of this book, except to illustrate the general patterns of the circulation of slaves from indigenous slave networks and the Company slave network. Marcus Vink gives an overview of these networks: "The Dutch Indian Ocean slave system drew captive labor from three interlocking and overlapping circuits of subregions: first the westernmost, African circuit of East Africa, Madagascar and the Mascarene Islands (Mauritius and Reunion); second the middle, South Asian circuit of the Indian subcontinent (Malabar, Coromandel, and the Bengal/Arakan coast); and last the easternmost, Southeast Asian circuit of Malaysia, Indonesia, New Guinea (Irian Jaya), and the southern Philippines."[71] The Company purchased slaves from indigenous or other European slave traders throughout these regions. Furthermore, the guarantee of supplying slaves was often included in treaty clauses between the Company and indigenous polities. The supply of slaves fluctuated according to local political and economic circumstances. Famines in regions disrupted by natural or human disasters stimulated the supply of people being sold into indigenous and European slave trades. Regions where decentralized polities were engaged in constant hostilities, like the island of Bali, generated a constant supply of slaves for the Dutch.

Slaves taken from all of these regions fed the labor demands of the major Company nodes, particularly those with the largest urban centers – including Batavia, Colombo, and the Cape – the rural hinterlands of these towns, as well as the slave-based agricultural economies of the Moluccas and the Cape of Good Hope. Whatever their origins, once slaves

---

[70] Fox, "For Good and Sufficient Reasons," p. 249.
[71] Vink, "'The World's Oldest Trade': Dutch Slavery and Slave Trade in the Indian Ocean in the Seventeenth Century." *Journal of World History*, 14(2), 2003, p. 139.

entered Company territories, they were subject to Company slave laws. Vink estimates that overall in the late seventeenth century there were approximately 4 thousand Company slaves and 60 thousand privately owned slaves in Dutch Indian Ocean territories. The average mortality rate of 20 percent, increases the numbers of slaves actually acquired but lost through death and desertion.[72] Slaves were a far more important form of labor than Company prisoners and exiles. Chapter 3 analyzes the conditions of possibility for forced migration and the complexities of bondage in the imperial capital of Batavia in the mid-eighteenth century. The Company's criminal records give some insight into the way the legal system affected individuals accused and convicted of crimes and how some of these people became part of the network of forced migration as criminals sentenced to penal transportation across its imperial web.

[72] Ibid., p. 176.

VOC Batavia
&
the Indies Archipelago
c. 1750

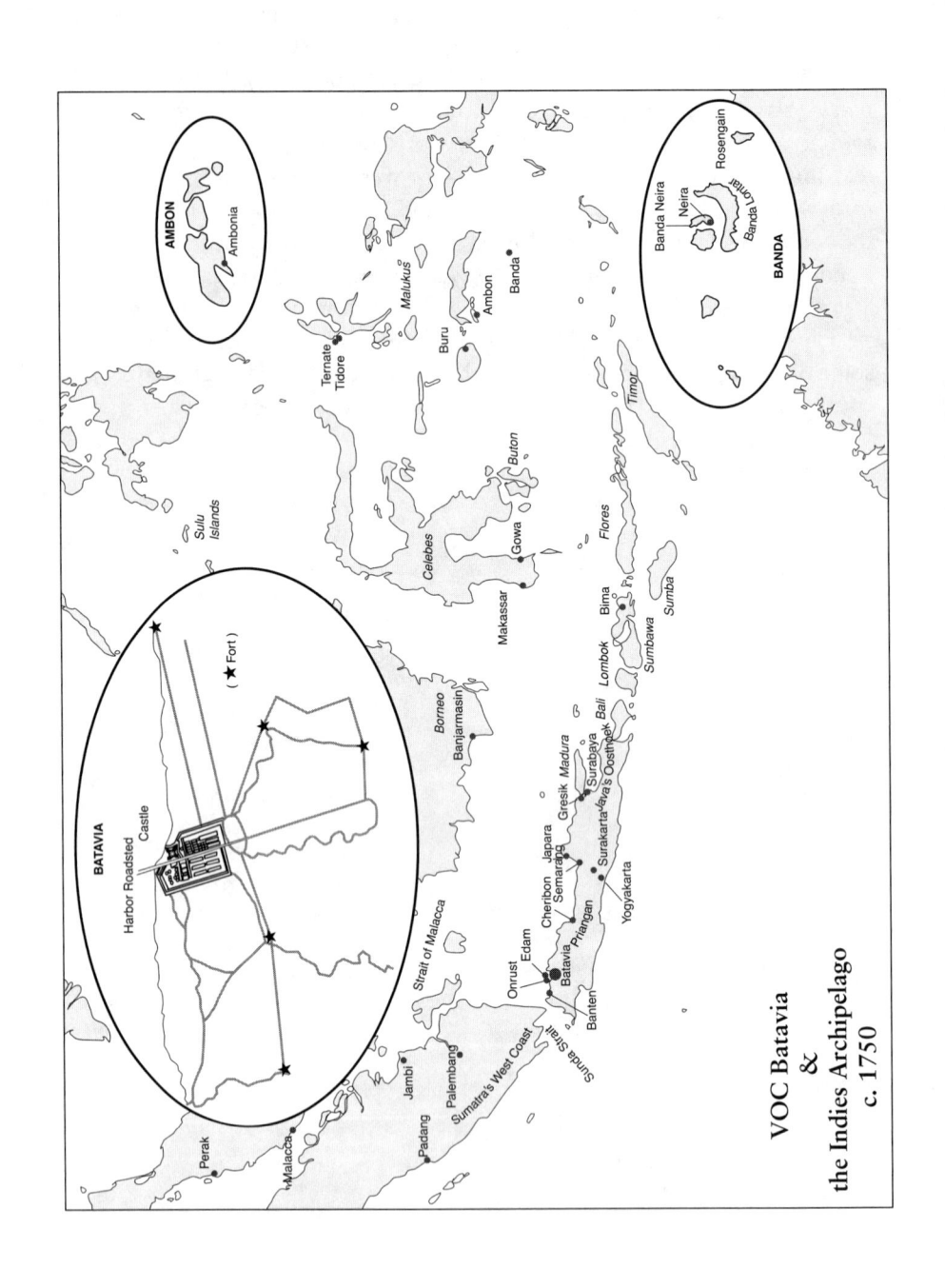

3

Crime and Punishment in Batavia, circa 1730 to 1750

Batavia grew into the capital of the Dutch East India Company through the evolution of its legal, administrative, political, transportation, and communication networks that provided the template for the evolution of other nodes in the empire. Located on the eastern coast of Java, Batavia was, from 1619, the seat of the Company's High Government at the center of power, though it was by no means omnipotent in its control over the imperial web. The Company's aim was to make Batavia the major entrepôt on the Straits of Malacca, filtering trade from the Indian Ocean and South China Sea. By 1730, the inner city population of Batavia was nearly 24,000 and the Company had invested massive amounts of money and labor to stimulate its growth.[1] The Company's network of forced migration facilitated slave labor in Batavia and throughout the empire through the slave trade; it used penal transportation and political exile to bolster the rule of law by banishing criminals and political opponents from Batavia to other Company nodes, including the Cape of Good Hope.

This chapter examines the institutions of law and governance in Batavia through the criminal record of the Council of Justice that produced convicts for potential banishment. It focuses particularly on the period before and after the massacre of Batavia's Chinese population in 1740 to demonstrate both the Company's efforts and its failures to enforce the rule of law. From the outset, the Company took steps to maintain control of its population, primarily its own servants and the slaves under its jurisdiction. The criminal record shows, however, the limitations of Company sovereignty, as people resisted being governed by committing crimes they hoped to get away with undetected. The unlucky ones who got caught

---

[1] Raben, Batavia – inner city: population 1729, "Batavia and Colombo," p. 312.

were branded as criminals and, with their freedom curtailed, became vulnerable to forced migration in similar ways to slaves.

Status and Crime in Batavia

As it emerged in Batavia, Dutch colonial society was somewhat of a misnomer. Europeans in Batavia, particularly women, were mostly of Asian birth or descent on the maternal side and, over time, so were many Company employees of all ranks. The imperial capital was a colonial city whose residents had an increasingly tenuous link to both European birth and social norms. Slavery was one of the most visible institutions that separated VOC imperial settlements from their headquarters in the United Provinces, and it was the focus of much attention by commentators writing about Batavia for a European audience. There were more slaves in Batavia than any other category of residents; huge numbers were owned by and labored for the Company and, on a more modest scale, for everyone else living in the city. The VOC elite tried to legislate sumptuary laws to control public displays of wealth that upset the strict social hierarchy of the Company and its chain of command as the pinnacle of power and prestige. Among other restrictions, the extensive sumptuary code of 1754 limited the use of slaves as public status symbols by enumerating how many slaves Batavian residents could have in their public retinue according to their rank and even what clothes their slaves could wear. Despite laws regulating the use of slaves as icons of status, the Company and individual slave owners feared their slaves. Company decrees tried to regulate slaves' behavior in banning public gatherings, the handling of weapons and the use of stimulants that might all lead to individual acts of violence, or, worse still, uprisings.[2] The Company's legal record shows the extent to which these laws were broken and what the consequences were for slaves apprehended, tried, convicted, and sentenced. These records also show the high level of social interaction between all the lower classes in the city, including ordinary Company servants and how and why some of these people broke the law and became convicts subject to imprisonment and/or penal transportation.

Examining in detail how the Company's legal system operated in Batavia provides insight into the mechanisms of the law, the social milieu of the Company's capital, and how the Company sought to control the people under its jurisdiction. The criminal records for the mid-eighteenth

---

[2] Jean Gelman Taylor, *The Social World of Batavia: European and Eurasian in Dutch Asia*. Madison: University of Wisconsin Press, 1983, pp. 66–71.

century demonstrate the great variety of social relationships between men and women of all legal categories and identities who inhabited Batavia's social landscape and how the Company punished transgressions against laws designed to keep control of these people for its own ends.

The imperial elite in Batavia was far more concerned with the comfort and privilege of their own households, their positions within the Company, and the protection of their status and patrimony than they were with life in the houses and on the alleyways and wharves of the town. In this status-driven environment, the lower classes were not considered worth contemplating by Company elites, except for their shortcomings. Profits from trade relied on good governance and the Company protected its privileges through its legal system. Only glimpses into the lives of common folk have been preserved in official Company archives or contemporary traveler's accounts, and most of them are particularly unflattering to common Company servants whom Governor-General Reynst in 1615 declared unequivocally were "the scum of our land."[3]

Social historians have recently begun redeeming the reputation of ordinary soldiers and sailors by examining journals and letters, and reconstructing voyages that tell of their experiences at sea and on land and counter such caricatures as Reynst's with details from the lives of real people. Legal scholars have tended to focus on the evolution of structures of legality rather than the implementation of law at the mundane level of common criminality. Social historians who do focus on crime are by definition dealing with individuals who transgress social boundaries.[4] Hendrik Niemeijer suggests, quite rightly, that the best vantage point to observe ordinary public social life in Batavia is from the *serambi*, or front porch, the hub of activity for urban households.[5]

Pamela McVay's examination of crimes and criminality in the Dutch East India Company during the seventeenth century is one of the few exceptions to the neglect of the perspectives and experiences of Company

---

[3] Charles R. Boxer, *The Dutch Seaborne Empire, 1600–1800*. London: Penguin Books, 1965, p. 244.
[4] Interest in these questions, most notably within the field of comparative urban studies, has increased since the 1990s. See Raben, "Batavia and Colombo" and Pamela McVay's study on crime in Batavia, Timor, and Ternate entitled "'I Am the Devil's Own': Crime, Class and Identity in the Seventeenth Century Dutch East Indies," unpublished dissertation, University of Illinois at Urbana-Champaign, 1995. F. W. de Haan, *Oud Batavia*. 3 Deel. Batavia: G. Kolff & Co., 1922. De Haan's book also included one of the early analyses of slavery under the Dutch East India Company.
[5] Hendrik Niemeijer, *Batavia: Een koloniale samenleving in de 17de eeuw*. Amersfoort, Neth.: Uitjgeverij Balans, 2005, p. 18.

servants. Using the Company's criminal records, McVay demonstrates that the highly mobile populations of the main port cities, including Batavia, tended to generate correspondingly high levels of common crime among the lower ranks. In contrast, the small stable garrison towns like Ternate and Timor tended to encourage greater compliance to respectable norms that were reinforced by Church institutions. The consistent pattern in criminal records shows that the Company arrested a far higher proportion of their own servants and slaves than any other population group and that these men (for overwhelmingly it was men who fell foul of the law) were punished more harshly than high-ranking officials who committed crimes.[6]

High-ranking officials of the Company who committed crimes, or more accurately whose patrimonial networks within the Company did not shield them from prosecution by their peers, were more likely to be tried in Batavia than in the other colonies. Small-scale profiteering was endemic among Company servants, and the amassing of fortunes through private trade by Company elites was expected, despite most of this trade being illegal in the eyes of the Company. By the end of the Company era it was a Dutch witticism to spell out the VOC initials as standing for *Vergaan Onder Corruptie* – "collapsed through corruption."[7] Occasionally, the Seventeen Gentlemen made a more determined effort to control their imperial elites through the appointment of supposedly "independent" officials who were ordered to investigate these activities.

Pamela McVay convincingly argues this was the case with Nicholaes Schagen, who was prosecuted by the Seventeen Gentlemen's commissioner-general, nobleman Hendrik Adriaan van Reede van Mijdrecht tot Drakenstein in 1687. Appointed as Director of Bengal, Schagen came under the scrutiny of Van Reede, partly it seems because Schagen and his wife Sara Aletta van Genegen were unconnected through family to the elite Company networks that would have protected them. Bengal was considered the ripest fruit for plucking personal profits among high-ranking officials, so that Schagen was not alone in succumbing to temptation. Schagen's wife was equally active in the pursuit of private profit on behalf of her family, and such activities by women were not as strictly scrutinized as those of Company officials. Although Schagen's case involved illegal trade in copper and a minor trade in cloth by his wife, it was opium trade in Bengal that provided the greatest opportunity

---

[6] McVay, "I Am the Devil's Own," pp. 78–81.
[7] Boxer, *Dutch Seaborne Empire*, p. 229.

for smuggling and profiteering. Nevertheless, Schagen was able to avoid conviction by basing his defense on appeals to his rank and honor while simultaneously disparaging those of lesser officials called as witnesses against him. He was suspended and recalled to serve as a magistrate in Batavia on the Council of Justice, the court that was actually hearing his trial, and after his acquittal he was sent to a less profitable governing post in Ambon.[8] By stark contrast, in 1722, twenty-six ordinary-ranking people, including eleven European storekeepers, were executed in Batavia under the orders of the same court for smuggling.[9]

Causes célèbres provide a window through which one can spy on the relationship between Company elites and the VOC's legal system.[10] These scandalous cases highlight how status determined access to and treatment under the law during the Company era. Civil cases, particularly marital disputes, were far more complex and could involve countersuits in courts based in the Netherlands. Such was the case, according to Leonard Blussé, of the opportunistic Dutch lawyer Johan Bitter, who in 1676 arrived in Batavia practically penniless and married an older wealthy Batavian widow Cornelia van Nijenroode. Herself a "child of the Company," Cornelia was the daughter of a Dutch Company merchant and his Japanese concubine but had been raised in Batavia and made an advantageous first marriage to an ambitious Company official, Pieter Cnoll. Despite widow Van Nijenroode's considerable efforts to protect her fortune against her avaricious and abusive second husband by appealing directly to the High Government, Bitter was able to manipulate his legal knowledge and access to courts in both Batavia and Holland to get at her money by arguing that under the laws of Holland he was entitled to half her money and usufruct rights to her assets as her husband.[11] Legal machinations of this

---

[8] McVay, "I Am the Devil's Own," chapter 1, pp. 6–25.
[9] Boxer, *Dutch Seaborne Empire*, p. 228.
[10] The 1722 case of conspiracy leading to the execution of the wealthy Batavian burgher Peter Erberveld has been the subject of intense scrutiny. The recently published Batavia-Jakarta bibliography has thirteen entries detailing articles dealing with this one particular case. The arrest and imprisonment of the former Governor-General Adriaan Valkinier following the Chinese massacre in 1740 has also drawn considerable attention. See Ewald Ebing and Youetta de Jager, comps., *Batavia-Jakarta, 1600–2000: A Bibliography*. KITLV Bilbiographic Series no. 23. Leiden: KITLV, 2000, p. 867. For marital disputes highlighting gender relationships within the eighteenth-century Batavian elite, see Leonard Blussé, *Bitter Bonds: A Colonial Divorce Drama of the Seventeenth Century*. Princeton, NJ: Markus Wiener Publications, 2002, and his first analysis of the case in *Strange Company*. For a thorough analysis of elite gender relations in VOC Batavia see Taylor, *Social World of Batavia*.
[11] Blussé, *Bitter Bonds*.

kind were only available to elites. Cornelia's sad case shows how colonial elite families sought the protection of the highest level of the Company's colonial government to protect their interests, even though they could not rely on the partiality of courts in the United Provinces.

The City of Batavia

A close examination of the Batavian criminal record shifts the emphasis away from the theoretical analysis of Company law toward its practical application in everyday life. It recalibrates the social history of Batavia from an emphasis on elites toward a fuller understanding of the broad spectrum of the city's social landscape. In so doing, one gains a glimpse into the daily lives of ordinary European and indigenous Company servants, Company and privately owned slaves, and Chinese and indigenous urban residents. This limited attempt at revealing "outcast Batavia" is a corrective to studies of the city that focus on the monumental, institutional, and elite representations of the "Queen City of the East."[12] This chapter considers the middle decades of the eighteenth century, roughly 1730 to 1750, partly because of constraints imposed by the archives. There is a gap in the Batavian criminal records between 1691 and 1728 that precludes an examination of the earlier period of the eighteenth century.[13] The middle decades are also those most readily accessible in the corresponding Cape criminal records and registers, which allow some sense of continuity between these two colonial urban contexts as viewed through penal transportation from Batavia to the Cape.

Records of the bureaucratic and legal institutions in Batavia through which the Company governed give considerable insight into how the ruling elite of the Company perceived the people they ruled. In these records, and in practice, the VOC categorized people according to gender, ethnicity, religion, and status of freedom and generated an enormous archive for historians interested in the population of Company settlements. These detailed pictures of Company settlements were not consistent because population categories changed over both time and geographical

---

[12] Pauline Milone, "'Queen City of the East': The Metamorphosis of a Colonial Capital," unpublished PhD dissertation, University of California, Berkeley, 1966. This was a common name for Batavia during the early Company era. See, for example, Susan Abeyesekere, *Jakarta: A History*. Singapore: Oxford University Press, 1987, p. 3; and Boxer, *Dutch Seaborne Empire*, p. 275.

[13] Meilink-Roelofsz, Raben, and Spikerman, eds., *De archieven van de VOC*.

context.[14] For example, Batavia's population categories were quite different from the Cape's because the specific ethnic categorization of people in Batavia determined their rights of residence and their legal status under Company law.

These categories were also the lens through which the VOC perceived who lived under the jurisdiction of its laws and who did not. Leonard Blussé invokes Furnival's notion of a plural society to analyze Batavia under Company rule. "From the outset, the population of Batavia consisted of different (ethnic) groups who lived more-or-less segregated, according to their own customs, but who met at the marketplace, each group carving its own niche in the local economy. In this respect Batavian society did not differ much from the type of society found in the harbor principalities of Java, where culturally heterogeneous groups lived in separate wards under their own chiefs."[15] This is the case to a certain extent, particularly in regard to civil law and the governance of daily life.

The record of the criminal courts presents another picture of Batavia's diverse population meeting not only in the marketplace but also everywhere else in the city and its environs.

The spatial segregation of population groups was one part of a complicated and pluralistic administrative system which was called into being in order to control a multi-ethnic society... The plural structure offered a practical solution to the Dutch authorities... The Company was neither able nor willing to impose its legal system on the Asian population and left complicated issues such as civil jurisdiction to indigenous political leaders... Despite its intentional plural structure, jurisdictions and boundaries blurred. The result was a fragmented authority structure, in which the Company government unquestionably stood at the apex, but many other sources of power persisted... Internal cleavages, class distinctions, interest groups, and ambiguous categories within the legal groups fragmented the formal plural structure at all levels[16]

Raben thereby suggests that ethnic separation occurred more in theory than in practice.

[14] Raben, "Batavia and Colombo," chapter 4, "Registration Mania," pp. 77–116. For ethnic categories at the Cape of Good Hope, see Richard Elphick and Robert Shell, "Intergroup Relations: Khoikhoi, Settlers, Slaves and Free Blacks, 1652–1795," in Richard Elphick and Hermann Giliomee, eds., *The Shaping of South African Society, 1652–1840*, 2nd ed. Cape Town: Maskew Miller Longman, 1989, pp. 184–242.
[15] Leonard Blussé, *Strange Company: Chinese Settlers, Mestizo Women and the Dutch in VOC Batavia*. Dordrecht, Holland: Foris Publications, 1986, pp. 4–5. See also J. S. Furnivall, *Netherlands India: A Study of Plural Economy*. Cambridge, UK: Cambridge University Press, 1939.
[16] Raben, "Batavia and Colombo," pp. 197–199.

The impression of distinct ethnic quarters was partly an illusion created by the administrative divisions of the city, even in those quarters inhabited by Europeans who also housed their slaves of South and Southeast Asian, and, sometimes, African descent. Gender relations fundamentally disrupted this neat parceling of the population because when women were recorded in population figures they were given the ethnic status of their husbands or fathers no matter where their place of birth. Traveler's accounts of Batavia give a much clearer notion of the early Creole composition of Batavia's population despite official designations of status and ethnicity. Even taking into account the ethnic quarters of Batavia, these observations undermine the impression that mixing of different ethnic groups occurred only in public spaces. The criminal record of Batavia clearly shows ubiquitous and multiethnic social interactions through the type of crimes committed against or in cooperation with people across the population spectrum.

The choice of the mid-eighteenth-century period as the focus of this chapter is not completely arbitrary in terms of broader historical events on Java that affected the Company and its capital city. The early 1720s encompassed the Second Javanese War of Succession (1719 to 1723) in which the ruler of the inland Javanese empire of Mataram, Amangkurat IV (r.1719 to 1726), was barely able to hold onto power in the face of both internal and external challenges. This war was followed by the more unstable reign of Pakubuwana II (r.1726 to 1749) that prompted the Third Javanese War of Succession (1746 to 1757). The result of these wars was the division of the Mataram empire into the courts of Jogyakarta and Surakarta under the 1755 Treaty of Giyanti. This treaty was negotiated and ratified by the VOC, the second most powerful empire on the island.[17]

Throughout this period the Company was deeply embroiled in the political and military intrigues in Java, but becoming an imperial power through a strategy of engagement in indigenous affairs was financially disastrous for the VOC. Although the Javanese court assumed debt repayment for military services rendered, this was hardly a fraction of the expenses incurred by the Company in its political and military endeavors. Intersecting these two dynastic wars was an event in Batavia known contemporarily as the 1740 Chinese rebellion or massacre (depending on

---

[17] Merle Ricklefs, *A History of Modern Indonesia Since c.1300*, 2nd ed. Stanford, CA: Stanford University Press, 1993, pp. 86–96.

one's perspective). This event permanently changed the demographics and the character of the city. An examination of the whole mid-century period therefore gives an immediate sense of "before" and "after" this disaster, and shows how the Company courts defined and prosecuted crime during these decades.

In her history of Jakarta (Batavia), Susan Abeyesekere calculates the apex of Batavia's "Golden Age" to be around 1730.[18] By this time all the major legal, administrative, civil, and military institutions were in place, and the city had grown into one of the urban splendors of Asia. "The Dutch molded their cities on the basis of European, even Dutch, aesthetic, military, and social conceptions superimposed on the original geography of the Asian soil."[19] At the symbolic center of Batavia, although actually located overlooking the harbor on one side and the town on another, was the Castle. Its imposing façade was the focal point of the city's fortifications that included the city walls and gates and outlying fortresses. While imposing, the city's defense system was virtually useless, giving an indication of Batavia's sense of security and prosperity. Decades of urban security had shifted the emphasis of urban construction from the upkeep of military fortifications to the building of major civilian institutions.[20] This was particularly evident in the construction of Batavia's majestic Dutch-style Town Hall, which was completed in 1710 and represented the apex of civilian power in juxtaposition to the Castle as the center of Company power. The civilian Court of Aldermen was housed in this building that also contained a prison wing.[21] This was the time when Batavia inspired many a sailor-poet or eloquent traveler to expound upon its beauty:

> O lovely Batavia, that holds me spellbound,
> There your Town Hall with its proudly arching vaults
> Rears its profile! How splendid is your situation!
> Your broad Canals, replenished with fresh water, beautifully planted.
> Need bend before no city in the Netherlands...
> The Tiger's Canal, of which Batavia well may boast,
> Throws up proudly to the skies a row of Palaces
> And glitters from end to end with jewels of architecture...
> O'ershadowed by an avenue of eternal spring green...
> How does Batavia charm the stroller then![22]

---

[18] Abeyesekere, *Jakarta*, p. 38.
[19] Raben, "Batavia and Colombo," p. 9.
[20] Ibid., p. 17.
[21] Abeyesekere, *Jakarta*, pp. 18–19.
[22] Jan de Marre, a Company seaman and poet, wrote this poem during a visit to Batavia in the early eighteenth century. Quotes in Taylor, *Social World of Batavia*, p. 52.

The main boundary distinction was between the areas inside and outside the city walls. Inside these walls were located the major civil and military buildings, too numerous to mention, but including a variety of churches, schools, hospitals, orphanages, two courts and prisons, shops and markets, Company storehouses, artisan quarters and workshops, and many hundreds of private dwellings ranging from luxurious mansions to crowded tenements.

The entire city was crossed by a series of canals. Although Francois Valentijn commented in the 1720s on the glory of the city's sixteen canals lined with tamarind and flowering trees, he saved his most glowing praise for the Tiger's Canal. "The *Tijgersgracht* possesses uniformly beautiful buildings, the most exquisite of the town. The beauty of this elegantly planted straight canal surpasses anything I have ever seen in Holland."[23] One of the most famous depictions of this canal is that of the Danish artist and Company servant, Johannes Rach, whose studio in Batavia produced drawings of magnificent country houses and street scenes commissioned by the Batavian elite. Rach's drawing of the *Tijgersgracht* depicts a scene of complete order and visual harmony, with well-proportioned canal houses and spotless streets where boats could be seen gliding serenely down the calm, clean canal.

The people portrayed in the drawing give a human element to this idealization. In the center of the image is a barge, complete with Dutch trumpeter heralding the presence of a "high mightiness," who appears to be a Councilor of the Indies. Another elite Company official accompanied by his European wife and their numerous slaves of diverse ethnic origins are just about to step into their slightly less lavish canal boat. Traders, laborers, and slaves of different ethnicities and religions, as indicated by their skin color and clothes, as well as women and children (and the ubiquitous street dogs) are bustling on the sidewalks and in canal barges of all shapes and sizes going about their business. The *Tijgersgracht* drawing captures in a single image the Company's own vision of social hierarchy and prosperity in Batavia.

The Company's government was able to realize the ideal of order, proportion and uniformity, so pleasing to the Dutch eye, in the initial layout of the inner city. "Batavia-town formed a rectangle of about 2,250 meters in length and 1,500 meters across. It was cut in two almost equal parts by the river Ciliwong or Great River as the Dutch used to call it. Each

---

[23] Francois Valentijn quoted in Blussé, *Strange Company*, p. 15.

part was intersected by a canal that ran parallel to the long sides of the rectangle. These were themselves intersected at right angles by several cross-canals. Eight streets – all of them thirty feet wide – further emphasized the grid pattern of the town. The entire city was enclosed by high coral rock walls and twenty-two bulwarks. Four gates led to the bridges that spanned the surrounding deep city moat."[24]

Although the Company made considerable effort to enumerate the population along ethnic lines, equally and neatly divided, these censuses did not accurately portray the reality of the city's daily life. Considering that women and children were mostly defined by their husband's or father's ethnicity, and that very few European and Chinese born women ever settled in Batavia, definitions of ethnicity and ethnic city quarters immediately become subjective.[25] These figures are at best an indicator of overall population figures and a rough profile of the male population. They are also evidence of an emerging *Indische* (Dutch-indigenous) and *Batawi* (indigenous Batavian) culture in the city during the eighteenth century.

Batavia's Inner City and Hinterland Population

The population of the inner city reached its peak of nearly 24,000 people in about 1730 and thereafter went into decline. One reason for this decline was the frequent malaria epidemics that started in the early 1730s and devastated the town with depressing regularity. The movement of the Company elite out of the city and their construction of lavish country estates attest to this gradual urban decline.[26] The Company elite

---

[24] Blussé, *Strange Company*, p. 23.
[25] Peter Nas points out that the studies on ethnic composition of colonial Indonesian towns have been determined by the perspective of the white male Dutch officials who wrote the documents that constitute the archives. In this sense, population tables and statistics can give only an indication rather than any accurate portrait. Peter Nas, "Introduction: A General View of the Indonesian Town," Peter J. M. Nas, ed., *The Indonesian City: Studies in Urban Development and Planning*, Verhandelingen KITLV, no. 117. Dordrecht-Holland: Foris Publications, 1986, pp. 6–7. Many scholarly studies have been based on these figures as constituting some kind of reality on the ground rather than Dutch perceptions of ethnicity. See, for example, Raben, "Batavia and Colombo," and Frank Spooner, "Batavia 1673–1790: A City of Colonial Growth and Migration," Ira Glazier and Luigi de Rosa, eds., *Migration Across Time and Nations: Population Mobility in Historical Context*. New York: Holmes and Meier, 1986. See also Gerrit Knaap, "The Demography of Ambon in the Seventeenth Century: Evidence from Colonial Proto-Censuses," *Journal of Southeast Asian Studies*, 26(2), September 1995, pp. 227–241.
[26] Taylor, *Social World of Batavia*.

literally headed for the hills, where it was cooler and had fresher air and water. In general, Europeans remained a minority in the city, with free European burghers representing an even smaller proportion of the population. Batavia was quintessentially a cosmopolitan town despite its Dutch-inspired architecture and layout, built by the labor of Chinese immigrants and slaves from all over South and Southeast Asia, the western Indian Ocean islands, and the east coast of Africa. Very few free Javanese lived within the city, the majority living in the outer *kampung* (compounds). Most ethnic groups could be found all over the city, and the widespread ownership of domestic slaves added to the urban mix.[27] The constant movement of Company personnel was represented most visibly in the triannual arriving and biannual departing of the fleets.[28] The sudden influx of hundreds of sailors of diverse ethnic origins into Batavia roadstead, and inevitably into town, was a feature of the city's population that was not enumerated in the census.

The fleets traveling between Europe and Asia were only part of the Company's shipping. Many other ships also entered Batavia's harbor. The Company's intra-Asian trade was a complex network of shipping and trading routes in the Indian Ocean and South China Sea. The crews of these ships often comprised as many Asian as European sailors. Added to this was the vibrant Chinese junk trade between Batavia and the South China Sea that stimulated the migration of Chinese to the city both as temporary sojourners and as rural laborers in the *Ommelanden* (outer districts). The continual importation of slaves and the Company slave trade through Batavia was another factor in the constantly changing population of the city. The population of Batavia was changing in terms of ethnicity and size. The Company's use of indigenous auxiliary troops from various Asian ethnic groups shifted the population of the compounds up and down by several thousand in a short space of time.[29]

Remco Raben's population figures for Batavia's inner city and outer districts show the fluctuation of these turbulent decades with a general tendency toward the depopulation of the inner city and the growth of the agriculturally based population in the outer districts.[30]

---

[27] De Haan, *Oud Batavia*; Raben, "Batavia and Colombo," p. 116.
[28] J. R. de Bruijn, F. S. Gaastra, and I. Schoffer, *Dutch-Asiatic Shipping in the 17th and 18th Centuries*. 3 vols. Rijks geschiedenkundige publicatien, grote serie, nos. 165–167. Den Haag: Martinus Nijhoff, 1979–1987; Boxer, *Dutch Seaborne Empire*, p. 221.
[29] Raben, "Batavia and Colombo," p. 145.
[30] Ibid., Appendix 3, pp. 312–314, 326–328.

	Inner city	Outer districts	Total
1729	23,701	78,957	102,658
1739	18,302	68,229	86,531
1749	14,141	77,015	91,156
1759	16,914	111,172	128,086

Furthermore, the ethnic breakdown of the population shows the Company's sensitivity to these categories. The Company's ethnic categorization of the inner city population included European, Mestizo, Mardijkers, Chinese, Moor, Malay, Javanese, Makasserese, and other subcategories. Slaves were not enumerated by ethnic category because they comprised a single legal category regardless of their ethnicity. These ethnic categories had implications for the treatment of individuals so defined in terms of the application of civil law. Whether tried by the Court of Aldermen or the Council of Justice, they were all subject to the Company's criminal laws. The drop in the Chinese population of the inner city from 4,199 in 1739 on the eve of the massacre to 1,590 in 1749 is not surprising. That decade also saw a sharp decline in the numbers of Malays and Javanese in the inner city, from 215 in 1729 to 92 in 1739 with a threefold increase over the next ten years.[31] These numbers are striking testament to how few free people from the Indies archipelago lived in the inner city. This was no coincidence. The Company sought to control the purchase of property in the city, and it limited the proportion of the indigenous population who could hold title to land. These figures would have been much higher had the ethnic origins of women and slaves been enumerated in the population figures.

The European population overwhelmingly lived in the inner city. Only about 2 percent, or 1500 Europeans, lived in the outer districts between 1729 and 1759. The Company's enumeration of Batavia's outer districts shows even greater sensitivity to the ethnic origins of the population living in these hinterlands. Apart from Europeans, Mestizos, Mardijkers, Chinese, Moors, Malays, Makasserese, and Javanese, other ethnic categories of people living in the outer districts included Ambonese, Bandanese, Bugis, Timorese, Balinese, Butonese, Manados, Sumbawas, and Bimas. As for the city, slaves living in the outer districts were enumerated as a separate category. The point in listing these ethnic labels is to demonstrate the Company's sensitivity to the origins of people living in its

[31] Ibid.

domain. The precise breakdown of these ethnic groups is not as important, except to mention that the Balinese and the Javanese were the most populous groups averaging about 33,000 between 1729 and 1749, increasing to a total of 54,597 in 1759, with the Javanese comprising 32,385 of the total. Slaves averaged 14,700 between 1729 and 1749, increasing to 17,111 in 1759. The biggest population shift in this period was therefore seen in the increase from 1749 to 1759 of the Chinese population from 10,042 to 23,615 and in the Balinese and Javanese populations listed above. By contrast, the European population of the outer districts averaged 289 for each decade. Thus, outside the Batavia city walls, the Company was overwhelmingly engaged in ruling an Asian population.[32]

Batavia's fate was sealed by the Company's development of sugar plantations in the outer districts during the late seventeenth century. The rapid expansion of the sugar industry in Java, controlled mostly by Chinese entrepreneurs, brought large numbers of Chinese and indigenous laborers into the region. Moreover, the uncontrolled exploitation of these lands resulted in a shortage of fresh water to the city as irrigation diverted river waters that naturally flowed from the mountains to the sea. The clearing of natural forests for plantations added to the problem by encouraging soil erosion that silted up the city's canals and natural waterways causing stagnant water that became a breeding ground for malaria, typhoid, and dysentery.[33] The pristine images of the *Tijgersgracht* belied the unhealthiness of the urban environment for its residents and visitors, a theme that increasingly came to dominate written accounts of the city.

The Chinese Massacre and Batavia's Decline

The collapse of the sugar industry due to changes in worldwide supplies to the European market after the 1720s caused the ecological and social crises that led to the Chinese massacre in 1740. Unregulated immigration of Chinese men to work on the sugar plantations resulted in a large number of unemployed workers by the 1730s. The Company responded by stepping up the arrest and deportation of illegal Chinese immigrants under tightened vagrancy laws. The Company had attempted to regulate the migration of the Chinese to Batavia by implementing a residency permit system in the 1690s. This system required all Chinese people in the city to carry an official Company-issued token or risk

---

[32] Raben, Inner city: population: 1729–1959, Ommelanden: population: 1729–1759, "Batavia and Colombo," pp. 312–315 and pp. 326–329.

[33] Blussé, *Strange Company*, pp. 26–28.

arrest.[34] Those arrested under this regulation were tried by the Court of Aldermen. The punishment of banishment for illegal Chinese residents of Batavia was common, and the Company deported them to their homeland on a fairly consistent basis or, alternatively, banished a smaller number to the Cape of Good Hope.[35] This system was supposedly in force for other indigenous ethnic groups but was never implemented.[36]

The increase in the number of arrests of Chinese immigrants under the residency permit system, combined with the corruption associated with issuing and implementing the permit regulations, led to wild rumors among the threatened Chinese population in the outer districts. One rumor that circulated widely was that the Company had publicly stated its intentions to exile all Chinese people to Ceylon but that its secret unstated intention was to throw them overboard at sea. The Company had indeed issued a resolution on July 25, 1740, ordering all suspicious Chinese people, whether in possession of a legal permit or not, to be arrested. If found to be unemployed they were supposed to be exiled to Ceylon.[37] Because the Company had already banished unregistered Chinese people found without permits in Batavia, and also those convicted of crimes, the apprehension that circulated among Chinese laborers had some basis in reality. The Company's resolution added fuel to the rumor that the Company's true aim was to drown all unwanted Chinese people in their midst. To forestall a potentially hideous fate, armed Chinese laborers in the outer districts attacked the sugar mills and vented their anger on their community leaders who had been cooperating with the Company. The rioters then breached the city walls, intending a general attack. Meanwhile, Chinese residents inside the city did not apparently join them in large numbers.

It was a hopeless attack, easily put down by the Company and its auxiliary troops, but nevertheless it led to massive retaliations inside the city on October 9 and 10, 1740. It appears that a fully fledged pogrom took place with Europeans and indigenous city dwellers attacking and plundering nearly seven thousand Chinese residences and businesses, killing many of those who lived there, minimally numbering at least a thousand. The High Government had not ordered the massacre but neither did it take measures to prevent or limit the ensuing carnage. "Five hundred

---

[34] Willem Remmelink, *The Chinese War and the Collapse of the Javanese State, 1725–1743.* Verhandelingen KITLV. no. 162. Leiden: KITLV Press, 1994, p. 125.

[35] James Armstrong, "The Chinese at the Cape in the Dutch East India Company Period." Unpublished paper presented at the UNESCO Slave Route Project Conference, Robben Island, Cape Town, 1997.

[36] Raben, "Batavia and Colombo," p. 212.   [37] Remmelink, *Chinese War*, p. 126.

Chinese who were shut up in the jails of the Town Hall were brought out one by one and killed. For a week the town blazed with fire and the canals ran red with blood."[38]

Many Chinese Batavians who escaped the massacre joined the war already raging inland.[39] The Chinese population of Batavia's inner city was virtually obliterated overnight. In 1739, it numbered 4,199. A year later it was only 112. In the same year, the Chinese population of the outer districts declined from 10,574 to 1,826.[40] The 1740 massacre changed the demographics of Batavia permanently. The Company no longer allowed the Chinese to reside within the city walls, although their numbers eventually recovered in the outer districts. During the course of the 1740s, thousands of Chinese people also took up residence near the city at the new Chinese compound set aside for their occupation in the shadow of the city walls and were enumerated in the inner city population figures. After the 1740 massacre, the Company attempted to ensure that only Christians could buy property within the city walls, theoretically excluding all Asians other than the Christian Mardijkers. Although this encouraged the development of supposedly ethnic-based compounds, the Company did not and could not completely enforce ethnic exclusivity within the city.[41]

The development of the outer districts had its corollary in the harbor and port of Batavia with the seasonal influx of Company sailors, who by the mid-eighteenth century were mostly not of European origin. The Batavia roadstead was filled with ships and sailors from all over the world. In the waters off the coast of Batavia lay numerous atolls and tiny islands that dotted the bay. The Company used the small islands of Onrust and Edam as workshops and shipyards.[42] The Island of Edam also operated as a prison and holding site for prisoners and exiles waiting for the next departing fleet. It would be difficult to overemphasize the level of activity taking place in the port itself, which was, after all, the reason for being of the city.[43] Although the Chinese junk trade declined after

---

[38] Abeyesekere, *Jakarta*, p. 26. Those prisoners killed are likely to have been in the Court of Aldermen jail not the Castle.
[39] Remmelink, *Chinese War*, p. 126.
[40] Spooner, "Batavia 1673–1790," p. 52; Raben, Batavia – Inner City: population 1739–1759, Batavia – Ommelanden: population 1729–1959, "Batavia and Colombo," pp. 312–315 and pp. 326–329.
[41] Raben, "Batavia and Colombo," p. 176.
[42] Dirk Schaap, *Onrust: Het Nederlandse duivelseiland*. Utrecht: A. W. Bruna Uitgevers, 2002.
[43] Some historians argue that Batavia asserted ascendancy as a port through its role as the Company's imperial capital alone, because it was geographically inferior to Colombo and Malacca as a natural entrepôt for the region's trade. See, for example, C. van Dijk, "Java, Indonesia and Southeast Asia: How Important Is the Java Sea?," in V. Houben and

1750, the major functions of the port remained fairly stable for the whole period.

The second half of the eighteenth century witnessed the decline of inner city Batavia as residents who could afford to do so fled the increasingly unhealthy environment. The Company employed convicts and Javanese from Ceribon to dredge the canals by hand. The canals had been used as general sewers and thus waterborne diseases, combined with endemic malaria, ensured that people who dredged the canals had been virtually handed a death sentence. The "miasma" theory of airborne disease that predominated during this era shaped how people explained the unhealthy climate of the city. Contrast Valentijn's earlier glowing description of Batavia's canals with that of the Swedish traveler Stavorinus in the second half of the eighteenth century:

The stagnant canals, in the dry season, exhale an intolerable stench, and the trees planted along them impede the course of the air, by which in some degree the putrid effluvia would be dissipated. In the wet season the inconvenience is equal; for then these reservoirs of corrupted water overflow their banks in the lower part of town, and fill the lower stories of the houses, where they leave behind them an inconceivable quantity of slime and filth.... [I]t poisons the air while it is drying, to a considerable extent.[44]

The decline of Batavia's urban environment did not result in any change in its role as the Company's capital, and the symbolic seat of power remained at the Castle. As the Company's major transit port, the fleets still gathered in the harbor at the end of their outbound journey from Europe and their yearly homebound journey. The governor-general and Council of the Indies as the High Government functioned as the focal point for decisions regarding trade and relations with foreign powers in the empire. Sickness and death among the many commoners existed in stark contrast to the pomp and displays of wealth of the Batavian elite.[45]

H. Maier, eds., *Looking in Odd Mirrors: The Java Sea*. Semaians 5. Leiden: Rijksuniversiteit te Leiden, 1992, p. 299.

[44] Stavorinus quoted in Abeyesekere, *Jakarta*, p. 39.

[45] These displays of wealth amazed travelers who dwell particularly on the details of the bejeweled Batavian women. The Company too found these displays of wealth intolerable, perhaps because they threatened the status symbols of the Company's uppermost echelons. Governor-General Jacob Mossel implemented the Sumptuary Code of December 30, 1754: "Measures for Curbing Pomp and Circumstance." Taylor has analyzed this code to great effect showing how it reveals the extent of displays of wealth unparalleled in European cities outside of court cultures. She argues that the sumptuary laws were also designed to downgrade Asian symbols of status important in this "Indische Society." Taylor, *Social World of Batavia*, pp. 66–71. For the application of these laws at the Cape, see Robert Ross, *Status and Respectability in the Cape Colony, 1750–1870: A Tragedy of Manners*, Cambridge, UK: Cambridge University Press, 1999, pp. 9–16.

Batavian Courts in the Mid-Eighteenth Century

Despite the varied fortunes of Batavia as "Queen City of the East" during the seventeenth century, the Company's administrative and judicial systems remained quite stable for the whole of the mid-eighteenth century. No major structural changes occurred after the entire system was in place by the 1720s. The VOC had implemented administrative and judicial measures to regulate the lives of people within its realm to fulfill its primary objective of generating trade and income. It made a crucial distinction between civil and criminal law and its courts focused on the latter to severely punish people of all categories and statuses who broke the law. Punishments were also aimed at discouraging others from similar acts. Another layer in the disciplining of the Company and civilian European population existed within the Dutch Reformed Church that had the power to censure its congregation. The Church authorities, themselves Company servants, wielded disciplinary power regularly with the authorization of the Company and constituted a significant force in enforcing social norms in Batavian colonial society.[46]

The Company had employed its own jurists in the seventeenth century to develop a Conflict of Laws theory to determine the applicability of law, jurisdiction, and enforcement in specific cases, and this theory was adopted throughout the Company's empire.[47] By and large, civil law was left under the control of ethnic authorities, some of whom were specifically endorsed by the Company officials in Batavia. The Court of Aldermen tried civil cases and criminal cases of non-Company Europeans and other residents of the city. The spatial and ethnic fragmentation of Batavia was reflected in the security considerations of the Company. Law and order were maintained by the Court of Aldermen and their servants, a bailiff and his *caffers* (who were the executioner's assistants and a nascent police), and the night patrols of the city.[48] The Court

---

[46] For the most thorough treatment of this topic see Niemeijer, *Batavia*.

[47] M. B. Hooker, *Concise Legal History of Southeast Asia*. Oxford: Clarendon Press, 1976, pp. 187–194. This issue was taken up by Hugo Grotius in *Mare Liberum*. Hooker points out that "[t]he administrative system which made possible juristic work of this type continued, but it was not until 1847 that legal pluralism in Indonesia became formalised in the constitution of the Netherlands East Indies," p. 94. Daniel Lev claims by contrast that the Company "couldn't have cared less" about local law "except where commercial interests were at stake." Daniel S. Lev, "Colonial Law and the Genesis of the Indonesian State," *Indonesia*, no. 40, 1980, p. 58. This is not an accurate assessment of the Company's legal system. The Company was intensely concerned with matters of security and control within all the settlements and colonies.

[48] Raben, "Batavia and Colombo," p. 213.

of Aldermen met in the Town Hall where it also administered its own jail.[49]

At the pinnacle of Batavia's judicial system was the Council of Justice, the highest Company court in the city and the Company's empire. It was composed of the highest-ranking Company officials and the *Fiscal*, equivalent to a public prosecutor. The Council of Justice tried all cases involving Company personnel and Company slaves.[50] Ball argues that by the mid-eighteenth century the Council of Justice was also trying cases from the Priangan highlands, usurping the authority of the Javanese Regents and other Javanese legal personnel and impinging upon their sovereign right to govern.[51] The Council of Justice could adjudicate any case it decided was in the Company's interests, and it frequently did so within Batavia, or by bringing cases to be heard by the Batavian court. This certainly appears to have been the case when in 1742 the Company arrested Carangassan van Balij, a slave of the old Governor-General Johannes Thedens; three other slaves belonging to Javanese residents of Batavia; the Javanese sergeant Bappa Mania; and the free Malay *caffer* Sleeman, along with two slaves of the Bantenese Prince Pannabahan; all of whom were accused in the same case of murder.[52] Theoretically at least, some of the accused lived under the jurisdiction of the Javanese Regent and ordinarily would have been tried by the Javanese court. Nevertheless, the jurisdictional complexities of this particular case were overridden by the Company's demand for order and justice. The case was heard by the Council of Justice.

Despite the separate spheres of civilian and criminal courts in Batavia, a closer examination of Company court records reveals that the Council of Justice tried a variety of cases outside its ordinary jurisdiction. Court records do not state explicitly what process determined whether certain criminal cases came before the Council of Justice rather than before the Court of Aldermen. Unfortunately, unlike the Court of Aldermen, records are not available in their entirety for the Company period and the seventeenth-century records have been conserved in much more complete form. This has somewhat skewed the way historians have been able to write about the history of crime and punishment in Batavia. Nevertheless, the Company produced copious quantities of notes from many of its legal cases. The records from the Council of Justice for the period between 1730 and 1750 alone run into seventy-three volumes averaging

---

[49] Milone, "Queen City of the East," p. 278.
[50] De Haan, *Oud Batavia*, vol. 1, p. 141.   [51] Ball, *Indonesian Legal History*, p. 54.
[52] NA: VOC 9403: Civile en Criminele Processen van Batavia 1742–1743, case 10.

several hundred pages each.[53] In spite of the enormity of these records it is unlikely that they contain complete documentation pertaining to the criminal cases that came before the Council of Justice in Batavia. Nor are they a compilation of the complete number of crimes dealt with by the court. The various cases bound within these huge volumes suggest that either a sampling of cases, or those considered the most serious, were preserved.

Unlike the census records that, despite their shortcomings, simply enumerate and categorize people, the criminal records provide some insight into the daily lives of individuals who came into contact with the court, either as those accused or as witnesses. While these cases likely represent only a fraction of the crimes actually committed, they are illustrative of both colonial society and judicial control. For example, a soldier tried for desertion had by definition been unsuccessful in his quest, but it is the frequency of these unsuccessful attempts to leave the Company that lead us to imagine how many more Company servants were actually able to flee permanently and create new lives for themselves outside the Company's domain. Conversely, the occasional discovery and trial of a deserter who returned to a particular Company settlement years later suggests that the Company had a long memory in the pursuit of people it had condemned as criminals.

Of course, all criminal records have their shortcomings. The mediation of scribes and translators who wrote these records are only the first two layers of removal from the actual words spoken by people who gave testimony in court. Threats and applications of torture, which were not uncommon in Company courts, also shaped what people said and would admit to having done, although the records do not take this into consideration. We will never know what actually went on, but one of the features of the Company's criminal records is the inclusion of some written testimonies purporting to be verbatim accounts. The testimonies in these cases do give a sense of immediacy in time and place that suggests they were close to the perspectives of what the interviewes thought actually happened during the event described.

The overwhelming image that emerges from the Council of Justice archives is that common Company servants were prosecuted for much the same crimes as the next most common set of criminals, slaves. Desertion is by far the most common form of crime committed by Company artisans, soldiers, and sailors, particularly the last group who were severely

---

[53] Meilink-Roelofsz, Raben, and Spikerman, eds., *De archieven van de VOC*.

punished if their ships sailed without them. The amount of time absent did not necessarily count in the apportioning of punishment, although there does seem to have been some differentiation between absenteeism and desertion. Egbertus Schrauers, a sailor from Amsterdam, was convicted of habitual desertion rather than absenteeism. Various forms of assault, escalating from fighting to manslaughter and murder, were the next most common category of crimes. Even sick patients residing in the hospital were not immune from or above starting fights.

Related to the punishment for bodily crimes was prosecution for self-inflicted wounds and attempted suicide. Suicide was a serious crime, but, in contrast to Cape Town, not one case of suicide, even slave suicide, was recorded by the records of the Batavia Court of Justice in the years 1729 to 1730, 1731 to 1732, 1735 to 1736, 1740 to 1741, and 1742 to 1743. The absence of suicide cases points to the limitations of court documents preserved in the modern archives rather than the absences of the crimes themselves. As would be expected in Batavia, theft was an equal opportunity crime. All categories of people, including both men and women, were caught thieving and smuggling a range of goods including money, opium, pepper, and coffee bushes.

Crimes of transgressive sexual acts were viewed as especially serious by the Company. Although the Company nominally controlled the Church, and minor infractions such as public displays of marital discord were mediated and censored within the sanctity of the congregation, more serious sexual transgressions were punished as crimes. This is the arena where most burgher women appeared before the court. Anna Maria Keppelaar from Batavia, wife of Gouert Christiaan van Draame, committed adultery with Alexander van Bougies, slave of the *landdrost* (civil commissioner/prosecutor) Justinus Vink in 1735 and 1736. This was a particularly heinous crime in all Company settlements. Not only were the lovers of different social statuses, but also the three women slaves who facilitated their liaison, Cassandra van Batavia, Isindra van Sumbawa, and Sitti van Boegis, were all slaves belonging to the cuckolded husband.[54]

Sex between a burgher woman and a slave was punished as the crime of adultery because it was an unacceptable inversion of sexual roles, whereas the sexual abuse of slave women by their masters was tacitly condoned by colonial society and rarely punished. The only other case involving a burgher woman was another case of adultery between Cornelia

---

[54] NA: VOC 9375: Civile en Criminele Processen van Batavia 1735–1736, case 13.

Groenevelt and Company Assistant Adriaan van Rije who were at least social equals, although even their crime was disastrous for the individuals so condemned.[55] The most severe punishments for sexual crimes were meted out for rape, which was comparatively rare in the criminal records, and sodomy, which was all too common.

Sodomy between two men was a capital crime and, although difficult to prove because it required eyewitnesses to the act, was pursued avidly by the courts. Latani van Ternate, a Company slave in Batavia, was charged with attempted sodomy, but this was often a crime uncovered in the confined conditions of shipboard life. The young sailor, Marten Jansz van Shartegenbosch found this out to his peril in 1735, as did the provost Jan de Kree from Rotterdam and his lover Leendert Uijtemans from Dantzig who were brought to trial in 1742.[56]

Serious cases of malfeasance above and beyond low-level private trade were transferred for trial to Batavia from the Company's other settlements regardless of whether it was a major node like Colombo or a minor settlement. Several high-and middle-ranking Company officials in Colombo who were entrusted with the administration of the Orphan Chamber had their cases of financial mismanagement forwarded to the Council of Justice for consideration.[57] A case of smuggling brought by a Jewish merchant resident in Cochin to the Council of Justice in Batavia confirms this point. Samson Rotenberg accused two Company merchants Jan de Roode, Petrus Albertus van der Parra, and the bookkeeper Adriaan van Ravenstijn of smuggling, and the case came before the Council of Justice. This illustrates how areas in which the Company did not exercise sovereignty, such as Cochin, could still result in charges being brought against Company officials engaged in illegal trade.[58] One of the most serious scandals of this kind took place in the 1680s when illegal trading between Japanese merchants and Company officials resulted in the Shogun executing thirty-eight of the Japanese people and deporting the head of the Dutch trading post in Deshima, Andreas Cleijer, who was shipped off to Batavia by the Shogun on pain of death should he return to Japan.[59] There was absolutely nothing the Company could do to prevent

[55] NA: VOC 9375: Civile en Criminele Processen van Batavia 1735–1736, case 20.
[56] NA: VOC 9375: Civile en Criminele Processen van Batavia 1735–1736, cases 12 and 7; NA: VOC 9403: Civile en Criminele Processen van Batavia 1742–1743, case 11.
[57] NA: VOC 9375: Civile en Criminele Processen van Batavia 1735–1736, cases 28 and 29.
[58] NA: VOC 9403: Civile en Criminele Processen van Batavia 1742–1743, case 7.
[59] Boxer, *Dutch Seaborne Empire*, p. 228.

the expulsion of its chief merchant, and indeed Batavia would have been at pains to placate the Shogun and thereby protect its right to trade on Deshima Island.

The negotiation of trading relations where the Company did not exercise sovereignty also involved the negotiation of what was considered criminal. Treaties between indigenous powers and the Company sometimes included provisions for the extent of Company control over criminal acts committed by its employees. Small-time smuggling by individuals in Batavia, though endemic, sometimes came to trial particularly if it involved trading with the Company's enemies (the English, for example), which was the case with the Batavian burgher, Daniel Fredrickszoon, and the scribe of the Resident of Ceribon, Louis Loiuszoon. European foreign merchants traveling as passengers on Company ships were subject to close scrutiny and were probably outside the networks of smuggling that informed them who to pay off to escape detection, something Nicolas George from Macedonia and his free Malay servant Augustijn found out when they were charged with illegally importing opium to Batavia.[60]

The VOC attempted to control shipping and travel around its core regions as an extension of sovereignty to the shipping networks and territories. It did so by criminalizing unauthorized ships and their sailors as pirates or smugglers. The Company tried to implement a pass system similar to the one the Portuguese had initiated in their Asian empire as they sought to dominate trading and communication networks. Trying to prevent indigenous shipping was a hopeless task, although occasionally Chinese and Malay seafarers were caught in the Company's surveillance system and charged with unpermitted travel and suspected piracy. Thirteen free Malay sailors were charged with this crime in the Batavia court between 1731 and 1732, and two Chinese sailors were brought from Ceribon to stand charge for the same crime between 1735 and 1736.[61] These cases were the proverbial drops in the ocean, but they do demonstrate that some attempts were made by the Company to control shipping lanes and regulate indigenous trading networks in areas considered to be its sovereign domain.

A detailed study of the records that survive for the year in which the Chinese massacre took place indicates how the Company court functioned at a time of crisis. For the period, eighty-one cases are recorded in

---

[60] NA: VOC 9403: Civile en Criminele Processen van Batavia 1742–1743, case 23.
[61] NA: VOC 9358: Civile en Criminele Processen van Batavia 1731–1732; NA; VOC 9375: Civile en Criminele Processen van Batavia 1735–1736.

the two volumes of sentences for the years 1739 to 1741. The cases handled by the Council of Justice do not strictly accord with the theoretical division of jurisdiction with the Court of Aldermen, suggesting the imposition of precedence by the Company court. These cases do, however, give a full picture of the range of crimes committed and dealt with by the Company's highest court. First, there is no indication of the impending crisis sparked by the Chinese massacre in the cases dealt with prior to this event. The Council of Justice does not appear to have heard any cases of illegal Chinese residents in Batavia or the outer districts.

Just a few months before the massacre, however, a Company sailor, Jan Schimmel of Arnhem, working in one of the ship repair yards, was convicted of assault with a knife against the Chinese Tsauw Tanko.[62] Schimmel had been walking near a street corner in Batavia when he came to the house of the Chinese Tsauw Anko. Another Chinese person, Gina Tjan, was carrying a basket of biscuits that Schimmel willfully destroyed, and he began beating Gina. Tsauw Anko asked Schimmel why he was attacking Gina whereupon Schimmel got out his knife. Tsauw tried to diffuse the situation and started to pick the biscuits up off the ground when Schimmel attacked him with the knife, wounding him in the left eye and damaging his nose. Gina and several other Chinese bystanders witnessed this attack. Schimmel was eventually apprehended and taken to the Company's prison where he confessed to his crime.

Interestingly, in his summary Cornelis Phillips, advocate prosecutor, said that such attacks needed to be deterred "in a land of patient justice" and that the prisoner should be made into an example through the severity of his punishment. He recommended corporal punishment and branding, followed by ten years banishment to hard labor in chains. The court reduced his sentence to five years, although at the time of sentencing Schimmel had no idea he would serve his sentence out at the Cape of Good Hope.[63] The fascinating thing is that Schimmel's crime and punishment, which was made into an example by the Court, occurred only a month before the Chinese massacre. This indicates what a complete surprise the Chinese uprising must have been for many ordinary people living in Batavia because there is no sense that Schimmel was being made an example because he attacked a Chinese person, but rather because he randomly attacked an innocent civilian.

---

[62] NA: VOC 9391: Civile en Criminele Processen van Batavia 1739–1740, case 24.
[63] NA: VOC 9391 and 9393: Civile en Criminele Processen van Batavia 1739–1740, case 25; NA: VOC 9305, September 10, 1740.

Prior to the outbreak of violence leading to the massacre, no cases involving a Chinese person as the accused had come before the Council of Justice. When the massacre did take place, not one person was brought before the Council of Justice and convicted of a crime committed against any Chinese person. The remaining Chinese residents of Batavia and surrounds were not so fortunate. The Council of Justice tried a number of "bulk cases" involving a multitude of those accused in the months following the "recent troubles," as the uprising and subsequent massacre were euphemistically referred to in the criminal records. In total twenty-three cases involving 252 Chinese men came before the court.[64]

In only two cases was a woman accused of a crime connected with the event. Oeij Saunio van Batavia, wife of Ong Pieko (who was also known as Tsji Piet), was brought before the court with her husband under suspicion of rebellion. Both were released without further punishment after no evidence or confession was forthcoming.[65] Poengoet van Batavia, wife of the Chinese prisoner Jan Tjamko, could be and was arrested but released when no confession was extracted under torture.[66] Both these women were born in Batavia and were married to Chinese men who had probably purchased them as locally born slaves and manumitted them to become their wives.

At the conclusion of eight cases, fifty men were executed by hanging. Afterward their bodies were publicly displayed, and their property was confiscated by the Company.[67] In one case, the men who were sentenced to death by hanging were sentenced also to having their bodies thrown in the sea and their property confiscated by the Company. The Council of Justice did not provide an explanation in the case records for why it ordered the symbolic acting out of the fantasy that had driven the Chinese to rebel in the first place.[68] In only three cases were Chinese people involved accused directly of rebellion. The first was Oeij Saunio of Batavia and her husband, mentioned above, who were found innocent and released. Jan Tjamko was sentenced to banishment for life in chains

---

[64] NA: VOC 9391: Civile en Criminele Processen van Batavia 1739–1740, cases 29, 30, 31, 32, 33, 34, 35, 36, 37, and 38; NA: VOC 9394: Civile en Criminele Processen van Batavia 1740–1741, cases 4, 5, 20, 26, 32, 33, 34, 36, 38, 39, 45, and 46.
[65] NA: VOC 9394: Civile en Criminele Processen van Batavia 1740–1741, case 20.
[66] NA: VOC 9394: Civile en Criminele Processen van Batavia 1740–1741, case 30.
[67] NA: VOC 9391: Civile en Criminele Processen van Batavia 1739–1740, cases 29, 30, 31, 32, and 34; NA: VOC 9394: Civile en Criminele Processen van Batavia 1740–1741, cases 36, 38, and 39.
[68] NA: VOC 9391: Civile en Criminele Processen van Batavia 1739–1740, case 34.

to labor without rest. Oeij Tenkie, Tan Soenko, Tsi Jauwko, and Kauw Tongko were found guilty and hanged.[69]

For 113 men in 12 cases the punishment was banishment for life to hard labor in chains.[70] No details are contained in the sentences about where these men were to be banished. This was not at all unusual in cases of the penal transportation of convicts; not all criminals were sentenced to specific places of banishment. Penal transportation depended upon the Company's shipping networks that were seasonal and regional, so it is likely that these communication patterns and transportation networks played a role in where some convicts might be transported. It is often only when a person appears in the criminal registers at the Cape that one can know with certainty that the individual has arrived in Africa. This applied to convicted Company servants as well as other categories of criminals. Finally, in seven cases involving ninety people, the accused were released without further punishment and required to obtain new residence permits.[71] The fate of these men is unknown once they disappeared from the Company records.

Not everyone tried in the same case received the same punishment. Each individual was sentenced according to their status, the evidence and witnesses against them, and whether they confessed to the crime of which they were accused. It is possible that those Chinese people who were executed had been arrested in possession of weapons, something that would virtually have proved their guilt in the eyes of the Court. As confessions were extracted under torture, it is probable that some, or perhaps many, innocent people were punished for crimes they did not commit. In all the cases against the Chinese of Batavia, the Council of Justice upheld the "rule of law" and due process within the court no matter the outcome. It is interesting to note that the Council of Justice presumed that the burden of guilt for the event lay with the Chinese of Batavia themselves.

Like the Chinese, free Javanese residents of Batavia were not exempt from prosecution by the Council of Justice. Three such cases related to the uprising came before the court. In one case, two Javanese people,

---

[69] NA: VOC 9394: Civile en Criminele Processen van Batavia 1740–1741, cases 20, 34, and 39.
[70] NA: VOC 9391: Civile en Criminele Processen van Batavia 1739–1740, cases 29, 30, 31, 32, 33, 36, 37, and 38; NA: VOC 9394: Civile en Criminele Processen van Batavia 1740–1741, cases 26, 34, 45, and 46.
[71] NA: VOC 9391: Civile en Criminele Processen van Batavia 1739–1740, cases 33, 35, 36, and 37; NA: VOC 9394: Civile en Criminele Processen van Batavia 1740–1741, cases 4, 5, and 20.

Biganti and Bandie or Panrie, were fined and released after being arrested for illegal residency.[72] In two cases the Javanese people involved were accused of rebellion, implying that they lived under the jurisdiction of the Company. Three were executed by hanging and one, Gabok, was apparently found not guilty but was banished for life to a place chosen by the court.[73] This was more commonly the fate of many Chinese people under Company jurisdiction in Java who were forcibly migrated to the Cape for their crimes or for illegal residency.

Although no European was brought before the courts accused of assault, murder, rape, arson, or theft arising from the massacre, the Seventeen Gentlemen were highly critical of how the event unfolded and was handled by Company officials and courts in Batavia. Governor-General Adriaan Valckenier and Councilor of the Indies Gustav Willem Baron van Imhoff had apparently argued about how to handle the initial phase of the Chinese uprising before the massacre occurred. Delays in the Company's military response had led to precious time being lost and Valkenier was blamed for mishandling the situation.[74] He was already on his way to the fatherland to plead his case when orders for his arrest arrived in Cape Town. He was subsequently arrested at the Cape and taken back to Batavia where he was imprisoned in the Castle awaiting trial until his death a few years later.

This was definitely the most high profile case in the mid-eighteenth century Company court records. It was rare for blame to be laid at the feet of the governor-general of the Indies, the most powerful man in the Company outside Europe. The Council of Justice did adjudicate criminal cases against high-ranking Company officials from all over the empire and was also the court of appeal. In 1740, a case that involved illegal trading by two Company officers was sent to the Batavian court by the *Fiscal* (prosecutor) of Colombo, Johan de Mauregnault. As the case expanded into multiple prosecutions, it was still under investigation a year later with evidence being sought from Company officials and burghers in both Colombo and Cochin.[75] Another case of appeal came from the Banda *Fiscal*. It involved an accusation of murder against Jacob Renouw from Lyon, a soldier serving in Banda, who apparently killed

---

[72] NA: VOC 9391: Civile en Criminele Processen van Batavia 1739–1740, case 28.
[73] NA: VOC 9391: Civile en Criminele Processen van Batavia 1739–1740, cases 37 and 40.
[74] Remmelink, *Chinese War*, p. 126.
[75] NA: VOC 9391: Civile en Criminele Processen van Batavia 1739–1740, cases 11, 12, 13, and 39; NA: VOC 9394: Civile en Criminele Processen van Batavia 1740–1741, case 49.

Sergeant Jan Jacobsz de Wit. Renouw, was found guilty by the Batavian court and executed by firing squad.[76] Similarly, there was an appeal in a case brought from the Ambon *Fiscal* regarding the murder of a lawyer by the burgher Daniel Pietersz Holthuijsen. This case was held over by the Court of Justice in Batavia pending further evidence.[77] Two cases involving ships' captains confirm that sentences for high-ranking officers did not involve corporal punishment even though a similar crime when committed by a common sailor would have resulted in a severe whipping. Four officers on the ship *Haapburg*, including the Captain Gillis Oudemans, were accused of corruption. They were all fined, demoted, and banished to the fatherland.[78] When Christiaan Duijff, captain of the ship the *Ketel*, endangered and damaged his vessel in the Sunda Straits, he was suspended and demoted.[79] Each of these cases demonstrates how the Company's legal network extended from its settlements back to the capital, Batavia. However, not all serious cases were forwarded to Batavia by local *Fiscals*. This was a more common practice in the Indies archipelago, the region closest to Batavia.

The overwhelming majority of cases involving the Company's servants involved accusations of being absent without permission. Although these cases were dealt with perfunctorily by the Council of Justice, details of the whereabouts of individuals while absent were not given unless it was mitigating evidence (for example, if someone were sick or in hospital). Thirteen cases of desertion were heard between 1739 and 1741, probably a smaller number of cases than usual given the events of the year. Cases of desertion that involved a sailor missing the sailing date of his ship were treated with greater severity than other cases that involved being absent for the same amount of time.

Harmanus Flasse from Antwerp, a sailor on the ship *Crabbendijk*, was absent for three weeks and missed his ship's departure for Japan. He was sentenced to banishment for one year of labor in chains and had his wages confiscated.[80] Gerrit Rietvelt from The Hague was absent for eight months from his ship the *Lagapolder* when it sailed for China without him, and he received the same punishment with the added pain of corporal punishment in the form of a sound whipping.[81] Arnoldus van

---

[76] NA: VOC 9394: Civile en Criminele Processen van Batavia 1740–1741, case 47.
[77] NA: VOC 9394: Civile en Criminele Processen van Batavia 1740–1741, case 48.
[78] NA: VOC 9394: Civile en Criminele Processen van Batavia 1740–1741, case 30.
[79] NA: VOC 9394: Civile en Criminele Processen van Batavia 1740–1741, case 27.
[80] NA: VOC 9394: Civile en Criminele Processen van Batavia 1740–1741, case 29.
[81] NA: VOC 9394: Civile en Criminele Processen van Batavia 1740–1741, case 15.

Suijlen from Utrecht, a sailor on the ship *Karssenhoff*, had deserted for five months when he was apprehended and convicted. This offense was no one-night drinking binge. Van Suijlen received the sentence of being brought to behind the Town Hall to the execution yard, bound to a pole and whipped. He was further sentenced to two years hard labor in chains on the Company's public works with the confiscation of one month's wages and the costs of the court. The court also ordered that, because Van Suijlen was obviously sick at the time of his trial, he had to go to the Company hospital to be cured before beginning his sentence.[82]

Gerrit Hulsebos Cramer from Amsterdam, sailor on the ship *Westerdijxharn*, was absent for only eight nights and did not miss his ship's departure. However, during his brief sojourn he got into serious mischief because he was also convicted of fraud. For his sins he was sentenced to three half days in the "iron maiden," a harsher form of stocks, and to penal transportation with hard labor on Edam Island.[83] This is one of the few cases where a site of banishment is mentioned directly. The ordinary riff-raff of Company servants got into all manner of trouble. There were five cases of assault, three of theft (one involving a Chinese accomplice), one of manslaughter, and two cases of homosexual sex. Punishments for theft varied widely. Cornelis Brand from Winckel in North Holland, a sailor on the ship *Papenberg*, was another prisoner who ended up serving his sentence of hard labor at the Cape.[84]

The last two cases involving sex crimes are interesting because they show that the court took each case on its merits. The stated punishment for sodomy under Company law was death. In cases of attempted seduction or suspected sodomy, or where the status of the accused parties was different, punishment varied. In the case brought against the galley boy Jan Coenraat Ribbe from Lipstad and the trumpeter Jan Michiel Loup from Melt, the former was sentenced to corporal punishment followed by twenty-five years hard labor in chains at the Company's works on the prison island of Rosengain in the Banda archipelago, while Loup was banished to the fatherland and warned never to return to the Company's territories.[85]

One February evening in 1740, twelve company servants, mostly sailors, broke into a crate of Company brandy, stealing about sixteen

[82] NA: VOC 9394: Civile en Criminele Processen van Batavia 1740–1741, case 9.
[83] NA: VOC 9394: Civile en Criminele Processen van Batavia 1740–1741, case 17.
[84] NA: VOC 9391: Civile en Criminele Processen van Batavia 1739–1740, case 24.
[85] NA: VOC 9394: Civile en Criminele Processen van Batavia 1740–1741, case 42.

bottles and partaking in a drinking binge at one of Batavia's outpost fortifications. Their revelry resulted in arrest for being drunk and disorderly. The Council of Justice decided their disobedience was so flagrant that it threw the full weight of its legal machinery into their case. Fourteen separate documents were brought to bear in the prosecution, including five different examinations and confessions, various notes from their ship's registers, notes from the court, and a statement from the prosecution amounting to 102 points summarizing the case and recommending harsh sentencing. Sijbrand Schordijk, a quartermaster from The Hague, was the highest-ranking prisoner and one of the ringleaders of the theft. He was sentenced to corporal punishment and ten years banishment to hard labor in chains, while Arij Heijman, a lowly sailor, was sentenced to five years banishment and hard labor.[86] All the prisoners were convicted of various forms of banishment and hard labor, but these two men ended up at the Cape of Good Hope. Their destination of banishment was not a part of their original sentence; it becomes clear where they were sent only when they appear in the criminal registers of the Cape a few years later. The vast majority of cases where Company servants are banished to the Cape occur in this manner. Very rarely did the Court specifically mention a place of banishment, including the Cape and sometimes even Robben Island.

The next major category of cases recorded by the Council of Justice between 1739 and 1741 involved the prosecution of slaves. Of the eleven cases that came before the court involving eighteen slaves, over half of those involved had attempted escape. Three of these cases also involved theft, and there was only one case of theft in which the slaves did not try to escape. This was a case forwarded from Malacca involving two slave women belonging to Daniel Koek, the old burgher captain. The court actually reduced the recommended sentence from fifty years banishment and hard labor for Flora and twenty for Anna to twenty-five and fifteen respectively.[87] Only one other case involved a woman, Joenko van Bima, slave of the Captain of the Malays Carie Bitjara. She had given refuge to Claus van Mandhaer, slave of the widow Leblancq, apparently not realizing he had committed a murder. Claus van Mandhaer was executed and Joenko van Bima received a beating and three years hard labor in chains.[88] Cases involving any form of serious attack by a slave resulted in execution.[89] Only five slaves brought before the court belonged to the

---

[86] NA: VOC 9391: Civile en Criminele Processen van Batavia 1739–1740, case 9.
[87] NA: VOC 9394: Civile en Criminele Processen van Batavia 1740–1741, case 13.
[88] NA: VOC 9394: Civile en Criminele Processen van Batavia 1740–1741, case 41.
[89] NA: VOC 9394: Civile en Criminele Processen van Batavia 1740–1741, cases 35 and 41.

Company, the others being privately owned. Batavian slave owners of all ethnicities were granted access to the court to punish their errant slaves and regularly availed themselves of this right.

Occasionally cases involving slaves give some insight into the circulation of slaves across the Company's empire. The widow Mevrouwe Elizabeth Angelica Burlamachi owned a twenty-eight-year-old slave named Harman van Cabo de Goede Hoop, who was also known by his alias Aron papoea. From his name it might appear that Harman was born at the Cape and sold in Batavia, but his alias is probably a more accurate description of his homeland, with "papoea" indicating his origins in the eastern archipelago on the island of New Guinea. Harman had been accused of disturbing the peace, along with two other slaves. Upon closer investigation, it appears that he had actually helped one of the Water Fiscal's *caffers* (guards/police), who was a *peranakan* (locally born) Chinese resident when he had been pushed into the Jonkers Canal by another slave. Harman's mistress testified on his behalf and he was released without punishment, unlike Jason van Siam, slave of the burgher Pieter Donker, who actually committed the deed and was given the sentence of being whipped, branded, and banished to ten years hard labor in chains.[90]

Finally, as we have seen, Europeans came before the Council of Justice in the more serious cases. For example, in one of the rare cases involving a Dutch woman, Metta Christina Woordenberg, wife of the under-merchant Elso Sterrengberg, was accused of a sexual liaison that bordered on bigamy. Their marriage was dissolved and Woordenberg was sentenced to fifty years in the *Tuchthuis* (the women's prison in Batavia also known as the *Spinhuis*), an extraordinarily harsh sentence in a city with a high mortality rate. Nothing is mentioned about her lover.[91] The case could have been tried by the Court of Aldermen except that bigamy was a criminal offense and the Company may well have insisted on prosecuting such a serious transgression of European social norms. Moreover, Woordenberg would also have attracted censure by the church, as her behavior obviously did not go unnoticed.[92] While it was common

---

[90] NA: VOC 9391: Civile en Criminele Processen van Batavia 1739–1740, case 9; NA: VOC 9393: Civile en Criminele Processen van Batavia 1739–1740, case 9.

[91] NA: VOC 9391: Civile en Criminele Processen van Batavia 1739–1740, case 18.

[92] Pamela McVay examines a case in 1661 where a woman married a man already engaged and was sentenced to fifty years in the *tuchthuis*. McVay, "I Am the Devil's Own," p. 37 and p. 98. Travel writers documenting life in Batavia often commented about the European women convicted of adultery who were incarcerated in the *Spinhuis*. See, for example, Marijke Barend-van Haeften, *Oost-Indië gespiegeld: Nicholaas de Graaff, een schrijvend chirurgijn in dienst van de VOC*. Zutphen: Walburg Pers, 1992, pp. 165–167. Margreet van Till analyzes how the Poor House also operated as an institution of

practice for married European men to sexually exploit their female slaves, the same option did not hold true for European women. Occasionally, European women from other colonies were sent to the women's prison in Batavia because there was nowhere to imprison them in the smaller colonies. These cases were rare exceptions, however, and at the Cape of Good Hope the court usually resorted to imprisoning women on Robben Island if necessity dictated such harsh punishment.

Penal Transportation to the Cape

From the analysis of the Council of Justice court records around the year 1740, at least five Company servants from four different cases were transported to the Cape of Good Hope.[93] It is possible that a number of others were also sent to the Cape and either died en route or slipped through the Cape's records. Chinese names in particular could be unrecognizable from one Dutch transcription to the next.[94] In a diametrically opposite problem, the use of generic slave names like "January" or "Cupid" makes it extremely difficult to identify specific individuals in the archival records, particularly when convicted slaves are not identified by their master's name. In the eighty-one cases that came before the court involving 340 people, 145 of those convicted were sentenced directly to banishment and at least a dozen more were sentenced to hard labor on the Company's works and could be sent away. The cases involving Chinese prisoners from the massacre to some extent accounts for the high proportion of banishment in these years and skews the number of convictions because it is very rare to see criminal cases involving more than three or four people. However, it would not be an exaggeration to estimate

---

incarceration in Batavia during the mid-eighteenth century. This was used for the institutionalization of both the poor and the insane. Company servants, free burghers, and indigenous residents of Batavia were incarcerated in the Poor House if they were determined to be insane by the judgment of the bailiff, the warden of the jail, and the town surgeon. Citizens could be pronounced insane by the magistrates if they had committed public violence and be sentenced to the Poor House. This institution also operated as an asylum for the rich insane, who had separate and more lavish accommodation provided (and presumably paid for by their families). There was an attempt at gender segregation of those determined to be insane. European women were incarcerated in the orphanage for their protection from male residents of the Poor House. Margreet van Till, "Social Care in Eighteenth Century Batavia: The Poor House, 1725–1750," *Itinerario*, 19(1), 1995, pp. 18–31.

[93] NA: VOC 9391: Civile en Criminele Processen van Batavia 1739–1740, cases 6, 24, 25; NA: VOC 9393: Civile en Criminele Processen van Batavia 1739–1740, case 9.

[94] Armstrong, "Chinese at the Cape." James Armstrong has skilfully managed to piece together various transcriptions of Chinese names to trace people through the archives.

that 75 percent of desertion cases for Company servants or escape for slaves involved some form of banishment and hard labor. Banishment was also used in mitigating the death sentence, but this was rare in the mid-eighteenth century.

The greatest number of cases brought before the Council of Justice therefore involved Company servants, mainly the common European sailors, soldiers, and artisans who comprised the bulk of the Company's free (as opposed to slave) personnel. McVay's study on criminality in Batavia during the seventeenth century indicates that public punishment in the form of humiliation was far more common in this period than it was by the mid-eighteenth century. The use of the "wooden horse," where a prisoner sat on something akin to a carpenter's sawhorse and had weights tied to his feet and was subject to public harassment and mild assault, was not commonly used in the eighteenth century, at least in cases in which banishment was also part of the sentence.[95] Beatings and branding were standard public punishments for even minor crimes. In cases where Company servants appeared before the court more than once, particularly if they committed a crime while under the status of convicted criminal, punishments could be extremely harsh.

Banishment was one of the most frequently imposed of the harsh penalties and was also used, although infrequently, in commuting the death sentence. Banishment took place on three levels:

1. To the fatherland – that is, back to the United Provinces.
2. To a specific place within the Company's realm.[96]
3. To banishment outside "all the forts, cities, and places under the jurisdiction of the Company under pain of harsh penalty should they return."[97]

Only Europeans were banished to the fatherland, but they were also banished to remain outside the realm of the Company. Criminals of all ethnic groups were banished to the Cape, where they were used as forced labor on the Company's public works.[98] In many respects, becoming a criminal overshadowed other forms of personal classifications for the individual being punished. This applied to both free people and slaves.

---

[95] McVay, "I Am the Devil's Own," p. 30.
[96] NA: VOC 9383: Marten Claaszoon, 1737; NA: VOC 9393: Matthijs Janzoon, 1737; NA: VOC 9386: Jan Andrieszoon, 1738.
[97] For example: NA: VOC 9387: Marten Claaszoon, 1738.
[98] Armstrong, "Chinese at the Cape," pp. 25–27.

Once an individual was classified as a Company prisoner, that status took precedence over their former rank. Despite their previous statuses, all prisoners generally worked under the same conditions, although at the Cape there was a distinction made between the allocation of rations to European and slave prisoners. In Batavia, with its extensive aritsan quarter, storehouses, docks, and work yards, as well as the ship repair docks on Onrust and Edam Islands, there was ample opportunity to employ convict labor. It is unlikely that European convicts would have been sentenced to dredge the city's canals because their labor was too valuable, and the value of their labor would also support the logic of mitigating the death sentence for other crimes they committed.[99]

Banishment was most commonly imposed on Company criminals who broke out of their chains and escaped from imprisonment.[100] Lodewijk Rets from The Hague was a third-ranking master stationed at the Siam office until he was charged with committing insubordination and desertion, along with three of his sailor friends.[101] Rets and Gerrit van den Berg, also from The Hague, were apparently the ringleaders as they were sentenced to ten years hard labor, whereas the other two deserters received only a year or less. Rets and Van den Berg were beaten and branded at the place of execution before being riveted in chains and sentenced to banishment.[102] Rets was still in Batavia the following year, where as a chain-ganger he met up with Arnoldus van Zuijlen, who had been convicted of desertion in 1741 and was working in chains on the Company's public works.[103] They both eventually broke out of their chains and escaped with two more of their fellow chain-gangers.

Rets and Van Zuijlen evaded recapture for seven weeks while running rampage around the back alleys of Batavia, assaulting and robbing a Javanese man and hiding out in civilian housing in the town. They resisted apprehension from two *caffers*, Baspa Mina and Laeijer van Malaijo, who both testified at the hearing. When they were eventually arrested, they each were sentenced – in the typical formula of serious crimes – "to be

---

[99] McVay, "I Am the Devil's Own," pp. 28–31.
[100] This contrasts with McVay's analysis for the seventeenth century who describes the penalties for repeated disobedience as being ever higher fines followed by banishment only on the fourth conviction. McVay, "I Am the Devil's Own," p. 28. I have found that second offences consistently led directly to banishment.
[101] NA: VOC 9403: Civile en Criminele Processen van Batavia 1741–1742, case 49.
[102] NA: VOC 9308: Lodewijk Rets, 1741.
[103] NA: VOC 9394: Criminele Processen van de Raad van Justitite op Batavia 1740–1741, case 9.

brought to the customary place of execution and handed over to the executioner, to be then tied to a post and scourged on his bare back until bloodied, to be branded and afterwards riveted in chains." The unfortunate Rets was sentenced to twenty-five years banishment with hard labor on the Company's public works. Van Zuijlen was sentenced to the same punishment but with only five years hard labor. To rub salt into their wounds, they were ordered in the usual fashion to pay court costs.[104] While Rets and Van Zuijlen both ended up at the Cape, the other two prisoners, Joseph Teelje and Willem Janz, were banished somewhere else, possibly back to the artisans' quarter of Batavia where they had all originally been laboring.

Skilled artisans were less likely to be banished in the first instance if their labor was required in Batavia. The courts therefore helped the Company regulate its labor supply through sentences of imprisonment with hard labor or banishment with hard labor. Jacobus Bunnegam, a carpenter on Onrust Island in the Batavia roadstead, was originally sentenced to ten years banishment in 1734 for forgery. But his valuable skills resulted in his being retained in Batavia to work in chains in the artisan quarter. Eventually tired of this no doubt painful fate, Bunnegam went into a drunken rage and threatened a fellow Company soldier with an axe. He was sentenced to corporal punishment in front of the other chain-gangers in the artisan quarter before receiving an extra five years on top of his original sentence.[105] Bunnegam stated in his own defense that he was too drunk to remember what had happened, but was ignored by the court. The criminal records document many cases of this kind. Drunkenness was a common but invariably unsuccessful defense, as in the case of Willem Butting from Amsterdam, a ship's quartermaster, whose drunken disobedience against a superior officer resulted in his banishment to the fatherland. This particular case is interesting because the prosecutor talked specifically about having to make an example of Butting to keep the subalterns under control.[106] The Company sought to maximize control over its own personnel and labor force and used the courts to impose discipline, often by imposing penal transportation with hard labor as punishment.

Keeping the subalterns under control was clearly a major preoccupation of the Council of Justice. Many of the cases brought against European

---

[104] NA: VOC 9306: Lodewijk Rets, 1743; NA: VOC 9308: Lodewijk Rets, 1744.
[105] NA: VOC 9298: Jacobus Bunnegam, 1733; NA: VOC 9300: Jacobus Bunnegam, 1744.
[106] NA: VOC 9357: Willem Cornelis Butting, 1730.

Company servants involved cases of assault against Chinese or other Asian residents in Batavia. The case notes show just how intimately the underclasses of Batavia shared common urban space. This interaction led to cases of cooperation among members of different ethnic groups to commit crimes.[107] In 1729, one Jan Dirkszoon Groen from Amsterdam, a ship's quartermaster, conspired with Ephraim Pauluszoon, a chainganger in the Company's artisans quarter; David Alexander, a Mardijker; Jenap from Bali, a free Balinese who owned a small boat; and Jonas from Makassar, a free Makassarese. These men stole fifty bags of pepper from the west-side store house, transporting them with the help of hired Chinese coolies using a Chinese prauw to ship the goods for concealment on the Island of Onrust. This elaborately planned theft went awry when they were spotted loading the stolen goods by Ismail and Japar from Batavia, two assistants of Commissioner Fredrick Julius Coijes.[108] Pauluszoon and Groen were beaten and branded, then riveted in chains and sentenced to fifteen and twenty-five years banishment with hard labor respectively. Both were transported to the Cape to serve out their sentences.

Theft was a serious crime, particularly if it was an obvious case of illegal trading against the Company. When Marten de Wilde from Sloteijn and Hendrik Wessel from Hogenvos joined with three other sailors and assisted two quartermasters, Jan Schaaf from Amsterdam and Claas Ernstmeijer from Enkhuizen, in stealing a quantity of gunpowder, the Council of Justice showed no mercy, possibly because the illegal sale of gunpowder was a direct military threat to the Company. It is not clear from the case notes to whom they planned to sell the gunpowder but it is not unlikely that it would have been to an enemy of the Company, an offense therefore bordering on treason. Quartermasters were far higher ranking Company servants than common sailors, and their position entailed both trust and temptation. The court tended to treat quartermasters who stole from the Company stores they supervised with great severity in an attempt to discourage such behavior. Schaaf and Ernstmeijer were executed by hanging. The other prisoners were sentenced to whipping, branding, and riveting in chains to labor for twenty-five years in banishment. Wessel and de Wilde appear a few years later in the Cape criminal records, while the fate of the other sailors is unknown.[109]

---

[107] NA: VOC 9305: Jan Schimmel, 1740.
[108] NA: VOC 9352: Jan Dirkszoon Groen, 1729.
[109] NA: VOC 9303: Marten de Wilde, 1738.

Free Javanese people also came under the jurisdiction of the Council of Justice when the case involved a crime against a Company subject. In April 1732, two Javanese men, Singa Carta, also known as Doggol, and Raxa Nanga, were arrested on suspicion of murdering the Company soldier, Hendrik van den Bosch. This case is particularly interesting because it shows how the social boundaries between the underclasses of Batavia were simultaneously blurred and maintained. Van den Bosch belonged to a contingent of soldiers stationed outside the city walls. His compatriots knew that he often left the Company's barracks and crossed over the nearby river to visit a Javanese woman. He was first reported missing on October 2, 1731 when he did not report for the evening roll call, and by the next day a party of soldiers was sent out to look for him. Two days later his naked body was discovered with many wounds on his hands, arms, shoulders, and head, and his throat had been cut. There were over thirty wounds on his body all of which seemed to have been inflicted by a "native weapon." The soldiers said that they knew Van den Bosch had money when he left the barracks and intended to buy sex from a Javanese prostitute working for the Javanese man they knew as Doggol, who was known as a procurer. Singa Carta denied this during his interrogation under torture. He asserted that Van den Bosch was murdered by the now-deceased Singa Dinanta and his accomplices, Astra Troena, Dita Marta, Hangsan, and Dita Poespa, because the soldier had had sex with Ombol Satja di Raxa's wife in the house of Raxa Nanga.

The Court also interrogated Singa Carta's wives, Oela Paneela and Mandol, who could not or would not throw any further light onto the case and were released. The case dragged on until February 1732 and Singa Carta and Raxa Nanga consistently maintained their innocence even during interrogation under torture. Without these confessions or witnesses, the Court's hands were tied and they eventually banished the men under suspicion of murder instead of executing them for the crime.[110] Both Javanese men were eventually banished to the Cape, although the details of their initial imprisonment and transportation are not known.

Free indigenes were the rarest category of prisoners forcibly sent to the Cape. This could be a result of the limits of Company jurisdiction or sovereignty depending upon the nature of the Company node where the crime was committed. In the same year that Singa Carta and Raxa Nanga were banished, thirteen men identified as "free Javanese" were

---

[110] NA: VOC 9359: Singa Carta alias Doggol, 1732.

arrested in Banda and sent to Batavia for trial under suspicion of piracy and unauthorized travel. The men were actually from Minangakabau in Sumatra and claimed that a storm had blown their boat off course and that they were forced to take shelter at the first island they found. Unfortunately for them, their boat was loaded with ammunition and Company officials decided they were lying. They had specifically broken one of the Statutes of Batavia dealing with unauthorized travelers. Each of these men was sentenced to ten-years banishment in chains and was eventually transported to the Cape.[111]

Indigenous slaves, however, were one of the most common categories of prisoners sent to the Cape. Slaves were one of the most important sources of labor throughout the VOC realm, as well as a valuable private commodity traded across the imperial grid.[112] For obvious reasons, the Council of Justice did not banish slaves to the fatherland and hence to freedom. Yet the Company did not hesitate to banish slaves within its imperial web, despite the implications of denying the slave's owner of an asset. Under Company slave codes, slaves had specific rights as human beings, and slave owners were not at liberty to kill their slaves. However, the Company enforced the right to punish slaves for their crimes in disregard of ownership rights.

Slaves were the next most common category of people after Company servants whose crimes led to sentences of banishment. Their punishments were often identical to those meted out to Company servants, and desertion by Company slaves and servants resulted in a similar punishment for both. Company slaves Catjoeng from Bougies and January from Bengal, who had both already been confined to chains for prior convictions, were brought before the court for attempting to escape. They were sentenced to be flogged in the presence of other chain-gangers before they were banished.[113] Slaves who verbally threatened their owners but did not touch them were treated similarly to Company servants convicted of insubordination. This did not apply just to Company slaves. Even if privately owned by other Asians, slaves who threatened their owners were brought

---

[111] NA: VOC 9360: Juda, 1732.
[112] James Armstrong and Nigel Worden, 'The Slaves, 1652–1834,' in Elphick and Giliomee, eds., *Shaping of South African Society*, pp. 109–143. For an interesting vignette on an individual Company servant's speculative slave trade, see: James Fox, "'For Good and Sufficient Reasons': An Examination of Early Dutch East India Company Ordinances on Slaves and Slavery," in Anthony Reid, ed., *Slavery Bondage and Dependency in Southeast Asia*. St Lucia: University of Queensland Press, 1983, pp. 246–247.
[113] NA: VOC 9381: Catjong from Boegies, 1736; NA: VOC 9386: January from Bengal, 1738.

before the Council of Justice and sentenced to corporal punishment and banishment.[114]

In the case of Cupido van Boegies, slave of the Merchant Jan Schreuder, who was accused of threatening his master, testimony reveals his master's fear of attack was the motivation for bringing the slave to court. Stated fears of a slave attack often resulted in the banishment of the slave concerned. In the relatively rare event of slaves actually physically attacking their owners (as opposed to the common beatings meted out by owners to their slaves), the death sentence was mandatory. There is considerable confusion in the testimony of witnesses about whether Cupido van Boegies actually directed his threats to his own wife Margaretha, also one of Schreuder's slaves, or to his master, Schreuder wasted no time in clarifying the issue. He called for the Fiscal's and the bailiff's assistants, the *caffers*, who acted as a police force in the town. *Caffers* had powers of arrest and were also called upon to administer "domestic correction" to slaves, as well as being employed as executioner's assistants. For the price of twelve stuivers, any slave owner could have their slaves beaten by the *caffers* at the place of execution behind the Town Hall.[115]

De Haan claims that in the early seventeenth century the *caffers* in Batavia were black African slaves of the Portuguese, originally from Angola and Mozambique, who were used specifically for the purpose of policing the town.[116] By the end of the seventeenth century, locals were also recruited into the *caffers*, who were distinguished from other Company servants by their bright uniforms.[117] It is only when the *caffers* appear in the criminal records, either as police or as criminals, that they can be identified as individuals. While the use of African slaves as *caffers* in Batavia seems to have been short-lived, in the Company's major African colony at the Cape, the majority of *caffers* were, paradoxically, Asian political prisoners and criminals sentenced to banishment by Batavia and Colombo.[118] Colonies like the Cape, which always suffered

---

[114] NA: VOC 9382: Ourson from Sendauw, 1737; NA: VOC 9385: Cupido from Boegies, 1738; NA: VOC 9387: Carang Assan from Bali, 1738.

[115] NA: VOC 9385: Cupido from Boegies, 1738. See also Barend-van Haeften, *Oost-Indie gespiegeld*, p. 160, and quote from Francois Valentijn, p. 163.

[116] Part of the problem with analyzing the *caffers* in detail is that subsequent historians have largely relied on De Haan's description for their own impressions of these servants of the law. See, for example, Jacobus la Bree, *De Rechterlijke Organisatie en Rechtsbedeling te Batavia in de XVIIe Eeuw*. Rotterdam and 'sGravenhage: Nigh & Van Ditmar N.V., 1951,. pp. 87–88.

[117] De Haan, *Oud Batavia*, vol. 2, p. 305.

[118] Armstrong and Worden, "The Slaves," p. 128; Ross, *Cape of Torments*; Shell, *Children of Bondage*, pp. 189–194; Kerry Ward, "'Crimes and Misdemeanors:' Forced

from a chronic labor shortage, ultimately used the system of forced migration to its own advantage, employing many of those exiled in a number of different forms of public labor. Reclassifying people as "criminals," or more usually "chain-gangers," largely overrode distinctions between ethnicities and statuses in terms of the daily treatment of prisoners, while conversely maintaining law and order in the Company realm.

The VOC Network of Penal Transportation and Exile

The Cape of Good Hope was a significant node in the Company's network of forced migration in regard to the slave trade, penal transportation, and political exile. Not all Company nodes were linked to the circuits of forced migration constituted by penal transportation and political exile. The Company colonies at Batavia, Colombo, Ambon, Banda, and the Cape were the major sites involved for cases tried in Batavia. As imperial capital and largest Company city, Batavia sent far more prisoners to these other colonies than it received.

The exile of indigenous rulers by the Company was also a part of the network of forced migration. The sites chosen to receive convicts and exiles were ones in which the Company had the largest proportional garrison presence to ensure the security of prisoners. Ceylon was the most visible and accessible site of exile from Batavia, both for the Company and for indigenous political prisoners. Prisoners sent to Ceylon were much more likely to gain access to networks of religion and communication outside Company control than those sent to other sites. Links between Ceylon and the archipelago were ancient and part of indigenous shipping networks of the Indian Ocean.

Exiles considered a security risk in Ceylon because their potential access to indigenous networks threatened their incarceration were transferred to the Cape of Good Hope. Banda and, to a lesser extent, Ambon, were not major sites for the exile of political prisoners but commonly received convicts from Batavia. Chapter 5 explores the long-range evolution of the Cape from its inception as a refreshment post to its evolution as a settler colony. The Cape participated in the network of forced migration from its very beginning because of its unique geographical position and its role as the major transit point for the Company's transportation network. Robben Island as a secondary site of banishment and imprisonment was crucial to the Cape, not only in terms of forced migration. The Cape also

Migration and Forced Labor in the Dutch East India Company Empire," unpublished paper presented at the African Studies Association Conference, Chicago, October 29, 1998, to November 1, 1998.

incorporated or evolved other subordinate nodes in the southwest Indian Ocean. These nodes were linked through various Company sub-circuits, including the full range of the network of forced migration – slavery, penal transportation, and exile. While the Cape intersected with multiple Company networks, it simultaneously established a reputation as being the most far-flung and isolated site for penal transportation and political exile.

This glimpse into the underclass social world of Batavia through the criminal record gives some indication of the motivations and limits of Company control in the daily lives of the city's inhabitants. Company servants, free indigenes, Chinese traders, and slaves were categorized and enumerated in great detail by the Company's bureaucracy. The city itself was designed to keep ethnic groups separated in their own neighborhoods. Even a brief survey of the crimes people committed is enough to demonstrate that the Company's urban planners could not strictly limit interaction among people in their daily lives and on the streets where Company surveillance was, at best, partial. Cases of crimes committed by high-ranking Company officials also reveal that the VOC was unable to control its own elite, and it was widely accepted that they were enriching themselves at every opportunity at the Company's expense, though few were prosecuted for their crimes. These records underline the limitations of Company control because, for every case of desertion that failed, there were no doubt many more that succeeded. The unauthorized massacre of Batavia's Chinese population in 1740 was a crisis of governance and the rule of law that dramatically exposed the limitations of Company institutions and power in the capital.

Forced migration in the form of penal transportation was one way for Batavia to decrease the number of criminals in the town, and it also provided a deterrent to its own servants' criminal behavior. The forced migration circuit between Batavia and the Cape of Good Hope was just one of multiple circuits in this extensive network used to maintain civic and political order in the posts, settlements, and colonies that comprised the Company's territorial nodes.

This chapter has explored the conditions of possibility for the emergence of an imperial network of forced migration that emanated from and was grounded in the social world of the empire's capital. Chapter 4 demonstrates how this one particular circuit of forced migration operated in one of its main receiving nodes. That is, how it affected the Cape of Good Hope, from its inception as an imperial refreshment node, and how it subsequently shaped the contours of its social world.

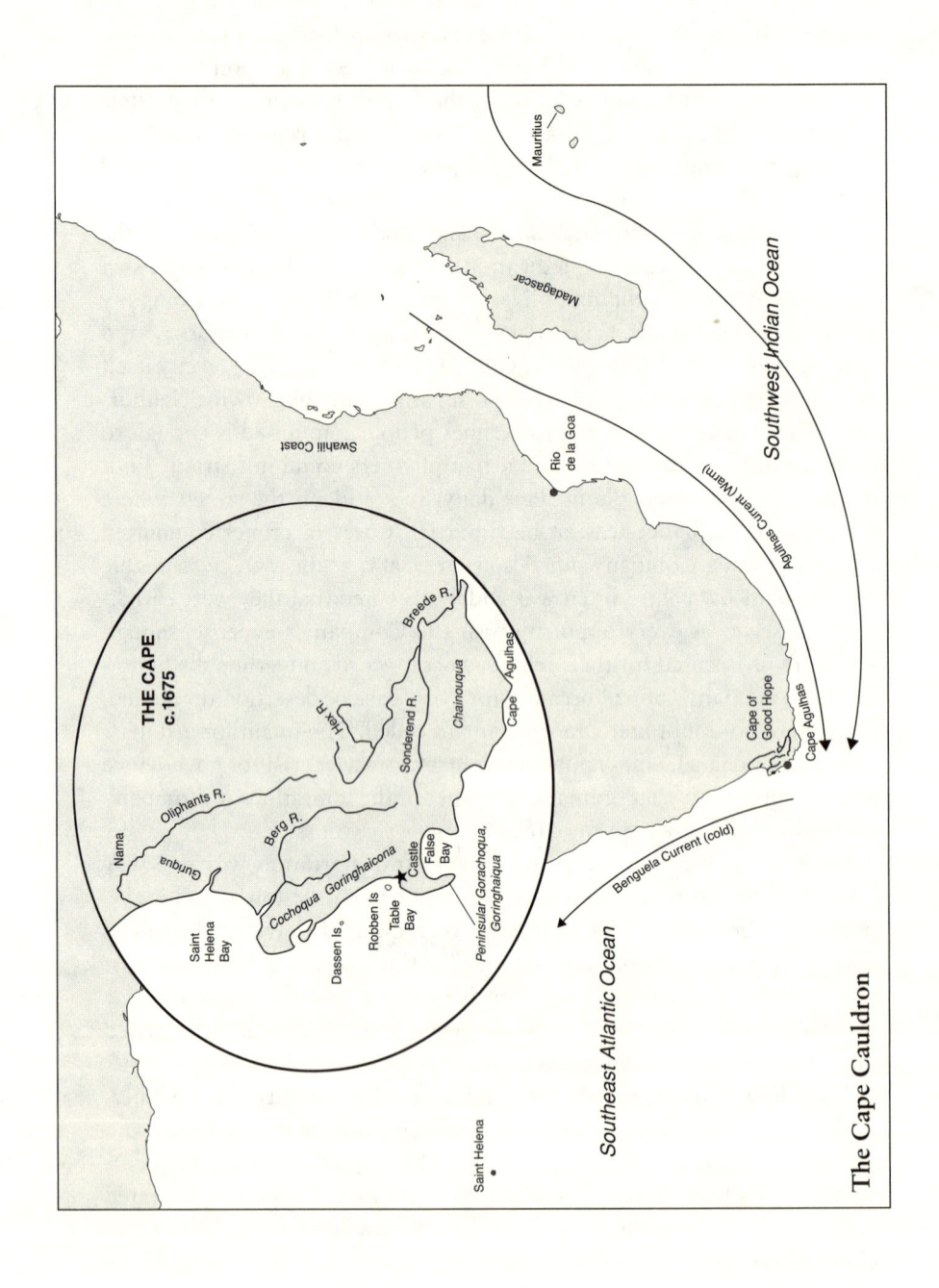

The Cape Cauldron

4

The Cape Cauldron: Strategic Site in Transoceanic Imperial Networks

The "Cape Cauldron" evokes the nautical perspective of the turbulent meeting of the southeast Atlantic and southwest Indian Ocean waters, a treacherous zone for ships sailing between the Atlantic and Indian Oceans and a region where they had to touch land to take on fresh water and supplies.[1] It was perilous to attempt this voyage without reprovisioning. Thus the Cape of Good Hope and other safe harbors for anchoring in this oceanic zone became strategically vital nodes in European transportation networks throughout the age of sail. The Cape had a long history of being one of these sites. After its settlement by the Dutch East India Company in 1652, it eventually developed into the Company's sole settler colony outside the Indies archipelago that resulted in a Dutch-speaking elite and slave-based society that survived the break up of the Company empire. The Cape Cauldron also refers metaphorically to the unsettling and destabilizing effects the forced migration of convicts, exiles, and slaves had on the settler society at the Cape of Good Hope.

From the outset the VOC settlement of the Cape aimed to produce victuals and supplies for Company fleets plying the oceans between Europe and the Indies. Company officials at the Cape had to negotiate relationships with established Khoekhoe polities in the region. They used various strategies from cooperation to outright hostility to fulfill the Company's basic requirements from this imperial node. Not until the late seventeenth

---

[1] This chapter takes its name from a reference to the region of the ocean produced by the "vigorous mixing and stirring of the Indian and Atlantic Ocean water masses... dubbed the 'Cape Cauldron.'" Joanna Gyory, Lisa M. Beal, Barbie Bischof, Arthur J. Mariano, and Edward H. Ryan, "The Agulhas Current" and "The Benguela Current," http:oceancurrents.rsmas.miami.edu, accessed on July 26, 2007. Robin Knox-Johnston, *The Cape of Good Hope: A Maritime History*. London: Hodder and Stoughton, 1989, pp. 1–48.

century did the Seventeen Gentlemen order treaties to be signed with Khoekhoe polities that legitimated, in theory, the Company's territorial sovereignty that, in turn, signaled the Cape's transition to a permanent colony. Over several generations, Company servants who had become settlers in this node made increasing demands on the Company elite, the High Government in Batavia, and the Seventeen Gentlemen for the recognition of their rights and economic interests. The Cape did not operate as a merchant trading entrepôt, plantation spicery, or bulk commodity producer like other major Company nodes. Although by the mid-eighteenth century it had developed a dynamic economy based on primary produce and urban merchant activity that was still very much linked to the Company and foreign shipping for its major markets.

However, the Cape settlement was also almost from its origin part of the Company's network of forced migration that fundamentally shaped its development. Slaves, convicts, and exiles were all present from the early years of the settlement and formed part of the social spectrum of freedom and bondage in this evolving colonial society. The slave trade in the southwest Indian Ocean stimulated a sub-circuit of forced migration from the Cape to Mauritius and other southern African sites. Minor Company settlements in this region, all of them temporary, were part of a sub-circuit of forced migration, transportation, and legality that focused on the Cape, instead of Batavia, as their primary Company authority.

Ships at the Cape before the VOC Settlement

The period of freewheeling trade by European merchants in the Indian Ocean during the last decades of the sixteenth century was replaced by the organization of East India Companies, given charters by their states for monopoly trade in specific zones dividing the world into imaginary realms. The Dutch East India Company was one of several European East India Companies that replaced independent trading voyages that characterized the late sixteenth century. The Portuguese global empire had been the dominant European presence in the Indian Ocean since the end of the fifteenth century with its headquarters in Goa on the west coast of India. Having established colonies in Angola and Mozambique located respectively on the west and east coasts of southern Africa, the Cape of Good Hope was not vital to the Portuguese imperial networks. Each of the East India trading companies developed its own transportation networks that included refreshment stations favorable to their own interests in the transoceanic zone between the Atlantic and Indian Oceans.

The Peninsular Khoekhoe who lived at the Cape of Good Hope prior to the invasion by the Dutch East India Company had already engaged in over a century and a half of barter trade with passing European ships. Although they were not seafarers, they were well aware of seasonal shipping patterns.[2] Ships wanting to replenish their supplies of water, forage for food, and barter for sheep and cattle first had to pass by a small, flat, uninhabited island on their way into the majestic bay. The Khoekhoe were only intermittently willing to trade their livestock, so other sources of food had to be found. It was Robben Island that provided the most regular supply of food and water, albeit mostly seals (after which the island was named by the Dutch), penguins and seabirds. By the beginning of the seventeenth century, the Cape had evolved into a familiar replenishment site for European ships and Robben Island was used regularly as a postal exchange spot.

The first attempt by the English to regularize trade with the indigenous people on the mainland was in 1613 when a Khoekhoe man, Coree, was kidnapped and taken to Britain to learn English to be returned to the Cape as an ally of the English East India Company, which he did to his own advantage. Around the same time, the English Company made an initial move to occupy the Cape by stranding ten prisoners there to fend for themselves, but these men were either killed by the Khoekhoe or carried off by passing ships eager to replenish their depleted crews. This was not a concerted effort to set up a penal colony. It was a common strategy of maritime European powers to banish prisoners as an exploratory party before committing to territorial settlement, and this particular experiment in that was deemed a failure. Despite the English declaring sovereignty over the Cape in 1620, they did not pursue further occupation and their claim was ignored by Europeans and unknown to the Khoekhoe.

Instead, after Coree's demise, they induced another Khoekhoe man, Autshumao (whom they called Harry) to sail with them from the Cape to the Indies and back to be trained as an English-speaking intermediary for the livestock barter trade. The chances that other Khoekhoe individuals boarded ships voluntarily or against their will are more likely than not, and travelers' accounts are sometimes suggestive in this regard but no

---

[2] For the best treatment of the Company settlement at the Cape upon which follows the same narrative of historical events depicted early in this chapter see Nigel Worden, Elizabeth van Heyningen, Vivian Bickford-Smith, *Cape Town: The Making of a City*. Cape Town: David Phillip, 1998, chapters 1 and 2, pp. 11–84.

further records have been found.[3] Not long after his return to the Cape, Autshumao and some of his followers took up residence for several years on Robben Island from which vantage point they were supplied with livestock and poultry by the English to raise for use by the fleet. Autshumao and his people were Goringhaicona Khoekhoe (also called Watermen or Strandlopers) who had previously subsisted by foraging along the shoreline. Their move to Robben Island was feasible because they were not pastoralists, and caretaking English livestock provided alternative subsistence to beachcombing. Robben Island, Nigel Penn observes, was absolutely crucial to the early success of the Cape as a refreshment post because it provided a reliable and accessible alternative source of food to the unpredictable mainland barter trade with the pastoral Goringhaiqua and Gorachoqua (Peninsular) Khoekhoe.[4]

The Cape of Good Hope had a Janus-faced reputation as a site of unparalleled beauty and as the "Cape of Storms" for its seasonally tempestuous waters. Its name "Good Hope" initially indicated that this was the route to India, but over time it symbolized for most seafarers relief from depravations at sea. A 1659 account by a German sailor Albrecht Herport vividly expresses the feeling of many travelers on first sight of the Cape of Good Hope:

[I]n the early morning there was a glad shout from the foremast of "Land! Land!" which caused no little joy among us all. About an hour later we ... recognized it for the coast of Africa and for the Promontory Caput bonae Spei whither we were bound. About 3 in the afternoon we passed between [sic] the Roben and Taxen [Dassen] Islands, and came safely into the harbour and dropped anchor there: that same night we must strike our yard and topmast [sails] because of heavy winds. And water was now issued freely, which caused so great a joy among us, that it cannot be described in words, and would appear incredible to any who had not himself experienced it, since before this many had only one desire, once again to drink his fill of water before his death, which desire however he could not fulfill until now. Next day ... our Master was very well received by the Commandeur at the Fort, who at once sent us 2 cows and 6 sheep, as also all sorts of green vegetables such as cabbage; and among these also radishes, which we, for our

---

[3] The French Director-General of Madagascar, Etienne de Flacourt, who visited Saldanha Bay in the *Saint Laurent* on October 14, 1648, tried unsuccessfully to enslave local children. "The Director-General wished to take two boys with him to France, but the Hottentots would have none of it. He brought out his two Madagascar Negroes in uniform and wearing swords, but instead of admiration this called forth only mirth." Jose Burman, *The Saldanha Bay Story*. Cape Town: Human and Rousseau, 1974, p. 14.

[4] Nigel Penn, "Robben Island, 1488–1805," in Harriet Deacon, ed., *The Island: A History of Robben Island, 1488–1990*. Bellville: Mayibuye Books, University of the Western Cape, and Cape Town: David Phillip Publishers, 1996, pp. 1–14.

great longing and hankering for fresh food, ate with leaves and stalks, and drank the lovely fresh water as if it had been good new wine.[5]

Herport's moving account conveys that many a sailor, soldier, and passenger died within sight of the Cape or were carried ashore incapacitated by illnesses contracted during their arduous sea journey. Scurvy was rife on European ships and was the scourge of the oceans throughout the early modern period. Over the course of the Company's existence nearly one million people traveled from Europe on board Company ships, but only approximately one-third of the Company's servants ever returned.[6] The Cape functioned as a hospital (and all too often a graveyard) for those who could not travel further and a respite for those continuing on their voyage. A few decades after the founding of the Dutch post in 1652, travelers' expectations were a little higher, and the Cape gained its enduring reputation as the "tavern of the seas," a port where not only the necessities of life, but also its more inebriating and illicit pleasures, were readily available to those who could afford them. This development depended upon the growth of wine production and the evolution of the Company post into an urban settlement with free burghers engaged in the tavern trade.[7]

The "Caabse Vlek" – The Cape Village

The Company's Cape settlement was bounded by its imperial context from the outset. In the evocative words of one of South Africa's founding economic historians, C. W. de Kiewiet: "What began as a cabbage patch on the way to India became the most vital strategic point, with the possible exception of Malacca, in the entire Empire of the Dutch East India Company. Jan van Riebeeck's instructions were precise. The Dutch East India Company had no desire to tame the wilderness, nor to find

---

[5] Albrecht Herport, 1659, quoted in R. Raven-Hart, ed. and trans., *Cape of Good Hope 1652–1702. The First Fifty Years of Dutch Colonisation as Seen by Callers*, vol. 1. Cape Town: A. A. Balkema, 1971, p. 55.

[6] Femme S. Gaastra, *The Dutch East India Company: Expansion and Decline*. Zutphen, Netherlands: Walburg Pers, 2003, pp. 81–91.

[7] Kerry Ward, "'Tavern of the Seas?' The Cape of Good Hope as an Oceanic Crossroads during the Seventeenth and Eighteenth Centuries," in Jerry Bentley, Renate Bridenthal, and Kären Wigen, *Seascapes: Maritime Histories, Littoral Cultures, and Transoceanic Exchanges*. Honolulu: University of Hawaii Press, 2007, pp. 137–152; Pieter van Duin and Robert Ross, "The Economy of the Cape Colony in the Eighteenth Century," unpublished paper, Intercontinenta 7, Center for the History of European Expansion, Leiden, 1987.

new homes for Dutchmen over the sea ... [His] duty would be done if he provided the Company's vessels with fresh meat and vegetables, for the settlement at the Cape was not a separate venture. It was a cog in a great commercial system."[8] De Kiewiet's imagery is evocative but cogs are identical components of a machine.

This book argues that the Cape was a unique node in the networks of empire. Furthermore, to understand the Company's imperial web it is necessary to examine or imagine each Company node through its intersection with the various imperial networks that shaped the conditions of possibility for the extension of partial sovereignty. When the Cape was established primarily as a refreshment post, it simultaneously became a penal colony and a slave society linked to the Company's networks of forced migration. This development is only explicable within the dynamics of the Company's transportation and forced migration networks in the Indian Ocean that linked the Cape to other Company settlements. These imperial networks first and foremost shaped the conditions and contours of the Cape settlement.

The first commander of the Cape settlement, Jan van Riebeeck, was a child of the first Dutch imperial age. His father, Anthoni van Riebeeck, a native of Culemborg, was a ship's surgeon for the Dutch West India Company who died in Brazil in 1639, the year his son sailed to Batavia in the same capacity for the Delft Chamber of the Dutch East India Company. After calling at Gorée Island, a major node for the west African slave trade, his ship was wrecked at Sierra Leone and it took another year for Jan van Riebeeck to reach Batavia. Van Riebeeck was a member of a well-connected family; he was second cousin to one of the Company's governors general, Antonio van Diemen, and this kinship was enough to secure his safe passage to promotion. After a stint as assistant scribe in Batavia, he was given various assignments in Aceh, Formosa, and Deshima. While posted as a merchant in Tonkin, Van Riebeeck fell from grace after one of the periodic crackdowns on privateering in the Company. He was tried in Batavia by the Court of Justice, convicted of private silk trading, and sentenced to a fine and temporary banishment to the fatherland in 1648, all without demotion, penalty, or loss of wages. This meant that the High Government did not take the charge too seriously and that he was also likely protected by his family connections. Because Van Riebeeck was not

---

[8] C. W. de Kiewiet, *A History of South Africa: Social and Economic*. London: Oxford University Press, 1941, p. 4.

sentenced to permanent banishment from Company territories, he could hold out hope of another assignment with the VOC.

It was on his return journey to the Netherlands that his ship *Coningh van Polen* called in at the Cape of Good Hope for replenishment and to check on the crew of the wrecked *Haarlem*, who were stranded there guarding salvaged cargo. These shipwrecked sailors had built a wooden fort and bartered with the Khoekhoe for supplies. It was their success that encouraged the Dutch to consider a more permanent settlement. After arriving in Holland, Van Riebeeck married Maria de la Queillerie, from an old French Huguenot family, and the couple lived in Amsterdam between his assignments with the Dutch West India Company. The Seventeen Gentlemen asked him to comment on a report considering the potential of a Cape settlement, and, having done so to their satisfaction, he was appointed to head the mission.[9]

The period leading to the mid-seventeenth century was one in which various European claims to sovereignty over the Cape were not brought to fruition by occupation. Once the VOC occupied the Cape of Good Hope in 1652 to forestall such a move by the English, it claimed exclusive rights to the resources of the area. It made supplies available to foreign ships only if a surplus was available after the Company's ships were serviced. Despite a persistent fear of invasion by rival European powers held by Company officials, which was sometimes well founded, the VOC maintained exclusive control of this oceanic crossroads for the next 143 years. Territorial control beyond the harbor was not such a simple matter. Company officials expressed insecurity about their occupation rights when faced with competing claims by displaced Khoekhoe and other European maritime powers.

The Cape was part of a subregional shipping and trading zone, most intensively focused on the southwest Indian Ocean, but also extending to St. Helena in the Atlantic Ocean and the Mascarenes in the Indian Ocean. It formed one of several strategic refreshment posts that were

---

[9] These biographical details of Jan van Riebeeck and of the early years of the Cape are well known in South Africa, having been incorporated into school histories during the apartheid era. The following sources provide variations of this narrative. H. B. Thom, ed., *Journal of Jan van Riebeeck, Vol. 1: 1651–1655*. Published by the Van Riebeeck Society. Cape Town: A. A. Balkema, 1952, pp. xvi–xxvi. Hymen Picard, *Masters of the Castle: A Portrait Gallery of the Dutch Commanders and Governors of the Cape of Good Hope*. Cape Town: C. Struik, 1972, pp. 15–39; A. J. Böeseken, *Jan van Riebeeck en Sy Gesin*. Kaapstad: Tafelberg, 1974, pp. 1–50.

planned, established, and sometimes abandoned in the crucial southeast Atlantic–southwest Indian Ocean zone.[10] The concept of a zone is used here to bring into a single framework a series of strategic ports on islands and on the African coast that functioned primarily as refreshment stations, although over time they became increasingly differentiated from one another as settlements developed according to the economic imperatives of distinct European imperial networks and an evolving global capitalist economy.[11]

The Dutch East India Company networks were developing during the mid-seventeenth century, and nodes were established in Ceylon, the Indonesian archipelago, and South Asia. The refreshment node at the Cape of Good Hope was a worthwhile experiment designed to help facilitate the trading network between Europe and Asia. The Company's occupation at the Cape meant that the Portuguese were no longer the sole European presence in the southern African coastal region.[12] Founding an imperial node at the Cape also signaled that the Company had not yet given up the possibility of conquering the Portuguese settlement in Mozambique despite its unsuccessful bid for dominance in 1605.[13] As discussed previously, hostilities between European states had important implications for their empires and chartered companies. This was one of the limitations of sovereignty in the Dutch East India Company

[10] Grant Evans, "Between the Global and the Local There Are Regions, Cultural Areas, and National States: A Review Article," *Journal of Southeast Asian Studies*, 33(1), February 2002, pp. 147–162. This extended review by Evans of O. W. Wolters, *History, Culture, and Region in Southeast Asian Perspectives*, Revised Edition. Ithaca, 1999, is very suggestive in revising the Southeast Asian debates on what constitutes a coherent region of analysis. It is these debates on the nature of "Southeast Asia" that have made me rethink the Cape in a regional perspective.

[11] The outer limits of the larger network of refreshment stations include the Canaries and the Cape Verde Islands, Ascension and the Azores, Trinidad, Cadiz, and Bahia, all of which were tied into the trans-Atlantic navigation that included potential stops at the Cape in a multistop journey. For a discussion of these navigation routes see Maurice Boucher, *The Cape of Good Hope and Foreign Contacts 1735–1755*. Pretoria: University of South Africa, 1985, p. 10.

[12] In contrast to this argument regarding refreshment stops, the Portuguese and Luso-African settlement of Luanda in Angola developed because it stimulated a violent slaving frontier into the interior that provided African slaves to the Brazilian colonial slave market. Its role as a refreshment post for Portuguese shipping was minor to the dominant dynamics of the slave trade in the region. Joseph C. Miller, *Way of Death: Merchant Capitalism and the Angolan Slave Trade, 1730–1830*. Madison: University of Wisconsin Press, 1988.

[13] Eric Axelson, *Portuguese in South-East Africa, 1600–1700*. Johannesburg: Witwatersrand University Press, 1969, p. 129. Worden, Van Heyningen, and Bickford-Smith, *Cape Town*, p. 27.

empire because it meant that Portuguese imperial nodes could not be challenged unless the United Provinces was at war with Portugal. Thus did war and peace between European states extend to animosities and allegiances for their ships, trading posts, and settlements in the rest of the world.

Three ships were assigned to the fleet that made the voyage to the Cape of Good Hope in 1651. Commander Jan van Riebeeck was on the flagship *Drommedaris*, accompanied by the *Reijger* and the *Goede Hoop*. The fleet and its crew were in good enough shape to pass by the Canary Islands without stopping, and, although they were eventually short of water and fresh food, they managed the journey to the Cape without stopping.[14] The first few months at the settlement were taken up with surveying Table Valley, choosing a site with access to water to build a mud fort, foraging for green vegetables, fishing to secure food for the party, planting the first vegetable garden, and establishing regular barter relations for cattle from the Goringhaiqua and Gorachoqua (Peninsular) Khoekhoe of the region of the Cape peninsula (see Map 4).

Jan van Riebeeck's daily diary, ordered by the Seventeen Gentlemen to gather intelligence, documents minute details of the daily life of the settlement: the comings and goings of all the people, their health and illnesses, the weather conditions they endured, the state of building fortifications, the condition of the gardens, news of passing ships, relations with the indigenes, and daily exhortations to God for their safe-keeping. Van Riebeeck had accepted the assignment to set up the refreshment post at the Cape of Good Hope as his path to redemption after being convicted as a criminal and banished from a lucrative career in Asia. He made every effort to ensure the success of the enterprise, but constantly reminded his superiors that he was too talented to endure for too long in a second banishment as chief farmer to a mundane refreshment post on the southern tip of Africa. He wanted to return to his merchant status in Asia.

One of the major challenges of Van Riebeeck's command was to ensure the discipline of his own people. The Company order to set up a supply post for their ships was a hardship assignment for all its servants and involved consistent heavy and unrewarding labor. The Cape could not have been further from most Company servants' dreams of adventure and fortune in Asia. Insubordination in the fledgling outpost could not be tolerated because it put the whole settlement at risk.

---

[14] Thom, ed., *Journal of Jan van Riebeeck*, vol. 1, pp. 1–34.

The first soldier to defy the captain of the *Goede Hoope* was sentenced to fall from the yardarm and to receive fifty lashes. The second, Gerrit Dirckssen of Elssen, was given one hundred lashes for insulting a superior officer. A couple of months later Dirckssen, along with three of his fellows, deserted the post. This caused such fear of revolt and further desertions among the commanding officers that the next person to complain about the unrelenting diet of fish was condemned to receive one hundred lashes, as was another fellow who refused to confess to having said that he wished he'd gone along with the deserters. The would-be deserter was also sentenced to be dropped three times from the yardarm and, for safe keeping, was ordered to serve onboard the yacht to minimize the chance he would incite others.

A week after the deserters had left the fort, they straggled back to beg pardon for their serious crime. During their interrogation, Jan Blanx confessed that their goal had been to reach the Portuguese settlement at Mozambique (thus compounding their crime by deserting to a Dutch enemy) and from that point to board a ship for home. They had been stopped in their tracks by a mountain range (later named the Hottentot Hollands) that inhibited their further progress along the shoreline and returned to the settlement to plead for mercy from their superior officers. The Company could not afford to lose any labor, and executions may have incited an uprising because many men had interceded on the prisoners' behalf against the death penalty.

So the four deserters were tried and sentenced by the governing council headed by Jan van Riebeeck and their lives were spared. Jan Blanx was tied to a pole and had a bullet shot over his head in mock execution and was then keel-hauled and received 150 lashes and, along with his three mates, ordered "to work as a slave in fetters for two years doing the common and all other dirty work." He survived his ordeal and along with his coconspirators was relieved from wearing chains on New Year's Day 1653 as a gesture of the commander's magnanimity.[15] The alternation of punishment and forgiveness was an important principle in meting out Company justice, as Jan van Riebeeck knew from personal experience.

Moreover, illness and death plagued the settlement and the governing council desperately wanted to maximize as much active labor as possible. For the next few years, Company servants at the Cape and visiting soldiers and sailors from Dutch ships were disciplined mainly

---

[15] Ibid., pp. 61–72.

for theft (especially of food), assault, leaving their posts, and mutinous mumblings.[16] Desertion was also a problem, but this could only be punished if it was unsuccessful and, all too often, Company servants stowed away on passing ships never to be seen again. For the first decade of the settlement, conditions were so harsh that two serious episodes of mass desertion were uncovered, underlining the tenuous nature of this Company post.[17] Crimes committed on board ship were handed over for trial at the Cape but in at least two cases, one of sodomy and the other of mutiny, the offenses were so serious that Van Riebeeck and his council concluded, "Especially since persons with a thorough knowledge of the law are required... it was decided by a majority of votes not to deal further with the matter here at the Cape but to send the offenders with the documents mentioned to Batavia where the High Court of India has its seat and the case could be tried properly."[18]

Meanwhile, Van Riebeeck attempted to consolidate relations with the cattle-owning people he called Saldanhars, the Cochoqua Khoekhoe, who arrived at the Cape seasonally to graze their livestock. The Dutch originally had hoped that Autshumao, with whom Van Riebeeck was forced to communicate in English, would have enough influence to ensure successful bartering arrangements.[19] It proved more difficult than anticipated to induce the Khoekhoe to trade their cattle and sheep for copper and tobacco. The possession of livestock was vital to the Company settlement, and Van Riebeeck's journal reflects his frustration in seeing thousands of healthy cattle pass by the gates of the fort while not being able to gain lawful access to them. Khoekhoe society was based on migratory pastoralism within specific regions controlled by particular polities under the loose leadership of a senior man. The Khoekhoe were often in competition for livestock and resources, particularly for access to the pasture and water on which they depended on for their wealth and livelihood. To the extreme vexation of the Company, the Khoekhoe were not readily willing to trade away the basis of their wealth.

Interactions with the Khoekhoe were governed by the initial instructions of the Seventeen Gentlemen and the Statutes of Batavia. The

---

[16] Donald Moodie, comp., trans., and ed., *The Record, Or a Series of Official Papers Relative to the Condition and Treatment of the Native Tribes of South Africa, Part 1. 1649–1720.* Originally published in 1838. Photostatic reprint published: Amsterdam and Cape Town: A. A. Balkema, 1960, p. 252.
[17] Worden, Van Heyningen, and Bickford-Smith, *Cape Town*, pp. 31–33.
[18] Thom, *Journal of Jan van Riebeeck*, vol 2, p. 254 and pp. 259–260.
[19] Ibid., vol. 1, pp. 49–72, 123.

development of the Law of Nations in the early seventeenth century included the recognition of the sovereignty and independence of heathen nations and recognized the jurisdiction of their own laws and customs. This law affected the way the VOC operated throughout its charter area. The option of titles of discovery or of occupation based on claims of *terra nullius* were not applicable in the East Indies. "Neither was this possible from the point of view of local inter-State custom which counted treaty-making, cession of territory or conquest among its normal legal institutions."[20] The Company's legal network extended to the Cape and determined the boundaries of relationships with the indigenous inhabitants. The Khoekhoe of the Cape were considered free nations governed by their own laws and could not be legally enslaved. Van Riebeeck's first written orders to his subordinates, read aloud at the very outset of the settlement, underlined the absolute necessity of peaceful coexistence with the indigenous inhabitants and promised severe punishment if transgressions occurred.

Nevertheless, it was tempting for the Dutch at the Cape to envisage a different scenario. Jan van Riebeeck was not above pondering in his journal about the alternatives to peaceful coexistence after eight frustrating and perilous months eking out a subsistence at the Cape on a diet in which penguins and cabbages were featured all too often on the menu.[21]

The Saldanhars with thousands of cattle and sheep came so close to our fort that their cattle nearly mingled with ours. Could not, however, get the bartering properly under way. Today we had ample opportunity of depriving them of 10,000 head of cattle had we been allowed to do so. Once we had possession of so many cattle... we should have no fear of the English touching here and spoiling the cattle trade... These people daily give us sufficient cause by stealing... many savages could be captured without a blow as they always come to us unarmed; they could then be sent to India as slaves.[22]

Van Riebeeck's reflections indicate his perception of the utility of a macro-network of forced migration in the empire as a means to achieve local

---

[20] C. H. Alexandrowicz, *An Introduction to the History of the Law of Nations in the East Indies (16th, 17th and 18th Centuries)*. Oxford: Clarendon Press, 1967, p. 41.

[21] It was an offense to complain about the meager provisions given to the garrison in the early years of the Company settlement. On September 28, 1652, one Harmen Vogelaer was sentenced to receive 100 blows with the butt of a musket for "expressing among the men discontent with the provisions issued, and wishing the devil to take the purser for serving out penguins instead of beef and pork." "Abstract of Convictions before Commander and Court of Justice of the Fort Good Hope, during the Command of Mr van Riebeeck, 1652–1662," in Moodie, ed, *The Record*, p. 252.

[22] Thom, *Journal of Jan van Riebeeck*, vol. 1, pp. 111–112.

ends at a particular node and in turn signal the decentralized character of the Company empire. The policy of using extreme force locally to achieve desired economic ends within the Company's empire as a whole was not without precedent. The conquest of the nutmeg and mace producing Banda islands in the Moluccas during the 1620s was accompanied by the almost complete destruction of Bandanese society in the name of establishing a Dutch monopoly over these valuable spices. The conquest included the massacre of most of the Bandanese ruling elite and the enslavement through forced migration of the surviving remnants of the Bandanese population.[23]

By 1657, desperation to stabilize the food supply and the growth of herds in the Cape settlement prompted the Company to release of some of its servants to become free burghers on allocated farmland along the Liesbeek River. The Khoekhoe resisted this encroachment on their grazing lands through intermittent violence, and stock theft was prevalent on both sides. The Company was by no means able to assert control over the region. Meanwhile, Van Riebeeck was desperately attempting to conclude treaties with other leaders of the Cape Khoekhoe polities to ensure the protection of the vulnerable Company post. On July 5, 1658, the Company concluded its first official peace treaty with the Goringhaiqua Khoekhoe led by Gogosoa. The treaty was one of mutual protection and trade and not one that ceded territory to the Company, although areas of exclusive rights to pasture were defined. It was sealed by handshakes all around.[24] The treaty seems to have been concluded on Gogosoa's side to ensure the release of his son, Osingkhimma (Shagger), who had been taken hostage by the Company in its latest effort to prevent incursions into its stock and in retaliation for assaults on members of the VOC settlement.[25]

Hostage-taking was common practice in many of the VOC disputes with indigenous polities over which it had no jurisdiction and was often combined with political exile to various Company nodes. At the Cape node, Robben Island was the farthest place of exile utilized for indigenous hostages. This was the first official treaty of the Company concluded with the Khoekhoe and it proved not particularly enduring. Nevertheless,

---

[23] Leonard Andaya, *The World of the Muluku: Eastern Indonesia in the Early Modern Period*. Honolulu: University of Hawaii Press, 1993; Willard A. Hanna, *Indonesian Banda: Colonialism and its Aftermath in the Nutmeg Islands*. Philadelphia, PA: Institute for the Study of Human Issues, 1978.

[24] "Kaap de Goede Hoop, 5 Juli 1658," in Heeres and Stapel, eds., *Corpus Diplomaticum. Tweede Deel (1650–1675)*, pp. 121–123.

[25] Thom, *Journal of Jan van Riebeeck*, vol. 2, pp. 300–302.

it was entered into the *Corpus Diplomaticum* (treaty records) of the Company alongside the treaties concluded with other indigenous polities in the Company's charter realm. Once the Khoekhoe realized the Dutch were extending their occupation of the land and denying them grazing rights, relations deteriorated into sporadic violence and recurrent struggles over livestock.

Historians of South Africa have not analyzed treaty-making with the Khoekhoe in the context of the Company's empire. In this case, the treaty was significant on a number of levels, in the main because it indicated official recognition of the sovereignty and independence of the Khoekhoe polities at the Cape. The Company's legal code defined the *modus operandi* of relations between the Company and the Khoekhoe polities in terms of international law. After signing the treaty, Company documents continuously referred to their breaking the contract in terms of an accumulation of Khoekhoe "guilt," which was used to justify revenge and reparations on the part of the Company.[26]

By 1657, Autshumao had outlived his usefulness and fallen from grace with the Company. He had been accused of duplicity and was implicated in the murder of a Dutch shepherd boy. Autshumao was the first African person banished by the VOC to Robben Island and was accompanied by members of his family and his followers. The official journal entry for July 10, 1658 stated: "About 9 o'clock the ex-interpreter, or, as the English used to call him, King Harry, was removed... from his kingdom in this furthest corner of Africa to the Robben Island." He was officially a hostage of the Company and not a convicted criminal under Company law.[27]

The same year, the Company decided to send Doman, alias Anthony, another leader of the Goringhaiqua Khoekhoe, to Batavia to learn Dutch and to be indoctrinated as a Company translator and ally. Elphick speculates that this visit to the VOC imperial headquarters was the beginning of Doman's determined hostility to the Company, as he recognized the dangers of Dutch settlement for his own people through his experience of the resistance of the Bantenese to Dutch incursions in Java.[28]

---

[26] For example, "As these Kaapmans are piling up infringements of the peace concluded with them, there is no reason why they should not be thoroughly punished sometime. On May 19, 1659, the Council resolved, "Since we see no other means of securing peace with these Cape people, we shall take the first opportunity practicable to attack them... We shall capture as many cattle and mean as we can... The prisoners we shall keep hostage. Thom, *Journal of Jan van Riebeeck*, vol. 3, pp. 36–37 and p. 48.

[27] Thom, *Journal of Jan van Riebeeck*, vol 2, p. 309.

[28] Richard Elphick, *Kraal and Castle: Khoikhoi and the Founding of White South Africa*. New Haven, CT: Yale University Press, 1977, p. 109.

Perhaps more importantly, Doman was exposed to the full range of slavery in Batavia, the implications of which could not have escaped his attention. He also observed the use of arson by the Bantenese in their resistance against Batavia and learned to use firearms.[29] The Goringhaiqua had promised to cooperate in recapturing runaway slaves and deserters for the Company in return for payment, but Doman's visit to Batavia exposed him to a fully developed colonial slave society and alerted him to the Company's potential plans for the permanent settlement of the Cape.

Upon his return to Africa in 1658, Doman became an unceasing enemy of the Company, and emerged as an important leader in the First Khoekhoe-Dutch War fought between 1659 and 1660. The Khoekhoe insisted that the land over which the war was fought had been theirs for centuries. In negotiations for peace that took place at the fort in April 1660, Gogosoa, leader of the Goringhaiqua stated, "As for your claim that the land is not big enough for us both, who should rather in justice give way, the rightful owners or the foreign intruder?" Van Riebeeck replied, "Their land had thus justly fallen to us in a defensive war, won by the sword, as it were, and we intended to keep it."[30] During the first period of Company rule at the Cape until the 1670s, the Khoekhoe were understood to be governed by their own laws and were not punished under Company law for crimes committed against the Company. They could, however, be held hostage.

The Company did its best to play one Khoekhoe polity off against another, but the Khoekhoe leaders were equally astute in using Company alliances for their own ends.[31] Political relations between the various Khoekhoe polities at the Cape were shifting and often hostile. The most loyal Khoekhoe interpreter for the Company was Krotoa, a Cochoqua woman of high-ranking birth. Krotoa was known to the Company by her Dutch name, Eva, and was about ten years old when she became a servant in the Van Riebeeck household, living alongside the family's slave women. She became a skilled multilingual negotiator between the Khoekhoe and the Company. V. C. Malherbe identifies Krotoa as a "culture broker" and indeed this was her role as an interpreter, but her subsequent tragic life shows the difficulties of negotiating this role.

Shortly before the Van Riebeeck family left for their long-awaited reassignment to Asia in 1662, Krotoa was baptized as Eva into the Reformed

---

[29] Thom, *Journal of Jan van Riebeeck*, vol. 3, p. 47.
[30] Ibid., p. 196.
[31] Shula Marks, "Khoisan Resistance to the Dutch in the Seventeenth and Eighteenth Centuries," *Journal of African History*, 13(1), 1972, pp. 55–80.

faith, a crowning moment for Maria van Riebeeck. She continued her role as interpreter under the new Commander of the Cape, Zacharias Wagenaer, who also encouraged her marriage to a Company servant, the Danish surgeon Pieter van Meerhoff. Van Meerhoff was assigned to manage Robben Island, and it is in this state of semibanishment from the mainland that Krotoa's addiction to alcohol began to manifest itself. After Van Meerhoff's death during a slaving expedition to Madagascar, Krotoa declined rapidly. She died in 1674, having been alienated from both her European and her Khoekhoe communities.[32]

Labor was a constant and pressing issue for the settlement. Even with the authority to requisition soldiers from ships to assist on land, the settlement required a sufficient and regular supply of new labor, especially for building. Jan van Riebeeck had at first entertained fantasies about the potential of the Cape to prosper under free labor "for which we require some married Chinese and other free Mardijkers or even Hollanders who could be allowed under some conditions to occupy some land." Even before the Company personnel had built their first permanent structure in their muddy camp during the autumn of 1652, the new commander's vision for Africa was filtered through a vision of empire.[33] In his diary he notes:

[E]ven if there were thousands of Chinese or other tillers they could not take up or cultivate more than a tenth part of this land. It is moreover so fertile and rich

---

[32] For a sensitive biography of Krotoa, see V. C. Malherbe, *Krotoa, Called "'Eva": a woman between*. Cape Town: Centre for African Studies, University of Cape Town. Communication No. 19, 1990. Krotoa progressively fell from favor with the Company, largely due to her alcoholism, and was periodically banished to Robben Island. She died on July 29, 1674. Her children were raised by a freeburgher who later moved to Mauritius. Krotoa's daughter Pieternella later returned as a married woman to the Cape. Many South Africans, including Afrikaners, now choose to trace their descent from Krotoa who has become a powerful symbol in post-apartheid identity politics. For a fascinating and archivally based fictionalized account of these events and the early decades of the Dutch settlement at the Cape and Mauritius see Dan Sleigh, *Islands*.

[33] Van Riebeeck's musings about the potential for Chinese labor at the Cape are well known among Cape historians. For the most comprehensive account of the Chinese at the Cape see James Armstrong, "The Chinese at the Cape in the Dutch East India Company Period." Unpublished paper presented at the UNESCO Slave Route Project Conference, Robben Island, Cape Town, 1997. For a recent account of these events see Karel Schoeman, *Early Slavery at the Cape of Good Hope, 1652–1717*. Pretoria: Protea Book House, 2007, pp. 27–28. See also Melanie Yap and Dianne Leong Man, *Colour Confusion and Concessions: The History of the Chinese in South Africa*. Hong Kong: Hong Kong University Press, 1996, pp. 5–6.

that neither Formosa which I have seen, nor New Netherland which I have heard of, can be compared with it.[34]

The commander repeated his request to Batavia, but finally received a definitive response from the High Government in 1657, who had a completely different perspective on the priorities of migration in the empire:

> We would have liked to have sent you some Chinese volunteers for agricultural purposes, but all were unwilling and could not be persuaded to go. We might carry out your suggestion to send you the insolvents working in chains here, but as they are for the most part indebted to private parties at Batavia, the latter would object strongly against their removal to the Cape. Besides the difficulty will arise, that if other Chinese debtors who are at large are informed that their comrades have been sent into exile, they will, fearing the same thing will happen to themselves, certainly run away to Bantam. This would cause serious loss to the Company and to the public.... You will therefore observe that it would be very injudicious to send any Chinese to the Cape against their inclination, so that you need not depend upon them for help.[35]

Van Riebeeck had seen first hand the impressive agricultural development of Formosa by free Chinese migrants. He probably did not know that at the very moment he was fantasizing about the potential of Chinese settlers for the Company. The Chinese in Formosa (Taiwan) had already begun fomenting a rebellion that would result in the defeat of the Dutch and their expulsion from the island in 1662.[36] James Armstrong points out that the Cape commanders pleaded with the Batavian authorities until the end of the seventeenth century to send out enough industrious Chinese laborers to farm at the Cape. Company officials had an empire-wide perspective of the potential of various imperial networks to be used in supporting any one node. The migration network was particularly appealing to a settlement with severe labor shortages. Hundreds of Chinese people were shipped by Batavia to the Cape during the Company period, but as exiles and not as free settlers, as Cape authorities had wished. These exiled Chinese and other Asian peoples from the Indies archipelago, Ceylon, and India, were often considered more of a liability to the colony

---

[34] Thom, *Journal of Jan van Riebeeck*, vol. 1, pp. 35–36.
[35] Governor-General and Council of the Indies to Commander Van Riebeeck, January 31, 1657, reproduced in H. C. V. Leibbrandt, ed., *Precis of the Archives of the Cape of Good Hope. Letters and Documents Received, 1649–1662. Part II*. Cape Town: W. A. Richards & Sons, Government Printers, 1896, pp. 2–5.
[36] Tonio Andrade, *How Taiwan Became Chinese: Dutch Spanish and Han Colonization in the Seventeenth Century*. New York: Columbia University Press, 2006.

than the asset the seventeenth-century rulers had imagined.[37] Considering the fundamentally important position of the Chinese community in Batavia for the welfare of the Company headquarters in the seventeenth century, it would have been highly unlikely for the Company to intervene in the local system of debt bondage by exiling debtors to remote places. Batavia was too dependent on Chinese labor and credit to risk alienating this valuable community during this era.[38] Instead, the High Government began sending a steady trickle of *bandieten* (convicts) and *bannelingen* (exiles) to the Cape to be used as forced labor for the Company. This was a mixed blessing as they had to be kept under some surveillance, and that required additional labor the Cape did not easily have to spare. The first Chinese convicts arrived at the Cape in 1654.[39]

Among these first convicts to arrive at the Cape from Batavia also included, unusually, a woman. Groote Catrijn, as she was called at the Cape, was a slave woman from Pallacate on the Coromandel Coast living in Batavia who was sentenced to death by the Company court in Batavia for accidentally killing her lover after he assaulted her. As the crime seems to have been committed in self-defense, the sentence was commuted to banishment for life to the Cape. She arrived at the Cape on the return fleet in 1657. Mansell Upham has traced Groote Catrijn's life at the Cape. Like other Company settlements, free women were in such short supply that it was not uncommon in the seventeenth century for Company servants, free burghers, and, increasingly free black men to buy female slaves with children whom they then manumitted and married.[40] In Groote Catrijn's case, she had a child by a Company soldier but later married the free black man, Anthonij van Bengale.

These first convicts began the pattern for the Cape and, especially, Robben Island to be used as a penal colony for arriving prisoners, particularly, from Batavia and Colombo. One of the early male convicts from Batavia, Domingo of Bengal, was sent to the Robben Island prison explicitly to relieve one of the Company servants to labor back on the mainland.[41] By the end of May 1658, the Cape settlement was comprised

---

[37] Armstrong, "Chinese at the Cape," pp. 6–8.
[38] Leonard Blussé, *Strange Company: Chinese Settlers, Mestizo Women and the Dutch in VOC Batavia*. Dordrecht, Holland: Foris Publications, 1986, chapter 4.
[39] Armstrong, "Chinese at the Cape," pp. 13–14.
[40] Robert C.-H. Shell, *Children of Bondage: A Social History of the Slave Society at the Cape of Good Hope, 1652–1838*. Johannesburg: Witwatersrand University Press, 1994; Hans F. Heese, *Groep sonder Grense: Die rol en status van de gemengde bevolking ann die Kaap, 1652–1795*. Belville: Wes Kaaplandse Instituut vir Historiese Navorsing, 1984.
[41] Schoeman, *Early Slavery*, p. 36; Thom, *Journal of Jan van Riebeeck*, vol 2, p. 314.

of eighty Company servants, fifteen incapacitated servants, twenty Dutch women and children, fifty-one free burghers, ninety-eight healthy and sick Company slaves, and seven exiles.[42] The proportions of these groups at the Cape would change over time with exiles comprising by far the smallest group. Nevertheless, within the first decade of the settlement, the full spectrum of unfree labor had begun to emerge.

Under the General Instructions and the Statutes of Batavia, the VOC was not allowed to enslave the indigenous population of the places it settled. This was a practical as well as a legal decision for the Cape because the small Company settlement could not have prevented enslaved indigenes from escaping. Van Riebeeck realized the strategic importance of Robben Island as a penal settlement not only for his own men but also for the Khoekhoe people he wanted isolated from the mainland. However, none of these measures helped with the labor crisis. From the outset of the settlement Van Riebeeck had requested permission from Batavia to acquire or receive slaves from other Company nodes.

To meet his labor needs two years after the founding of the Cape settlement, Van Riebeeck ordered the first Company slaving journey from the Cape to Madagascar.[43] Slave labor was considered a desirable supplement to Company servants and free burghers. Only one Company slaving voyage was sent to Dahomey in West Africa, and this was a secret mission ordered by the Seventeen Gentlemen because Dahomey fell outside the VOC charter domain. The territory west of the Cape of Good Hope was the monopoly realm of the Dutch West India Company, which was for a short time in the seventeenth century the leading slave-trading enterprise in the Atlantic slaving system. One VOC fleet on its way from Europe to Asia in 1658 had captured an enemy Portuguese ship with 174 Angolan slaves who they kept as a prize; some remained at the Cape for the Company, others were allocated to the burghers, and the remainder was sent on to Batavia. Of those who stayed at the Cape, many escaped. This proved to be the Cape's only direct contact with the Atlantic slave trade because the Company's transportation and legal networks did not intersect with these other networks of the slave trade.[44]

---

[42] Worden, Van Heyningen, and Bickford-Smith, *Cape Town*, p. 26.
[43] Westra, Piet, and James C. Armstrong, eds., *Slave Trade with Madagascar: The Journals of the Cape Slaver Leijdsman, 1715*. Cape Town: Africana Publishers, 2006. See also Robert Shell, ed., *From Diaspora to Diorama*. Cape Town: Ancestry24, 2003.
[44] James Armstrong and Nigel Worden, "The slaves, 1652–1834," in Elphick and Gilliomee, *Shaping of South African Society*, pp. 111–112.

Slaves at the Cape were provided through contacts with slaving networks the Company tapped into at various strategic nodes in the Indian Ocean grid. Over the whole Company period and until the end of the slave trade, roughly 63,000 slaves were brought to the Cape. According to Robert Shell's estimates, 26.4 percent came from East Africa, 25.1 percent from Madagascar and Mauritius, 25.9 percent from India and Ceylon, and 22.7 percent from the Indies archipelago.[45] The proportion of slaves being imported to the Cape from each of these regions shifted during the 150 years of Company rule. The African mainland did not become a significant source of slaves until the 1770s, with the exception of a small peak in trade in the late 1720s and early 1730s. In the seventeenth century, the majority of slaves had come from Madagascar. For much of the eighteenth century, at least half came from the south Asian subcontinent and Ceylon, and a fifth came from the Indies archipelago. By the late eighteenth century, slaves from India and Ceylon were no longer traded in great numbers, but there was a sharp increase of slaves coming from the east African mainland through the port of Rio de la Goa on the Mozambique coast. Shell calculates that creolization of Cape slaves (the period when locally born slaves were in the majority) did not occur until the 1760s. Even so, the colony remained dependent on imported slaves. Unlike other major Company settlements, the Cape node was not previously part of an indigenous slave trade network that could be tapped for labor. Official Company policy to depend on slave labor at the Cape was only clarified in 1717, by which time the Cape had already extended a slave-trading circuit to meet up with the west Indian Ocean slave trade networks.[46]

The Cape's Southwest Indian Ocean Sub-Circuit

The island of Mauritius in the western waters of the Indian Ocean was well known to European shipping as a refreshment post and source of valuable ebony, a hard wood used in ship building. When the VOC first decided to open a small logging and refreshment post on the southeast

---

[45] Shell, *Children of Bondage*, pp. 40–41.
[46] Ibid., pp. 47–48; Patrick Harries, "Making Mozbiekers: History, Memory and the African Diaspora at the Cape," in Benigna Zimba, Edward Alpers, and Allen Isaacman, eds., *Slave Routes and Oral Tradition in Southeastern Africa*. Eduardo Mondlane University. Maputo, Mozambique: Filsom Entertainment, 2005, pp. 91–123; Nigel Worden and Gerald Groenewald, eds., *Trials of Slavery: Selected Documents Concerning Slaves from the Criminal Records of the Council of Justice at the Cape of Good Hope, 1705–1794*, second series no. 36. Cape Town: Van Riebeeck Society for the Publication of South African Historical Documents, 2005, pp. xi–xii.

coast of Mauritius in 1638, the French had already established their own logging and refreshment camp on a different part of the island. The second leader of the Company post was Adrien van der Stel, whose wife Maria Levens gave birth to her first child, Simon, on the island in 1639. Simon van der Stel would grow up to become the first governor of the Cape of Good Hope. The High Government in Batavia kept the Company settlement in Mauritius to a minimum, but the VOC used it as a dumping ground for convicts from Asia. By 1641, Van der Stel had begun sending slaving missions to the Bay of Antongil in Madagascar, a major point for the Malagasy slave trade with the Swahili coast, the Omanis and Portuguese, as well as the English, French, and Dutch. The Malagasy chiefs controlled a sophisticated slave trade that serviced many of the Indian Ocean forced migration networks. Mauritius itself was not a source of slaves; it was just the opposite – the island lent itself to ideal conditions for escape and maronage (the formation of communities of escapees) which slaves and convicts alike soon realized. Jan van Riebeeck organized the dismantling of the Company post in 1658 because it was no longer serviceable, for falling ebony prices made it unprofitable, and therefore a waste of valuable manpower.

The post was reopened in 1664 under orders from the Cape's new Commander, Zacharias Wagenaer. This time the small settlement on Mauritius functioned as an outpost of the Cape. It was subordinate to the interests of the Cape and Batavia, both of which sent settlers and convicts to the island. The Cape functioned as the nearest site of Company governance for Mauritius. In return, Company officials in Mauritius sent serious criminal cases to the Cape to be tried because they were under its legal jurisdiction. For several decades, Mauritius was a useful refreshment post and staging point for the slave trade, although it was finally dismantled permanently in 1710 when its Company inhabitants were dispatched to the Cape or Batavia.[47] The Company later opened another trading, slaving, and penal outpost under the control of the Cape on the African mainland at Rio de la Goa that operated from 1719 to 1731, giving the Cape a direct link with the southernmost reaches of the monsoonal shipping and trade networks of the east African coast.[48]

---

[47] D. Sleigh, *Die Buiteposte: VOC-buiteposte onder Kaapse bestuur 1652–1795*. Pretoria: Haum Uitgevers, 1993, pp. 639–679; Megan Vaughan, *Creating the Creole Island: Slavery in Eighteenth-Century Mauritius*. Durham, NC: Duke University Press, 2005, pp. 4–19.

[48] Ibid., pp. 679–716.

The Company settlement at the Cape of Good Hope was first centered on the fort, warehouses, wharf, and garden. The *Caabse Vlek* (Cape hamlet) was an apt description of the settlement beyond the Company buildings. By the early 1670s, the VOC had finally committed itself to a permanent settlement. By 1679, when the new stone Castle was complete, the Company's intention to invest in the site had been established. From then on the Cape hamlet developed into a small port town with both a free and an unfree population whose physical space was dominated by Company buildings including the Company Slave Lodge, hospital, warehouses, and barracks. Its main fortifications were constructed with Company servant and slave labor between the years of 1665 and 1679, although the surrounding moat took much longer. As Wayne Dooling points out, the VOC used a combination of punishment and reward to induce its own employees to work harder. If necessary, the Company requisitioned slaves owned by free burghers and employed the Khoekhoe who lived in the vicinity of the castle as day laborers.[49]

The fortifications of the Cape had already extended beyond the original fort before building at the castle was complete. The hedge of bitter almonds and brambles planted to protect the first farms had, by the early 1670s, expanded to redoubts and post-houses along the shoreline on Robben Island and at the base of the Hottentot Hollands mountains.[50] Further batteries and outposts were built with the extension of cultivation along the whole Cape Peninsula coast. These sections of the city continued to be developed into the eighteenth century.

A significant portion of the Company's labor force was thereby dedicated to building, manning, and maintaining these posts and fortifications with labor supplemented by convicts and exiles. Fortifications and outposts were also built along the west coast of the Cape region at Saldanha and St. Helena Bays. The Company's strategy of extending its fortifications was aimed at protecting its territorial and market sovereignty against European rivals and also helped protect the expanding rural economy from indigenous attack.[51]

---

[49] Wayne Dooling, "The Castle: Its place in the History of Cape Town in the VOC Period," in Elizabeth van Heyningen, ed., *Studies in the History of Cape Town*, vol. 7. Cape Town History Project in association with the Center for African Studies. Cape Town: University of Cape Town Press, 1994, pp. 9–31.

[50] U. A. Seeman, *Fortifications of the Cape Peninsula 1647–1829*. Cape Town: Castle Military Museum, 1997.

[51] Sleigh, *Die Buiteposte*.

Free and Forced Migration and Sojourns at the Cape

The VOC instituted various circuits of free and forced migration that intersected at the Cape node and comprised an important dimension of the Company's peopling of empire. At first, European settlement at the Cape was both temporary and fluctuated seasonally. The Company outpost was not considered a permanent node of the empire until the late 1670s, and this shift was accompanied by a definitive decision to establish sovereignty over the land it occupied or wanted to occupy through treaty. Therefore, early European migration to the Cape was part of the sojourning patterns of the Company that scattered its personnel – administrators, merchants, sailors, soldiers, and artisans – around its various settlements on a temporary basis as its imperial networks were being established.

European Company personnel crossed the Atlantic Ocean and were assigned settlements in the Company's emerging imperial web, but they could also apply for transfer from one to another node.[52] Its voluntary permanent postings required an application for burgher status by Company personnel through which they could obtain release from Company service in favor of permanent residence. Conversely, free burghers at the Cape could also apply to be reinstated by the Company as servants. The precarious nature of farming in the early decades meant that a significant proportion of free burghers did just that or they deserted.[53] It was not common for individuals with extended careers in the Company to be resident in a single place. Given the high mortality rate among both land-based and seafaring people in the Company's domain, even supposedly temporary postings could prove to be an individual's final resting place.

The Company's migration network allowed multiple forms of the circulation of people within its domain and these patterns were gendered in specific ways. The temporary sojourning circuit of seafaring workers was composed overwhelmingly of men. The slave trade and voluntary permanent migration included the largest proportion of women. Even so, the number of women slaves who experienced forced migration to the Cape remained between 20 and 30 percent of the total number of slaves. Men were overwhelmingly preferred for slave labor.

---

[52] Philip Curtin, *Cross-Cultural Trade in World History*. Cambridge, UK: Cambridge University Press, 1984, pp. 1–15; Robin Cohen, *Global Diasporas: An Introduction*. Seattle: University of Washington Press, 1997. p. 178.
[53] Worden, Van Heyningen, and Bickford-Smith, *Cape Town*, p. 20.

It was not until a commitment to a permanent settlement of the Cape was made in the 1670s that one could claim that a stable European migration took place. Company servants who became burghers could petition for their wives and children to join them, but a minority availed themselves of this opportunity. To bolster production in the rural sector, the first sponsored voluntary migration of civilians occurred, with the Company offering refuge to several hundred male and female French Huguenots who were allowed to settle and were given land at the Cape to farm.[54] These early voluntary migrations only slightly shifted the gender ratio of European residents at the Cape from an overwhelmingly male population to a higher ratio of women and a higher rate of family creation. Nevertheless, European residence at the Cape continued in the form of small-scale migration from Europe, small numbers of Company personnel who decided to settle permanently at the Cape, and far larger numbers of temporary residents and seasonal sojourners.[55]

Not all European migrations, whether temporary or permanent, were made voluntarily. The Cape served as penal settlement for the Dutch East India Company's Indian Ocean empire for almost the entire period of Company rule. Unlike most colonies of other early modern European powers, the Cape did not receive convicts directly from Europe across the Atlantic Ocean. Europeans were transported as convicts to the Cape throughout the Company period but came only from within the Company's Indian Ocean empire. Company servants transported to the Cape as convicts were by definition male. Although female European convicts were sent from the Cape to Robben Island, there were few European women transported to the Cape from elsewhere in the empire. The exception was Mauritius, which was under the direct jurisdiction of the Cape, and was required to send criminal cases to be tried there. European women in Company settlements were sometimes sentenced to penal transportation for imprisonment in Batavia's *Spinhuis* (women's prison). From 1722 to 1757 fewer than twenty women were transported to the Cape as convicts and at least a quarter of these died en route.[56]

---

[54] Robert Ross, *A Concise History of South Africa*. Cambridge, UK: Cambridge University Press, 1999, p. 23.

[55] See, for example, Adolphe Linder, *The Swiss at the Cape of Good Hope 1652–1971*. Basel: Basel Afrika Bibliographien, 1997.

[56] Helena Liebenberg, "Introduction to the Documents of the Court of Justice at the Cape of Good Hope regarding Convicts and Exiles," p. 20. TECP Project, CJ 3186, 1722, 96–97.

From the beginning, the Cape settlement depended upon slave labor and was connected through this labor to the slave-trading circuits of the Company's network of forced migration. The vast majority of slaves at the Cape came from the various Indian Ocean networks of slave-trading. Although the majority of slaves brought to the Cape during the Company period were men, this trade also produced the greatest proportion of women brought to the Cape as slaves.[57] The Company at the Cape utilized slave labor obtained from indigenous slave trading networks onto whose existing patterns of forced migration it overlaid its own slave trading circuit. Slaves from the southwest Indian Ocean – mainly Madagascar, Mauritius, and Mozambique – were traded within a network connecting the Indian Ocean to the Red Sea. Slaves from India or Ceylon were either transported directly across the Indian Ocean or were shipped from their homelands to Batavia and then transported back across the Indian Ocean to the Cape. Slaves from Southeast Asia came from many island polities across the archipelago that fed into subregional slave trades, especially from Makassar and the Bugis region of South Sulawesi, the Moluccas, and the extensive local slave trade from Bali.[58]

Company officials at the Cape sent slaving expeditions only to the southwest Indian Ocean including Madagascar, Mauritius, and the region around Mozambique. However, slaves were also sold at the Cape through the private trade of Company officials and burghers speculating on the slave market and from individuals on foreign ships who did likewise. The Company's slave trade was minor in terms of its proportion to overall trade but significant in terms of its effect on the evolution of colonial societies, particularly at the Cape.[59]

The ethnic origins and identities of these slaves from the eastern Indian Ocean were therefore as complex as their places of origin. Asians who were forcibly migrated as exiles, criminals, and political prisoners were most often incorporated into the Cape's free black population if they survived their sentences. A few of these people managed to be repatriated

---

[57] It would be interesting to compare this form of forced migration with impressments both as a recruiting strategy for the merchant companies and navies in Europe, as well as impressments and capture at sea. J. R. Bruijn, F. S. Gaastra, and I. Schoffer, *Dutch-Asiatic Shipping in the 17th and 18th Centuries*, vol. 1. Rijks geschiedenkundige publicatien, grote serie, nos. 165–167. Den Haag: Martinus Nijhoff, 1979–1987, pp. 143–172. For the latter see Boucher, *Cape of Good Hope and Foreign Contacts*, p. 118.
[58] Armstrong and Worden, "The Slaves," pp. 109–143.
[59] Ibid., pp. 115–117.

to their homelands. Again, the overwhelming majority of Asian exiles and prisoners sentenced to the Cape were men, although the wives and children of high-ranking men often accompanied them into exile. James Armstrong has traced the transportation to the Cape of Chinese men, mostly sent from Batavia, who had been convicted of crimes or exiled as illegal residents. In effect, their forced migration by the Company gave the Chinese trading diaspora a trans-Indian Ocean dimension that incorporated the Company's circuit of forced migration to the Cape.[60]

Consolidation of Company Control at the Cape

The legal system developed by the Dutch East India Company at its headquarters in Batavia, endorsed by the directors in the Netherlands and later extended to the Cape and other of its imperial nodes, articulated two interwoven strands of the rule of law. The first was the specificity of the legal code as it applied to the particular conditions encountered in Batavia. The second was the imperial dimension. Batavia, as headquarters of the VOC outside Europe, created the template for the Company's legal code. Provisions within the Statutes of Batavia allowed other Company nodes to pass their own local laws and resulted in variations on the Company's legal codes.[61] At one end of the spectrum, the VOC trading post on Deshima Island in Nagasaki Bay existed solely with the permission of the Shogun in Edo, and the Company had no right to pass laws beyond control of their own personnel and slaves. At many posts like Surat the VOC was one European trading presence among others in a port city controlled by a local polity. In this case, the Company's attempts to extend its legal system were mitigated by its limited sovereignty. At the other end of the spectrum lay the Cape of Good Hope, where an increasingly assertive and localized settler society developed around the eighteenth century and, despite the initial intentions of the Seventeen Gentlemen, began to demand rights beyond those granted under Company policy and law.

The free burgher population expanded rapidly from 9 in 1657 to 1,334 in 1700 and around 15,000 by the end of the Company period.[62]

---

[60] Armstrong, "Chinese at the Cape."
[61] "The Government at Batavia was *primus inter pares* among the governments of the various possessions. The administration of the *buiten comptoiren* (outposts), and especially the important posts was – *mutas mutandis* – everywhere on the same lines." C. G. Botha, *History of Law, Medicine and Place Names in the Cape of Good Hope. Collected Works*, vol. 2. Cape Town: C Struik, 1962, p. 157.
[62] Schutte, "Company and Colonists," p. 298.

Proportionate with their numbers, Cape colonists sought to maximize their participation in the governance of the colony. Burgher representation on the governing bodies of the colony was minimal and largely advisory until the late eighteenth century. VOC authority weakened in the rural areas and was practically nonexistent in the frontier zones.[63] While Company officials at the Cape sometimes balked at the policies emanating from Batavia, the Cape burgher population did likewise to its local Company authority. Indigenous African resistance to Company sovereignty did not arise in terms of the law but took place on the terrain of conquest and territorial incorporation instead.

The Cape of Good Hope was a peculiar node within the Company's imperial web because it fell outside other indigenous trading and imperial networks and because its main frontier was made internal by the expansion of the rural territories over which the Company government had increasingly less control. The main colonies had jurisdiction over their subregions and were able to pass regulations specific to their needs. They were also the courts of first appeal for criminal cases in which smaller posts, like Mauritius or Rio de la Goa, did not have sufficient administrative capacity.[64] The High Government in Batavia did not attempt, and could not apply, equal levels of control over all Company nodes. The network of forced migration was only one particular VOC imperial circuit that incorporated the Cape into the empire as the farthest link in its chain of bondage.

The ability of the refreshment station at the Cape to adequately service the VOC fleets took several decades from the establishment of the settlement in 1652. Allowing Company servants to become free burghers was designed to save the Company their wages and to offset the costs of maintaining the Cape settlement by levying various taxes upon them.[65] This was the settlement policy followed by the Company in its major

---

[63] Wayne Dooling, "'The Good Opinion of Others': Law, Slavery and Community in the Cape Colony, c.1760–1830," in Nigel Worden and Clifton Crais, *Breaking the Chains: Slavery and Its Legacy in the Nineteenth-Century Cape Colony*, Johannesburg: Witwatersrand University Press, 1994; Nigel Penn, *The Forgotten Frontier: Colonist and Khoikhoi on the Cape's Northern Frontier in the 18th Century*. Athens, OH.: Ohio University Press, 2005.

[64] Van Kan's survey of the Statutes of Batavia as applied to all the *buiten comptoiren* supports his contention that the Statutes of Batavia were indeed the basis of law governing both the center and periphery of the Company's empire. J. van Kan "De Bataviasche Statuten en de Buitencomptoiren," *BKI*, 100, 1941, pp. 255–282.

[65] J. L. Hattingh, "Grondbesit in die Tafelvallei. Deel 1: De Eksperiment: Vryswartes as Grondeienaars, 1652–1710," *Kronos*, 10, 1985, p. 32.

colonies, Batavia, Ceylon, and the Molaccas. All had concentrations of free burghers who were intended to provide the basis of a community loyal to the Company and help consolidate its sovereignty. This strategy was supposed to, but rarely did, reduce the need for a large permanent garrison at each of these crucial trading and plantation settlements.[66] The first Cape commander Van Riebeeck set out the legal position of burghers under the Company as follows:

> They will be subject to the same civil laws and regulations as are in force in the Fatherland or in India, or such other as it may hereafter be deemed necessary to enact in the interest of the Company or for the common good.[67]

All free burghers were obliged to take an oath of loyalty to the States-General, the directors of the Company and their servants. They were not "free" in the sense of being outside legal control of the Company and coming under Company law, and the Company reserved the right to forcibly reenlist free burghers into the Company as a criminal sentence. Reenlistment for a free burger was a harsh punishment that normally entailed being transferred to another Company node. It was, in effect, a sentence of penal transportation. However, banishment for Cape burghers was most often imposed locally to Robben Island as a criminal sentence without the accompanying punishment of forcible reenlistment.[68] Whereas in the early lean years free burghers availed themselves of the opportunity to reenlist to escape poverty, increasingly the potential for forcible reenlistment and penal transportation was later resented by them.

The Company's power to banish inhabitants under its jurisdiction was common throughout the empire. What differed among the settlements were the patterns of imposing this punishment. The Cape was tied into the circuit of exile and penal transportation emanating mainly from Batavia and Colombo. It used Robben Island as its main site of banishment, and to a lesser extent Mauritius and Rio de la Goa when these sites were available, but it did not often send criminals to Batavia or Colombo. As the Company established rural outposts, a few of which developed into small towns, the government's range of internal incarceration sites was

---

[66] Schutte, "Company and Colonists," p. 289.
[67] Thom, ed., *Journal of Jan van Riebeeck*, vol. 2, p. 90.
[68] Theuntje van Warden, a burgher's wife, was one of the first European civilians sentenced to criminal transportation, having apparently caused quite a stir in the small community by slandering the other women of the Cape. On September 7, 1663, she was "sentenced to retract the slander in public, to ask forgiveness of God and justice, to be bound to a post for one hour, and to be banished to Dassen Island for six weeks." Abstract of Criminal Convictions before the Court of Justice, Cape of Good Hope, 1662–1672, in Moodie, ed., *The Record*, p. 311.

extended. Exiles and convicts were sent to Company outposts to perform public labor. Occasionally, exiles were banished to rural settlements or farms and the free burghers had no say in the matter.

During the first years of the Cape settlement the government consisted of the Council of Policy, headed by the commander and the highest-ranking Company officers who, at the beginning of settlement, also tried criminal cases. From 1656 on, this body also met with additional officers who comprised the Council of Justice and the military court. From 1657 on, burgher councilors were granted positions on the Council of Justice on cases dealing with burghers in an advisory capacity only. Free burghers were not officially part of the Council of Policy, although in practice they were regularly consulted about matters of importance to their welfare. Even with a burgher presence on the governing and judicial bodies of the Cape, decisions were vested in Company officials and were not subject to the approval of free burghers. The commander (who from 1671 held the rank of governor) had final veto power over all decisions in the courts and government. Governance was therefore tied very much into Company rule and patronage.

As the halfway-station for the journey between the Netherlands and Batavia, the Cape was often visited by councilors of the Indies and governors-general en route. Occasionally, councilors of the Indies were specifically sent to the Cape by the governor-general in Batavia or the Seventeen Gentlemen to review the Cape government and make recommendations for reforms. When these high-ranking visitors were at the Cape, they outranked the Cape governor and became the *de facto* rulers of the colony, able to institute reforms without approval of the Cape officials. During early 1685, there was actually a clash of wills between two visiting commissioners. Ordinary Councillor Rykloff van Goens, Jr. was prevented by Commissioner Hendrick Adriaan van Rheede tot Drakenstein from taking two Company slaves and repatriating a number of Asian convicts to Batavia when he departed the Cape. Van Rheede was the more senior officer and objected to Van Goens's plan.[69] The official separation of the Council of Policy and the Council of Justice came from Van Rheede's orders to Governor Simon van der Stel. Van Rheede also ratified Van der Stel's treatment of the Khoekhoe in negotiations for the Company.[70] Moreover, the appointment of governors and

---

[69] M. W. Spilhaus, *Company's Men*. Cape Town: John Malherbe, 1973, pp. 109–110.
[70] Schutte, "Company and Colonists," p. 292; Hilton Basil Fine, "Administration of Criminal Justice at the Cape of Good Hope 1795–1828." unpublished PhD dissertation, University of Cape Town, 1991, pp. 108–125. Hahlo and Kahn outline the details of

high-ranking officials to the Cape came from the recommendations of the High Government in Batavia to the Seventeen Gentlemen who ratified the new appointments. In this way, the VOC's imperial hierarchy was strengthened and maintained at the highest level of appointments and promotions.

In the first few decades of settlement, the Cape was clearly a hardship posting for an ambitious Company official. Van Riebeeck himself begged to be removed to the Indies almost from the moment he arrived in Africa.[71] By the end of the seventeenth century, with the districts immediately adjacent to the Cape Peninsula having been allocated in land grants for mixed wheat, wine, sheep and cattle farming, even the Cape governors had begun to profit from their postings to Africa. They would never amass the fortunes made from trade in some of the Company's Asian nodes, but some could and did style themselves as a landed aristocracy, holding court at the Castle of Good Hope.

With the decision to make the Cape settlement permanent in the late seventeenth century, the Company made a more concerted effort to attract free settlers to the Cape. Between 1679 and 1707, the Seventeen Gentlemen offered free passage from the Netherlands to the Cape of Good Hope. Until 1717, free land grants were also available. The district of

---

the development of these bodies. At first the Council consisted of the commander and the ships' captains. From 1656 the commander, *secunde* (second in charge), garrison sergeant, and bookkeeper comprised the Council, with the fort constable and two corporals added for judicial and military matters. After 1660, the *Fiscal* and surgeon served on the Council and over the next twenty-five years, as the settlement grew, further officers were appointed. When the VOC fleet was present, the ships' captains and highest-ranking officers could be added to the Council. If the highest-ranking officer outranked the Cape governor he would preside over the Council. The governor could override the majority decision at his discretion. The minutes and decisions of Council were recorded by the secretary, and signed by all present. H. R. Halo and E. Kahn, *South African Legal System and Its Background*. Cape Town: Juta, 1968, pp. 537–539.

[71] Van Riebeeck was already seeking promotion out of the Cape before he took up the commission. After one year in Africa, his request to be transferred reflected a fair assessment of the position of the Cape in the imperial scheme of things for an ambitious Company officer: "I will now, to conclude, most humbly, respectfully, and earnestly pray, that your Honors will think of removing me hence to India... for, among these dull, stupid, lazy, stinking people, little address is required as among the Japanese, Tonquinese and other precise nations thereabouts, who... give enough to do to the brains of the cleverest Dutchman; and here there is nothing to be done, except to barter a few sheep and cattle..." Extract from a despatch from Commander Van Riebeeck to the Chamber XVII. April 14, 1653. Quoted in Moodie, ed., *The Record*, p. 32. In 1662, Van Riebeeck was promoted to Governor of Malacca. His Indies-born son, Adriaan van Riebeeck, reached the pinnacle of the Company hierarchy in 1709 as governor-general. Moodie, ed., *The Record*, p. 254.

Stellenbosch was established in 1679, Drakenstein in 1685, and Franschhoek in 1688, thereby expanding the borders of the colony well beyond the Cape port settlement.[72] The biggest single influx of free settlers to the Cape came around 1688 when French Huguenots fleeing persecution in Europe were encouraged to settle there. The arrival of 180 Huguenots boosted the free burgher population considerably. As the settler population grew and extended beyond the established grain, wine, and mixed farming regions into places where more pastoral farming activities could take place, they also became increasingly linked through kinship networks that reproduced hierarchies of settler elites and marginalized farming clans.

By the end of the seventeenth century, there were 1,334 free burghers at the Cape, and the boundaries of the colony stretched well beyond the immediate protection of the Castle garrison. While security was supplemented by the extension of fortifications, free burghers were interested in their own communities' protection. However, they did not prove to be reliable defenders of the Company's interests.[73] The Cape of Good Hope was a slave colony completely dependent on slave labor to extend the rural and urban economy, with the Company itself being the largest slave owner. The extension of legal institutions was designed to uphold this social hierarchy at the Cape. This included dominance over the Khoekhoe who, as their own communities disintegrated through the conquest of their land and confiscation and theft of their cattle, were increasingly incorporated into colonial society as semi-bonded labor in the rural areas, though they were not legally enslaved.

Local institutions of administration and law were established in these settler districts, establishing a pattern of local administration that lasted until the end of Company rule that was also retained under the British. In 1682, four of the leading settlers in the Stellenbosch district formed the *Heemraden* (Council). In 1685, a Company official was appointed as *Landdrost* (magistrate) to oversee the Council. This body served as a district council and had jurisdiction over petty civil cases between settlers, and in such cases the *Landdrost* served as public prosecutor. The *Landdrost* and Council were assisted at the interdistrict level by settlers appointed as *Veldcornets* (district constables). The constables basically policed the local regions but none of these officials were initially empowered to deal with criminal cases. They were obliged only to collect evidence

---

[72] Hattingh, "Grondbesit in die Tafelvallei," p. 32.
[73] Schutte, "Company and Colonists," pp. 298–300.

to be presented to the Court of Justice and to forward all cases to the Castle for trial.[74]

VOC-Khoekhoe Relations to the End of the Seventeenth Century

The outcome of the First Khoekhoe-Dutch War was not decisive and a cycle of stock theft and land occupation by settlers prompted reprisals from the displaced Khoekhoe. In the 1660 peace negotiations with the Company officials, Goringhaiqua and Gorachoqua leaders were forced to cede sovereignty over the land around the Cape settlement to the Company.[75] Tensions in both free burgher and Khoekhoe communities increased with the extension of pastoral farming within and beyond the borders of the Company colony and resulted in competition over natural resources.[76] A significant shift in the legal status of the Khoekhoe in terms of Company jurisdiction occurred in the early 1670s. Firstly, Gogosoa's son, Osingkhimma, signed a treaty on April 19, 1672, selling the Cape to the VOC. In an extract of Resolution of the Council of Policy, the Company reasoned their demands for a series of treaties with Khoekhoe leaders in terms of establishing sovereignty over the Cape:[77]

> The Commissioner [Aernout van Overbeke] stated to the meeting that he had been reflecting whether it might not be both practicable and serviceable to the Company... that we should try to enter into an agreement with some Hottentoos.... whereby they should declare us to be the rightful and lawful possessors of this Cape District, and its dependencies, lawfully sold and ceded to the Company, or to us the Company's servants, for a specified sum of money; in order thus more firmly to establish our masters in their right of property... it was resolved and determined to enter into such an agreement accordingly, in the first place with

---

[74] Wayne Dooling, *Law and Community in a Slave Society: Stellenbosch District, South Africa, c.1760–1820*. Communication no. 23. Cape Town: Centre for African Studies, University of Cape Town, 1992, pp. 2–3. Dooling argues that the rule of law must be understood at the local level, and that at the Cape, settlers mediated access to the law to maintain control over community membership and exert power over their slaves and servants. His argument about the incomplete hegemony of settler rule must, however, be extended to the level of imperial law and the power of the central court to banish settlers convicted of serious crimes and to slave codes that were determined by the Council. Nevertheless Dooling's argument about the strength of local institutions of law in the transition to British rule is extremely convincing.

[75] Elphick, *Kraal and Castle*, pp. 111–114.

[76] R. Elphick and V. C. Malherbe, "The Khoisan to 1828," in Elphick and Giliomee, eds., *Shaping of South African Society*, p. 12.

[77] Extract of Resolution of Council, April 13, 1672. Moodie, ed., *The Record*, p. 317.

the Hottentoo Captain Manckihagou, alias Schacher, as hereditary sovereign (*Erf Heer*) of the lands, on which the company has already established her residency at the Cape, and in its district;... and also hereafter to do the same without delay, with the other neighbouring Hottentoos....

The important articles in the treaty were: first, the article in which Osingkhimma ceded the Cape of Good Hope in perpetuity to the Company; second, the article in which Osingkhimma agreed to be the enemy of the Company's enemies, particularly any European power that might attempt to settle at the Cape; third, the article in which the Company reserved the right to adjudicate any disagreement between the Khoekhoe nations; and, finally, the Khoekhoe obligation to pay an annual tribute to the Company in livestock.[78] Two weeks later, on May 5, the Company signed an identical contract with "the minor Prince D'houuw, hereditary sovereign of the country called by us Hottentoos Holland, and its dependencies, assisted by the Hottentot chief Dackkgy (alias Cuyper) *stadhouder* (regent) and guardian of the prince, and the captain Oyth'key, his counselor and representative."[79] In return, Company officials documented that they had given the Khoekhoe leaders goods amounting to four thousand reals of eight. In effect, the Khoekhoe leaders were ceding control within European law over their own lifeblood and submitting themselves to Company jurisdiction within these lands.

These treaties were drafted and signed under Commissioner Arnout van Overbeke, commander of the return fleet, who was a member of the Council of Justice in Batavia. He had been instructed to negotiate the purchase of the Cape to resolve the ongoing disputes between the Khoekhoe and the Company.[80] Colonial history is replete with such unequal treaties.[81] In this case the treaties cleared the way for further military action against the Cochoqua.[82]

The Cape treaties need to be seen in the context of the extension of territorial sovereignty by the Company throughout its empire. Company treaties with indigenous rulers legitimated Company sovereignty on two levels. First, in terms of European international law, the treaties foreclosed any attempt by rival European powers to make territorial claims in the

---

[78] Moodie, ed., *The Record*, p. 318.   [79] Ibid, pp. 318–319.
[80] "Kaap de Goede Hoop, 19 April 1672," in J. E. Heeres and F. W. Stapel, eds., *Corpus Diplomaticum Neerlando-Indicum. Versameling van politieke contractenen verdere vedagen door de Nederlanders in het Oosten gesloten. Tweede Deel (1650–1675)*, Bijdragen tot de Taal- Land- en Volkenkunde*, pp. 466–467.
[81] Elphick, *Kraal and Castle*, p. 124.
[82] Marks, "Khoisan Resistance," p. 67, fn. 50.

vicinity of Company settlements.[83] Second, they were also meant to alter the power relationships between the Company and indigenous polities through the official extension of Company jurisdiction over territory in its possession. The Cape treaties were signed before the outbreak of the Second Khoekhoe-Dutch War (1673 to 1677). Military actions taken by the VOC had resulted in considerable losses of livestock for the Cochoqua people. Thereafter, the Cochoqua, under their leader Gonnema, concluded a peace treaty with the new Cape commander Joan Bax.[84] From this time onward, the Company began to assert its jurisdiction over the Khoekhoe polities, intervene in their disputes, and enforce the Company's decisions.[85]

It is not at all likely that the Company and Khoekhoe leaders shared a common perception of these treaties being binding in perpetuity. The Company's insistence on ascribing European concepts of royalty to the Khoekhoe leaders, thereby granting legitimacy to conclude such treaties under international law, were clearly an invention for that purpose. Company documents during this era reveal that many Company officials understood that Khoekhoe concepts of territorial sovereignty were different, but they knew nothing about Khoekhoe cosmology that centered on the intimate connection between people and the land. It was painfully obvious to the Khoekhoe that they lost rights to the use of their land and were forced to pay tribute to the Company. The last of these treaties signed in 1677 signaled a shift in the Company's perception of its own sovereignty over the Cape. This treaty was legitimated solely with respect to the Company's own imperial legal system for the enforcement of its own rules by whatever means necessary.

The final major assault took place against one of the Company's own Khoekhoe allies, the Chainouqua clan of Dohra, after which his herds were confiscated by Van der Stel and he was imprisoned temporarily on Robben Island. The Seventeen Gentlemen rebuked Van der Stel for taking these actions against a Company ally.[86] The strategies left to the Khoekhoe were to flee, submit to tribute demands from the Company, or, as increasingly was the case, become incorporated into the rural colonial labor force alongside Company slaves.

---

[83] Worden, Van Heyningen, and Bickford-Smith, *Cape Town*, p. 36.
[84] Elphick, *Kraal and Castle*, pp. 132–133.
[85] Elphick and Malherbe, "The Khoisan to 1828," p. 14.
[86] Ibid., pp. 14–17.

The treaties validated an extension of jurisdiction that had been in practice since the beginning of 1672. Prior to this time, the Khoekhoe who were accused of crimes against the Company were ransomed by members of their own community with no further punishment or were turned over to their community for punishment specific to their crimes after the payment of ransom to the Company in the form livestock. In early 1672, five Khoekhoe men were taken into custody by settlers and brought to the Company castle for stock theft.[87] Instead of accepting the usual ransom, the Council of Justice insisted on convicting them under Company criminal law and sentencing them to banishment on Robben Island. This was not the same as banishment of hostages, which had become common practice, but, rather, a criminal conviction entered into the Company's criminal roll and carried out under the standard procedures for criminal sentences.[88]

The legality of this conviction under Company law is dubious, because it occurred prior to the signing of the treaty establishing Company sovereignty over the Cape. Elphick proposes that the case was argued by the *Fiscal* (prosecutor) on the basis of the applicability of the Laws of Nature and the Laws of Nations to the Khoekhoe and therefore the Company's rights to inflict punishment for crimes contravening these universal laws.[89] Despite the philosophical arguments underpinning the prosecution, the meaning of the conviction would have been clear to everyone present, for the sentence was carried out under the standard

---

[87] That same year, the first conviction of a European burgher for the manslaughter of a Khoekhoe took place. Willem Willemsz fled by ship to the Netherlands before his arrest. He was convicted in absentia and banished from the Cape for life. But he returned to the Cape with a written pardon from the Prince of Orange. The Cape authorities thought the pardon was a fake and banished him to Robben Island pending the pardon's verification. After being banished from there to Batavia, he again illegally returned to the Cape and was banished again, this time to Mauritius for life. Meanwhile, his wife had lived in concubinage with another man, for which she was banished to the *Spinhuis* in Batavia and her lover to Robben Island. Several historians have written both about the suicide of Sara and about the Willemsz case as foundational in the evolution of the Cape's legal system. See A. J. Böeseken, "Die Verhouding tussen Blank en Nie-Blank in Suid-Afrika aan die hand van die Vroegste Dokumente," *South African Historical Journal*, 2, November, 1970, p. 10; Elphick, *Kraal and Castle*, p. 184; Robert Ross, "The Changing Legal Position of the Khoisan," in *Beyond the Pale: Essays on the History of Colonial South Africa*. Johannesburg: Witwatersrand University Press, 1994, pp. 174–175. This case clearly shows the subservience of the Cape to the legal hierarchies in the empire and the effective use of banishment in the circuit of forced migration. Moodie, ed., *The Record*, pp. 326–355.

[88] Elphick, *Kraal and Castle*, p. 127.   [89] Ibid., p. 184.

procedures for criminal convictions, including the spectacle of public flogging and branding before being hauled off to Robben Island.[90] The Khoekhoe were now subject to Company law and not their own.

One sad event pondered by historians reveals how the Company elite had rationalized their legal decisions regarding the applicability of VOC law to the Khoekhoe. A young Khoekhoe woman living in the Cape village, Sara, hanged herself in December 1671. Sara had been raised in the settlement and employed as a servant by a free black family and consequently was tried for the crime of suicide and sentenced postmortem under Company law to have her body defiled. Suicide was a complicated cultural crime in any slave society because slave suicide was the ultimate act of personal resistance and simultaneously a crime against property. Sara's case was more ambiguous because she was legally free. This is an interesting case, because it set out clearly the grounds upon which Company jurisdiction was extended to Khoekhoe who had been acculturated into European society.[91] After the signing of the treaties, conformity to the "Dutch way of life" or residence in the household of a person under Company jurisdiction was no longer necessary to prove grounds for prosecution.

---

[90] Extract from the Journal kept in the Fort of Good Hope, January 10 to March 11, 1672, in Moodie, ed., *The Record*, pp. 316–317.

[91] The Court of Justice determined on December 18, 1671 that "a certain Dutch female Hottentot, had this morning hanged and thus strangled herself... as the said female Hottentot [Sara]... had resided from her childhood with the Company's servants or free men... and had thus acquired the full use of our language and of the Portuguese, and become habituated to our manners and mode of dress; and as she had also frequently attended Divine service, and had furthermore, (as is presumed) lived in concubinage with our, or other German people, not having any particular familiarity with her kindred or countrymen... It is concluded that the said Hottentot can not be any longer considered as having led the usual heathenish or savage Hottentot mode of life... and this animal then, has not only – actuated by a diabolical inspiration – transgressed against the laws of nature, which are common to all created beings; but also – as a consequence of her said education – through her Dutch mode of life – against the law of nations, and the civil law – for, having enjoyed the *good* of our kind favor [sic] and protection, she must consequently be subject to the rigorous punishment of *evil*; seeing that those who live under our protection, from whatever part of the world they may have come, and whether they be Christians or heathens, may be justly called our subjects – And as this act was committed in our *territorium*, and in a free man's house under our jurisdiction; which should be purified from this foul sin, and such evil doers, and enemies of their own persons and lives visited with the most rigorous punishment." Moodie, ed., *The Record*, pp. 315–316. Sara's corpse was sentenced to judicial defilement and her property confiscated. Kerry Ward, "Knocking on Death's Door: Mapping Spectrums of Bondage and Status through Marking the Dead at the Cape," Worden, ed., *Contingent Lives*, pp. 391–413.

The extension of territorial sovereignty by implication changed Company jurisdiction from being embodied in people to being resident on the land. The criminal roll for 1678 records five Khoekhoe, who were known subjects of Osingkhimma, as being convicted of repeated livestock theft and sentenced to be hanged under Company criminal law.[92] By the end of the seventeenth century, the Khoekhoe increasingly came under Company jurisdiction and were tried and sentenced to the death penalty, the ultimate imposition of legal sovereignty over the individual. The Khoekhoe were recognized as free and equal before the law, but increasingly not as sovereign subjects of their own independent polities.[93] This process was consistent with a shift toward definitions of territorial jurisdiction emanating from Batavia and points to the important distinctions between imperial nodes. The signing of the treaties in the late seventeenth century was therefore a turning point in the philosophy and practice of Company rule at the Cape.

Elphick and Malherbe point to one of the symbolic markers of this new sense of sovereignty as manifested in the Company. With the arrival of the new Governor, Simon van der Stel, in 1679, the Company began to assert its authority to approve the appointment of new Khoekhoe chiefs and bestowed upon them an engraved copper-headed cane as a mark of office. In doing so, the Company symbolically asserted its own sovereignty and the subservience of the Khoekhoe polities as clients of the Company rather than as equal allies. These copper-tipped canes became a marker of allegiance to the Company by Khoekhoe leaders and were items of prestige, but they were not equivalent to indigenous regalia imbued with cultural and spiritual power as objects. Regalia in Southeast Asian polities contained mystical powers that were part of the authentification of kingship and the power of these objects was not entirely in the control of the beholder. Company authorities in Batavia recognized the cultural meaning of these objects and sometimes held regalia "hostage" to extract cooperation from indigenous rulers.

At the Cape, both the Company and the Khoekhoe were aware that the relationship embodied in the copper-tipped cane was a creation of the VOC. When Khoekhoe leaders wanted to break their treaties with

---

[92] Abstract of Criminal Convictions before the Court of Justice in the Castle of the Cape of Good Hope 1672–1682, Moodie, ed., *The Record*, p. 383.
[93] Ross, "The Changing Legal Position of the Khoisan," *Beyond the Pale: Essays on the History of Colonial South Africa*. Johannesburg: Witwatersrand University Press, 1994, pp. 166–182. I disagree with Ross' argument that the Company had a nonterritorial concept of the extension of jurisdiction at the Cape.

the Company they returned the cane to the governor at the castle. The cane had no meaning outside this relationship. The Company employed a somewhat similar strategy in its relationships with the indigenous clans in Formosa. A rattan cane with a silver tip emblazoned with the Company's insignia was presented to village heads to symbolize their relationship as vassals of the Company's highest-ranking official at Fort Zeelandia. The Company began an annual ritual of reclaiming and reassigning the staffs as a strategy to fix a system of rotating authority of elders to replace the more fluid indigenous system of village councils. The invented Dutch rituals and regalia symbolizing lord-vassal relations between the Company and the Formosans were only partly successful.[94] In Formosa, as at the Cape, this symbolic subservience could also be made manifest by the use of force. Simon van der Stel demonstrated this in 1693 when, cane or no cane, he banished Dohra, leader of the western Chainouqua clan, to Robben Island for "disloyalty."[95]

The Van der Stel Dispute

A shift in governance at the Cape began with the governorships of Simon van der Stel (1679 to 1699) and his son Willem Adriaan (1699 to 1707). While the settled regions of the western Cape were under the control of the Company and were governed through Company law and administration with the establishment of formal districts,[96] the expanding frontier was "illegally" inhabited by pastoral farmers outside the official Company realm who were locked in a perpetual struggle with the Khoisan over resources of land and labor.[97] In 1685, Simon van der Stel signed the last formal peace and cooperation treaty at the Cape of Good Hope with the Namaquas of the west coast region, which was supposed to ensure the safety of free trade.[98] Curiously, Governor van der Stel invited the exiled Makassarese noble Daeng Mangale and his servant to join his entourage to Namaqualand.[99] Whether Van der Stel sought out Daeng Mangale's company for social or political purposes is unknown and both explanations are likely. It is probable this invitation would not have been approved by Batavia as falling within the prince's conditions of exile, but

---

[94] Andrade, *How Taiwan Became Chinese*, chapter 9.
[95] Elphick and Malherbe, "Khoisan to 1828," pp. 14–15.
[96] Dooling, *Law and Community*, pp. 2–3. [97] Penn, *The Forgotten Frontier*.
[98] "Kaap de Goede Hoop, 14 October 1685," Heeres and Stapel, eds., *Corpus Diplomaticum, vol. 3*, p. 387.
[99] Spilhaus, *Company's Men*, p. 123.

it is interesting to speculate how the Cape burghers would have responded to their governor seeking the companionship of a prisoner of state exiled as an enemy of the Company by the Batavian authorities. No comment on Daeng Mangale's role in the expedition is made in the official diary of the expedition, nor on the languages members of the party used to communicate.[100] That Daeng Mangale was included in the governor's party is just one example of the complex inversions of status that took place at the Cape.

The father–son governorships of the Van der Stels were indicative of the patriarchal networks within the Company elite. Simon was born in Mauritius, the son of the commander, Adriaan, who was promoted to a high-ranking post in Ceylon, where he died. Adriaan van der Stel was also a child of the Company whose mother was a Christianized Portuguese-Indian from the Coromandel Coast. After his father's death, Simon was raised in Batavia and sent to the Netherlands for education. He married into one of the wealthiest regent elite families in Holland, the Six-Hinlopens. Simon van der Stel used his connections to be appointed commander at the Cape of Good Hope, taking his children but leaving his wife in Amsterdam. It was under his rule that the town developed its civic buildings and the formal extension of rural towns began, the first of which was named in his honor, Stellenbosch. Simon van der Stel was also instrumental in searching for mineral resources, particularly copper, in Namaqualand. After his retirement to his country estate Constantia, he oversaw his slave labor force to produce a fine wine that bore its name and gained fame for the Cape in Europe.[101]

Over time, divisions of wealth within the Cape became more marked within the settler population and among Company personnel. The 1685 decree by Commissioner Van Rheede under instructions from the Seventeen Gentlemen included a provision to set up the office of Independent *Fiscal*. The *Fiscal*, appointed by and directly answerable to the Seventeen Gentlemen, was part of their effort to counter the increasingly independent power base of the Company elite in the colonies.[102] The *Fiscal* was granted a seat on the Council of Policy, and the position was retained for the rest of the Company period.[103] These measures by the Seventeen

---

[100] Gilbert Waterhouse, ed., *Simon van der Stel's Journal of His Expedition to Namaqualand, 1685–1686*. London: Longmans Green, pp. 3 & 113.
[101] A. J. Böeseken, *Simon van der Stel en Sy Kinders*. Kaapstad: Nasou Beperk, 1984.
[102] Visagie, *Regspleging en Reg*, p. 46.
[103] Botha, "Administration of the Cape of Good Hope, 1652–1834," p. 232.

Gentlemen were of limited success due to resistance by the Company's imperial elite.

The apparent creation of a ruling family with rural estates and a patrimonial network at the Cape that favored allies of the Van der Stels against other free burghers proved to be a recipe for discontent. Willem Adriaan van der Stel's governorship culminated a trend in the Cape toward territorial expansion begun under his father's reign. He authorized the extension of the frontier of occupied territory beyond the arable south-western Cape further into the interior where pastoralism was the only practical form of land use. During the governorship of Willem Adriaan van der Stel, conflicts between the Company elite and their close settler allies against that section of the Cape colonists who felt alienated from the profiteering of the Company came to a head. Many of the disaffected colonists were themselves mostly wealthy men in direct competition with the Van der Stels and their clique for marketing their produce to the Company.[104] The colonists found allies in the poorer sections of the settlers' colony removed from the regent class of the Van der Stels.

In 1705, the governor's opponents drafted their complaints in a petition to Council of the Indies sent directly to the Seventeen Gentlemen. The main instigators, the farmers Henning Hüsing and his nephew Adam Tas, were eloquent and determined in their opposition to the favoritism they believed was undermining the livelihood and rights of their fellow free burghers.[105] In his diary, Adam Tas noted disparagingly that the Governor had induced free blacks, including ex-convicts, to sign his petition.[106] Van der Stel had the Council of Justice banish one of his critics to Batavia for insubordination and imprisoned others, including Adam Tas, in a castle cell where he spent the next thirteen months. The governor drafted a counter-petition to the Seventeen Gentlemen to answer the charges of corruption which was partly an attempt to undermine the reputation of the Cape burghers who opposed him.

---

[104] Penn, *Forgotten Frontier*, pp. 30–31.
[105] Leo Fouché, ed., A. J. Böeseken, rev. and J. Smuts, trans., *The Diary of Adam Tas 1705–1706*. Van Riebeeck Society 2nd series, no. 1. Cape Town: Van Riebeeck Society, 1970. Fouché's introduction is a classic example of the historical interpretation of a conservative racist in apartheid South Africa. He attributes Willem Adriaan's actions to his "mixed blood" that created a "throw-back ... half Oriental" that lead him to manifest Oriental ostentation and despotism, p. 11. Instead, both Van der Stels used access to resources for their own profit in ways not dissimilar to many other Company elite officials at other posts around the empire. The difference in this situation was the presence of free burghers who were in competition with the Company.
[106] Schoeman, *Early Slavery*, p. 378.

The Seventeen Gentlemen were sensitive to the charges of profiteering that were laid against Willem Adriaan. They had Van der Stel removed from his post and his properties auctioned off but did not pursue any further punishment.[107] Du Toit and Giliomee have characterized this incident as "basically a refreshment post dispute which revolved around the question of who was to produce the supplies."[108] A more nuanced reading by Schutte of the incident focuses on the increasingly localized sentiments of the petitioners, Van der Stel's response, and the actions of the Seventeen Gentlemen in light of shifting regent factions in the Netherlands. He further identifies how both the colonists' and Van der Stel's petitions were drafted to appeal to the Seventeen Gentlemen as the sovereign rulers of Cape.[109] Significantly for this book, Schoeman emphasizes the wrath the free burghers directed toward Van der Stel because he included ex-convicts who had become part of the free black population as his signatories in his counterpetition. They questioned the honor of the governor in putting ex-convicts on equal social footing with free burghers.[110]

The dispute between the free burgher faction and Governor van der Stel contains several implications for the Cape within the VOC imperial web. It is significant that Van der Stel had one of his opponents immediately banished to Batavia. This was possibly a strategy to warn other colonists of the implications of defying Company power. The Company was fully within its legal rights to exile people living within its jurisdiction. Within the free burghers' petition was a complaint against Van der Stel regarding the governor's manipulation of the local labor supply.

> Should a freeman require a man-servant for agriculture, and ask the Governor for such a man on loan out of the Company's service, he is never... given by the Governor... And if it happens that he wishes to get rid of a man in his service, he does not allow a burgher to have him (although he is a fit man for farm work), but sends him away from his farm to Batavia or Ceylon, not desiring that he should live with any other person afterwards, or remain in the Castle.[111]

The colonists' complaint, whether real or imagined, indicates a sense in which the governor was able to assert his authority and access to imperial networks and use these powers in ways that were not available

---

[107] Schutte, "Company and Colonists," pp. 304–305.
[108] Andre du Toit and Hermann Giliomee, *Afrikaner Political Thought: Analysis and Documents, Volume One: 1780–1850*. Cape Town: David Philip, 1983, p. 5.
[109] Schutte, "Company and Colonists," pp. 305–307.
[110] Schoeman, *Early Slavery*, pp. 375–381.
[111] H. C. V. Liebbrandt, ed., *Precis of the Archives of the Cape of Good Hope: The Defense of Willem Adriaan van der Stel*. Cape Town: Government Printers, 1897, p. 60.

or acceptable to the colonists. It is an indication the colonists felt they had no access to the wider imperial networks of the Company and that they considered themselves victims of Company rule because of the potential that the Company might punish them with exile or exclude them from the Company labor supply.

Batavia sought to reassert its supreme authority in the face of local discontent against Company officials at the Cape. In the aftermath of the Van der Stel dispute, the governor-general and the Council of the Indies authorized Cornelis Johan Simons to act as commissioner during his return journey to Europe. Simons reiterated to the Cape authorities "that the Statutes of Batavia were to supersede all *plakaaten* issued [at the Cape] on the same subjects of which it treated."[112] This was confirmed a year later in correspondence from the Seventeen Gentlemen. By 1715, the Cape Council of Justice again appealed to the governor-general to clarify which regulations took precedence. They were told once more that the Statutes of Batavia were to be applied where they did not conflict with local Cape laws.[113]

With this decision, the first crisis of local authority was over, although tensions between the Company and colonists remained unresolved. Locally born colonists were balking increasingly against the Company's monopolies and assertions that its interests were primary. Class interests were diverging between the rich and poor among both rural and urban free burghers. Early in the eighteenth century, the predominant forms of access to land at the Cape had shifted from freehold grants to loan farms that required the payment of rent to the Company and could revert to Company ownership at the end of the grant period or upon nonpayment of rent. Although the colonists needed access to Company markets they increasingly resented the monopolistic practices of the Company that kept a stranglehold on the local economy and controlled their access to farming land. The colonists were not able to challenge the Company's control over the provisioning trade because they had no direct access to harbors or shipping networks, both of which remained firmly in the hands of the VOC.

---

[112] C. G. Botha, "The Common and Statute Law at the Cape of Good Hope during the 17th and 18th Centuries," in *History of Law, Medicine and Place Names in the Cape of Good Hope*. Cape Town: C. Struik, 1962, p. 46.

[113] Cornelis Johan Simons had been independent *fiscal* at the Cape from 1690 to 1694, then governor of Ceylon. He was instructed to act as commissioner to review the situation at the Cape by the governor-general and council of the Indies on his return to Europe in 1708. Botha, "Common and Statute Law," pp. 43–46.

Cape Town as a Transoceanic Port City

The colonists pursued their interests on land and viewed the sea as important only insofar as the ships that traversed the oceans created a market for their goods when they came into harbor or could take their produce to other markets overseas. The perspective of the Cape as an oceanic crossroads taken in this chapter, shifts the analytic focus from the dynamics of colonial settlement on the land to the process of the movement of people within an empire along networks that connected imperial nodes through seaborne transport networks. It thereby disrupts a territorial center-periphery analysis of empire by showing how and why various imperial networks were created, how they linked nodes in the imperial web, and how one locality was connected to other localities as well as to the entire imperial web. At the Dutch East India Company node at the Cape of Good Hope, this is particularly relevant because the evolution of this colony depended primarily upon its links with multiple networks by sea and upon the density of the shipping network itself for its existence.

Ship numbers entering the Cape roadstead fluctuated seasonally and annually depending on a number of factors. First, the state of alliances between the United Provinces and other European states determined which ships had permission to enter Table Bay. Company officials could deny anchorage or provisions to foreign ships, although supplying these services was profitable for the Company, and more particularly for the colonists, so it became increasingly problematic for the Company to deny these demands or to curtail private trade. Between 1700 and 1714, over one thousand ships anchored in Table Bay, with only 64 percent of these belonging to the Company. During the mid-eighteenth century these numbers fluctuated and they increased significantly in its later decades.

Combined with the annual fluctuation in the number of ships was the seasonal nature of shipping. Ships were most commonly in harbor for approximately a month during the southern hemisphere summer and autumn (December to May), and this created a massive seasonal fluctuation in the average annual urban population of the Cape.[114] The population of the Cape was therefore tied to its role as a port city with a similar seasonally based pattern to other port polities in the Indian Ocean dependent on monsoon winds for their main trading and shipping networks.

---

[114] Worden, Van Heyningen, and Bickford-Smith, *Cape Town*, pp. 52–53. The main source for information about Company shipping is Bruijn, Gaastra, and Schoffer, *Dutch-Asiatic Shipping*.

The patterns of these sojourning populations to the Cape were quite different in size and duration from most other Indian Ocean ports, including those operated by other European empires. In particular, the exclusively European shipping network that connected at the Cape isolated the Company colony from broader patterns of trade in the Indian Ocean region and from alternative African and Asian shipping networks. The Cape, therefore, never became a major trading entrepôt.

Nevertheless, the ethnic composition of ships' crews changed over the course of the Company period. There was an increasing proportion of Asian and African crews sailing on European ships from the mid-eighteenth century onward. This different composition of ships' crews provisioning at the Cape, rather than the Cape's participation in regional trade networks, intensified the cosmopolitan nature of the Cape's already ethnically diverse colonial population. However, in stressing the European nature of shipping networks, one concentrates on the ownership of vessels and not on the people who were sojourning at the Cape and the other refreshment stations in these transoceanic networks.

Cape Town emerged during the Company period as a littoral society fundamentally engaged with the provisioning of ships at the intersection of multiple imperial networks of trade, information, and migration across the Atlantic and Indian Oceans. The Dutch imperial networks are of primary importance because the Company, by virtue of its territorial possession of the Cape and its harbors, was able to control access to these shipping networks as they intersected with the city. David Hancock's characterization of the Atlantic world has direct resonance for the Cape.

[T]o accentuate inter-imperial behaviour over intra-imperial behaviour would be to miscast reality. One really needs to present both. In its identification of a community more-or-less oceanic, the Atlantic history perspective, if it is to be anything more than boiled-over imperial history, must accentuate cross-boundary exchanges... At the same time, it extends our understanding of how real people constructed their commercial, social and cultural lives out of plural demands and influences, especially how marginal members of society wove together threads from local and international sources to create syncretically new social phenomena and cultural forms.[115]

---

[115] David Hancock, "The British Atlantic World: Co-ordination, Complexity, and the Emergence of an Atlantic Market Economy, 1651–1815," *Itinerario*, 2, 1999, p. 10. Peter Linebaugh and Marcus Rediker's conceptualization of the emergence of a

Historians of the Indian Ocean have already acknowledged that the multiplicity of long-term and complex networks of association across and around this ocean makes it difficult to define a unified concept of the region.[116] Eric Tagliocozzo's long-term overview of common experiences in the transformation of the Indian Ocean is analyzed in terms of large-scale economic and social processes.[117] He employs Michael Pearson's concept of "littoral societies" as communities extending from the coast that are influenced by their relationship with the port, an influence that weakens with geographic distance.[118]

This concept of a littoral society has the advantage of integrating the harbor town with its hinterland in a way similar to earlier analyses of Southeast Asian indigenous port polities. Tagliocozzo identifies three major littoral regions on the boundaries of the Indian Ocean: the eastern littoral including Southeast Asia, the northern littoral incorporating South Asia, and the western littoral of East Africa. Incorporating East Africa within an analytical category of the Indian Ocean schema takes into account the major dynamics of indigenous trading networks on the African coast and within regional African-Arabic and cross-oceanic patterns of trade, balancing the conceptualization of the Indian Ocean region within its major continental and subcontinental coastlines.[119]

multiethnic, trans-Atlantic working class is also evocative of the Cape. "The circular transmission of human experience from Europe to Africa to the Americas and back again corresponded to the same cosmic forces that set the Atlantic currents in motion." Peter Linebaugh and Marcus Rediker, *The Many-Headed Hydra: Sailors, Slaves, Commoners, and the Hidden History of the Revolutionary Atlantic*. Boston: Beacon Press, 2000. p. 2.

[116] Both Abu-Lughod and Chaudhuri leave the southwest Indian Ocean out of their units of analysis. See Janet Abu-Lughod, *Before European Hegemony. The World System A.D. 1250–1350*. New York: Oxford University Press, 1989; K. N. Chaudhuri, *Asia Before Europe: Economy and Civilization of the Indian Ocean from the Rise of Islam to 1750*. Cambridge, UK: Cambridge University Press, 1990. Richard Hall's popular history does make an attempt to traverse the length and breadth of the ocean. *Empires of the Monsoon: A History of the Indian Ocean and Its Invaders*. New York: Harper Collins, 1998.

[117] Eric Tagliocozzo, "Trade, Production and Incorporation: The Indian Ocean in Flux, 1600–1900," *Itinerario*, 1, 2002, pp. 75–106.

[118] Michael Pearson, "Littoral Society: The Case for the Coast," *The Great Circle*, 7, 1985, pp. 1–8.

[119] The unifying factor of urban forms in *Gateways of Asia* is that "[t]he foundations of most if not all Asian port cities ultimately rests on indigenous fishing villages ... It would not be too much to see the origins of Asian sea faring in the myriad of fishing communities which, to a very large extent, still stretch along much of the littoral of the continent and its islands." Frank Broeze, "*Brides of the Sea* Revisited," pp. 10–11 in

One of the limitations of examining only port towns or littoral societies is that such a focus downplays the importance of shipping as the process of transporting people. Incorporating the movement and migration of people brings settlers, slaves, sojourners, sailors and soldiers, convicts, and exiles into the same analytical framework and illustrates the working of the Company's transportation and migration networks as they connected to the Cape. It also brings into focus both rulers and ruled as engaged in different forms of migration.[120] Also, revitalizing the concept of refreshment station within oceanic networks shifts expands the regional orientation toward Atlantic and Indian Ocean divisions to a transoceanic perspective.[121] The Cape could therefore be directly compared with the islands of St. Helena in the southeast Atlantic and Mauritius in southwest Indian Ocean, or Mozambique in the same region as they were all, at one level, refreshment posts. Boucher points out that by no means did all European ships stop at the Cape of Good Hope in the seventeenth and eighteenth centuries.

Frank Broeze, ed., *Gateways of Asia: Port Cities of Asia in the 13th to the 20th Centuries*. London: Columbia University Press, 1997. See also Frank Broeze, ed., *Brides of the Sea: Port Cities of Asia from the 16th to the 20th Centuries*. Honolulu: University of Hawaii Press, 1989; J. Kathirithamby-Wells and John Villiers, eds., *Southeast Asian Port and Polity – Rise and Demise*. Singapore: Singapore University Press, 1990; Anthony Reid, "The City and Its Commerce," in *Southeast Asia in the Age of Commerce 1450–1680, vol. 2: Expansion and Crisis*. New Haven, CT: Yale University Press, 1993, pp. 62–131.

[120] This perspective contrasts with that of Ross and Telkamp who claimed that "cities were superfluous to the purposes of colonists... [f]rom the point of view of the colonists, the cities were... necessary evils, as they were parasites on the rural producers, competing with the colonists in the process of surplus extraction." Robert Ross and Gerard Telkamp, "Introduction," in Robert Ross and Gerald Telkamp, eds., *Colonial Cities: Essays on Urbanism in a Colonial Context*. Dordrecht: Martinus Nijhoff, 1985, p. 1. Robert Ross also analyzes the growth of Cape Town in a comparative colonial context within an analysis of its integration into a world capitalist market. Robert Ross, "Cape Town (1750–1850): Synthesis in the Dialectic of Continents," in Ross and Telkamp, eds., *Colonial Cities*, pp. 105–122.

[121] John Thornton has powerfully argued that any consideration of the Atlantic world must have as one of its central premises the examination of the role of Africans in the making of this oceanic world. This differs from the Indian Ocean arena where indigenous oceanic trading networks were ancient but did not directly reach South Africa, even with regard to the slave trade. Stressing the multiple elements of the Atlantic port city and their origins in European colonialism bears direct comparison with the main functions of Cape Town. It was European ships harboring in colonial Atlantic port cities that transported goods and people from the interiors of the lands bordering the ocean, similarly to the Cape of Good Hope. John Thornton, *Africa and Africans in the Making of the Atlantic World, 1400–1800*, 2nd ed. Cambridge, UK: Cambridge University Press, 1998.

Cadiz, the Brazilian coast and the islands of the Atlantic and Indian Oceans sheltered many ships; St. Helena in particular was used by British East Indiamen... Portugal, with an anchorage at Mozambique... made little use of Dutch facilities in Southern Africa.[122]

Moreover, once the French had secured a base in the Mascarenes (Mauritius and Reunion) and Madagascar, they no longer needed to stop at the Cape. The implication of taking a regional perspective is that the Dutch Cape begins to share commonalities with settlements like Jamestown on St. Helena for the English, Port Louis in French Mauritius, and Cape Verde, Luanda (Angola), and Mozambique Island for the Portuguese.[123] Even so, this gives a somewhat static picture of this vibrant zone.

During the early modern period, the major European shipping powers were constantly trying to wrest control of these strategic ports from one another, or to look for alternative sites to rival those already established. Jamestown in St. Helena was colonized by the Portuguese, British and Dutch and reconquered by the British. Similarly Dutch, French, and British ambitions in Mauritius and Madagascar were originally aimed at establishing victualling stations, as well as engaging in the slave trade in the latter island.[124] The Dutch failed to maintain posts at both Rio de la Goa and Mauritius partly because the consolidation of the Cape made these other posts superfluous in terms of allocating the precious Company resources necessary to secure a self-sustaining settlement.[125] In the mid-1660s, French aspirations to establish a refreshment post at Saldanha Bay up the west coast near the Cape of Good Hope were forestalled mainly by the Company's sending a garrison of soldiers to occupy the territory.[126]

"Ceremonies of possession" were by the mid-seventeenth century more formulaic among European powers than they had been in the conquest of

---

[122] Maurice Boucher, "The Cape and Foreign Shipping, 1714–1723," *South African Historical Journal*, 6, November 1974, p. 5.
[123] Nigel Worden, "Cape Town and Port Louis in the Eighteenth Century," in Gwyn Campbell, ed., *The Indian Ocean Rim: Southern Africa and Regional Co-operation*. London and New York: Routledge Curzon, 2003. pp. 42–53.
[124] Vijayalakshmi Teelock, *Mauritian History: From Its Beginnings to Modern Times*. Moka, Mauritius: Mahatma Gandhi Institute, 2001.
[125] P. J. Moree, *A Concise History of Dutch Mauritius 1598–1710*. London: Columbia University Press, 1998.
[126] Sidney Welch, *Portuguese and Dutch in South Africa 1641–1806*. Cape Town: Juta Press, 1951, pp. 216–217.

the New World.[127] Both the French and the Dutch took pains on several occasions between 1664 and 1671 to knock down each other's wooden marker posts and thereby claim possession of Saldanha Bay, although the matter was eventually settled by changing political fortunes in France, which caused them to literally abandon their stake.[128] These seemingly trivial defacements of wooden markers were the subject of diplomatic incidents that could justify hostilities between European powers. The Company also perceived competing claims to the region of Natal as a threat to its stability at the Cape, though the area was not colonized until the nineteenth century under British rule.

There were as many failures as successes in this coastal zone to set up viable refreshment and trading posts. The Cape of Good Hope was by no means the only or even the best potential provisioning harbor at the southern tip of Africa, but it did become the major European colony in the region. Taken together, these attempts at territorial possession, if not settlement, make the refreshment zone of the southeast Atlantic Ocean and southwest Indian Ocean fertile ground for rethinking concepts of region and oceanic spheres in the history of early modern colonialism.

This was also a vulnerable zone for piracy by European and Arabic ships, although the latter were confined to the Indian Ocean zone. Piracy was the flip side of legitimate trade and war in the early modern period, and the Dutch East India Company was, not surprisingly, concerned with the potential for pirate activity at the Cape, although St. Helena, Madagascar, and Mauritius were far more vulnerable to pirate activity than the Cape of Good Hope. There are several reasons why the Cape was spared excessive piracy of their ships. First, the Cape settlement presented fairly slim pickings as a site of potential plunder, considering its main economic strengths lay in the rural economy and the tavern trade rather than in movable wealth like gold or slaves. Second, the Indian Ocean islands of Madagascar and Mauritius were linked through both piracy and the slave trade to the commercial networks of the eastern North American seaboard, rendering them a more attractive safe haven and target than the Cape.[129] Finally, the Company's insistence that its

---

[127] Patricia Seed, *Ceremonies of Possession in Europe's Conquest of the New World, 1492–1640*. Cambridge, UK: Cambridge University Press, 1995.
[128] Burman, *Saldanha Bay Story*, pp. 28–34.
[129] Arne Bialuschewski, "Pirates, Slavers and the Indigenous Population in Madagascar, c1690–1715," *International Journal of African Historical Studies*, 38(3), 2005, pp. 401–425.

ships sail together in large armed fleets and the use of the Cape by other European powers as a rendezvous point made it less likely that individual ships could be seized in open waters.

Buccaneers operating in the Atlantic Ocean, particularly around Jamaica and the Caribbean, were sometimes commissioned by European powers operating as mercenaries who profited from their raiding parties. These piracy networks extended as far as the Cape: even Captain William Kidd visited the Cape in January 1697, although Governor Simon van der Stel did not act against him because he had not committed offenses against the Company or its allies at the time.[130] Arne Bialuschewski argues that in the late seventeenth century, competition between Dutch and colonial American traders for slaves in Madagascar centered on their respective ability to provide arms to Malagasy polities in which the Americans were able to out-supply the Dutch.[131] The broad patterns of pirate activity tend to support the contention that the whole area was linked to illicit trans-Atlantic shipping as well as to more localized concentrations of piracy. As such, these shipping networks also break down an easy analytical division of Atlantic and Indian Oceans.

Tavern of the Seas

The evolution of an urban free burgher population dependent on the provisioning, tavern, and accommodation trade in Cape Town contributed to its emerging reputation as "the tavern of the seas." Gerald Groenewald argues that tavern culture was a major site in the multiethnic social world of the resident and transient underclass at the Cape. This trade was also increasingly important in generating wealth that created town-based members of the Cape burgher elite. In the eighteenth century, a broad range of urban residents were involved in various aspects of the tavern trade.[132] The appellation of *de Indische Zeeherberg* (tavern of the Indian Ocean) was already in common use by the eighteenth century when the

---

[130] Welch, *Portuguese and Dutch*, pp. 502–523.
[131] Bialuschewski, "Pirates, Slavers," p. 416.
[132] Susan Newton-King, "Company Castle and Control: The Social, Moral and Emotional World of Servants and Slaves of the Dutch East India Company in Seventeenth and Eighteenth Century Cape Town." National Research Foundation, South Africa, 2002; Gerald Groenewald, "The Culture and Economy of Taverns, Inns and Lodging Houses in Dutch Cape Town 1652–1795," PhD dissertation, University of Cape Town, forthcoming.

Swedish surgeon-botanist Carl Peter Thunberg traveling to the Cape in 1772 described it as

(a)n inn for travelers to and from the East Indies, who, after several months' sail may here get refreshments of all kinds, and are then about half way to the place of their destination, whether homeward or outward bound.[133]

The Cape was one of a series of refreshment posts established along major shipping routes between the Atlantic and Indian Oceans. It was also part of an economic zone composed of legitimate and illegitimate trade on land and legal and illegal shipping and plunder at sea. Any history of the Dutch Cape needs to keep both land and sea in sight, as this was the perspective of the world inhabited by those who lived at the time. Although the Cape of Good Hope developed into a Company colony that was an exceptional node in its empire, if given different historical circumstances it might have been located somewhere else, potentially at the site of the deep-water port at modern Mossel Bay in the southern Cape, known as Aguada de São Bras by the Portuguese. The Portuguese may have established a provisioning port at this site had they not already had access to Angola and Mozambique in the same general oceanic region.[134]

Compared to these Portuguese colonies in the Cape Cauldron, the Cape was exceptional because it was not, like they, tied directly into multiple imperial and indigenous trading networks extending from the coastal region to the African interior. The Cape remained, instead, tied to its primary function as a strategic provisioning post for the mainly European ships who anchored there at the halfway point of their transoceanic voyages. Slave labor for the colony was obtained through the Company's network of forced migration and through a sub-circuit of forced migration to Madagascar and Mauritius. Slaves acquired in both capacities stimulated the growth of the Cape's economy, but neither of these expendable settlements on the southeast coast of Africa displaced the Cape in its provisioning trade or as a settler colony in the Company's imperial web.

Batavia's links to the Cape were maintained not only through the Company's transoceanic shipping network but also through the extension of the Company's legal network that reinforced the primacy of Batavia

---

[133] Carl Peter Thunberg quoted in Charles Boxer, *The Dutch Seaborne Empire 1600–1800*. Middlesex, 1973, p. 273. Boxer's chapter on the Cape is entitled "The Tavern of Two Seas," pp. 273–301.

[134] Knox-Johnston, *Maritime History*, pp. 1–48; Coates, *Convicts and Orphans*, pp. 21–40.

in imperial law and governance. The following chapters explore how the circuit of forced migration in the form of political exile and penal transportation brought exiles and convicts to the Cape from Asia and how people in bondage at the Cape helped change the course of its evolution as a colonial society in unforeseen ways.

Shaykh Yusuf's Indian Ocean Network

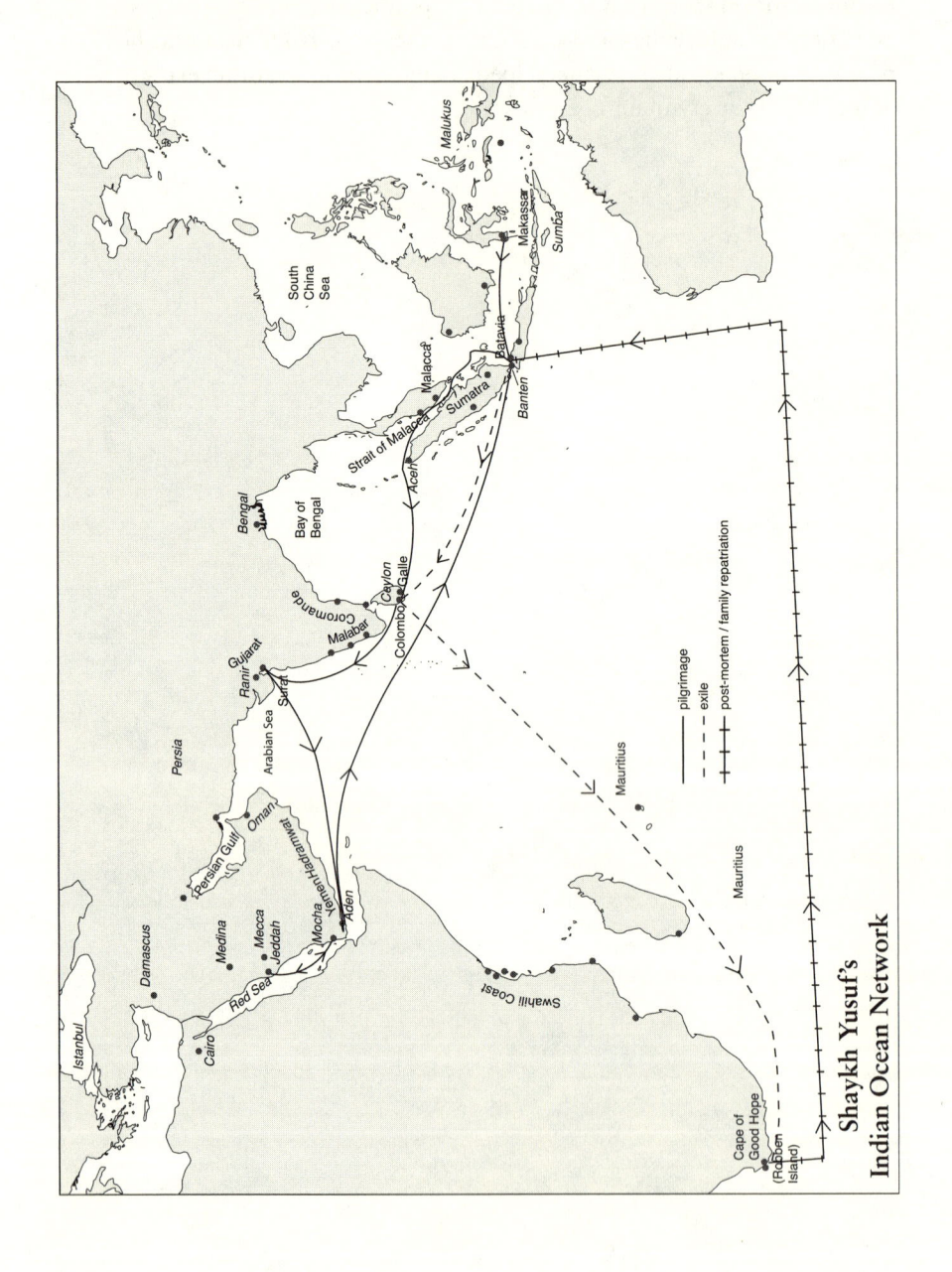

5

Company and Court Politics in Java: Islam and Exile at the Cape

The Cape of Good Hope was a crucial node in the Company's circuit of political exile emanating from Batavia. Although no coherent policy or overarching strategy governed the Company's use of exile, it became an important political tool in relations with indigenous polities because the Company could physically remove and relocate individuals who threatened its interests. The High Government used exile in much the same way as did indigenous polities who had their own circuits of exile within networks of forced migration. The Company's use of exile reveals the strengths and the limitations of its imperial nodes and networks. Company sites like Colombo, one of its most secure nodes, nevertheless intersected with indigenous Indian Ocean networks of religion, culture and communication the Company could not control. While the Company could impose physical restraints on people it exiled, it could not completely restrict their ability to communicate with and promulgate alternative networks of authority.

The Cape of Good Hope demonstrates very clearly the limits of Company sovereignty, to, on the one hand, be the only Company node completely outside indigenous Indian Ocean networks and, on the other, a site where these networks were extended through the agency of exiles and slaves themselves who transmitted Islam to the southernmost tip of Africa. Religious leaders banished in the Batavia-Cape exile circuit became powerful and sometimes charismatic nodes in and of themselves as condensed points for the transmission and transformation of Islamic practice. Moreover, they disrupted the Company's efforts to enforce strict social hierarchies in its empire. Some high-ranking Company officials were complicit in this social inversion by befriending high-ranking exiles under their care, although they suffered no censure for doing so. When the Company sought to undermine the prestige of exiles through harsh measures of incarceration and punishment, it could not entirely prevent the recognition of their status and power by people living at the Cape. Company officials were aware of both the limitations of banishment as a political tool and of the potential for exiles to undermine the control over people the Company sought to consolidate through its network of forced migration. The circuit of exile from Batavia to the Cape therefore changed the course of Indian Ocean networks, and, in at least one case of the repatriation of an exile to Java, facilitated an Islamic rebellion against the Company.

This chapter presents one narrative of many that could be written about the unforeseen consequences of exile for the Dutch East India Company's empire. Although archival sources for this hidden history are severely limited because they consist of personal communication, some even fragmentary, but, as highlighted in this chapter, they present compelling evidence of this important counter-dynamic in the Company's imperial web.

Performative Practice, Contracts, and the Culture of Legality

Company sovereignty was manifested through internal relations with its own subjects and external relations with foreign powers. It was cemented through the performative acts of oaths taken and contracts signed by individual Company subjects and rulers of foreign polities.[1] Oaths and treaties were formal and public commitments that carried the force of law. Individuals who lived within VOC jurisdiction took oaths of allegiance and office. Treaties were signed between representatives of the VOC and foreign rulers that established various rights and privileges between the parties that could be enforced through recourse to war or other direct political action. Exile and penal transportation were political and legal strategies used to enforce treaties and contracts with the Company and constituted part of its network of forced migration.

Treaties acknowledged the sovereignty of foreign powers and comprised an aspect of the public international law of most sovereign entities in the early modern period.[2] The Dutch East India Company signed

---

[1] For a summary of the history of oath taking and the political controversies surrounding the religious and legal debates with reference to England, see James Ednell Tyler, *Oaths; Their Origin, Nature and History*. London: John W. Parker, 1834.

[2] The opening chapter of *Mare Liberum* begins, "*By the Law of Nations navigation is free to all persons whatsoever.* My intention is to demonstrate briefly and clearly that the Dutch – that is to say, the subjects of the United Netherlands – have the right to sail to

treaties with foreign rulers on behalf of the States-General in the same way that the States-General of the United Provinces did with other European powers. However, as Leonard Andaya points out, it is not at all clear that these treaties were signed and sealed with the same cultural understanding of what the treaty relationship represented for all parties in terms of European legal concepts of the laws of nations. The VOC acknowledged and used these differences in understanding of treaty-signing to push its own advantage in international relations.[3] Extensive records were kept of these treaties compiled in the *Corpus Diplomaticum* (treaty records) that constituted the diplomatic memory and genealogy of the Company's public international law. Every new treaty was made and amended, or transgressions noted and aggressions justified, with reference to the entire history of treaties signed between the two parties.[4]

The negotiation of treaties and tributary relationships was as familiar to Southeast Asian polities as it was to European.[5] When the VOC negotiated treaties with oral societies, treaties were sealed through elaborate rituals and the swearing of oaths.[6] The negotiation of treaties in both writing and oratory was a performance of the formal recognition of sovereignty on the part of both parties. It was not necessarily a process of establishing relationships of equality between two powers. Moreover, as an added measure to ensure the integrity of this process, VOC servants had to swear an oath not to establish independent polities themselves in the territories where they served and to maintain the interests of the

---

the East Indies, as they are now doing, and to engage in trade with the people there." Hugo Grotius, *Freedom of the Seas*, p. 7.

[3] Leonard Andaya, "Treaty Conceptions and Misconceptions: A Case Study from South Sulawesi," *BKI*, 134(2–3), 1978, pp. 275–276.

[4] These treaties have been compiled and published in the six volumes. Heeres and Stapel, *Corpus Diplomaticum*. The original documents were made in a number of copies for the parties concerned, with simultaneous translations of the Dutch and the local languages. Southeast Asian languages often had their own script, so treaties were also often written in Arabic script of the Southeast Asian language as an intermediary translation. They were signed and sealed by those present and officiating in the name of the sovereigns of each polity.

[5] G. J. Resink, "The Significance of the History of International Law in Indonesia," in Soedjatmoko et al., eds., *An Introduction to Indonesian Historiography*. Ithaca, NY: Cornell University Press, 1965. Resink points out that the earliest documentary evidence of a treaty between an Indonesian ruler and a foreign power dates from approximately 132 C.E. The treaty was with the Heavenly Kingdom and the surviving copy is written in Chinese. It is only from the sixteenth century that Europeans become relevant in terms of Indonesian international law, pp. 359–363.

[6] Kenneth Bilby, "Swearing by the Past, Swearing to the Future: Sacred Oaths, Alliances, and Treaties among the Guianese and Jamaican Maroons," *Ethnohistory*, 44, 4, Fall 1997, pp. 655–689.

Company as paramount.[7] By the end of Company rule, oaths of loyalty taken by some regents and sultans in Java were replaced by an explicitly sworn fidelity to the *Stadhouder* (Vice-regent/Prince) as sovereign, the governor-general and the Council of the Indies as the *Stadhouder's* representative, and a recognition that the laws of Holland were to take precedence over local laws.[8]

Oaths and treaties did not only have meaning as symbolic performances. The VOC used these contractual performances as the bedrock of individual obligations and international alliances. Individuals bound by oaths of office and loyalty could be tried under a criminal court for breaking the terms of their contract or, at worst, for treason. The formal extension of VOC jurisdiction over its empire marked the transition of resistance against the Company from war to treason. Only people included under VOC jurisdiction could be tried as rebels or traitors. Those individuals clearly belonging to other nations, or falling in the borders between conquest and incorporation, could be punished only as prisoners of war or prisoners of state. Breaking the terms of treaties signed by the VOC with indigenous rulers was considered the basis for legitimate aggression and conquest. Both Company servants and indigenous rulers were exiled by the VOC on the basis of having broken their oaths or treaties. The use of forced migration by criminal transportation and political exile was one of the methods of control used by the VOC in establishing its legal right to rule within its jurisdiction and to manage its international relations with foreign powers. The performative practices of legality were implicitly and necessarily backed by military power and the threat of violence for their enforcement.[9]

Contracts included in the treaty records or *Corpus Diplomaticum* of the Dutch East India Company by their nature represented a negotiation of diplomatic protocols between the Company and the respective

---

[7] Consider, for example, the career of the English adventurer, James Brooke, who was recognized as the "Raja" and founder of Sarawak on the island of Borneo during the mid-nineteenth century after he was granted the territory by the Sultan of Brunei. David Chandler et al., *In Search of Southeast Asia: A Modern History*. Revised edition, edited by Joel Steinberg. Honolulu: University of Hawaii Press, 1987, pp. 148 & 200. For the oath of fidelity to the VOC see H. R. Hahlo and E. Kahn, *South African Legal System and Its Background*. Cape Town: Juta, 1968, p. 536.

[8] November 27, 1808, "Instructie voor den Sultan (sic) van Bantam: Eed voor den Sulthan," J. A. Van der Chijs, ed., *Nederlandsch-Indies Plakaatboek 1602–1811 (NIP)*, vol. 15, Batavia: Landsdrukkerij; 'sHage: M. Nijhoff, 1885, pp. 359–367.

[9] Gerrit Knaap and Ger Teitler, eds., *De Vereenigde Oostindische Compagnie tussen oorlog en diplomitie*, Leiden: KITLV Press, 2002.

indigenous polity. Indigenous diplomacatic and treaty documents became, as objects, part of the symbolic relations between polities and were contained within the court regalia as items of potent power.[10] As Leonard Andaya and Barbara Watson Andaya have argued, understandings of these contracts by the signatories were not necessarily the same. Cultural differences imbued the contracts with different meanings that were not explicitly expressed in their wording. Moreover, indigenous rulers, accustomed to their own form of treaty negotiation that established the nature of power relations between rulers rather than the extraction of specific concessions, misunderstood the purpose of signing these contracts.[11] These misunderstandings were sometimes resolved through action, particularly military intervention, that made their meaning for the Company obvious.

Not all VOC contracts were as one-sided as those with the Khoekhoe at the Cape of Good Hope. Many were not completely favorable to Company interests, reflecting the comparative political strength of the negotiating parties in ways that would have been familiar forms of political maneuvering. The contracts themselves concentrated on formalizing economic and political concessions in ways that were not necessarily phrased in the patron-client terminology of indigenous polities. The diplomatic protocols that surrounded the treaties were often formalized negotiations of cultural difference. Company officials were keenly aware of how their actions were being interpreted in indigenous courts and of the implications of these actions. As contracts were incorporated into the documentary regalia of indigenous courts partly as embodiments of oral traditions, the VOC thus also relied on oral recitations to explicate the treaties. Both signing parties were preoccupied with translations, signatures, and seals as the symbolic and legal legitimization of the documents.[12] One of the main cultural differences between VOC and indigenous interests was that the Company was focused on extracting specific economic concessions and extending its jurisdiction over defined territories, whereas indigenous rulers signed contracts acknowledging power relations with

---

[10] Barbara Watson Andaya, *To Live as Brothers: Southeast Sumatra in the Seventeenth and Eighteenth Centuries.* Honolulu: University of Hawaii Press, 1993, p. 145.

[11] Andaya, "Treaty Conceptions and Misconceptions," pp. 275–295; Andaya, *To Live as Brothers*, pp. xvi.

[12] Remmelink points out that the Dutch translators wrote in a "curious Company chancery Javanese," raising questions about how they were read and understood in the Javanese courts. Willem Remmelink, *The Chinese War and the Collapse of the Javanese State, 1725–1743.* Verhandelingen KITLV, no. 162. Leiden: KITLV Press, 1994, p. 280.

the Company to recognize tribute provisions and thereby best preserve their own dynastic succession.[13]

Company contracts are silent about the performance of diplomatic protocols that formed the negotiation leading up to the documents being signed and sealed. For this knowledge, other written Company sources in the form of reports and correspondence provide some of the context for these negotiations from the perspective of Company servants. Behind the formalities of diplomacy and the concluding of written contracts, the Company became deeply embedded in indigenous politics, especially in Java and the Indonesian archipelago. In many ways, the Company, with its capital in Batavia, operated along similar lines as other Indian Ocean polities, particularly in matters of diplomacy and war. Anthony Reid suggests that once Batavia was established as the Company's headquarters, the governor-general specifically discouraged indigenous rulers from conducting diplomacy directly and on an equal basis with the Dutch *Stadhouder*, despite protests of some Asian monarchs.[14] In these diplomatic negotiations, the governor-general assumed the role of a sovereign with the authority to ratify contracts, although, in principle, sovereignty ultimately rested in the United Provinces.

Nevertheless, the Company was a polity unlike any indigenous polity in the Indian Ocean region. Its bureaucratic organization, trading practices, rationale, and maintenance of an empire comprised of colonies and outposts were permanently subservient to the interests of the whole and not rival imperial centers in the making. While the Company intervened in countless succession disputes in Southeast Asian polities, it is significant that its own political crises and structures of career advancement through promotion and patrimonial networks prevented disruption to the overall functioning of the empire. The death of a governor-general, for example, did not cause the same level of political crisis as the death of an Asian monarch because power in the VOC was invested in the office and not in the charisma of the person holding it. It was also absolutely exceptional practice in Indian Ocean diplomacy that relations between polities, in this case between the VOC and indigenous polities, were not cemented through marriage bonds with the giving

---

[13] See also Ann Kumar, *Java and Modern Europe: Ambiguous Encounters*. Richmond, UK: Curzon Press, 1997. Kumar argues that contracts acknowledged already existing concessions between the VOC and indigenous rulers, p. 33.

[14] Anthony Reid, *Southeast Asia in the Age of Commerce, 1450–168*, vol. 2, *Expansion and Crisis*. New Haven, CT: Yale University Press, 1993, p. 241.

of royal daughters from tributary polities as wives for the dominant king.[15]

Although familial networks of the Company elite were perpetuated through strategic couplings, these marital relations were internal to the Company and the United Provinces. The Company remained aloof to the myriad ties of mutual obligations and generational networks that were bound into elite indigenous familial bonds, particularly within the Southeast Asian archipelago. The basis of personal power within the Company and indigenous polities remained separate and thereby precluded the possibility that the Company could be incorporated into power relations with them on the latter's terms. This separation of politics and marriage fundamentally structured the conduct of relations between the Company and indigenous polities.

Barbara Watson Andaya has examined the changing fortunes of the Jambi and Palembang kingdoms in southeast Sumatra and their respective relationships with the VOC using, "the image of European account books to invoke the notion of indigenous 'balance sheets' by which human memories were constantly recalculating the mutual obligations incurred through interaction with other individuals or communities."[16] Southeast Asian rulers developed their entourages through various forms of kinship arrangements that were essential to their own rule and to their relations with other rulers. The "balance sheet" imagery highlights cultural difference precisely because Company officials *literally* structured relations with indigenous rulers through abstract notions of "accounting" in the forms of trade accounts, the inventories of specific tribute payments, and the signing of contracts that encoded these items in their memory. Yet despite notions of equality in the concept of "balance" it was still an accounting of asymmetrical reciprocities codified in law and exchange relations.[17]

Exile as a Tool of Empire

From the Company's perspective, its diplomatic ties with indigenous polities were created and maintained through contracts that applied to the

---

[15] Ibid., pp. 238–239.
[16] Andaya, *To Live as Brothers*, p. xvii; Anthony Day, "Ties That (Un)Bind: Families and States in Premodern Southeast Asia," *JSEAS*, 55(2), May 1996, pp. 384–409. Day suggests that the family as an analytical category has been neglected in Southeast Asian historiography because of the focus on "male 'power' and historical 'structures' and that 'families and family values' served to bind people together to become historical agents which we can call 'states' in premodern Southeast Asia," p. 384.
[17] Andaya, *To Live as Brothers*, p. 145.

polities themselves and not to individual rulers. The Company had little intrinsic and no familial interest in the survival of any one particular ruling dynasty. Thus was a new rationale introduced into indigenous politics through relationships with European colonial powers like the VOC. The Company was able to exercise the power of imprisonment and banishment of indigenous rulers and their followers, and sometimes their execution, free of consequences for its own ruling elite. Indigenous polities relied much more on the strategy of hostage-taking and internal banishment or assassination to subdue high-ranking rivals within their courts. However, indigenous rulers were not able to impose these punishments systematically on the VOC. The occasional assassination of a Company official was greeted with demands for restitution backed up by the threat of military intervention. However, Company officials were, in fact, replaceable.

The High Government's systematic use of exile underpinned its diplomatic relations with indigenous polities that were formalized in the signing of contracts. In support of this system, Batavia created a network of exile sites throughout its empire that enabled it to choose specific places of banishment according to the High Government's perceptions of the danger of particular prisoners. Batavia used the nature of its far-flung domain to help consolidate its interests within particular archipelagic polities, and, most especially, at the center of the Company empire in Java.

The organization of the Company bureaucracy included the transfer of personnel between disparate postings. Over generations this practice created an imperial patrimonial system that linked the European-based upper echelons of the Company in their role as patrons to Company officials within the empire. It formed the basis of an expatriate elite that to some extent shared knowledge about the wider framework of the Company's imperial domain. Promotion and transfer of the highest-ranking officials took place across the full range of colonies. Even a cursory glance at the family tree of Jan van Riebeeck, to name only one example, shows how this system of intermarriage linked the fortunes of many elite families across the empire. Jan van Riebeeck's familial relationship with the then Governor-General Antonio van Dieman had smoothed the way to his initial promotions in Batavia. While his earlier disgrace probably precluded him from the very highest office, his children fared better. His son Abraham's daughter, Johanna-Maria van Riebeeck, married Governor-General Joan van Hoorn in 1706.[18] This opened the way

---

[18] A. J. Böeseken, *Jan van Riebeeck en Sy Gesin*. Kaapstad: Tafelberg, 1974, pp. 234–238.

for Abraham van Riebeeck to be appointed governor-general in succession.

Company officials actively sought promotion from less prominent and profitable Company settlements to those where they could further advance their personal interests, aiming for the pinnacle of power in the governor-generalship in Batavia.[19] Unlike regional indigenous leaders who sought to strengthen their own position and challenge to overthrow the center of power, the Company's chain of command remained internalized and intact. Batavia Castle and the increasingly lavish civic buildings of the imperial capital functioned as an "imperial court," incorporating both European and Asian protocols of power. The strength of the Company's bureaucracy was that promotion within the system was often accompanied by a move geographically, for example, from merchant in Surat to governor in Colombo. The Cape of Good Hope, as it developed from refreshment post to a settler colony, was unique in the Company's colonies outside Batavia for creating a free burgher population that over generations permanently identified with their new homeland and not with either the imperial center in Batavia or, increasingly, with the overlordship of the Company in Europe.

Court Politics: The Protocols of Exile

The official diplomatic memory of the Company as embodied in the treaties remains silent about negotiations regarding exile and succession, as these documents represent the resolution phase of political crises or relationships. In a general sense, political dealings between European and Asian polities constructed an agreed-upon protocol of diplomacy largely designed to facilitate the conclusion of treaties.[20] Although diplomacy was often mediated through translators, European traders and envoys took considerable pains to understand the local protocols so they could bargain with Asian polities. During the mid-seventeenth century these diplomatic relations were widespread, and envoys from Southeast Asian polities traveled to Europe as well as the courts of the Ottoman, Mughal, and Chinese empires. There was a shared understanding of the realm of international diplomacy, if not its specific protocols. The

---

[19] Jean Gelman Taylor, *The Social World of Batavia: European and Eurasian in Dutch Asia*. Madison: University of Wisconsin Press, 1983. See especially Appendices 1–3, pp. 183–207.
[20] C. H. Alexandrowicz, *An Introduction to the History of the Law of Nations in the East Indies (16th, 17th and 18th Centuries)*. Oxford: Clarendon Press, 1967, p. 185.

Company inserted itself into this realm by asserting its authority to conduct diplomatic relations on its own behalf without the intervention, but still ultimately in the name, of the States-General of the United Provinces.[21]

While the Company conducted its diplomatic relationships much like any other Southeast Asian power, one of the main differences was that the Dutch were excluded from marriage ties to indigenous states. Remmelink observes that: "Politics and polygamy tied the Javanese elite into a Gordian knot of stupendous proportions. Marriages cemented the bonds that no other relationship seemed to provide."[22] The Company did, however, intervene in archipelagic politics by negotiating military support for particular rulers in exchange for payment in cash and kind. This type of relationship was not unusual in interstate relations in the region. Exile played a specific role in these diplomatic ties.

The use of exile and hostage-taking was common practice among archipelagic states. Hostage-taking most often took the form of imprisoning noble women and children within the court to ensure the loyalty of their male relatives in times of crisis. The Company played a particular role in this strategy by both adopting it for their own purposes and by aiding their allies through assisting with the exile of their allies' enemies as a form of punishment. Punishment within indigenous courts "ranged from the death penalty to a fine but usually meant removal from office, either to be placed at court, banished to a place on Java...or exiled outside Java. The last option required the help of the Company and was mainly used in case of rebellious princes of the blood or very high officials. It was also expensive, for the king still had to pay the keep of those exiled to what the Javanese called *Pulo Kap* (the Cape Colony) or *Selong* (Ceylon)."[23] This was not necessarily always the case, as the Company often paid the subsistence expenses of exiled nobles and their entourages, particularly when they became impoverished. However, whenever possible, the Company extracted these expenses from their remaining relatives or rulers.

This strategy of political exile was not confined to relationships with the Javanese courts. The Company operated a far-flung network of exile that it used to bolster its own power and that of its allies. The governor-general even replicated these court strategies by keeping hostages at the Batavia Castle. With respect to the Cape, Batavia was the point of origin

---

[21] Reid, *Expansion and Crisis*, pp. 233–245.   [22] Remmelink, *The Chinese War*, p. 18
[23] Ibid., pp. 16–19.

for most but not all exiles as a number of them were also sent directly from Ceylon. The VOC's military power within the archipelago enabled it both to sell its military technology to the highest bidder and to enter into military allegiances with particular rulers to further its own ends. The Company backed up this military power by controlling exile sites within the archipelago and extending them to the Cape and Ceylon. In this way, the Cape entered the consciousness of indigenous elites in the Indies archipelago and Ceylon as a place of exile over which they had no access or control. The geographical extent of the Company's empire was an element of its political strength vis-à-vis indigenous polities.[24] The castles and forts maintained by the Company operated as strategic centers of Company "court" politics, including the exercise of political and judicial power and ceremony, and, ultimately, as sites of imprisonment and exile.

While the stone and mortar of VOC castles and fortresses performed both a military and a diplomatic function, the treaties as documents were often perceived by Southeast Asian elites as objects of royal regalia imbued with an intrinsic and sacred power. The investment of royal letters as objects with the sovereignty of the king by whom they were written was one distinctive feature of diplomatic protocol in Southeast Asia, as compared to the Indian Ocean and Sinic sphere.[25] The symbolic power of documents extended to the writing of diplomatic treaties between indigenous polities. Barbara Andaya captures the culture gap that existed in diplomatic relations between indigenous polities and the VOC:

Stored with the community's ritual objects, such indigenous contracts were normally revered rather than consulted... In the seventeenth and eighteenth centuries, these attitudes were puzzling to Europeans. In Dutch eyes, treaties were certainly a declaration of friendship, but their primary purpose was to facilitate trade and to list specific commercial arrangements to which both sides were bound. They were not in any way "sacred" and could be altered or renegotiated to suit changing circumstances.[26]

Thus, although the *Corpus Diplomaticum* of the VOC reflects largely the European practices of treaty writing, the meanings of the treaties and

---

[24] Henk Niemeijer's analysis of the relationship between technology and power in the Indies during the Company period confirms part of this analysis, asserting the existence of strategic diplomacy. Hendrik Niemeijer, "De Geveinsde vrede: Eer, protocol en diplomatie in de machetsverhouding tussen de Verenigde Oost-Indische Compagnie en Ternate omstreeks 1750, " in Knaap and Teitler, *Tussen Oorlog en Diplomatie*, pp. 309–336.

[25] Reid, *Expansion and Crisis*, p. 235.   [26] Andaya, *To Live as Brothers*, p. 146.

the protocols of diplomacy through which they were composed and concluded were much more a form of negotiated practice between European and Asian cultural expectations. Over time, indigenous polities began to pay more attention to the clauses contained within these treaties rather than focusing solely on their symbolic power as objects.[27] The Company was not unaware of the symbolic importance of regalia as objects of kingly power in the archipelago and sometimes manipulated the possession of these objects to its own ends. The Company in fact sometimes held these regalia "hostage" as an exercise of power.

In 1719, for example, the governor-general, Hendrick Zwaardecroon, refused to return the Jambi regalia to its king, Kiai Gede, until the king repaid his debt to the Company.[28] Batavia's exile of deposed rulers could, however, backfire. Several attempts by Batavia to retrieve the royal regalia of Kartasura that the deposed Javanese ruler, Amangkurat III, had secretly taken with him into exile to Ceylon in 1709 failed to achieve results, causing a diplomatic crisis between Batavia and the Kartasura court of Pakubuwana I.[29] Batavia's source of intelligence was by no means infallible, and in this case the High Government had utterly misjudged the significance of its actions in exiling a ruler still in possession of the regalia of state; it had confiscated the wrong objects and the sacred *pusakas* (regalia) remained beyond their reach.

The major sites of exile were those in which the Company felt most secure in its control of the surrounding region, usually a combination of the largest garrisons and the least possibility of intervention by neighboring polities. Of all the Company nodes, the Cape fulfilled these requirements most completely. It combined security, distance, and isolation in a unique configuration to the advantage of the Company. Of all VOC exile sites, including Batavia, it was the least likely to be captured through conquest by indigenous or neighboring polities. As one of the most expensive of the Company outposts to keep, it is not surprising that the Seventeen Gentlemen and the High Government looked to maximize the use of the Cape settlement in ways that would not significantly increase expenditure.

---

[27] Leonard Andaya notes that in one of the Bugis chronicles reflecting back on the period during the signing of the Treaty of Bungaya in 1667, the chronicler warns about the duplicity of the Company officials in Batavia in treaty negotiations. Andaya, "Treaty Conceptions," p. 291.

[28] Andaya, *To Live as Brothers*, p. 170.

[29] M. C. Ricklefs, *War, Culture and Economy in Java 1677–1726: Asian and European Imperialism in the Early Kartasura Period*. Sydney: Asian Studies Association of Australia in association with Allen & Unwin, 1993, pp. 153–159.

For these reasons, the Cape became tied to the fortunes of various archipelagic polities in unforeseen ways. The Company's network of exile was a political strategy that simultaneously bound together its imperial realm and wove the Cape into the fabric of Southeast Asian polities.

The consequences for the development of the colonial society at the Cape were profound. While exiles arriving at the Cape were perceived by Company officials and colonists alike as a dangerous population, the aristocratic elite of the exiles simultaneously presented a social dilemma for the small colony. The Company was forced to house and sustain exiles and their entourages, most often attempting to keep these people away from the town. In so doing, it inadvertently provided the circumstances under which Islam at the Cape appears to have been propagated among slaves and the free black population. Some of these exiles were prominent Islamic scholars who practiced, and, in all likelihood, transmitted their faith to willing recipients from their isolated abodes at the Cape.

The influence of religious scholar-exiles in the spread of Islam was felt beyond their deaths or repatriations. There is strong evidence to suggest that Islamic practices developed at the Cape of Good Hope in the late seventeenth and early eighteenth centuries had an impact on the course of political and religious opposition to the Company in Java during the latter part of the century. The Cape exerted an influence on archipelagic polities both in the imaginative realm as a place of exile, and in the realm of politics with the reinsertion of high-ranking exiles, their families, and retinues returning from Africa to resume their roles in court. These consequences of the network of exile were almost entirely out of the control of the VOC. Apart from being able to restrict the physical movement of people, the Company was unable to restrain the movement of ideas and beliefs generated by those whom it sentenced to exile. In attempting to consolidate political influence in one part of its empire, the VOC inadvertently created conditions with the potential to undermine their control in other areas.

It is beyond the scope of this book to detail every case of political exile to the Cape. Several hundred people were exiled to the Cape during a period of over one hundred and thirty years. This chapter constructs a narrative account of specific cases of exile that demonstrate the diversity and interconnectedness of political exile over a century of Company rule. The individual case studies presented here elucidate the imperial dimension of localized situations by analyzing the consequences of the Company's networks of exile, both at the local archipelagic, or sending level, and at the Cape, or receiving level. The scale of the entire network can be imagined when considering that the Cape was but a single albeit important exile site in the Company's empire. In presenting a coherent narrative along the Batavia-Cape circuit, this book nevertheless suggests that this particular circuit could be replicated in detailed accounts many times over, at the Cape or other major sites of exile, such as Ceylon or Banda.[30]

Exile was a familiar dimension of court politics in the archipelagic region of Southeast Asia. Indigenous written sources in the form of *babads*, epic poems, or chronicles that explore historical themes of particular regions and dynasties, are replete with metaphors of exile in indigenous polities, and of specific historical references to places of exile and people sent into exile.[31] Most of the examples and metaphors of exile within the *babads* make no reference to relations with the Company, underlining the frequency and significance of exile within indigenous politics.[32] These sources provide an indigenous perspective on exile different from that in Company records, and the *Babad Tanah Jawa* is particularly interesting in this respect.[33] Remmelink's transcription of this Javanese *babad* into an historical narrative highlights the indigenous perception of relatively autonomous political realms existing alongside the Company.

The exile of members of the Javanese court elite occurs both through the machinations of the king and under pressure from the Company. Exile

---

[30] For an examination of the Malay networks with Ceylon see A. Hussainmiya, *Orang Rejimen: The Malays of the Ceylon Rifle Regiment*. Bangi: Unversiti Kebangsaan, Malaysia, 1990. See also Winius and Vink, *Merchant-Warrior Pacified*, for links to South Asia.

[31] *Babads* differed significantly in form. Some are secular histories comparable to Western history writing; others wove fantasy and history into a more mythical interpretation of the past. See Ann Kumar, "Javanese Historiography in and of the 'Colonial Period': A Case Study," in A. Reid and D. Marr, *Perceptions of the Past in Southeast Asia*. Singapore: Heinemann Educational Books, 1979, pp. 187–206. Even the more "historical" *babads* vary significantly according to the perspective and vested interests within versions of the same events. See Virginia Matheson, "Strategies of Survival: The Malay Royal Line of Lingga-Riau," *JSEAS*, 17(1), March 1986, pp. 5–38.

[32] Nevertheless, there were attempts to explain the rise of the Company's power in terms of indigenous concepts of kingship and spirituality. Ricklefs points out that one of the Javanese myths surrounding the Company was that the Dutch rulers in Batavia, embodied in the mythical figure, Baron Sakendher, were the descendents of the royal house of Pajajaran and by descent related to the Goddess of the Southern Ocean. Ricklefs further surmises that the VOC were ignorant of their incorporation into Javanese mythology. M. C. Ricklefs, *The Seen and Unseen Worlds in Java, 1726–1749: History Literature and Islam in the Court of Pakubuwana II*. Honolulu: Allen and Unwin and the University of Hawaii Press, 1998, pp. 13–14.

[33] Remmelink gives an account of the debates around the use of *babads* as historical sources. See Remmelink, *The Chinese War*, p. 207.

as a political weapon was both commonplace and familiar, with Batavia, Ceylon, and the Cape as the most prominent sites.[34] In this *babad*, description of events between 1725 and 1745 leading to the collapse and division of the Javanese state, exile is depicted as a plight that essentially consisted of removal from the center of the Javanese universe – the court. Exile to Batavia is not depicted as qualitatively different from exile to Ceylon or the Cape. Nor is exile seen as being necessarily a permanent condition, as petitions for the return of exiled relatives and reinsertion into court politics are woven throughout the *babad*. One group of exiles returning to Java from Ceylon was thereafter called the "Ceylonese party" within *kraton* (palace) politics.[35] In this *babad*, exile appears in many forms, including in the dreams of the king, in premonitions of personal downfall, and as portents of disaster.[36]

The Cape is prominent as *"Pulo Kap"* (Cape Island) in these indigenous accounts. However, it is also clear that Javanese chroniclers were not primarily concerned with the exact geographical nature of the Cape settlement. One can speculate that at first the Javanese assumed the Cape was an island similar in nature to Ceylon or other islands in the archipelago, or that they were referring specifically to Robben Island as representative of exile at the Cape. Ann Kumar's analysis of the various Surapati *babads* describes Javanese fantasies about the nature of the Cape that makes it qualitatively different from other places of exile.

Surapati was an early eighteenth-century hero and leader of anti-Company resistance around whom many legends arose. Although Surapati died in battle against the Dutch in 1706, his descendents and followers continued resisting the Company and were eventually either killed or captured and exiled to the Cape and Ceylon. Nevertheless, within the West Javanese *babad* describing Surapati's life, it is during his magical youth that the Cape comes into prominence. When Surapati is rejected as a young boy by his royal father and exiled from the court, he wanders

---

[34] Remmelink, *The Chinese War*, chapter 6, "The Babad," pp. 214–244. See also Anthony Day, "The Drama of Bangun Tapa's Exile in Ambon, the Poetry of Kingship in Surakarta, 1830–58," in Lorraine Gesick, *Centers, Symbols, and Hierarchies: Essays on the Classical States of Southeast Asia*. New Haven, CT: Yale University Southeast Asia Series, 1983, pp. 148–151. Day transcribes a *babad* wherein the exiled King Pakubuwana II speculates about the Dutch "Admiral" in charge of the Ambon garrison: "The Admiral looks very much like grandfather Pangeran Mangkumbumi.... Could he be descended from Mangkumbumi at the time when he was exiled [*sinelong*]? He does not move like a Dutchman." The specific meaning of *"sinelong"* was "exiled to Ceylon."

[35] Remmelink, *The Chinese War*, p. 152.   [36] Ibid., pp. 236, 240–241.

until captured as a slave and is taken aboard a ship that travels "to the Cape Island, *the dwelling-place of the banished*" (my emphasis).[37]

Kumar notes that in these *babads* it is extremely difficult to distinguish between the historical and the fantastic, as both are often described in similarly realistic terms. While it is historically untrue that Surapati journeyed to the Cape, other historical figures within the *babads* were indeed exiled to the Cape, like Tuwan Seh (Shaykh Yusuf of Makassar).[38] The *babad* even specifies the journey between Batavia and the Cape as being nine days – an impossibly speedy sailing time – as if it were chronicling actual events. Kumar speculates that this voyage to the Cape was attributed to Surapati's life because it "was a remarkable feat appropriate to the career of a young hero."[39] However, it is not the act of exile that is extraordinary. It is Surapati's return from the Cape that makes the journey remarkable, perhaps because it was the most "foreign" place of banishment to imagine and from which to return.[40]

The Java-Makassar-Cape Nexus

The links between Java, the Cape, and Makassar through the network of forced migration were particularly strong and demonstrate how the circuit of exile operated in the Company empire. Company officials at the Cape no doubt engaged in speculation about the exiles who arrived in their midst from the other side of the Indian Ocean.[41] Political exiles and criminals from the archipelago arrived in a steady trickle from the beginning of the settlement. In 1680, Governor Simon van der Stel requested that this flow be stopped because the exiles were encouraging slaves to escape and the garrison was too small to pursue them. Governor-General

---

[37] Ann Kumar, *Surapati: Man and Legend. A Study of Three Babad Traditions*. Australian National University, Center of Oriental Studies, Oriental Monograph Series, no. 20, Leiden: Brill, 1976, p. 52.
[38] Ibid., p. 382. [39] Ibid., p. 323.
[40] Nancy Florida's analysis of the *Babad Jaka Tingkir* from the Surakarta *kraton* archive collection highlights the importance of concepts of exile within indigenous literature. Nancy Florida, *Writing the Past, Inscribing the Future: History as Prophecy in Colonial Java*. Durham, NC: Duke University Press, 1995, p. 401. John Pemberton's discursive analysis of the emergence of "Java" as both an imagined and real "realm" situates the pivotal intervention as being the Dutch partition of the Javanese kingdoms in 1745, wherein *Walandi* (Dutch) became simultaneously the symbolic mirror image of, and subsumed within, *Jawi* (Javanese). John Pemberton, *On the Subject of "Java."* Ithaca, NY: Cornell University Press, 1994, p. 70.
[41] It is beyond the capacity of this chapter to detail the biographies of all the political exiles sent to the Cape. The multiplication of examples would not alter my argument. I am not arguing these are the only influential people who propagated Islam at the Cape.

Rijkloff van Goens responded by saying that in the interests of the Company it was not possible to comply with their request at the time.[42]

In the autumn of 1681, the arrival of at least a dozen political exiles from Makassar (composed of three princes and members of their families and entourages) underlined the Cape's inability to control the influx of prisoners from abroad. Cape Company officials resolved to separate and isolate these Makassarese exiles because rumors were circulating that the prisoners were in secret communication with each other and were trying to discover the strength of the Cape garrison.[43] Fearing that the Makassarese were conspiring to seek vengeance against them, the Company decided to place some of them hostage on Robben Island, some in inland Company posts, and to keep the three Makassarese princesses hostage in a room at the Rustenberg manor house, a few miles distant from the Castle, with a personal slave woman provided by the Company to attend each one of them.[44]

The apprehension with which the Cape authorities viewed the arrival of the Makassarese exiles was justified in terms of the political situation in the archipelago. The Company's relationship with the Makassarese kingdom was turbulent to say the least. The VOC and their Bugis allies, led respectively by Cornelis Speelman and the legendary Bugis leader Arung Palakka had militarily defeated the Makassarese kingdom of Goa in 1667. Under the terms of the peace concluded in the Treaty of Bungaya, the Company occupied the Makassarese Fort, Ujung Pandang, renaming it Fort Rotterdam, and claimed its jurisdiction over the surrounding area.

---

[42] A. J. Böeseken, *Simon van der Stel en Sy Kinders*. Kaapstad: Nasou Beperk, 1984, p. 122.

[43] The separation of exiles from the town was a common strategy employed by the Cape authorities. In the 1670s two Sumatran exiles were sent to the Constantia forest outside Cape Town. Their *kramats* (graves) indicate their status as Muslim saints. K. M. Jeffreys, "The Malay Tombs of the Holy Circle," pts. 1–6, *The Cape Naturalist*, 1, 1, November 1934, pp. 15–17; 1, 2, July 1935, pp. 40–43; 1, 3, July 1936, pp. 89–92; 1, 4, April 1937, pp. 118–121; 1, 5, June 1938, pp. 157–163; and 1, 6, June 1939, pp. 195–199. Adil Bradlow argues that oral tradition among Cape Town Muslims indicates that the smaller unmarked graves surrounding the *kramats* are the graves of their followers. Bradlow reasonably suggests that this is evidence of contacts between these isolated exiles and/or runaway slaves and people from the town and that these sites indicate the probable existence of an active Sufi *tariqah*. M. Adil Bradlow, "Imperialism, State Formation and the Establishment of a Muslim Community at the Cape of Good Hope, 1770–1840: A Study in Urban Resistance," unpublished MA thesis, University of Cape Town, 1988, pp. 120–121.

[44] Thursday, November 26, 1682, *Resoluties van die Politike Raad*, vol. 3, 1681–1707, pp. 54–55.

The VOC outpost at Makassar did not develop into an expanding settler node and remained dependent on local allies to maintain its position.[45] The Company realized that the strategic importance of this region lay in its relationship of suzerainty over the shipping lanes and through its ability to disrupt regional indigenous, Chinese, and rival European trade with many of the islands in the eastern archipelago, including the spice-producing islands of the Moluccas. A negotiated relationship with the Makassar and Bugis kingdoms in South Sulawesi was the only way to ensure the stability of Company trade with the eastern archipelago. Although the Company was never able to claim sovereignty over South Sulawesi, it entered into a series of important treaty relationships with indigenous polities in the area.

By far the most important of these alliances was with the Bugis kingdom of Bone under Arung Palakka. The Company went to great lengths to ensure that Arung Palakka remained a faithful ally, for without the Bugis alliance the Company would not have been able to conduct peaceful trade in the region. Many Makassarese nobles had been exiled to Batavia and other Company settlements following the Treaty of Bungaya in 1667. Many others had fled the region and taken refuge in Banten, eastern Java, and other archipelagic polities in what amounted to a Makassarese diaspora. The Makassarese had a well-deserved reputation for military prowess and were often welcomed in this capacity by their hosts. However, Governor-General Joan Maetsucyker considered them a dangerous and destabilizing influence in the region. It is not at all clear how much the Cape authorities knew about these developments in the wider world of the Company's empire. While written reports and personnel circulated information about conditions within other settlements, not all flows of information were recorded in Company documents.[46]

The Company did not always instigate cases of exile; it often did so on behalf of indigenous allies who used the Company's ability to ship people off to the far reaches of its empire to their advantage. It was

---

[45] Heather Sutherland, "Ethnicity, Wealth and Power in Colonial Makassar: A Historiographical Reconsideration," in Peter Nas, *The Indonesian City*, Verhandelingen KITLV, no. 117. The Hague: Martinus Nijhof, 1986. Sutherland argues that in Company outposts like Makassar the garrison was absolutely essential in protecting Dutch trading interests and that unlike the situation in Batavia, the Company was not concerned with extending political power or colonizing in the region. pp. 49–50.

[46] Leonard Andaya, *The Heritage of Arung Palakka: A History of South Sulawesi (Celebes) in the Seventeenth Century*. Verhandelingen, KITLV, no. 91. The Hague: Martinus Nijhoff, 1981. chap. 1-6; I. D. Du Plessis, *The Cape Malays*. Cape Town: Maskew Miller Longman, 1941.

Arung Palakka himself who insisted on the banishment of at least one of the Makassarese nobles who arrived at the Cape in 1681. Karaeng Lambengi, a young Makassarese noble from Goa, had incurred the wrath of Arung Palakka by allegedly seducing one of his wives while visiting the Bone court in 1675. As a matter of honor, Arung Palakka insisted that he be punished severely. It took months for the Company to finalize negotiations between Goa and Bone over this matter, resulting in the delivery of Karaeng Lambengi into the hands of the Company "to be banished to whichever spot chosen by the Company." The Makassarese noble also had to give one of his wives to Arung Palakka as retribution.[47]

Karaeng Lambengi appears as Crain Lambungi or Crain Lambengi in the Batavia records when he was banished to the Cape by order of Governor-General Maetsuycker and the Council of India.[48] He had already been kept prisoner for three years on Point Gelderland in Batavia Castle before arriving at the Cape accompanied by one of his wives and two slaves. Karaeng Lambengi, known as Crain Lambungu in the Cape records, was given an allowance of clothing, food, and money for his upkeep at the Cape.[49]

Another of the Makassarese exiles, Daeng Matoedje, the erstwhile King of Loeboe, died on the outward voyage to the Cape.[50] A more violent death befell Care Roepa, another of the Makassarese exiles, who ran amok while trying to escape from the Cape Castle. He was shot dead by members of the Company garrison in the attempt to control him.[51] This incident resulted in a strengthening of the Cape garrison (and in particular the Castle guard) and not surprisingly heightened local anxiety about the Makassarese exiles as a group at the Cape settlement.

Confusion exists for present-day historians as well as it did for VOC officials in the transcription into Dutch of the names and titles of people who were not from Europe. This makes tracing people through their travels in the Dutch archives and around the Company's empire extremely

---

[47] Andaya, *Arung Palakka*, p. 174.
[48] November 28, 1676, *Generale Missiven*, vol. 4, 1675–1685, p. 136.
[49] The Company was at pains to keep track of royal family links across its empire. The three "illegitimate" sons of Crain Lambingi, who died at the Cape, were returned to the archipelago and records were kept of what relatives they were living with at the time and what their links were to the Bone and Bima royal clans. *Generale Missiven*, vol. 5, 1686–1697, pp. 750–751.
[50] Böeseken, *Simon van der Stel*, p. 124.
[51] Ibid., p. 125. Another Makassarese royal, Daeng Tjitjo, also ran amok at the Cape on October 10, 1699, and was killed by the garrison. *Generale Missiven*, vol. 6, November 23, 1699.

difficult.[52] One of the most prominent Makassarese people exiled in 1681, Daeng Mangale, appears in archives and travel accounts variously as Daijn Manalle,[53] Daim Mengale,[54] Dain Bengale,[55] and Dain Bengali,[56] and by Leonard Andaya as Daeng Mangappa.[57] Daeng Mangale was the brother of Karaeng Bisei, who was also known as Mohammad Ali, Sultan of Goa. In 1678 Arung Palakka, outraged when he discovered that the VOC Commander of Fort Rotterdam had granted asylum to the Sultan of Goa and his family, appealed directly to Governor-General Van Goens against Commander Cops's decision to protect these Makassarese nobles. Andaya argues that Batavia relied so heavily on Arung Palakka's alliance (both in maintaining stability in South Sulawesi and for military assistance in Java) that they were quite willing to override the judgment of their own Company officials at Makassar.[58]

The Sultan and his family were thus exiled to Batavia, from whence Daeng Mangale was further exiled to the Cape, apparently on the insistence of his brother. Daeng Mangale was at first declared "a dangerous enemy of the Company," although Governor-General Van Goens and the Council of India granted him a stipend of six rixdollars per month over and above provisions and clothes for himself and his servants.[59] Upon their arrival at the Cape, the Makassarese prisoners were confined in the Castle and subsequently separated and housed at various outposts including Stellenbosch to "prevent them planning conspiracies."[60] A list of Makassarese princes and nobles and their attendants dispatched from

---

[52] James Armstrong's research on the Chinese exiles to the Cape shows exemplary techniques in piecing together bits of biographical information to verify the identity of certain individuals whose names have been transcribed in sometimes completely unrelated ways. See Armstrong, "The Chinese at the Cape."

[53] A. J. Böeseken, *Memoriën en Instructiën*, vol. 1, 1657–1699, Suid-Africaanse Argiefstukke. Belangrike Kaapse Dokument. Kaapstad, 1966, p. 217.

[54] CA: C501: 508ff. Letters despatched September 5, 1686, "Lijste de geregeleerde Maccasarschen princen en groten en dieselven dienaren." Thanks to Robert Shell for providing me with his transcriptions of this source.

[55] Francois Valentijn, *Description of the Cape of Good Hope with the Matters Concerning It, Amsterdam 1726*, pt. 1, second series, no. 2, edited and annotated by P. Serton. Cape Town: Van Riebeeck Society, 1971, pp. 224–225.

[56] NA: General Resolution – April 5, 1680.

[57] Leonard Andaya transcribes his name as Daeng Mangappa, brother of Sultan Mohammad Ali of Goa. See Andaya, *Arung Palakka*, p. 181.

[58] Ibid., p. 205.

[59] Böeseken, *Simon van der Stel*, p. 126; Böeseken, *Memoriën en Instructiën 1657–1699*, p. 217.

[60] November 26, 1682. *Abstract of the Debates and Resolutions of the Council of Policy at the Cape from 1651–1687 (Abstracts)* ed. George McCall Theal. Cape Town: Saul Solomon and Company Printers, 1881, p. 204.

the Cape in 1686 details seventy individuals.[61] The next year the garrison at the Cape increased by twenty men as a direct result of the increasing number of prisoners at the settlement.[62]

Nevertheless, Daeng Mangale gained the sympathy of the VOC Commissioner, Adriaan van Rheede tot Drakenstein, who interviewed him at the Cape Castle. Van Rheede ordered Governor Simon van der Stel to treat the "unlucky prince" with respect and tolerance, which probably led to Van der Stel inviting Daeng Mangale to accompany the official Company expedition to Namaqualand in August 1685, where Van der Stel was attempting to enter into treaty negotiations with the Namaquas. No other mention is made of the prince in the journal of this expedition.[63] One can only speculate about the nature of the conversations that took place between the prince and the governor and in what language during these long months of traveling in the Cape countryside. Upon arriving in Batavia, Van Rheede pled Daeng Mangale's case to Governor-General Johannes Camphuys and the Council of Policy, resulting in the repatriation of the prince and five of his entourage in April 1689.[64]

The repatriation of royal exiles was not unusual, particularly if accompanied by petitions from high-ranking Company officials or persistent petitions from the exile and his family. The final decision was dependent upon the continued exile of the individual and his family serving no further political purpose for the Company, or indeed to gain advantage from a grateful ruling family. Exiles were most commonly released when they were considered too old to be a direct political threat. Repatriated exiles were given permission to return to their homes or to the custody of family members elsewhere.[65]

Shaykh Yusuf in Islamic and Company Networks

By far the most important of the exiles to the Cape in the perception of the Company was Muhammad Yusuf bin 'Abad Allah Abu al-Mahasin al-Taj al Khalwati al-Maqassari. He was known by several names and

[61] CA: C501, September 5, 1686. Letters despatched.
[62] March 14, 1687, *Abstracts*, p. 231.
[63] Gilbert Waterhouse, *Simon van der Stel's Journal of His Expedition to Namaqualand, 1685–1686*. London: Longmans Green, 1932, p. 2
[64] Böeseken, *Simon van der Stel*, pp. 125–126.
[65] The repatriation of one of the Makassarese princes, Daeng Majampa, was supported by the Cape officials after he had petitioned them directly. In their letter to Batavia, the Cape officials stated that Daeng Majampa had behaved himself well and that as he was now an old man they supported his request to go home, October 30, 1692. Letters despatched to Batavia. CA: LM, vol. 37, p. 25.

most likely referred to as Muhammad Yusuf al-Maqassari. In Sulawesi he was called *Tuanta Salamaka ri Goa* (Our Gracious Master from Goa);[66] in Java, *Tuwan Seh*; and in Batavia and at the Cape of Good Hope, he was commonly referred to by the Dutch as "the moorish pope," Shaykh Josep van Makassar.[67] The historical significance of Shaykh Yusuf lies in part in his prominence in both indigenous and Company politics, meaning that his life has been documented in great detail and that many of his religious writings were preserved in both their original manuscripts and in subsequent translations.[68]

Modern accounts of Shaykh Yusuf's life usually draw upon both Dutch and Indonesian sources, as well as oral traditions in both South Sulawesi and the Cape. His fame has enabled the most coherent narrative of exile to the Cape in the Company period.[69] Shaykh Yusuf's life is also a prominent example of the extensive Islamic networks of pilgrimage, education, and politics in the Indian Ocean that linked the archipelago to Ceylon, India and the Arabian Peninsula, and finally to the Cape. The early details of his life are well documented and infused with mythical and mystical overtones.[70]

---

[66] Azyumardi Azra, *The Origins of Islamic Reformism in Southeast Asia: Networks of Malay-Indonesian and Middle Eastern Ulama in the Seventeenth and Eighteenth Centuries*. Honolulu: University of Hawaii Press; Crows Nest, NSW: Allen and Unwin, 2004, p. 87. The biographical section that follows draws on Chapter 5, "Seventeenth Century Malay-Indonesian Networks III: Muhammad Yusuf al-Maqassari," pp. 87–108.

[67] Makassar is the common name used by outsiders for the kingdoms of Goa and Tallo on the island of Sulawesi. Christian Perlas, "Religion, Tradition and the Dynamics of Islamization in South Sulawesi," *Archipel*, 29, 1985, pp. 107–135.

[68] Manuscripts of Shaykh Yusuf's writing are preserved in several archives including the South Sulawesi Archives and at the University of Leiden in the Netherlands. Abu Hamid, *Syekh Yusuf: Seorang Ulama, Sufi dan Pejuang*. Jakarta: Yayasan Obor Indonesia, 1994; Anonymous, *Memperingati 300 Tahun pendaraan Syekh Yusuf di Afrika Selatan: Katalog Naskah Tentang Syekh Yusuf*. Ujung Pandang: Universitas Hassanudin, 1994.

[69] B. F. Matthes, "Boegineesche en Makassarsche Legenden," *BKI*, 14, 1885; G. W. J. Drewes, "Sech Joessoep Makasar," *Djawa*, 6, 2, 1926, pp. 83–88; Jeffreys, "Malay Tombs"; A. A. Cense, "De verering van Sjaich Yusuf in Zuid-Celebes," in Taufik Abdullah, "Introduction," *Sejarah lokal di Indonesia Kumpulan Tulisan*. Yogjakarta: Gadjah Mada Universitas, 1985, pp. 234–236. Abdullah mentions the tendencies toward hagiographic renditions of Shaykh Yusuf's biography. Hamid, *Syekh Yusuf*; Yusuf da Costa and Achmat Davids, *Pages from Cape Muslim History*. Pietermaritzburg: Shuter and Shooter, 1994; Achmat Davids, "The Kramat at Zandvleit – Shaykh Yusuf of Macassar," unpublished manuscript, no date.

[70] William Cummings argues that Shaykh Yusuf's "life story" was a powerful moral and educational lesson for Muslims and that his students memorized details of his life and his texts, which were transmitted orally. William Cummings, *Making Blood White: Historical Transformations in Early Modern Makassar*. Honolulu: University of Hawaii Press, 2002, p. 155.

Shaykh Yusuf was born in 1627 into the royal house of Goa and was raised in the palace of the king, Sultan Alauddin Tumenangra ri Gaukanna (r.1593 to 1639).[71] His childhood Islamic education began in the palace under Daeng ri Tasammang and Arab and Achenese teachers who had migrated to South Sulawesi, followed by periods of tutelage under famous teachers at Islamic centers in Bontoala and Cikoang. This was the same period during which South Sulawesi was undergoing conversion to Islam, and court politics were reorganized in accordance with the new faith of the leaders. Shaykh Yusuf married a daughter of the Sultan of Goa, Mangarangi Daeng Maurabiya, before leaving to further his religious education. Miraculous signs that accompanied his childhood and his exceptional talent as a young scholar had destined him for fame and for the hand of the Sultan's daughter. Cummings argues that in this story the Sultan consults written texts to determine whether his daughter could marry below her rank instead of consulting royal courtiers. This indicates a shift away from oral traditions as the source of law to written texts that contained absolute truths.[72] Shaykh Yusuf was already leaning toward an interest in the mystical practices of Islam embodied in the *Tasawwuf*.[73]

At the age of eighteen, Yusuf began his educational journey and pilgrimage to the Haramayn (Mecca and Medina). En route he stayed at Banten where he struck up a friendship with the Crown Prince, Pangeran Surya, who was later to rule Banten as Abdul Fathi Abdul Fattah Sultan Ageng Tirtayasa, commonly known as Sultan Ageng. He studied under the famous Shaykh Nuruddin in Aceh on the far-west coast of Sumatra, acquiring *ijazah* (authority) of *tariqah* (order) Qadariyyah before departing for Arabia via Gujarat in 1649. His studies continued in Yemen where he obtained *ijazah* of the *tariqahs* Naqshbandiyyah and Ba'Alawiyyah before completing his pilgrimage to Mecca. After continuing his journey to study in Medinah under another famous teacher, he traveled to Damascus where he gained *ijazah* of the Khalwatiyyah and was granted the title, "*al-Taj al-Khalwati*" (the Crown of the Khalwati). Azyumardi Azra points out that written and oral traditions of South Sulawesi indicate that Shaykh Yusuf went to Negeri Rum (Istanbul) although this cannot be corroborated.[74]

---

[71] Andaya, *Arung Palaka*, p. 303.
[72] Cummings, *Making Blood White*, pp. 69–70.
[73] Abu Hamid, *Syekh Yusuf Makassar: Alim, Sufi, Author, Hero*. Ujung Pandang, Indonesia: University of Hasanuddin, 1994, pp. 79–84.
[74] Azra, *Islamic Reformism*, p. 92.

By this time Shaykh Yusuf, known as a "Jawi alim" (Javanese alim), was attracting his own students at the Masjidil Haram in Mecca, including hajj pilgrims from all over the archipelago.[75] Shaykh Yusuf's pilgrimage, although exceptional in the distinction of his scholarship, was not unusual in its basic elements. By the late sixteenth century the Muslim elite of archipelagic polities were well integrated into regional migrations to centers of Islamic education and to pilgrimage routes across the Indian Ocean. Although this Indian Ocean Islamic network has not been studied as a whole during this period, it is clear that a pilgrimage to Mecca had already become standard practice, particularly for potential rulers and scholars.

After a sojourn in Jeddah, Shaykh Yusuf returned to the archipelago. Written biographies and oral traditions of the Shaykh all differ on his movements after his return. Ricklefs and Perlas assert that he returned to Makassar and attempted to generate widespread Islamic reform through the influence of his teaching and organizing *tariqahs*. With the failure of his religious reform and a deteriorating political situation in Makassar in 1672, he left and settled in Banten, where he was welcomed by Sultan Ageng.[76]

In contrast, Abu Hamid, whose biography of Shaykh Yusuf forms the basis of subsequent biographies by Cape scholars like Achmat Davids, claims that the Shaykh arrived in Banten in 1664 and remained there because of the deteriorating political situation in his homeland. As Azra points out, it was not necessary for Shaykh Yusuf to go to Makassar to have influenced reformist movements there. His students returning from the Haramayn and Banten would have carried forth his teachings and practices. The persistent and widespread support of later requests for Shaykh Yusuf's return from exile, by both palace and populace, confirms his considerable impact as an Islamic scholar and charismatic leader despite his physical absence.

---

[75] This section on Shaykh Yusuf's education and immersion in Islamic networks is drawn from Hamid, *Syekh Yusuf Makassar*, and Azra, *Islamic Reformism*, chapter 5, pp. 87–108. One of Shaykh Yusuf's students during this period was Abdul Fattah Basir ad Dharir, whom Shaykh Yusuf later met in Banten and ordered to return to Makassar to spread the tariqah Khalwatiyyah in the region. Shaykh Yusuf also married a daughter of an Imam of Masjidil Haram, named Sitti Khadijah. Some sources imply she was reluctant to marry a non-Arab but was persuaded by her father. They had one daughter, Sitti Samang or Puang Ammang, before the woman died in childbirth. During his stay in Jeddah Shaykh Yusuf married another Shaykh's daughter, whose name is unknown, but their son's name was Daeng Kare Sitaba. It is not clear whether she accompanied Shaykh Yusuf back to the archipelago, Hamid, *Sheykh Yusuf Makassar*, pp. 3–7.

[76] Ricklefs, *War, Culture and Economy*, p. 295; Perlas, "Religion, Tradition," pp. 123–125.

By the early 1660s the deterioration of relations between the King of Goa, Sultan Hasanuddin Tumenanga ri Balla'pangkana (r.1653 to 1669), and the Company had begun. Disputes over jurisdiction, particularly the transfer of the disputed territory of Butung and Menado to Ternate and over the legal rights to salvaging shipwrecks had soured relations between the two parties precisely at the time of Shaykh Yusuf's return. Leonard Andaya argues that

> [t]he Company was interested in South Sulawesi affairs only insofar as they impinged on its principal concern: the spices of the Moluccas... the conflict over the interpretation of the meaning of "freedom of the seas" demonstrated the essence of the struggle between the Company and Goa. To enforce an economic monopoly the Company had to control the sea-lanes; but for Goa to accept the Company's restrictions was tantamount to relinquishing its sovereign powers and its pretensions to overlordship in the area. By the middle of the 17th century this basic irreconcilable difference between two ambitious powers boded ill for their future relations.[77]

The subsequent war resulted in the abdication and defeat of Sultan Hasanuddin achieved by the dual forces of Arung Palakka and the VOC. Interestingly, Andaya quotes a source claiming that in 1667 a copy the Treaty of Bungaya in Malay had been shown to the Sultan Ageng Tirtayasa of Banten (r.1650–1682), who commented that "those in Makassar had promised more than could and would be fulfilled."[78] Shaykh Yusuf was probably a party to the Sultan's deliberations over the treaty. In any case, it was clear that people in Banten were fully apprised of the unstable situation in South Sulawesi and that Sultan Ageng had extended an invitation to his childhood friend, Shaykh Yusuf, to seek refuge there as an honored member of his court. Shaykh Yusuf became a revered Mufti, royal advisor, and eventually son-in-law to the Sultan.

The Makassarese presence in Banten was considerably strengthened in the 1670s with the arrival of significant numbers of Makassarese nobles exiled with their followers to Java, totaling several thousand people. Unlike many indigenous rulers, Sultan Ageng was eager to offer refuge to the Makassarese to bolster his own armed forces in preparation for the looming confrontation with the VOC.[79] Sultan Ageng supported European rivals of the Dutch, indigenous traders, and provided sanctuary for deserters and escaped convicts from the Company.

One of these exiles was Daeng Mangappa, who arrived on November 9, 1674 with seven to eight hundred of his followers in Banten, where

[77] Andaya, *Arung Palaka*, p. 71.
[78] Ibid., p. 117.
[79] Ibid., pp. 208–211.

they settled for a year before moving onto east Java because of differences with the Sultan. The VOC considered these mobile populations of Makassarese nobles and their followers such a destabilizing influence in the archipelago that by the late 1670s there were attempts to force them back to their homeland in South Sulawesi. By 1680, Daeng Mangappa and his followers were seeking refuge in Palembang in West Java. It appears that to force his followers to return, the Company arrested Daeng Mangappa, and Governor-General Rijkloff van Goens exiled him to the Cape, where he arrived in 1681 and was known as the "unlucky prince" Daeng Mangale.[80]

As part of his court duties, Shaykh Yusuf had been tutoring Sultan Ageng's eldest son, Pangeran 'Abd al-Qahhar, in preparation for his pilgrimage to Mecca in 1674. The prince visited Istanbul on a diplomatic mission from Banten during his hajj journey. Relations between Sultan Ageng and the VOC had deteriorated during this period partly due to direct competition between Batavia and Banten over trade, and partly over suzerainty of the Ceribon region of Java.[81] Upon his return in 1676, Pangeran 'Abd al-Qahhar, now known as Sultan Haji, began making overtures toward the Company, most probably because his younger brother Pangeran Poerbaya had been chosen by their father as the Crown Prince.[82] He was able to secure Company support in preparation for an attempt to overthrow his father's rule. Achmat Davids overstates the Company's power over Sultan Haji in presenting the latter as a witless puppet of Western imperialism.[83] The political strategy of employing mercenaries was common in Southeast Asian polities, and the VOC had formalized this and other military alliances as a way to enhance its own influence in the region and gain economic advantage from rendering military service. Governor-General Rijkloff van Goens assured Sultan Haji of military support in return for signing a contract that guaranteed reparations and trade concessions once he became sole ruler.[84]

When the succession dispute in Banten broke into full-scale civil war during 1682, Shaykh Yusuf sided with the aging Sultan Ageng against his

---

[80] Ibid., pp. 212–227.
[81] Ceribon had been militarily defeated by the Company in 1681 and the Ceribon rulers were forced to conclude a treaty ceding sovereignty over the region to the Company. *Corpus Diplomaticum*, vol. 3, pp. 233–242.
[82] Suleman Dangor, *Shaykh Yusuf*, Mobeni: Iqra Research Committee, 1982. p. 15.
[83] Davids, "The Kramat at Zandvleit." pp. 10–11.
[84] For one detailed account of the intricacies of these relationships between the VOC and indigenous polities in Java see Ricklefs, *War Culture and Economy*.

usurping son. Although Sultan Ageng surrendered and was imprisoned by the VOC in Batavia, Shaykh Yusuf fled to the mountains with several thousand followers and started heading east, probably in an attempt to reach the coast and regroup in Makassar.[85] The Company enlisted the support of Surapati and his Balinese followers, who in the Dutch records was considered an escaped slave and bandit leader.[86] At this point, the Javanese and Dutch accounts of events differ widely.

According to the West Javanese Surapati *babad*, Surapati had sworn an oath of allegiance to the Company in 1678 and was appointed lieutenant in charge of a contingent of Balinese auxiliaries. Surapati was solely responsible for convincing Shaykh Yusuf to surrender, and he formally handed over the Shaykh to the Company in Ceribon in exchange for a considerable fortune in war booty.[87] Ricklefs claims that Surapati and his followers betrayed the Dutch and fled before Shaykh Yusuf was arrested.[88] Dutch accounts of the Shaykh's capture also contain mythical elements and stories that circulated in travelers' accounts. According to their version, Shaykh Yusuf finally surrendered to Lieutenant Van Happel who, dressed in Moorish attire and speaking fluent Malay and Arabic, had entered the Shaykh's camp accompanied by his hostage daughter, Asma. Van Happel then persuaded Shaykh Yusuf to surrender upon assurances of fair treatment and took the Shaykh, his family, and close followers to Ceribon, from where they were taken to Batavia. Many of Shaykh Yusuf's followers were either sent back to Makassar, or escaped and joined forces with Surapati, who was now regarded as a rebel by the VOC for having betrayed his oath of allegiance.[89]

Governor-General Cornelis Speelman and his Council of Policy were reluctant to keep Shaykh Yusuf a long-term prisoner in Batavia Castle because he was considered a grave security risk. He was revered as a saint by many of the Muslims in Batavia who collected his *sepah* (chewed betel nut) from the ground and treated it as a holy relic.[90] Shaykh Yusuf

---

[85] Shaykh Yusuf and Pangeran Poerbaya had a bounty on their heads from the Company of 1,000 rixdollars dead or alive. This was a fortune at the time, considering that a skilled Company craftsman in Batavia earned around 150 rixdollars per year. Opper, "Company Artisans," pp. 49–81.
[86] Ricklefs, *War, Culture and Economy*, p. 87.
[87] Kumar, *Surapati*, pp. 59–62.
[88] Ricklefs, *War, Culture and Economy*, p. 87.
[89] Hamid, *Shaykh Yusuf Makassar*, pp. 14–16; Ricklefs, *War Culture and Economy*, p. 87; Valentijn, *Oud en Nieuw Oost-Indies*, vol. 4, pt. 1, p. 123, February 19, 1684; *Generale Missiven* vol. 4, p. 658.
[90] Valentijn, *Oud en Nieuw Oost-Indies*, vol. 3, p. 123.

and his retinue were accordingly exiled to Colombo in 1684, where he lived without harsh restrictions being placed upon his writing or his religious practices.[91] As Ceylon was on the pilgrimage route from the archipelago to India, the Haramayn, the rest of the Arabian Peninsula, and the Ottoman Empire, the Shaykh had open communication with Muslim pilgrims from all over the Indian Ocean and Dar al Islam. Azra notes that Shaykh Yusuf used his time in Ceylon to write religious works and that his presence continued to attract scholars there. The Moghul emperor Aurangzeb was apparently aware of Shaykh Yusuf's presence in Ceylon and ordered the Dutch to provide for his well being.[92] The Company did nothing to isolate Shaykh Yusuf from the Islamic networks of the region while he was in Ceylon.

By 1689, political events in South Sulawesi prompted a concerted effort by the nobility of Makassar to seek Shaykh Yusuf's return. This petition for his return was supported by Arung Palakka's Goan wife, Daeng Talele, and the new Sultan of Goa, Kaerang Abdul Jallil. Bringing a ransom of 2,000 rixdollars to Fort Rotterdam, Commander Hartsink rashly agreed to their demands without first consulting with Batavia. When forwarding his request to Governor-General Johannes Camphuys, Hartsink advised that should Batavia refuse, it needed to send military reinforcements to Makassar "because the request had come from the common man, and the masses in Makassar hold this same Syaikh in such great love and awe as though he was a second Muhammad."[93]

Andaya speculates that the request for Shaykh Yusuf's return was an attempt by the Sultan of Goa to bolster his own political position relative to Arung Palakka.[94] Perhaps fearing Shaykh Yusuf's popular support, Arung Palakka secretly informed Batavia that he opposed the Shaykh's return and consequently the Company did not act upon the request. Nevertheless, this left Hartsink in a vulnerable position and a special Commissioner, Dirk de Haas, was sent to Makassar in 1691 to repair the already strained relations between Arung Palakka and the Company's local representative.[95] The authority of Hartsink was circumvented in

---

[91] November 30, 1684; *Generale Missiven* vol. 4, p. 709. Shaykh Yusuf and his family traveled on the *Coevorden* to Ceylon and was allocated 24 rixdollars per month for his upkeep.
[92] Azra, *Islamic Reformism*, p. 98.
[93] Hartsink quoted in Andaya, *Arung Palakka*, pp. 276–277.
[94] William Cummings, "Only One People But Two Rulers': Hiding the Past in Seventeenth-Century Makasarese Chronicles," *BKI*, 155, 1, 1999, p. 112.
[95] Andaya, *Arung Palakka*, pp. 277–278.

recognition that although he was dispensable, the alliance with Arung Palakka was crucial to the Company's power in South Sulawesi.[96]

Indigenous rulers were often able to circumvent the authority of local Company officials by appealing directly to the governor-general in Batavia. The complexities of power relations within the Company's empire and between the Company and indigenous polities often put local Company officials at a distinct disadvantage.[97] At the Cape, Company officials were loathe to take action against political exiles who transgressed local authority without first checking the status of the offender with Batavia or justifying further harsh punishment in terms of overt criminal activity.[98]

The renewed request by the Makassarese nobility in 1691 to Commissioner De Haas for Shaykh Yusuf's return quite possibly prompted Batavia's decision to send the Shaykh to the Cape of Good Hope. Shaykh Yusuf's exile in Ceylon had not been sufficient to neutralize his religious or political influence in the archipelago. It was also speculated that he was in direct communication with other Muslim leaders and that letters had been written to the Moghul court requesting assistance in freeing Shaykh Yusuf and other Muslim prisoners of the Company.[99]

It was Shaykh Yusuf's influence and status as an important prisoner of state, and the fact that Banten was still an independent polity outside the jurisdiction of the Company, that prevented him from being executed for rebellion. His status as a royal prisoner of state brought with it certain rights and obligations on the part of the Company. This social and political status allowed the Shaykh to go into exile accompanied by forty-nine members of his family, religious followers, and slaves.[100] Sailing on the Company flute, *Voetboeg*, Shaykh Yusuf and his retinue arrived at the Cape on April 2, 1694. They were officially received by Willem Adriaan van der Stel, the governor and son of the former governor, Simon van der Stel.[101]

---

[96] Ibid., pp. 278–280.
[97] See for example Hendrik Niemeijer, "A Feigned Peace?" Sultan Saifuddin of Ternate outreigned and outmaneuvered twelve different regional Company governors, while simultaneously relying on the support of Batavia to consolidate his own local power.
[98] See Chapter 6 for a case of rebellion on Robben Island where these issues of rank, status, and punishment are played out in detail.
[99] Böeseken, *Simon van der Stel*, p. 128.
[100] February 19, 1684; *Generale Missiven* vol. 4, p. 674. The High Government ordered Shaykh Yusuf must be treated according to his "status and stature."
[101] Shaykh Yusuf's magical and mystical powers prompted the story that when the ship had run out of fresh water, he ordered the sailors to draw water from the sea at the spot

After being housed in the Castle, preparations were made to relocate Shaykh Yusuf and his entourage to the farm, Zandvliet, which had been purchased by the Company for this purpose. The farm, belonging to Reverend Kalden, was located near the coast at the mouth of the Eerste River, at a spot that would eventually become known as the "Makassar Downs." Shaykh Yusuf was allocated an allowance of twelve rixdollars per month by order from Batavia.[102] Company records are not at all revealing about the details of Shaykh Yusuf's banishment to the windswept farm of Zandvliet that lies several miles from Cape Town near the coastline of False Bay. There were rumors that Shaykh Yusuf's settlement had become a safe haven for runaway slaves and other fugitives. Achmat Davids claims that, despite his advanced years, requests for the Shaykh's repatriation were again refused by Batavia in 1698.[103]

News of Shaykh Yusuf's death on May 23, 1699, by natural causes at the age of seventy-three, prompted an expression of great relief from Batavia.[104] One of the reasons cited is that the Company had calculated its expenses for maintaining the Shaykh and his entourage at 26,221.12 guilders, and it was eager to be rid of this financial burden.[105] The High Government had passed a general resolution on October 30, 1699, authorizing the repatriation of Shaykh Yusuf's two wives, daughters, and sons under the age of six. This was only a partial fulfillment of requests from the Sultan of Goa and, significantly, the principle Makassarese residents of Batavia who had petitioned the Governor-General Willem van Outshoorn for the repatriation of all members of Shaykh Yusuf's entourage. Batavia decided that all men and boys over the age of six should remain in exile at the Cape, presumably for fear of their taking up political opposition to the Company on behalf of their martyred saint and leader. Furthermore, in a typical Company financial decision, Shaykh Yusuf's slaves were ordered to be assessed for their monetary value and remain at the Cape in the service of the Company until they had worked off this

---

where he had dipped in his foot. To their amazement, the sailors lifted casks filled with fresh water. George McCall Theal, *History of South Africa Before 1795*. Originally published 1922. Cape Town: C. Struik, 1964, vol. 3, p. 263.

[102] Resolution, June 14, 1694, p. 511; CA: LM, p. 27.

[103] Jeffreys, "The Malay Tombs," pt. 2, p. 195. A letter from Radja Goa to Batavia dated February 19, 1697, specifically requests Shaykh Yusuf's return. Batavia decided that it was too dangerous to let Shaykh Yusuf return to Makassar. *Generale Missiven* vol. 4, February 21, 1698, p. 13.

[104] Letter despatched to Batavia, July 1, 1699. CA: LM, vol. 38, p. 41.

[105] Letter received from Batavia, November 23, 1699. CA: LM, vol. 37, p. 37.

amount to defray costs to the Company for the continued (but reduced) maintenance of the remaining exiles.[106]

In a courageous standoff, Shaykh Yusuf's wives stated to Company officials at the Cape that if the party could not leave together, they would all remain together. This may well have been an attempt to protect all the women in Shaykh Yusuf's family, including his two women slaves, Momina and Naima, not to mention the male children in the group. The party showed considerable resilience in refusing to be separated, while Batavia was receiving further requests and petitions from Makassar for their return.[107] Two years after Shaykh Yusuf's death, his entourage was still at the Cape and being supported by the Company.[108] Batavia's irritation was palpable in writing to the Cape that it would be most convenient if Shaykh Yusuf's widows would stop petitioning, and thereafter arrangements were made for the whole group's repatriation.[109] Most members of Shaykh Yusuf's family and entourage returned to Batavia on the Company schooners *Liefde* and *Spiegel*, finally arriving in Makassar in April 1705.[110]

According to Dangor, two imams in Shaykh Yusuf's entourage elected of their own free will to stay at the Cape. It is difficult to imagine why these men decided to stay at the Cape except in terms of their religious commitment.[111] Without the protection of their patron, minor political exiles were much more vulnerable to Company discipline. In general, only very high-ranking prisoners and politically important exiles were treated with the regard shown to Shaykh Yusuf. Hundreds of minor political exiles were sent to the Cape and lived in extremely harsh conditions, some suffering punishments similar to convicted criminals. Responding to further petitions in Batavia from the Makassarese court for the return of the remaining members of Shaykh Yusuf's followers, Cape officials informed Batavia that they had held Manjampa Singa on Robben Island after determining he was "dangerous." Manjampa Singa was particularly vulnerable because his exile had not been personally determined by resolution from Batavia. The Cape officials were therefore under no obligation to maintain him under the same conditions as Shaykh Yusuf.

---

[106] Extract from a General Resolution of the Castle of Batavia, October 30, 1699. CA: C: Inkomende Briewe, vol. 366, pp. 21–23.
[107] Letter despatched to Batavia, March 22, 1700. CA: LM, vol. 38, p. 74.
[108] Letter despatched to Batavia, May 29, 1701. CA: LM, vol. 38, p. 119.
[109] Letter received from Batavia, December 1, 1703. CA: LM, vol. 36, p. 37.
[110] Letter despatched from Batavia, May 5, 1705.
[111] Dangor, *Shaykh Yusuf*, p. 32.

When Batavia determined the conditions of exile, the Cape officials had much less room to maneuver. In the case of Manjampa Singa, the intervention of the Makassarese court prompted Batavia to order the Cape officials to repatriate him.[112]

The other member of Shaykh Yusuf's entourage who elected to remain at the Cape was one of his daughters, Sitti Sara Marouff, who had married the exiled Raja of Tambora, Abdul Basir, at the Cape.[113] Despite repeated requests from the Raja in an appropriately florid supplicating tone, Batavia would not allow him to be repatriated and so the couple remained in exile.[114] Their conditions of exile were quite extraordinary because the Cape governor had apparently befriended them. Francois Valentijn in his travel account of the Cape describes having met the couple at Vergelegen, Governor Willem Adriaan van der Stel's lavish country estate.[115] Speculations exist that the Raja of Tambora gave Van der Stel a hand-written copy of the Q'uran he had transcribed from memory.[116] Nevertheless, the Raja petitioned Batavia consistently to be allowed to return to his homeland on the island of Sumbawa, east of Java. His personal relationship with the Cape governor was of no benefit in these negotiations.

The marriage of Shaykh Yusuf's daughter to a high-ranking noble who was neither from Java nor from Makassar offers a tantalizing glimpse of elite family alliances that were forged in conditions of exile, which, under ordinary circumstances, may not have taken place. Hussainmaiya suggests that this was the case in Ceylon, where most of the high-ranking political exiles had been received.[117] Fortunately for him and his family, the Raja of Tambora's persistence finally paid off, and they were allowed to return to the Indies after his pardon in 1710.[118] He appears

---

[112] Letter despatched to Batavia, May 25, 1707. CAS: UCT, McMillan Collection, "Shaykh Yusuf," Annexure C, p. 3.
[113] Dangor, *Shaykh Yusuf*, p. 32. Raja Tambora had arrived at the Cape in 1698 by order of Batavia. CA: C362, Inkomende Briewe, February 3-September 18, 1698, p. 126.
[114] Letter received from Batavia, November 23, 1699. CA: LM, vol. 37, p. 37.
[115] Valentijn, *Oud en Nieuw Oost-Indies*, vol. 4, pt. 3, pp. 108–109.
[116] More than one Muslim exile performed this religious feat, including Tuan Guru whose hand written Qur'an is in private possession in Cape Town, as are other religious texts of this era. Achmat Davids, personal communication, April 1994.
[117] Hussainmiya, *Orang Rejimen*, pp. 1–87.
[118] Letters received from Batavia. August 13, 1697; November 20, 1699; January 28, 1701; November 30, 1702. CA: LM, vol. 36, p. 12; vol. 36, p. 39. Letters despatched to Batavia, March 10, 1708; March 17, 1710. CA: LM, vol. 38, p. 43b. *Generale Missiven* vol. 7, November 20, 1713, p. 9.

to have stirred up political opposition to the Company upon his return to Batavia because he was re-exiled to the Cape for "seditious conduct" in 1714.[119]

The Raja of Tambora is the only case of repeat political exile to the Cape that appears in the archives. At the time of his second exile, he was not the reigning king of Tambora, and the Company was exercising direct political power in the kingdom in apparent overlordship of the incumbent ruler.[120] The kingdom of Tambora itself was not a crucial polity in the broader scheme of the Company's empire. Far more attention was paid by Batavia to the political situation in the core areas of Java, Makassar, and the Molaccas. The Raja of Tambora was one of scores of minor rulers sent into exile by the Company.

Apart from being exiled twice, what makes the Raja of Tambora's case particularly interesting in terms of the dynamics of Company exile circuits is what it reveals and reinforces about the gendered dimension of the process. Women were not exiled as political prisoners in their own right. Women were, however, exiled alongside their husbands, fathers, and sons, and were particularly vulnerable once their male relatives died. Cases of exile have been calculated on the basis of the primary figure involved, and although the large entourage of Shaykh Yusuf was unmatched in any other case of exile to the Cape, it appears that there were other cases in which women and children were involved in the process. Taking this into consideration alters the demographics of exile to the Cape. Although their numbers cannot be calculated using Company records because insufficient details about these women exist, it does alert historians to another aspect of this network of exile, children born into exile. In some cases, these children born at the Cape returned to the archipelago and joined the court culture of their parental homelands having known nothing other than life in Africa.

During his second exile, Abdul Basir was accompanied by another of his wives, Care Sale, their children, and followers who made up a party of eight. The Raja remained pitifully dejected about his exile until released by death in 1719, shortly after his last petition to Governor-General Hendrik Zwaardecroon in Batavia.[121] Over the next several years, Care Sale

---

[119] Letter received from Batavia, 1714. CA: LM, vol. 38, p. 43b.
[120] *Generale Missiven* vol. 7, November 20, 1713, p. 8. The reigning Raja of Tambora was informed of the "old Raja's" arrest after he had already left for the Cape.
[121] Cape General Resolutions, April 25, 1719. Letter received by the Cape 1716–1717, no specific date. CA: LM, vol. 31, Index to Annexures. Letters Received 1716–1782, p. 18.

petitioned the Cape governor for financial assistance and to be allowed to return home. Her first petition detailed that she was living in town with her five children in extreme poverty, having lost most of her slaves to death through illness. Her request was forwarded to Batavia where it languished unresolved among the paperwork and meeting agendas at the Castle.[122]

Her next letter to the Cape governor again stressed her dire straits, pointing out that because her children were too young to work and the Company had confiscated the slaves allocated to her for her subsistence, her household was unable to survive on their present allowance and was short of food. The Cape officials resolved to increase her allowance by six rixdollars per month without incurring further cost to the Company. In a feat of imaginative accounting this amount was confiscated from the errant Prince of Ternate who had been imprisoned as a convict on Robben Island after having transgressed all acceptable proprieties and boundaries of political exile by opening up an illegal gambling house in the town.[123]

Javanese Royalty at the Cape

By the end of the seventeenth century, Batavia was deeply drawn into the intricate complexity of political intrigues that constituted the life of the Mataram empire in Java. In the course of what became known as the First Javanese War of Succession, the VOC assisted Pangeran Pugur against the reigning Kartasuran king, Amangkurat III, and his ally Surapati. Although Surapati was killed, his sons were able to consolidate their control over the mountain area of Malang in Eastern Java. Amangkurat III was arrested by the VOC and exiled for the remainder of his life to Ceylon. Pangeran Pugur installed himself in the Kartasura *kraton* and took the title of Susuhanan Pakubuwana I.[124] As payment for the Company's assistance, a contract was negotiated between the VOC and the new Mataram rulers recognizing the boundaries of Batavia and ceding to the Company sovereignty over the Priangan highlands, Ceribon, Sumanap and Caligawe. The Company was granted the right to build forts in Java and to station a garrison at the palace. It extracted substantial trade

---

[122] Cape General Resolutions, September 24, 1720. CA: LM, vol. 38, p. 43.
[123] Cape General Resolutions, November 24, 1722, and December 8, 1722. CA: LM, vol. 36, p. 38 and vol. 38, p. 43b.
[124] M. C. Ricklefs, *Modern Javanese Historical Tradition: A Study of an Original Kartasuran Chronicle and Related Materials*. London: SOAS, 1978, p. 8.

concessions and restricted the Javanese sphere of influence and right of passage in surrounding seas.[125] The results of this treaty were, on paper at least, a significant increase in Company jurisdiction in Java and its waters.

Not all the *kraton* elite was supportive of the new relationship between the Susuhanan and the VOC. A son of Pakubuwana I, Raden Suryakasuma (alias Saloringpasar), was accused by both his father and the Company of conspiring with the Balinese rebels and lords of Surabaya.[126] Saloringpasar took refuge in Semarang and sought protection from the Company. Despite requests from Pakubuwana I that Saloringpasar be returned to Kartasura for execution, Company officials at Semarang said they could not do so until they had approval from Batavia. Pakubuwana I then requested that Batavia exile Saloringpasar to the Cape of Good Hope instead of executing him. The Susuhanan specifically asked that his son not be sent to Ceylon because Amunkurat III was exiled there and was thought to be still in possession of the Kartasuran regalia. Pakubuwana I feared a challenge to his rule from the potential allegiance between the exiles and their ability to invoke the power of the royal regalia.[127]

Merle Ricklefs speculates about the Company's motives for exiling Saloringpasar to the Cape: "It is not clear why the VOC preferred his exile to his execution, for the Company usually cavilled neither at execution nor murder. Perhaps it felt, as Pakabuwana I doubtless suspected, that it could gain some leverage over the palace by being known as a safe refuge for recusant princes. Whatever the cause, this cannot have assuaged the Susuhanan's doubts about an ally, who had perhaps prevented him from having the royal *pusakas* and now certainly prevented him from executing a rebellious son."[128]

It is unlikely that the VOC was perceived to be doing Saloringpasar a great favor by exiling him to the Cape of Good Hope, and the conditions of his exile would certainly not have guaranteed the Company his gratitude. Before being transported to the Cape, Saloringpasar was held with his entourage on the Island of Edam in the Batavia roadstead to await their westbound ship, the *Gansenhoef*.[129] He was accompanied into

---

[125] Java-Mataram, *Corpus Diplomaticum* 633, October 5, 1705, pp. 242–251.
[126] The Company reported that Saloringpasar was linked directly with Surapati. ANRI: General Resolutions, Batavia: January 4, 1715.
[127] Ricklefs, *War, Culture and Economy*, pp. 120–121, 163.
[128] Ibid., pp. 163–164.
[129] ANRI: General Resolutions, Batavia, August 29, 1715. CA: C24, pp. 283–286, fn. 24, p. 69.

lifetime exile with his mother, two wives, mother-in-law, and followers totaling fourteen people.[130]

Upon his arrival in Africa, Saloringpasar, who was known there as Loring Pasir, was held in the Castle pending a decision by the Cape officials about where best to house him. After elaborate discussions, the governor, Maurice Pasques, Marquis de Chavonnes, decided that he would be safest if held inland to minimize his chance of being able to escape on a passing ship. Stellenbosch was chosen over Drakenstein as Saloringpasar's place of exile as he could be kept under close surveillance in this small village. Governor-General Christoffel van Swol had ordered that the Cape officials furnish Saloringpasar with a house for himself and his entourage.

The Cape officials organized the purchase of a property for 1,500 guilders from a highly respected burgher, Daniel Pheijl, even though Pakabuwana I had only provided an annual allowance of 337.5 rixdollars.[131] Considerable thought went into the purchase of this property, which reveals the extent to which the Company officials at the Cape went to great pains to ensure the basic needs of their royal prisoner. The property was carefully surveyed before the purchase and a detailed report submitted to the Governor and Council of Policy. The whitewashed house had two side rooms, an entrance area, a comfortable kitchen on the right-hand side behind the entrance, and a small room suitable for a pantry. At the back of the property there was another room suitable for servants' quarters. Although the buildings needed some work, the Company officials reported that Saloringpasar's servants could help with the necessary repairs. The property came with twelve morgen of land, suitable for growing corn and grapes, and had direct river access for water. This latter point was considered particularly important as the Company report stated that it was well-known that the Javanese nation required access to running water for frequent bathing.[132]

Saloringpasar and his entourage were accompanied to Stellenbosch by senior Company officials, in recognition of Saloringpasar's royal status. The merchant, Arent Protte, the Stellenbosch landdrost Nicholaas van der Heuvel, and undermerchant Bartholomeus de Wit led the way through the forty or so miles past the sandy Cape Flats toward the fertile rural

---

[130] *Generale Missiven*, February 18, 1715, p. 159.
[131] February 3, 1716. CA: C10, pp. 201–215, Resoluties van die Polititie Raad, vol. 5, pp. 13–14; Ricklefs, *War, Culture and Economy*, fn. 47, p. 353.
[132] February 18, 1716. CA: C10, pp. 227–264, Resoluties van die Polititie Raad, vol. 5, pp. 22–23.

landscape at the foot of the exquisitely rugged Hottentot Hollands mountains and then to the property that became the prince's new home.[133]

Along with the purchase of the Stellenbosch property, the Company provided Saloringpasar with 520 pounds of rice because it was presumed that the Javanese could not eat bread. Other provisions were to be supplied at cost from the Company stores.[134] After these elaborate arrangements were put into place, little is known about the daily life of Saloringpasir and his entourage. A brief crisis took place in 1720 when their Stellenbosch house burnt down after a fire started in the kitchen, an event that put the whole population of Stellenbosch at considerable danger from fast-spreading fire. Although no ulterior motives were suspected, the event did prompt some debate about whether it would be safer to house the royal exiles in the relatively isolated coastal fishing hamlet of Vischhoek. Instead, the aristocratic governor, Maurice Pasques Marquis de Chavonnes, ordered the rebuilding of the Stellenbosch house.[135]

It appears that Saloringpasir and his entourage were restricted in their movements on their property or in Stellenbosch. Batavia did not submit any further orders regarding the prince's exile at the Cape. In other cases of exile to the Cape, it is clear that the VOC considered prisoners of state as direct leverages in the political affairs of their homelands. Company-palace relations were more delicately handled at this stage and Saloringpasar was not used overtly as political capital. When the Company Resident at Kartasura, Christoffel Walling, casually asked a senior advisor of the Crown Prince, Pangeran Purbaya, what he thought would be the consequence of returning Saloringpasir to the court, Pakabuwana I immediately petitioned Governor-General Christoffel van Swol to have the Resident recalled and replaced.[136]

In 1717, as Saloringpasir settled into his exile at the Cape, the Company's fears regarding rebellion against Pakubuwana I by the lords of Surabaya and Madura came to fruition. As the rebellion spread in Java, Pakabuwana I sent one of his sons, Pangeran Dipanagara, to quell the strife east of Kartasura. Instead, Dipanagara joined the rebellion, which now involved Balinese strongholds in east Java ruled by Surapati's

---

[133] February 25, 1716. CA: C10, pp. 265–288, Resoluties van die Polititie Raad, vol. 5, p. 25.
[134] February 25, 1716 and March 3, 1716, Resolutions. CA: LM, vol. 38, General Index, p. 31.
[135] January 9, 1720, January 24, 1720, and February 13, 1720, Resolutions. CA: LM, vol. 38, General Index, p. 31.
[136] Ricklefs, *War, Culture and Economy*, p. 178–179 & fn. 50, p. 363.

sons.[137] Ricklefs notes that the VOC speculated Pakabuwana I had secretly endorsed Dipanagara's rebellion as a way to undermine Company power in Java without incurring its direct wrath.

Apparently, Pangeran Dipanagara was not a prominent figure in palace sources prior to the rebellion. He did have a reputation as a religious scholar, having transcribed the Old Javanese text, *Darma Sunya Keling*, a philosophical exposition concerning Siva-Buddhist mysticism. This form of mysticism defined redemptive leadership in terms of the qualities of a "just king," a role that Dipanagara adopted when he rebelled. Ricklefs speculates: "Dipanagara perhaps felt, or chose to assert, that he was a prince who could bridge the distinctions between the royal house and the rebels, and between Islam and the Hindu-Buddhist ideas still alive in Bali."[138] By the end of 1718, Pangeran Dipanagara had taken for himself the exalted title of Panembahan Erucakra, the title of the messianic just king in Javanese prophetical literature.[139]

If the intention of Pakabuwana I was to extract the palace from Company influence, his plan was thwarted partly through divine intervention. The Susuhanan's death in 1719, coupled with the Company's endorsement of Amangkurat IV as the successor to the throne, occasioned the outbreak of full-scale rebellion in the Second Javanese War of Succession. Amangkurat IV was totally dependent upon VOC support when the palace princes, including his brother Dipanagara and his son Mangkunegara, allied with the religious establishment against the new Susuhunan. The rebel princes and Islamic leaders of the palace appealed unsuccessfully to Amangkurat IV to break with the Company. Both Dutch and Javanese sources stress the Islamic religious element of this rebellion, although the rebellion also had the support of the Hindu-Buddhist Balinese. Ricklefs's translation of the Surakarta Major *Babad* confirms the Islamic overtones of what was considered a just war:

> The ulamas and hajis
> all wished to wage Holy War, ...
> It was the wish of God
> that they should all be destroyed;
> of the religious folk only a few remained,
> the rest dying in Holy War against the *kafirs* (infidels).[140]

---

[137] Ricklefs, *Modern Javanese Historical Traditions*, p. 10.
[138] Ricklefs, *War, Culture and Economy*, pp. 179–180.
[139] Ibid., p. 180; H. J. de Graaf, *Geschiedenis van Indonesië*. 'sGravenhage and Bandung: W. van Hoeve, 1949, p. 247. De Graaf calls Dipanagara a "Javanese Messiah."
[140] Ricklefs, *War, Culture and Economy*, p. 193.

The collapse of the rebellion was facilitated by illness and hunger ravaging supporters of both sides. Defeat was also partly due to the unstable alliances of the rebel princes. The losses suffered in numerous regional battles with Company and indigenous forces resulted in the eventual surrender of the surviving princes. Surapati III acted as a negotiator between the princes and the Company-Kartasura forces. By late June 1723, Pangerans Dipanagara, Purbaya, and Mankuegara had surrendered to the Company, apparently in exchange for a guaranteed pardon that was not forthcoming. Pangerans Dipanagara and Purbaya were taken as prisoners to Batavia, while Susuhunan Amangkurat III ordered the return of his son Mankunegara to the Kartasura palace. The Governor-General Hendrick Zwaardecroon then ordered the exile of Pangeran Dipanagara to the Cape of Good Hope, while the other major rebels were exiled to Ceylon.[141] Interestingly, the Surapati *babads* change the temporal sequence of Dipanagara and Saloringpasar to make them appear simultaneous.[142] It is not clear that the *babad* authors knew that Dipanagara's exile to the Cape of Good Hope would indeed result in the reunion of the brothers, although Company sources were aware of their relationship.[143]

Pangeran Dipanagara's journey on the *Herstelling* to the Cape of Good Hope was one full of personal tragedy. Dipanagara was accompanied into exile by members of his family and his entourage, as was appropriate for a royal prisoner of state. His two wives (Raden Ajoe daba and Raden Ajoe badrie), his three sons (Doerik, Amir, and Soebaira), and two of his servants (Derpa and Kebben) all perished on the outward voyage. By the time the ship reached Table Bay, the prince had lost his entire family.[144] Dipanagara, a prince of Kartasura who had claimed the title of the "just king" and deliverer of Java, was given over to the charity of his brother, Saloringpasar.

Dipanagara did not arrive alone at the Cape. Batavia scattered into exile the minor followers of the rebellion, particularly those identified as *mahometaanse tempelbesoekers* (roughly translatable as Muslim fanatics)

---

[141] Ibid., pp. 200–201. Thomas Stamford Raffles, *A History of Java*, 2 vols., 1815. Reprinted with an "Introduction" by John Bastin. Kuala Lumpur: Oxford University Press, 1965, p. 205.

[142] Kumar, *Surapati*, p. 193.

[143] CA: A1657, 22. March 26, 1720, *Generale Missiven* vol. 7, reports that Pangeran Dipanagara, brother of Loring Pasar, half brother of the rebellious pangerans, had gone into rebellion at the death of his father.

[144] CA: A1657, 20. August 16, 1723, Resolution of the Governor General and Raad van Indië.

and followers of Surapati III. The Company's return fleet to Europe that carried Dipanagara also brought two groups of these minor exiles to the Cape on the ships *Lindschoten* and *'t Slot Algdegonde*.[145] Batavia indicated that these prisoners were extremely dangerous and accordingly were divided into three groups to work in chains, one-third in the Company gardens, one-third in Newlands, and one-third in Rondebosch where they chopped wood for the Company.[146]

There is no indication in the local Company records that Cape officials realized the role played in recent Javanese politics by the new royal exile in their midst. Cape Company records for the next few years mention the Javanese princes only in terms of their requests for more maintenance. Dipanagara in particular was in dire straits because no provisions had been made for his support. Apparently, he vented his displeasure to the Stellenbosch *landdrost* and was personally reprimanded by the governor who advised him to refrain from his "impudent conduct." Dipanagara replied that he had meant no disrespect; however because his brother could not support him on his meager allowance and he had been reduced to eating locusts and insects, and "not being able to bear this any longer he had begged for God's sake for some food and clothing, such as the lowest of the Company slaves received, that he and his may be spared from death by cold and starvation." At first the Cape officials responded by warning him to "conduct himself in an orderly manner, as the Council was not justified to go in for more expense on his behalf and to write to his brother the emperor of Java for maintenance." Nevertheless, fearing that Dipanagara may be driven to desperation by the approaching winter, the Cape officials resolved to provide him forty pounds of rice monthly and clothing, the same allowances given to Company slaves.[147]

Pangerans Saloringpasar and Dipanagara, princes of the blood of the emperor of Java, spent the next few years in relative obscurity at the Cape. As usual, the Cape officials regularly calculated their expenditure on Batavia's behalf. The burden of keeping Saloringpasar was 2,025 guilders by November 1729, and the Cape resolved to seek from Batavia 26.5 rixdollars (66.5 guilders) per month to cover these costs.[148] More

---

[145] CA: A1657, 20. Inkomende Briewe, September 20, 1723. The names of these exiles were: Nalla gati, Seger, Delomong, Djos, Hombak, Djewa, Abas (who died en route), Soedja, and Praija Soeta.
[146] CA: A1657, 22. December 14, 1723, Resolution of the Cape.
[147] May 3, 1724, Cape Resolution. CA: LM, vol. 37, General Index, p. 11.
[148] November 24, 1729, CA: C24, pp. 283–286, Resoluties, p. 69.

interestingly, Saloringpasar petitioned the governor to have the Company punish for "vagabondery" six of his personal slaves whom he had brought with him from Java by ordering the men to the public works on Robben Island and the women to the Company Slave Lodge. After several months of this punishment the prince requested their return, deciding that they had been suitably chastened and would henceforth be obedient. The Company obliged in assisting the prince, as they would have any slave owner, with the domestic correction of his slaves.[149] In a remarkably complex display of power and authority, the royal exile and the Company collaborated to ensure the continued oppression of the slave population in the small colony. Modern claims that the royal exiles were unflinchingly champions of the oppressed must surely be modified, given the historical complexities of forced migration to the Cape.

The Cape governors and Company elite were not completely closed-minded to the plight of Saloringpasar and Dipanagara. The princes and their entourages had neither been molested by the Company nor had caused any trouble. The governor, Jan de la Fontaine, therefore sent a request to Batavia that they be allowed to leave rural Stellenbosch and return to the urban town environment of the Cape. Batavia agreed to this request and the princes thereafter took up residence somewhere in town.[150] Not one mention is made in the Cape Company records about fears that the princes were fomenting the spread of Islam at the Cape. Amazingly, given the backgrounds of both Saloringpasar and Dipanagara as religious scholars, this does not seem to have been an overt concern of Company officials at the Cape. They were therefore allowed free reign to practice their religion as other Muslims did, in private and as long as it did not come to the attention of the Company. It is difficult to believe that the presence of these powerful religious and royal men did not attract followers to Islam or that they were not active in discreetly seeking adherents to their faith at the Cape.

When Pangeran Dipanagara was first exiled to the Cape in 1723, Pangeran Mankunegara, the eldest son of the Susuhanan Amangkurat IV, was returned to the Kartasuran palace to the protection of his father. Before the ailing Amangkurat IV died in 1726, he passed over his eldest son to succeed him in favor of the sixteen-year-old Pakubuwana III. Because the new Susuhanan was still a minor, Patih Denurega was

---

[149] May 8, 1731. CA C26, pp. 115–146, Resoluties, p. 157, February 28, 1732. CA: C27, pp. 56–60, Resoluties, p. 195.
[150] February 23, 1733. CA: C27, pp. 407–411, Resoluties, p. 276.

appointed regent on his behalf.[151] Remmelink argues that because the political dispute between the Patih Denurega and Mankunegara was quite open in palace circles, it therefore came as no surprise that a trap was set for the prince (in the form of an alleged sexual scandal involving a minor wife of the Susuhanan), which led to his exile to Batavia.[152] Although Batavia was aware Mankunegara had been set up by the ambitious Patih, according to Ricklefs, Company officials feared that the prince would return to open rebellion against the palace and so sending him into exile was the preferred political solution.[153] A covered sudan chair carried Pangeran Mankunegara from the Kartasura palace to Semarang and then onward to Batavia. His entourage consisted of his second wife, Ragasmara, their son, a concubine, and other servants.[154] In a twist of fate, it was Mankunegara's refusal to marry one of the daughters of the exiled Pangeran Dipanagara that led to his downfall at the hands of the Patih. Pangeran Mankunegara was forced to live in exile in Batavia before being transported to Ceylon.[155]

Patih Danureja did not reap the rewards of his machinations against Pangeran Mankunegara. When the Susuhunan Pakubuwana II reached his majority in 1733 he immediately had Danureja arrested by the Company and sent into exile to Ceylon. The Company was apparently pleased to oblige, as it was keen to end the Patih's influence over the young king, figuring it would be to their advantage. This was a serious misreading of the intentions of Pakubuwana II, as he immediately began consolidating his control over the regional lords and insisting they pay tribute to him rather than to the Company. Pakubuwana II tried to centralize power in his own hands by cutting off direct contact between the Company and the local regents. His actions were particularly aimed at Cakraningrat IV, regent of Madura, whose loyalty the Susuhanan questioned, especially in relation to the VOC.[156]

Despite regular tribute payments by Pakubuwana II to the VOC, which offset the Company's huge expenses, the Susuhunan's relationship with the Company was strained over a number of issues. One of these was

---

[151] Ricklefs, *War, Culture and Economy*, (Patih-chief administrator) pp. 209–220.
[152] Remmelink, *Chinese War*, pp. 41–42 & 48.
[153] M. C. Ricklefs, *Jogyakarta under Sultan Mangkumbumi, 1749–1792: A History of the Division of Java*. London and Oxford: Oxford University Press, 1974, p. 109.
[154] Remmelink, *Chinese War*, p. 49.   [155] Ibid., pp. 50–56.
[156] Luc Nagtegaal, *Riding the Dutch Tiger: The Dutch East India Company and the Northeast Coast of Java,1680–1743*. Verhandlening, no. 171. Leiden: KITLV, 1996. pp. 212–213.

a dispute over criminal jurisdiction. Nagtegaal argues that around 1680 the Company had unofficially exercised the legal right to try Javanese accused of crimes against non-Javanese, even though they were subjects of the Susuhunan. By 1737, an agreement was reached whereby the VOC could try Javanese only in cases against non-Javanese within their own territorial boundaries. The Company therefore had no further legal jurisdiction outside these areas and was forced to restrict the enforcement of Company law on this basis.[157]

Meanwhile at the Cape, the aging princes Seloringpasar and Dipanagara began regularly petitioning the Cape Company officials to forward requests for their repatriation to Java.[158] In a poignant plea, Saloringpasar wrote that he was now sixty years old and could no longer stand the cold of the Cape winters and wanted to go home. The Cape officials, tiring of these frequent petitions, gave him permission to forward his request to Batavia. Sadly, Pangeran Saloringpasar died before approval arrived from Batavia, and while preparations for the departure of his family were being made, one of his widows also died at the Cape. Two years after Saloringpasar's last request to go home, his family finally boarded the Company ship, *Clarabeek*, bound for Java. Saloringpasar's body was disinterred and taken home for burial. Batavia ordered sufficient supplies granted to the seventeen members of the pangeran's entourage who traveled homeward.[159] Pangeran Dipanagara was not allowed to return home with his brother's entourage. In 1743, his petition to Governor Van Imhoff to have mercy on him and permit his return to Batavia with his wife, son, and four grandsons was refused.[160]

The middle decades of the eighteenth century were turbulent times for both the VOC in Batavia and the Mataram court at Kartasura. The burden of supporting these rapacious empires fuelled the outbreak of widespread common rebellion in Java. In 1740, the uprising of Chinese and Javanese residents in Batavia and surrounding rural plantation lands was aimed at both Chinese and indigenous elites cooperating with the Company and the Company itself. The ruthless massacre of Chinese residents in Batavia

---

[157] Ibid., pp. 215–216.
[158] CA: LM, vol. 31, Index to Annexures, p. 61.
[159] June 21, 1735, June 5, 1736, July 2, 1737, July 11, 1737, and July 23, 1737, Resolutions. CA: C29, pp. 182–185 & 420–421. CA: C30, pp. 202–203, 210–211, 212. The party was granted enough rice for four months, 100 lb sugar powder, 50 lb candy sugar, 10 lb pepper, six live sheep, and 100 rixdollars as provisions for their return journey.
[160] Requestien 26, 1743, March 14, 1743. Resolution, CA: C35, p. 153–154. CA: A1657, 31.

resulted in surviving Chinese and Javanese people fleeing the town to spread the uprising eastward. Dutch settlements were attacked all along the northeast coast of Java.[161]

By late 1741, the Susuhunan sided with the rebellion, thinking that the VOC was vulnerable enough to be finally expelled from Java. The Company begged Cakraningrat IV of Madura to assist them, and he agreed to do so in exchange for official recognition as a Company vassal. Cakraningrat thereby ended his own allegiance to Pakubuwana II, making his territorial ambitions clear. Madurese troops occupied and sacked the Kartasura palace in November 1742. However, the Company forced Cakraningrat IV to return the palace to the Susuhunan. The VOC then imposed a new treaty on Pakubuwana II, in which the Company was ceded sovereignty over west Madura and most of northeast Java. The treaty also forbade the Javanese people to sail outside Java, Madura, and Bali, thereby restricting Javanese trade virtually to the island.[162]

Returning Exiles: Cape Islam and Javanese Politics

Not surprisingly, Cakraningrat IV balked at the reinstatement of Pakubuwana II and the frustration of his territorial ambitions in Eastern Java. He forged an alliance with the descendents of Surapati in east Java and, using Balinese troops, attempted to prevent the consolidation of Company control in the region.[163] In 1745, the VOC formally removed Cakraningrat IV from power and declared him a rebel. When the tide turned toward a military victory for the Company, Cakraningrat IV escaped and was eventually captured. He was exiled to the Cape of Good Hope in 1746 and at least one of his sons was exiled to Ceylon.[164] One of his more pliable sons was installed as Company vassal in west Madura.[165] The VOC had successfully weathered its most serious political and military challenge in Java at great cost to its financial stability.[166]

The exile of Cakraningrat IV to the Cape did not appear to have made any major impression or demands upon local Company officials.[167] As a rebel against the Company (despite his royal status) he was originally sentenced to hard labor at the Cape. Nevertheless, when he arrived in

---

[161] Nagtegaal, *Riding the Dutch Tiger*, pp. 220–221.
[162] Ricklefs, *Modern Indonesia*, p. 92.   [163] Kumar, *Surapati*, pp. 41–42.
[164] NA: VOC 348. Register der Brieven. Batavia, September 14, 1748, p. 88.
[165] Ricklefs, *Modern Indonesia*, pp. 91–93.   [166] Raffles, *History of Java*, p. 223.
[167] De Graaf, *Geschiedenis van Indonesië*, p. 261. De Graaf notes that Cakraningrat IV was nicknamed Ngekap at the Cape and was numbered among the Cape Muslims.

Africa in late December 1746 on the *Fortuijn*, Company officials decided that for security purposes it was wiser to keep Cakraningrat IV, known at the Cape by the name Raden Djoerit, prisoner at the Castle. As an official prisoner of state, he was granted thirty rixdollars per month for his upkeep and was apparently not forced to labor. He was assigned two armed guards to escort him at all times to prevent his escape.[168] Cakraningrat IV made only one material demand on the Company, and that was for an allowance of rice because he was unable to eat bread.[169] Batavia refused to allow his repatriation to Java. By 1748, the Company had gained full sovereignty over Madura.[170] The next year, Company officials reported to Batavia that Cakraningrat IV had died at the Cape and had been buried according to Muslim custom. They were ordered to disinter his body and transport it back to Batavia.[171] Like so many other royal exiles, Cakraningrat IV never saw his homeland again, yet he was buried in royal fashion in the land of his ancestors.

The same year that Cakraningrat IV arrived at the Cape, Pangeran Dipanagara was finally given permission to return to Batavia.[172] There is no record whether the two royal exiles met while at the Cape. Pakubuwana II had requested Dipanagara's repatriation. It was not until 1751 that the prince, now an old man, was released from Company custody and was finally allowed to return to the Javanese court to live out the remainder of his life.[173] Prince Dipanagara, once heralded as the "just king" and "Javanese messiah'" left no visible trace on the Cape landscape nor in the oral traditions of Cape Islam and the archival sources available to historians. Nevertheless, it is inconceivable that a scholar and leader of his status did not share his faith and knowledge with those around him.

Coincidentally, the same year Dipanagara was welcomed home, Mankunegara's sons were again sent into exile from Java with his third

---

[168] October 12, 1646. Letter received from Batavia, December 29, 1746, Cape Resolution, CA: C38, pp. 247–248. December 30, 1746, NA: General Resolutions, December 31, 1746, *Generale Missiven*, vol. 11, p. 453. January 12, 1747, Cape Resolution, CA: C39, p. 42. December 5, 1747, NA: General Resolutions, vol. 777.
[169] January 12, 1747. Cape Resolution, CA: C39, p. 42. The Company granted him the same allowance they had given Pangeran Seloringpasar.
[170] February 20, 1748, NA: General Resolutions, vol. 778.
[171] August 26, 1749, Cape Resolutions, CA: C41, pp. 15–158.
[172] October 25, 1746, Cape Resolutions, CA: C83, p. 225.
[173] March 11, 1746, NA: General Resolutions, vol. 776, responding to a request from Pakubuwana II dated January 6, 1746, July 8, 1751. J. A. van der Chijs, ed., *Realia. Register op de generale resolutiën van het Kasteel Batavia, 1632-1805*. 3 vols. Leiden Gualth Kolff; Den Haag: Martinus Nijhoff; Batavia: W. Bruining, 1882-1885, p. 85.

son, Raden Mascaretti (or Mas Kreti), on board a ship bound for the Cape of Good Hope. There has been some confusion among historians of Indonesia about the details of Mangkunegara's exile. Ricklefs claims that he had been sent from Ceylon to exile at the Cape.[174] Unfortunately, there is no evidence to confirm this in the Cape Company archives. The fate of Mankunegara's family, however, highlights the density of the networks of political exile instituted by the VOC. Mankunegara was a man of extraordinarily high reputation at the Kartasura palace, and his exile had caused considerable discontent in court circles. His older son, known as Mas Said, eventually returned from exile in Ceylon and rose to prominence as Pangeran Adipati Mankunegara I after the 1755 partition of the Javanese court between Sultan Hamengkubauwana I in Jogyakarta and Susuhunan Pakubuwana III in Surakarta.[175]

It is through an unprecedented archival document, written by Mankunegara's third son, Raden Mas Kreti, that one glimpses firsthand the complexity of networks of political exile under the VOC. Raden Mas Kreti, in exile at the Cape, was encouraged to travel on the return fleet to Europe by Director General Hooreman and the Cape governor, Rijk Tulbagh, to plead his case for clemency directly to the Directors of the VOC's Enkhuizen Chamber. In a unique by-passing of Batavia's authority, most probably sanctioned by Hooreman, Raden Mas Kreti was allowed to travel directly to the United Provinces in 1778 without informing Batavia.[176] Having been granted the clemency he sought, he wrote his life story at the request of the Directors of the Enkhuizen Chamber during his return journey to the Cape, supposedly as a way to reiterate his fidelity to the Company for their mercy.[177]

In the letter, Raden Mas Kreti relates that in 1726 his father, Pangeran Azia Mankunegara, had been banished to Batavia by order of his brother Susuhanan Jakka (Pakubuwana I), "Emperor of Java." Mankunegara was housed with his retinue in the Vierkantsche Poort under the protection of the Company and allocated sixty rixdollars per month for his upkeep.

---

[174] Ricklefs, *Modern Indonesia*, p. 88.   [175] Ibid., pp. 94–98.
[176] Ricklefs was unable to verify reports about Mas Kreti's journey to Europe through the Company records pertaining to Batavia. He also claims Mas Kreti had been born to Mangkunegara during the latter's exile at the Cape. Ricklefs, *Jogyakarta*, p. 270. According to Mas Kreti's own testimony he was born in Batavia before going into exile to Ceylon with his family.
[177] September 20, 1778. Letter received, *Kaapse Archiefstukken 1778*, pp. 490–494.

In 1733, the Susuhunan sent an ambassador to the governor-general insisting that Mankunegara be sent into exile in Ceylon, along with his family. Raden Mas Kreti wrote that his father had six children by his wives (only the sons were mentioned). Radinmas Tintas Coesoemas and Pangeran Ti-Pati Mankoe Nagara (later known as Mas Said – who became Mankunegara I) were born in Java before their father was banished from the court. Raden Mas Kreti was born in Batavia only months before the family was sent into exile. His three younger brothers, Radinmas Ceylon, Radinmas Sam Sam, and Radinmas Rotto, were all born in Ceylon; the latter two died as children.

When Mankunegara died in 1739, Raden Mas Kreti's elder brother took his father's title and the three eldest sons returned to Batavia, arriving sometime in 1741. As this was the time during which the Susuhunan and the Company were at war, the princes were held under guard in Batavia and allocated sixty-five rixdollars per month for subsistence. Raden Mas Kreti's return to Java was short-lived and, as in 1750, the brothers were once more sent into exile. His two elder brothers and younger brother were sent to Ceylon, while at the age of seventeen Raden Mas Kreti was shipped off to the Cape. There is no obvious or documented political reason that served the Company's interests in making the decision to send Mas Kreti into exile at the Cape. However, it was not uncommon for the Company to separate groups of exiles by sending them to different sites of banishment. The exiles in Ceylon were allowed to return to Batavia a year later, while Raden Mas Kreti languished, apparently forgotten, at the Cape. By Raden Mas Kreti's own account, confirmed by the silence of the Company records, he lived quietly without restriction at the Cape, never once attempting to escape.[178] His impoverished circumstances prompted him to seek an allowance from the Company, which was granted at five rixdollars per month, pending confirmation from Batavia.[179]

During his first decade at the Cape, Raden Mas Kreti became acquainted with Governor Rijk Tulbagh. Although the details are unknown, their relationship must have been cordial and based upon mutual confidence, given Tulbagh's interventions on the young prince's behalf. This situation reiterates simultaneously the fluidity of social interactions and the inherent recognition of social status embodied in the political exiles

---

[178] Letter written by Raden Mas Kreti, *Kaapse Archiefstukken 1780*, pp. 491–492.
[179] Letter from Raden Mas Kreti, *Kaapse Archiefstukken 1780*, p. 492, April 12, 1757, Cape Resolutions.

of royal status at the Cape. Raden Mas Kreti was by all accounts an innocent victim of dynastic politics in Java, and his poignant story must have touched the Cape governor as much as it elicits sympathy across the centuries to present-day readers of his letter. Without his autobiographical account, very little trace of Raden Mas Kreti would have been left in the Company archives. In this respect his letter is a unique Company document, being also reminiscent of the *babad* narrative style.

While Raden Mas Kreti's account concentrates on the male line of his family, Company records do give some insight into his domestic arrangements. In 1759, Raden Mas Kreti requested the manumission of his slave Sarah van Bougies and his son Amsterdam van die Cape. He gave his own name and that of the burgher Frans Lens as surety.[180] Raden Mas Kreti had given no details of any wife or other family members who had traveled with him to the Cape, which was not surprising, given that he was still a teenager at the time. It can therefore be assumed that he created a family, like so many other men at the Cape, through the purchase of a slave woman who bore his children.[181]

One glimpse into Raden Mas Kreti's life at the Cape might possibly be found in what has become a famous passage in the writing of Cape Muslim history. Carl Thunberg's eyewitness account of the "Javanese New Year" celebrations in 1772 most probably refers to the festival of Eid Al-Fitr at the end of Ramadan. Thunberg describes the colorful and lively Cape Town apartment in which the celebration attended by both men and women took place:

[A] priest read out of the great book that lay on the cushion before the alter, the congregation at times reading aloud after him. I observed them reading after the Oriental manner, from right to left, and imagined it to be the Alcoran that they were reading, the Javanese being mostly Mahometans... [T]he principle man of the congregation at intervals accompanied their singing on the violin. I understood afterwards, that this was a prince from Java, who had opposed the interests of the Dutch East India Company, and for that reason had been brought from his native country to the Cape, where he lives at the Company's expense.[182]

---

[180] CA: LM, Requisition no. 114, 1759. Frans Lens was a Cape burgher. He may also have been a free black. See Leibbrandt, *Precis*, vol. 2, pp. 687 & 690.

[181] Robert C.-H. Shell, *Children of Bondage: A Social History of the Slave Society at the Cape of Good Hope, 1652–1838*. Johannesburg: Witwatersrand University Press, 1994.

[182] Carl Peter Thunberg, *Travels at the Cape of Good Hope 1772–1775*, ed., V. S. Forbes, Van Riebeeck Society, second series, no. 17. Cape Town: Van Riebeeck Society, 1986, pp. 47–48.

Raden Mas Kreti was the only Javanese prince living without restriction in Cape Town during this period.[183] As he was not under house arrest, Raden Mas Kreti seems to have had freedom of movement and association at the Cape. His social interactions seem most intimately tied to the growing Cape Muslim population, as is evidenced by Thunberg witnessing the Eid celebrations. Given Mas Kreti's family background and upbringing, it would be most likely that he was highly literate and learned in the traditions of Javanese Islam, as well as having been exposed to the Islamic teachings of the exiles in Ceylon and to pilgrims en route between the archipelago, India, and the Haramayn.

However, Raden Mas Kreti's social circle obviously included the Cape governor, Rijk Tulbagh, who allowed him to travel to the United Provinces six years after Thunberg's visit to the Cape. After appealing for clemency, Raden Mas Kreti returned to the Cape to await the Company's decision. His first appeal was turned down by Batavia with no explanation to the Company officials at the Cape forthcoming.[184] The prince was still a relatively young man in 1785 when the long awaited approval for his repatriation came through from Batavia. Aware that Raden Mas Kreti had lived in virtual poverty at the Cape, Governor Joachim Ammema, Baron van Plettenberg, exercised an unusual act of generosity on behalf of the Company in allocating the prince one hundred rixdollars to fit himself out for the voyage.[185]

It is impossible to guess the range of emotions Raden Mas Kreti and his family experienced during their voyage on the *Selwonderlog* homeward across the Indian Ocean. For the prince, a lifetime of exile as a prisoner of state of the Dutch East India Company was drawing to a close. His wife was undertaking an incredible journey from being a slave woman at the Cape to royal wife in the Javanese palace. His African-born son was leaving home to begin life as a royal courtier in Java. The family was being reunited with relatives they had not seen for decades or had never known. Raden Mas Kreti had already articulated his profound gratitude to his Company patrons on his journey from Europe back to the Cape in 1778. Once the prince had departed the shores of Africa, the Cape officials appear to have heard no more from their royal charge.[186]

---

[183] There is speculation by Forbes and others that this event describes Tuan Guru but this is unlikely. Thunberg, *Travels*, p. 48, fn. 140.
[184] CA: A1657, 31. Letter received from Batavia, October 20, 1779.
[185] Leibbrant, *Precis*, vol. 2, February 7, 1786, p. 789.
[186] CA: A1657, 24. Letter despatched to Batavia, 1786.

However, the extraordinary consequences of Raden Mas Kreti's life and exile at the Cape reverberated into the very heart of Javanese politics.

Raden Mas Kreti and his family were welcomed back to the Javanese court of Surakarta by his brothers, Mankunegara I and Pakubuwana III.[187] Ricklefs relates that:

> [Raden Mas Kreti] reportedly returned to Java in European dress, complete to the wearing of a wig. The Susuhunan allowed him to continue in this attire, but reportedly the Crown Prince forbade it. He ordered Kreti to throw away his wig, to grow his hair, and to take up a religious life, which he apparently did.[188]

It is not at all surprising that Raden Mas Kreti arrived at the Surakarta *kraton* wearing Dutch-style clothing, considering he was returning to Java after thirty-four years of exile at the Cape. Although he had been reported by Thunberg as wearing Javanese-style clothing in Cape Town, by his own admission he had worn Dutch-style clothing in the Netherlands.[189] Considering Raden Mas Kreti's complex sense of patronage and loyalty, as simultaneously a member of Javanese royalty and a grateful recipient of Company mercy, it is probable that the Crown Prince of Surakarta objected to his Dutch clothing because it demonstrated all too visibly his connections with the Company. Thereafter, Raden Mas Kreti seems to have faded peacefully into the background of *kraton* life. No mention is made about how Sarah adjusted to life as a royal wife in Java.

Raden Mas Kreti's eventual obscurity contrasts vividly with the rise to prominence of his son, Wirjakusuma, who was immediately embroiled in the radical Islamic circles at the *kraton*. As Ricklef notes:

> Wirjakusuma had thus presumably just arrived in Java for the first time in his life. But immediately he became the leader of what seems probably to have been a traditional Javanese religious movement... That Wirjakusuma became so quickly involved in such a group suggests the extent to which Javanese rebels and religious leaders maintained their traditions even in exile.[190]

---

[187] Ricklefs, *Jogyakarta*, p. 271. Ricklefs repeats the rumor that Raden Mas Kreti had been to Europe as a stowaway during his exile at the Cape but found no evidence to confirm this in the Company's Batavia archives. This confirms my speculation that the Cape officials acting under the authority of Director-General Hoorn bypassed Batavia in allowing the prince to travel to Europe.
[188] Ibid., pp. 287–288.
[189] Letter from Raden Mas Kreti, 1778, *Kaapse Archiefstukken 1778*, p. 493.
[190] Ricklefs, *Jogyakarta*, p. 287.

Ricklefs draws this conclusion quite plausibly on the basis of Company sources emanating from Semarang and Batavia. There is no mention of Raden Mas Kreti having another son at the Cape and Ricklefs confirms that Wirjakusuma was born in Africa. This supports the conclusion that Wirjakusuma is none other than Amsterdam of the Cape, the son born to Raden Mas Kreti and his Bouginese slave Sarah.[191] Raden Mas Kreti manumitted his family in 1757, which means that Amsterdam of the Cape was approximately thirty years of age when he traveled to Java. Amsterdam of the Cape would have been given a Javanese name from birth by his father, even though it does not appear in the Company records. Wirjakusuma was also educated by his father in the Javanese language and culture and Islamic practices and traditions, as befitting a son of royalty.

However, it is not necessary to assume that Wirjakusuma's religious authority stemmed from "a traditional Javanese religious movement." The practice of Islam at the Cape was already over a century old by the time Raden Mas Kreti and his family departed from Africa. Muslims of many diverse backgrounds and traditions mingled at the Cape as political and religious exiles, transported criminals, slaves, and eventually as part of the free black population in the small colony. Wirjakusuma's power and charisma came not from the unadulterated preservation of Javanese religious traditions. Instead, dynamic practices of syncretic Islam had emerged in the crucible of the Cape as a colony in the VOC's Indian Ocean empire.

Azra argues that by the eighteenth century, prominent religious scholars in the Malay-Indonesian networks of Islamic reform in the Indian Ocean were directly exhorting political leaders in their homelands to wage *jihad* against European colonists. Al-Palimbani from Palambang in South Sumatra was one of these leaders who lived in the Haramayn. He taught scholar-pilgrims from the archipelago and wrote to the Sultan of Mataram in 1772 and Pangeran Mangkunagara (in letters intercepted and translated by the Dutch) that it was their duty to kill those who did not embrace the true faith. Al-Palimbani also sent Pangeran Mangkunagara a *jimat* (amulet) written as a banner to protect him in battle.[192]

---

[191] M. C. Ricklefs, *Mystic Synthesis in Java: A History of Islamization from the Fourteenth to the Early Nineteenth Centuries.* Norwalk, CT: East Bridge, 2006. pp. 173–174.

[192] Azra, *Islamic Reformism*, pp. 111–143. Amulets in the form of writing were powerful religious objects in Sufism and in pre-Islamic Southeast Asian societies. For an example

Wirjakusuma's actions at the Surakarta palace were known to be directly anti-European, and his influence over the Crown Prince made him dangerous to Company interests. With the permission of the Susuhunan, the Company arrested Wirjakusuma and other religious leaders and banished them to Batavia. Apparently, he was found in the possession of mystical amulets and his personal *babad* (epic).[193] Born in exile like his father, Wirjakusuma was once again exiled by the Company from the land of his forefathers.[194] It is clear from this account that the Company's exile circuit operated at one level as an unintended conduit for religious and political movements that were diametrically opposed to its own religious values and political interests.

These narratives, woven across a century-long tapestry of archipelagic and Cape history, illustrate the operation of the Company's exile circuits. Except in the case of Shaykh Yusuf, the cases chosen for discussion in this chapter are not mentioned in Cape historiography. These particular choices by no means exhaust the range of possibilities. Other linkages in these exile circuits would have highlighted a different pattern and texture but with a similar underlying structure. The relationships and interactions of generations of exiles from the Molaccas would reveal an extra dimension to the historical narratives of this chapter, as would a more extensive narrative of the links between Ceylon, the Cape, and the archipelago through exile circuits.[195] The hundreds of political prisoners exiled as "rebels" because they fell within the borders of the Company's territorial jurisdiction, constitute yet another strand of exile. So, too, does the exile of many Islamic religious dissidents, often defined as "*Mohammedan paaps* or *priesters*" (Muslim popes or priests). The multiplication of examples would not, however, alter the basic configuration of the Company's imperial circuits of exile.

---

of the power of written amulets see Robert Ross and Sirtjo Koolhoff, "Upas, September, and the Bugis at the Cape of Good Hope: The Context of a Slave's Letter," *Archipel*, 70, 2005, pp. 281–308.

[193] Ricklefs, *Jogyakarta*, p. 287.
[194] Merle Ricklefs, *Mystic Synthesis in Java: A History of Islamization from the Fourteenth to the Early Nineteenth Centuries*. Norwalk, CT: East Bridge, 2006, p. 174.
[195] Hussainmiya, *Orang Regimin*; Karel Schoeman, "Bandiete en Bannelinge," in *Kinders van die Kompanjie: Kaapse lewens uit die sewentiende eeu*. Pretoria: Protea Boekhuis, 2006, pp. 496–513.

Exile and Islam at the Cape

The consequences of this circuit of empire for the Cape of Good Hope were profound on a number of levels. High-ranking exiles, often accompanied by their own subordinates and slaves, disrupted the colonial hierarchy that equated rank and privilege with ethnicity, religion, and freedom. A few royal exiles were at times treated as the social equals at the uppermost level of the Company elite in Cape society. Company officials were obliged to provide for high-ranking prisoners of state, sometimes assigning Company slaves for their own personal use. Cape officials were given orders from Batavia about the appropriate treatment of prisoners of state and had very little room to maneuver in altering their conditions of exile. Simultaneously, high-ranking, even royal, political prisoners who had been convicted of rebellion against the Company could also be treated like common criminals. Their formerly high status would have been recognized at the very least by the free blacks and slaves who came from their home regions. The presence of these exiles complicated the social order of the Cape in ways Company officials and colonists alike found most disturbing.

Nowhere was this more evident than in the propagation of Islam at the Cape. From the very beginning of the arrival of political exiles to the colony, Company officials feared the influence of these Muslims. Religious leaders like Shaykh Yusuf were isolated from the town because of the potential "danger" they posed in spreading Islam, especially to its slave population. Religious scholars like Pangeran Dipanagara lived in relative freedom in Stellenbosch and the Cape, primarily because the exile of these royal scholars was not directly associated with their religious activities. From the beginning of the eighteenth century, political prisoners defined as "Muslim" rather than primarily as royalty; were increasingly treated more like transported convicts, often being imprisoned on Robben Island. The exile credited with the establishment of the *madrasah* (religious school) tradition at the Cape, commonly known by the name Tuan Guru, had been a prisoner on Robben Island during the 1780s before his release in 1792.[196]

The process of forced migration to the Cape, with respect to the slave trade, penal transportation, and political exile is central, therefore, to

---

[196] Achmat Davids, *The History of the Tana Baru*. Cape Town: Committee for the Preservation of the Tana Baru, 1985, pp. 40–48.

debates about the propagation of Islam at the Cape. Protagonists in this debate have argued about the influence of prominent Muslim exiles vis-à-vis the forced migration of Muslim slaves as the prime source for local conversion.[197] Abdulkader Tayob rightly points out that "the memory of these political exiles and prominent personalities became an important part of Muslim religious consciousness and practices."[198] Even more significantly, those political exiles have become part of the collective historical memory of Islam at the Cape and have defined the parameters of the debate on Cape Muslim history.

This has created a focus on exiles who were identified with the circle of *kramats* (tombs) at the Cape, and on prominent ex-slaves who were fundamentally involved in the establishment of the first *madrasahs* and, after the VOC period, in the building of mosques in Cape Town.[199] Debates about the origins of Islam at the Cape have therefore centered on the institutional characteristics of community formation, drawing on limited historical sources that examine the basis of leadership, organization, and religious practice.[200] Although it is impossible to substantiate archivally the influence of the *tariqahs* in transmitting Islam at the Cape, there is convincing circumstantial evidence to suggest that for the late seventeenth and early eighteenth centuries, religious leaders like Shaykh Yusuf and their followers were key figures in disseminating the mystical practices of Islam among sections of the slave and free black population, probably even among those who were already Muslim, through the teachings of their *tariqahs*. Shaykh Yusuf was a *khalifah* (successor) of the Qadiriyyah,

---

[197] Frank Bradlow and Margaret Cairns, *The Early Cape Muslims. A Study of Their Mosques, Genealogy and Origins*. Cape Town: A. A. Balkema, 1978; Achmat Davids, *The Mosques of the Bo-Kaap*. Athlone: South African Institute of Arabic and Islamic Studies, 1980; Dangor, *Shaykh Yusuf*. Bradlow, "Imperialism"; Yusuf da Costa and Achmat Davids, *Pages from Cape Muslim History*. Robert Shell, "Islam in South Africa, 1652–1997," paper presented to the Van Leer Institute, Jerusalem, revised January 8, 1998.

[198] Abdulkader Tayob, *Islam in South Africa: Mosques, Imams and Sermons*. Gainsville: University of Florida Press, 1999, p. 23.

[199] For one of the most recent popular publications on the circle of kramats see: Mansoor Jaffer, ed., *Guide to the Kramats of the Western Cape*. Cape Town: Cape Mazaar (Kramat) Society, 1996.

[200] Adil Bradlow was the first to argue for the influence of the Sufi *tariqahs*, a position that has subsequently been taken up by Davids and Shell. Bradlow, "Imperialism." See also Yusuf da Costa, "The Influence of Tasawuuf on Islamic Practices at the Cape," in Da Costa and Davids, eds., *Pages from Cape Muslim History*, pp. 129–142. John Mason, "A Faith for Ourselves: Slavery, Sufism and Conversion to Islam at the Cape," *SAHJ*, 46, 2002, pp. 3–24.

Shattariyyah, and Rifaiyyah Sufi orders and their existence at the Cape is in all probability the result of the *isnad* (chain of transmission) from Shaykh Yusuf and his followers.[201]

Adil Bradlow suggests there were two formative periods in the propagation of Islam at the Cape; the first around the late seventeenth century with the initial arrival of high-ranking Muslim exiles to the Cape, and the second around the 1770s with the emergence of more open Muslim groups centered in town.[202] Historians have generally tended to place more emphasis on the latter period as the main indicator of community formation that led to building the first mosque in Cape Town under British rule in 1799. Evidence suggests that the transmission of Islam through verbal communication and recitation, cultural practices of religious ceremonies, the writing of religious texts, and the production of mystical talismans for sickness and protection were powerful, portable, and non-institutional means of worship and conversion.

The VOC recognized this by attempting to isolate exiles like Shaykh Yusuf, although they did not isolate all Muslim exiles. Moreover, the Cape criminal records contain at least two cases where a slave and an exile, both leaders of the Muslim community, wrote mystical amulets in Southeast Asian scripts for their followers that were later used as evidence of resistance and potential rebellion against the Company. Most of the defendants in these cases were executed by being broken on the wheel and their bodies exposed on the gibbet. Both cases indicate the Company's fear of the potential for Islam to become a catalyst for slave uprisings, although any serious slave resistance was punished in the same brutal way.[203] Unlike political developments in the archipelago that, during the eighteenth century began to focus specifically on religious difference as the basis of animosity against the Company, Islam at the Cape was not an overtly political force and did not promote organized resistance to colonial rule. Resistance was rather embedded in religious and ceremonial practices of Islam as the main expression of an alternative

---

[201] Azra, *Islamic Reformism*, p. 102.
[202] Bradlow, "Imperialism," pp. 126–127.
[203] Nigel Worden and Gerald Groenewald, eds., *Trials of Slavery: Selected Documents Concerning Slaves from the Criminal Records of the Council of Justice at the Cape of Good Hope, 1705–1794*. Van Riebeeck Society for the Publication of South African Historical Documents. 2nd ser., no. 36. Cape Town: Van Riebeeck Society 2005, pp. 355–384; 537–556; Ross and Koolhof, "Upas, September and the Bugis," pp. 280–308; Mason, "A faith for ourselves," pp. 3–24.

religious faith to Christianity, the faith of the VOC, and an alternative worldview.[204]

Analyses of Islam at the Cape during the Company era have been limited because of the difficulty in finding adequate archival and oral sources, making any systematic effort to link the propagation and practice of Islam at the Cape to those sites of origin of slaves and exiles in Africa or South and Southeast Asia somewhat speculative.[205] This chapter proposes that the depth of Islamic scholarship and practice of exiles to the Cape was much greater than has hitherto been recognized. Nor was the flow of knowledge entirely one way. Islamic practices formed at the Cape were part of the circuits of Islamic reform throughout the Indian Ocean. Although it is beyond the scope of this book to explore these issues in detail, general patterns of Islamic conversion and community in the archipelago are highly suggestive of practices that developed at the Cape during the eighteenth century.

Anthony Johns cautions against broad generalizations: "[T]he sheer diversity and extent of the region renders impossible the formulation of any single theory of Islamization, or pattern of Islamic life, or any periodization common to the region as a whole."[206] Nevertheless, Johns stresses the centrality of Sufi orders as the basis of Islamic education in the region. This process of institutionalizing Islamic education linked religious leaders in alliances with ruling elites in the cities and courts of the major archipelagic polities.[207] Ricklefs, Johns, and Reid all argue that the mystical forms of Islam espoused by the Sufi scholars were particularly well-suited to incorporation into preexisting Southeast Asian belief systems.[208] Their emphasis is on the spiritual power embodied

---

[204] Robert Ross, *Cape of Torments: Slavery and Resistance in South Africa*. London: Routledge and Kegan Paul, 1983; James Armstrong and Nigel Worden, "The Slaves, 1652–1834," in Elphick and Giliomee, *Shaping of South African Society*, pp. 143–161; Davids, "The Kramat at Zandvliet"; Shell, "Islam in South Africa."

[205] The main proponent of Cape Malay scholarship was I. D. du Plessis. See, for example, I. D. du Plessis, *The Cape Malays*. Cape Town: Maskew Miller Longman, 1941. For an incisive critique of I. D. du Plessis see Shamil Jeppie, "Historical Process and the Construction of Subjects: I. D. du Plessis and the Reinvention of the 'Malay," unpublished BA (Honors) thesis, University of Cape Town, 1987.

[206] A. H. Johns, "From Coastal Settlement to Islamic school and City: Islamization in Sumatra, the Malay Peninsula and Java," *Hamard Islamicus*, 4, 4, Winter 1981, p. 7.

[207] Ibid., pp. 7–10. Johns stresses this aspect partly in reaction to the secular tendencies in explanations of Islamization in Southeast Asia.

[208] Ricklefs, *Mystic Synthesis*, pp. 22–29.

in religious leaders, which was preserved through the "chain (*silsila*) of spiritual genealogy linking teacher and followers."[209] These features of Southeast Asian Islam were enhanced by the development of pilgrimage networks in the region, because Islamic scholars circulated in the Indian Ocean nodes, enhancing their status through training in the centers of Islamic learning in the Haramayn and the Arabian Peninsula. Moreover, these Sufi leaders were often linked with court elites through marriage alliances.

Religious and royal power could be embedded in royal genealogies, for example, in the way that Shaykh Yusuf married into the Goa and Banten royal families.[210] Sufism was also suited to the use and adaptation of Hindu-Buddhist traditions and to interpreting them within an Islamic context.[211] "The courtiers who promoted Sufi paradigms in the palace sought mystic and mundane unities between the seen and the unseen worlds, between doctrine and practice, between older Javanese ideas and Islamic mysticism, between God and themselves."[212] Pangeran Adipati Dipanagara, son of Susuhunan Pakubuwana I, who was exiled to the Cape, was an archetypal prince-scholar. Dipanagara had a reputation as a "connoisseur" of Siva-Buddhist mystical texts on the doctrine of non-duality that contributed to Javanese Islamic mysticism.[213] It is difficult to believe that during his period of exile at the Cape, a princely scholar of the caliber of Dipanagara, despite his deprivations, did not influence the spiritual life of Muslims at the Cape. The role of charismatic religious leader attributed to Shaykh Yusuf could also be applied to the exiles

---

[209] Anthony Reid, "The Islamization of Southeast Asia," in Muhammed Abu Bakr et al., eds., *Historia: Essays in Commemoration of the 25th Anniversary of the Department of History, University of Malaysia*. Kuala Lumpur: The Malaysian Historical Society, 1984, p. 17. Reid also stresses the importance of religious power transmitted through the veneration of dead saints, particularly through visitations to the tombs of holy men where offerings were made and intercession sought. This is a recognizable origin of the kramat tradition at the Cape.

[210] J. Kathirithamby-Wells, "Banten: A West Indonesian Port and Polity during the Sixteenth and Seventeenth Centuries," in Kathirithamby-Wells and Villiers, *Port and Polity*, p. 119.

[211] A. H. Johns, "Sufism as a Category in Indonesian Literature and History," *JSEAS*, 2(2), July 1961, pp. 15–19. Ricklefs suggests that this syncretic tradition was a vital part of eighteenth-century Javanese court culture. Ricklefs, *Modern Javanese Historical Tradition*, p. 2.

[212] Ricklefs, *Seen and Unseen Worlds*, p. 339.

[213] M. C. Ricklefs, "Unity and Disunity in Javanese Political and Religious Thought of the Eighteenth Century," *Modern Asian Studies*, 26(4), 1992, pp. 670–673.

like Dipanagara, Saloringpasar, and Mas Kreti. In combination, these features of Sufism that highlight the embodiment of spiritual power in charismatic leadership, the transmission of authority from *guru* (teacher) to *murid* (student), the mystical practices that transmit religious power in miraculous feats, and the veneration of saints are all recognizable features of early Southeast Asian and Cape Islam.

Given the concepts of power and knowledge implicit in this form of Islam, it is therefore understandable that Wirjakusuma could return to Java and immediately assume the role of a charismatic religious leader. The multitude of other elements that contribute to early Cape Islamic practices cannot be readily discerned from available archival sources. However, the form of mystical Islam that incorporated syncretic practices could also have incorporated these elements into the practice of Islam at the Cape forged over time during the Company period. Wirjakusuma offered to the religious circles of the Surakarta court a vibrant interpretation of Islam, conceived in the archipelago, carried over the Indian Ocean Islamic networks, and born in Africa.

This chapter presents a long and complicated narrative of the intimate links between the Company and archipelagic polities through diplomacy and politics. It demonstrates how these relations in Java were extended to the Cape of Good Hope through the Batavia-Cape circuit of exile. The Company's banishment of political and religious leaders from the Indonesian archipelago to the Cape had the unintended consequence of compromising Company power at the Cape. The transmission and propagation of Islam by exiles and slaves revealed the limitations of Company sovereignty. The Company could control people physically through forced migration or legal punishment, but isolation or execution could not guarantee that an individual's influence would not survive and, ultimately, flourish. Although forced migration limited agency by imposing legal categories of bondage, it could not limit agency through control of communication within indigenous networks of communication.

Chapter 6 continues this analysis by examining other unforeseen consequences of the Company's network of forced migration. As one aspect, the slave trade was crucial to the Cape's labor supply and both the Company and the colonists feared that slave resistance, and uprisings would challenge social control and undermine the rule of law. The circuit of exile and penal transportation to the Cape was therefore implemented to bolster Company sovereignty in other imperial nodes, especially Batavia as the Company's capital city. However, convicts and exiles did not only present a security risk to the Company at the Cape. They were also feared and resented by the burghers as threats to their social and economic interests. The use of Robben Island as an isolated site of exile at the Cape was not sufficient to prevent the settler-exile dynamics from subverting the original intent of the network of forced migration to contribute to the extension of Company sovereignty over its entire imperial web.

The Cape Colony c.1798

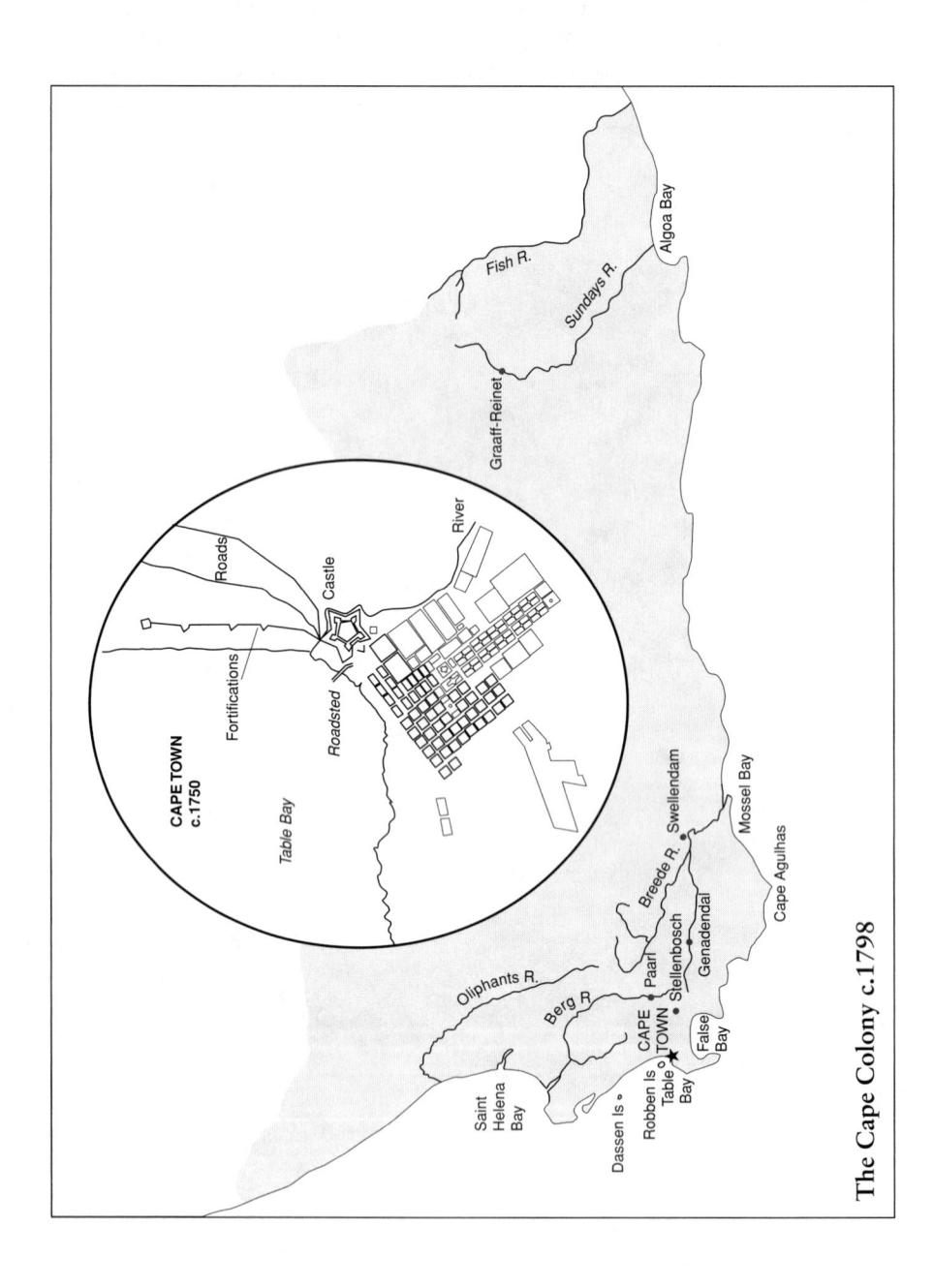

6

Forced Migration and Cape Colonial Society

By the mid-eighteenth century, a seafarer's first view of Cape Town from the deck of a ship was the formidable stone fortress protecting a small well-ordered European colonial town that looked expectantly out to sea. A sight that impressed many travelers most vividly on first arriving at the Cape, and one that many cartographers represented in disproportionate size, was the Company's gibbet. Situated just outside the town at a slight elevation, the scaffold was visible to ships entering the Cape roadstead. This was where corpses of the condemned were hung on display to rot. Another site of execution – the gallows – stood within a walled yard next to the Castle of Good Hope at the top of the main road going inland so all travelers would pass it. This was where sentences of public punishment, torture, and execution took place.[1] These sites, on display for all travelers and residents to see, epitomized the foundations of Dutch East India Company rule as clearly as did the Castle. The VOC's imposition of jurisdiction and monopoly of legal force over those who inhabited its settlements throughout its far-flung empire, as exemplified by these three sites – the gibbet, gallows, and Castle – enabled the Company to impose its will in the name of the law.

Places of execution at the Cape were just one of the signs and symbols of a system of discipline that incorporated ships at sea and settlements on land across the Indian Ocean. Company colonies and settlements in Africa and Asia were linked in a network of law that could impose both capital punishment and forced migration. However, the Company's control over people within and beyond its settlements was limited and partial, while evasion and resistance to its laws took many forms. Nowhere was

---

[1] Nigel Worden, "Space and Identity in VOC Cape Town," *Kronos*, no. 25, 1998–99, p. 76.

this more evident than at the Cape of Good Hope, where the sites of execution simultaneously displayed the Company's power in terms of the application of law and signaled its anxiety about those same individuals who posed a challenge to its authority, many of whom had arrived via the Company's circuit of forced migration through the Cape roadstead from which the sites of their potential demise could so readily be viewed.[2]

This contradiction between the Company's power and its limitations was obvious to Swedish naturalist and student of Linnaeus, Anders Sparrman, who visited the Cape in the early 1770s and expressed his horror upon beholding the site of execution:[3]

Heus Viator! (Hail Visitor). Here we stopped a little to contemplate the uncertainty of human life. Above half a score wheels placed round it, presented us with the most horrid subjects for this purpose; the inevitable consequences, and at the same time the most flagrant proofs of slavery and tyranny; monsters, that never fail to generate each other, together with crimes and misdemeanors of every kind, as soon as either of them is once introduced into any country. The gallows itself, the largest I ever saw, was indeed of itself a sufficiently wide door to eternity; but was by no means too large for the purpose of a tyrannical government, that in so small a town as the Cape, could find seven victims to be hanged in chains.

The contemplative tone of Sparrman's musings would probably not have been shared by people who made the journey to the Cape against their will – the convicts and exiles who were banished to the Cape under Company law, and those men, women, and children traded as slaves who were bound for perpetual servitude. For these people, passing by the barren landscape of the penal colony on Robben Island and being confronted at the harbor with the Castle and its sites of execution were ominous indications of their own potential fates as Company captives at the Cape. It is no wonder that many travelers to the Cape of Good Hope in the Dutch East India Company era noted, in effect, that the consolidation of Company sovereignty in this colony was achieved through the use of extreme violence to enforce the rule of law.

To recapitulate, the Cape colony had been established in 1653 as a transoceanic refreshment post for Company ships traveling to and fro between Europe and Asia, and the Company used this settlement as a

---

[2] Foucault, *Discipline and Punish*; Steven Pierce and Anupama Rao, eds., *Discipline and the Other Body: Correction, Corporeality, Colonialism*. Durham, NC: Duke University Press, 2006.

[3] Victor de Kock, *Those in Bondage: An Account of the Life of the Slave at the Cape in the Days of the Dutch East India Company*. Pretoria: Union Booksellers, 1963, p. 165.

central point in its transportation network. By virtue of its strategic location, the Cape became the most visited node in the Company's imperial web, despite being the node most isolated from European and indigenous Indian Ocean networks of trade with which the Company was primarily engaged.

The Cape economy developed on the basis of free burghers of European descent who relied primarily on slaves as their source of labor. From the perspective of the imperial capital Batavia, and Colombo, the capital of the Company colony in Ceylon, the Cape was an ideal site for penal transportation and political exile from their colonies. Despite protests by Cape Company officials against the effects of being a recipient of this particular circuit in the Company's network of forced migration, the Cape was forced to operate not only as a primary refreshment post but also as a primary recipient node of forced migration, becoming, essentially, one of the empire's foremost jails.

Robben Island was particularly important as a secondary site of banishment from the Cape. Nevertheless, even this isolated penal colony was potentially a site of organized resistance against Company sovereignty, as when an uprising by slaves, convicts, and exiles from the eastern regions of the Indonesian archipelago was uncovered in the mid-eighteenth century. This attempt to subvert Company authority was met with brutal force, as were at times crimes with far less threatening implications for Cape society.

The presence at the Cape of European convicts sentenced to penal transportation and hard labor along with political exiles (many of them high-ranking) and slaves, became another source of unrest and protest by Company settlers who were, theoretically, also subject to summary banishment by the Company. The appointment of Asian exiles and convicts as police, torturers and executioners' assistants by company officials at the Cape was the ultimate symbol of the paradox of forced migration. The Company felt secure enough in its control over these people to use them to uphold and implement laws that were the source of their own bondage. Individual acts of resistance by slaves, exiles, and convicts, however, disabused Company officials of this perception. The social and racial inversion of colonial power infuriated settlers and constituted another rallying point for their opposition to Company authority.

The Company's network of forced migration constituted both a source of labor and a source of resistance by people in bondage and by those who supposedly benefitted from this system at the Cape. These contradictions of sovereignty were not resolved during the Company period. The Cape of Good Hope had only limited control over its role as receiving node in the imperial network of forced migration.

Contours of Colonial Society at the Cape

The network of forced migration in the Dutch East India Company's empire consisted of three strands: the slave trade, penal transportation, and political and religious exile. In the evolution of colonial society, these forms of forced migration blurred social boundaries of status, ethnicity, and religion at the Cape. During the Company era, the difference between free and unfree people was not entirely determined on the basis of ethnicity. A small free black population emerged from manumitted slaves, time-expired convicts, and those who had been banished without further restrictions to their movements. In legal terms, the indigenous population was inalienably free, but by the eighteenth century, many Khoisan lived in conditions of servitude on settler farms while others lived in the town and became part of a free black population. Over generations, the free black population was increasingly differentiated in terms of wealth, with some becoming successful business and property owners and others remaining poor laborers.

Penal transportation and political exile made the boundaries of freedom and status even more indistinct. High-status political exiles to the Cape were prisoners, but some of them were also treated with respect due to their rank. Even in their strained circumstances as political exiles, they remained a visible reminder to the lower classes that their social betters were not exclusively European or Christian. The Cape governor was far more likely to acknowledge the status of an exiled Asian prince than to relate as an equal to a common Company servant from his own hometown. Yet, there were also royal Asian prisoners who fared little better than slaves. European convicts who arrived at the Cape under a sentence of penal transportation, whether previously Company servants or civilians, were also condemned to hard labor, often in chains, on the Company's public works. They toiled alongside Company slaves and Asian convicts and lived in comparable conditions. Nevertheless, some boundaries could not be transgressed, for no one categorized as European could be legally enslaved. Slavery was determined by maternal status, and with slave women bearing the children of Europeans either by consent or force, slaves born at the Cape were often not physically distinguishable from their masters. Cape Company servants and free burghers could likewise be sentenced to banishment to other parts of the Company's empire or to Europe.

Nor did difference in religious beliefs, particularly between Christianity and Islam, correspond with ethnicity or the status of freedom. European convicts were Christians, but this did little to alleviate their conditions of incarceration. Not all Christians were of European descent and emancipated slave women and their children had generationally been incorporated into both the free black and free burgher population, depending upon the status of their husbands and fathers. Free blacks, slaves, convicts, and exiles often shared the faith of Islam, and this created alternative networks of knowledge, authority, and status that were not under the control of the Company.

The contours of Cape colonial society were therefore more complicated in terms of the correlations among ethnicity, freedom, religion, wealth and gender than the simple categorization of people in the Company records might suggest. These complexities would have been visible to people living at the Cape in the mid-eighteenth century and were the source of considerable angst for many.[4] The tensions produced through this inversion of social boundaries were not exclusive to the Cape. They were most evident in the issuing of sumptuary laws in Batavia aimed at controlling the conspicuous display of wealth that disrupted an understood correlation between outward appearance and social position. Members of the Company elite were concerned that their social positions as the highest echelon of Batavian society were thereby being undermined. This concern was serious enough to warrant legal action to uphold their superior status.

As laws issued in Batavia were applicable throughout the empire, Company officials at the Cape amended these provisions according to local circumstances. This applied particularly to the clothes that free blacks and slaves were permitted to wear to be readily identified as such. Robert Ross's vivid description of the minute details of consumption to which these ordinances were applied, including the type of buttons or the fabric of clothing one was permitted to wear, underscores the importance of degrees of status and subordination and the constant need to enforce hierarchy in the face of deceptive appearances in the Company's colonies.[5]

The complex social landscape of bondage at the Cape was included in this attempt by the Company to control people in its midst. The spectrum

---

[4] Robert Ross, *Status and Respectability in the Cape Colony, 1750–1870: A Tragedy of Manners*. Cambridge, UK: Cambridge University Press, 1999, pp. 1–40; Richard Elphick and Robert Shell, "Intergroup Relations: Khoikhoi, Settlers, Slaves and Free Blacks, 1652-1795," in Elphick and Giliomee, *Shaping of South African Society*, pp. 283–323.

[5] Ross, *Status and Respectability*, pp. 1–40.

of forced migration, based fundamentally on the slave trade, but including penal transportation and political exile, was part of this equation as well. The treatment of all prisoners, exiles, and criminals alike was determined by their sentences or banishment orders issued by the court in the Company node in which their trial took place. Although the majority of convicts at the Cape were local, those who arrived through penal transportation most commonly came through Batavia or Colombo. Cape authorities applied these sentences as written and often utilized convicts as forced labor for its own needs.

Although there was constant demand for slaves at the Cape, the Company did not consider penal transportation a viable means to alleviate the general labor shortage. It responded instead by isolating political prisoners and convicts believed to pose the greatest danger, sending them to farms, isolated outposts, or small rural settlements. They also concentrated the majority of prisoners on public works where there was sufficient surveillance, like building the Company's fortifications. The natural isolation of Robben Island provided the safest prison for criminals convicted to hard labor and those transported from other colonies. Exiled prisoners of state and transported criminals entered the Cape's own disciplinary regime under conditions determined by courts at their place of origin, and their position was renegotiated after the sentence expired determining whether or not they remained at the Cape.

Colonial society at the Cape and the Company's disciplinary system were inextricably linked to the wider imperial web. Although slaves were by far the most important source of labor at the Cape, convicts banished to labor were an important and visible minority. They were exclusively used by the Company for their public works and constituted a significant unpaid portion of the Company's labor force. Yet for all this, these convicts were seen as a constant threat and far more trouble than they were worth. Fears of slaves and convicts conspiring together were borne out in various crimes and misdemeanors as well as serious escape attempts and minor rebellions tried by the Cape court. The Company further blurred these lines of authority and freedom by employing Asian prisoners and exiles as executioners' assistants and as a nascent police force in the town, known locally as "*caffers*." Inevitably, control and resistance went hand in hand as a consequence of forced migration to the Cape.

The Cape Government's Response to Forced Migration

Labor was a persistent and enduring problem for the Dutch East India Company's settlement at the Cape of Good Hope. Free burghers depended entirely upon slave and coerced indigenous labor supplemented by *knechts* (overseers), Company servants who had been released from their contracts. Jan van Riebeeck had first suggested to Batavia that the Cape settlement could be developed by "industrious Chinese" workers, either as free or unfree migrants. Subsequent governors repeatedly requested that Chinese migrants be sent to the Cape until the early eighteenth century, when their hope of getting them receded.[6]

For its part, Batavia began sending *bandieten* (convicts) and *bannelingen* (exiles) to the Cape within the first few years of its founding as a settlement. This was a mixed blessing because convicts and exiles required as much surveillance as slaves and were sometimes specifically sentenced to banishment on Robben Island. High-ranking exiles were often excluded from labor requirements altogether, further reducing the possibility that the Cape could derive needed labor from the Company's forced migration network. The Cape's role as a penal colony in the Dutch East India Company empire was therefore not entirely to its advantage.

By the early eighteenth century, Cape authorities began to object to being jailers for the empire. In 1715, Governor de Chavonnes sent a plea to the Seventeen Gentlemen to stem the tide of exiles to the Cape:

Regarding the convicts sent annually from Batavia, Ceylon and other places, we wish to state that we are being swamped with the rascals, this year again we received twenty-one and if it continues at that rate, the number will increase to such an extent that they may do a deal of mischief by running away, as has often occurred to the interior. They daily urge the slaves to run away and even provide them with arms. Further such people are very dangerous should an enemy attack the place and we wish you to consider whether for the future safety of the settlement it would not be advisable to locate these convicts on some convenient spot in India.[7]

The Seventeen Gentlemen duly responded to this plea and wrote to Batavia about the matter in a letter dated June 24, 1716: "The Governor and Council at the Cape...notify that it is not without anxiety and danger to be obliged to keep there so many convicts and prisoners sent thither from time to time from Batavia and Ceylon, and hence we have decided to advise you to be very sparing in sending any... [so] that the Government is not heaped up too much with those miscreants."[8]

---

[6] James Armstrong, "The Chinese at the Cape in the Dutch East India Company Period," unpublished paper presented at the UNESCO Slave Route Project Conference, Robben Island, Cape Town, 1997, p. 12.

[7] CA: Letters despatched from the Cape to Amsterdam, March 30, 1715.

[8] CA: LM, vol. 31. Index to Annexures, extract from letter dated June 24, 1716, Heren XVII to India.

Cape authorities responded optimistically to the Company Directors' response. They wrote fraternally to Colombo: "Glad to hear that you will henceforth send to the Cape as few convicts as you can; we have made the same request to Batavia, and hope you will not be burdened with that sort of person from there or elsewhere."[9] However, this order from the Seventeen Gentlemen was issued to no avail, and Batavia and Colombo both continued to send prisoners to the Cape. There is no indication that Batavia ever sought to alleviate the Cape's burden as penal colony for the Company's empire.

By 1749, the Council of Policy had resigned itself to having imposed upon them numerous convicts and exiles from the Indian Ocean. They were powerless to overrule the High Government in Batavia. Indeed, convicts and exiles were a noticeable presence in the town, and Cape authorities tried a new tactic to rid themselves of this potentially injurious population:

Considering that this place is so full of Eastern convicts, sent hither from India [i.e., Asia], who after the term of their imprisonment has expired, become free and remain free, competing with the poor whites of European descent in procuring their livelihood, and consequently very injurious to the latter... the council deem it necessary to take steps, in time, and write by first opportunity to Batavia for permission to send such convicts after the expiration of their terms of banishment back to the place whence they came.[10]

This step was implemented fairly consistently, but often at the request of the time-expired convicts themselves, who regularly petitioned the Cape authorities to be allowed passage on Company ships back to Asia. Male exiles who had not been subject to incarceration but banished to fend for themselves had sometimes earned enough money to purchase a slave woman whom they manumitted along with their children, forming stable family units. These men and ex-convicts who had served the time of their sentence, as James Armstrong points out, occupied an indeterminate status as "free exiles" who were not officially categorized by this term but who were absorbed into the urban underclass.[11]

At the same time, Company officials at the Cape sought an alternative location in the colony for keeping some of the convicts isolated from the town. The Company's *buiteposte* (outposts) were considered suitable

---

[9] CA: LM, Letters despatched to Colombo, July 25, 1716.
[10] Quoted in Elphick and Shell, "Intergroup Relations," in Elphick and Giliomee, eds., *Shaping*, p. 217.
[11] Armstrong, "Chinese at the Cape," p. 12.

sites where convicts could safely be put to productive labor.[12] There were suggestions that convicts could be kept permanently at St. Helena Bay to work at the fishing colony, but after considerable investigation this was rejected by the Council because it opened up too many opportunities for escape, either inland or on enemy ships passing by these waters en route to and from Cape Town. Instead, a number of convicts from Robben Island were taken seasonally between October and December to the islets in Saldanha Bay to labor on the oil works.[13] This deep-water harbor was also used regularly as a ship repair site for the Company and, with permission, for foreign ships. It had the advantage of keeping foreign ships isolated from the main settlement. Another problem that occurred to the security-conscious Company officials was that, should such a penal colony be established, it could be a security risk if enemies invaded the Cape from either St. Helena Bay or Saldanha Bay. Saldanha Bay was also considered vulnerable to pirate activity, so it was necessary to keep it as secure as possible.[14]

The suggestion was abandoned, but it does reveal that Company officials at the Cape were seriously concerned about the danger convicts and exiles posed to the colony and their own ability to control them.[15] The strategy of divide and rule, keeping small numbers of convicts as laborers in various outposts around the colony and occasionally spreading exiles around the small towns, helped supplement the Company labor pool and maintain security. Robben Island remained the most populous site for prisoners, where they were set to work on the lime-kilns or gathering stone for building use.

The ebb and flow in the source of slaves traded at the Cape had, over time, resulted in an ethnically mixed slave and prisoner population. Ethnic stereotyping of slaves was generated partly through channels of shared information throughout the Company's empire and was reinforced by specific local forms of slave resistance. One of the most feared forms of resistance was the murderous suicidal rage called "amok," considered

---

[12] For the most extensive analysis of the outposts under the control of the Company at the Cape see Dan Sleigh, *Die Buiteposte: VOC-buiteposte onder Kaapse bestuur 1652–1795*. Pretoria: Haum, 1993.

[13] Sealing and later whaling were the basis of the oil extraction. These industries attracted foreign vessels from as far as the North American colonies into Cape waters. Originally it was a barter post with the indigenous Khoekhoe. After settlers invaded and appropriated Khoekhoe land, Saldanha Bay was directly connected to the hinterland.

[14] Sleigh, *Die Buiteposte*, pp. 411–468.

[15] CA: A1657, vol. 31. Cape Resolutions, March 20, 1753.

a behavioral characteristic peculiar to men from the Malay regions and the eastern archipelago. Owing to fears of Asian slaves running amok, Batavia had issued an ordinance prohibiting the import of adult male slaves from the eastern archipelago in 1757. The Cape followed suit in 1767 by requesting the provision be extended to the trade in all male Asian slaves from Batavia to the Cape. Although Batavia attempted to enforce this embargo, it did not closely monitor or prevent the trade in personal slaves traveling on Company ships and officials at the Cape reissued the banning order again in 1784 and 1787.[16]

Shell's speculation that "those who came to the Cape from the East involuntarily as slaves, convicts or exiles, served the same purpose as [Batavia's] *mardijkers*, namely, strengthening the colony against invasion," does not accord with the repeated statements to the contrary by the Cape governors.[17] The Council of Policy at the Cape remained unreceptive to its role as imperial jailers, raising the same objections to the Seventeen Gentlemen and Batavia against the importation of convicts and political exiles until the end of Company rule. While the import of slaves continued to be important to the growth of the Cape economy, this was tempered by perceptions of the relative desirability of slaves from different regions. The consistency and longevity of these communications and official orders reveal the anxiety of Cape officials had regarding their ability to control its unfree and underclass population.

Crime and Punishment at the Cape in the Mid-Eighteenth Century

By the middle of the eighteenth century, Cape Town appeared to have much in common with other Company port towns of the Indian Ocean. However, it was uniquely isolated from European and indigenous trading networks in the region, save in its participation in the sub-circuit of slave trading in southeastern Africa. The Cape did not receive Asian ships in its roadstead, nor was there an indigenous shipping network that existed alongside or was displaced by the Company. Depictions of the Cape showing distinctive Asian-looking small craft were those of slaves, Chinese exiles, and free black fishermen who often sold their goods to ships in the harbor.

---

[16] Armstrong and Worden, "The Slaves," p. 117 and fn. 40, p. 171.
[17] Robert Shell, "The March of the Mardijckers: The Toleration of Islam at the Cape, 1633–1861," *Kronos*, no. 22, November 1995, p. 8.

In some respects, the social landscape of Cape Town bore similarities to other large Company settlements like Batavia and Colombo, with a status-conscious Company hierarchy at the top of the social ladder and the wealthiest European burghers occupying the next rung down. A land-based population of common Company servants and free burghers of European descent comprised the following rungs. These social groupings were seasonally augmented by the influx of Company sailors and soldiers into the port. The floating stratum of the Company was itself distinguished between army and naval officers, common soldiers, and sailors who fit into their respective social milieus at sea and while ashore. The urban underclass of Cape Town occupied the lower rungs of the social hierarchy and was composed of ordinary European burghers and free blacks including a small but visible group of Chinese people who had been exiled to the Cape from Batavia.[18] There were very few Khoekhoe people living in the town and surrounds by the mid-eighteenth century. On the lowest rungs were convicts of all ethnic groups and the large slave population upon whose labor the colony was erected. Throughout the eighteenth century, the slave population at the Cape is estimated as comprising over half of its total population, with the highest concentration being in the town.[19]

By the early 1730s, travelers to the Cape were confronted with a small bustling port town with a population of at least three thousand souls, three-quarters of whom were men, creating social problems not found in most colonial ports with larger indigenous populations.[20] Dominating the landscape on the left side of the beach was the Castle of Good Hope, a stone fortress and familiar symbol of the Company's presence in the main settlements of its empire. Continuing past the Castle was a line of low stone fortifications reaching along the coast to the mouth of a smallish

---

[18] Free blacks were categorized only as part of the town population. In the rural and frontier zones different appellations were applied including Bastard and Bastard-Hottentot. For a useful overview of these categories for the whole colony see Elphick and Shell, "Intergroup Relations," in Elphick and Giliomee, *Shaping of South African Society*, pp. 184–239.

[19] Robert C.-H. Shell, *Children of Bondage: A Social History of the Slave Society at the Cape of Good Hope, 1652–1838*. Johannesburg: Witwatersrand University Press, 1994, p. 156.

[20] Worden, Van Heyningen, and Bickford-Smith, *Cape Town*. The figure of 4,000 is calculated from the 1731 census by Governor Jan de la Fontaine and the estimates of the University of Cape Town History Project. The number includes estimates of slaves owned by individual Company servants that were not included in the official 1731 census, and speculations regarding the number of Khoekhoe living in town, pp. 50–51.

river. Past the Castle, a road leading inland wound its way around Devil's Peak to the south. The vague outline of windmills in the distance indicated settled farms spreading out toward the horizon.

Tracing the shoreline to the right of the Castle, one noticed the main jetty and the line of Company wharves, workshops, and warehouses that separated the shore from the town. The largest of these was a rectangular building that accommodated the naval stores and sailors. The town itself was set out on a grid pattern with a central street dominated by three large buildings: church, slave lodge, and hospital. Most of the surrounding houses were single-story buildings and at the top of the main street heading toward the mountain were the Company's gardens. Other garden lands and stables were situated on the gently rising land broken only by two stone reservoirs before the start of the vertical elevation of Table Mountain straight ahead and the lower elevation of the Lion's Head to the right. Along the bay on the opposite side of the town from the castle were two small batteries. The last one, situated near the foot of the Signal Hill, was called the Water-Kasteel and consisted of a partitioned building housing members of the garrison and prisoners in chains condemned to hard labor for the Company.[21]

Nigel Penn's description of Cape Town is far less idyllic than the neat white-washed houses and well laid out streets depicted by many visiting artists, invoking instead the potential danger of the streets at night:[22]

> By mid-century the town consisted of some 1,200 buildings. Because of the strong winds and the danger of fires thatch was an unpopular roofing material and the tendency was to build flat roofed houses which stood four feet apart from each other. Streets were unpaved, uneven and frequently muddy. At night they were unlit and their deep ruts and holes were especially dangerous to drunkards who had been known to drown in the puddles on the Parade. The streets were, in addition, unsanitary, with rubbish and night soil being dumped in them instead of in the sea. Domestic animals and outspanned oxen roamed the streets at will. The burghers' laundry was washed by slaves, in the streams which flowed from the mountain, whilst the town's canals were frequently clogged with filth. In these circumstances a fresh Southeaster was not always an unwelcome visitor.

Although the temperate Mediterranean climate of the Cape saved the colony from the scourge of tropical diseases that plagued Batavia, Cape

---

[21] Ibid., pp. 38–51. Otto F. Mentzel, *A Geographical and Topographical Description of the Cape of Good Hope. Pt. 1.* Translated by H. J. Mandelbrote. Cape Town: Van Riebeeck Society, 1921, pp. 98–122.

[22] Nigel Penn, "Daily Life in Eighteenth-Century Cape Town," *Cabo*, 4(1), 1986, p. 4.

Town suffered periodic smallpox epidemics in 1713, 1748, 1755, and 1767. These devastating outbreaks were invariably started when sailors coming into port gave their infected clothes to slave washerwomen to clean, thereby spreading the disease to the rest of the colony. The 1713 epidemic decimated the population, killing one-third of the town's inhabitants and nearly half of the Company's five hundred slaves.[23] When another epidemic broke out in 1755, Governor Rijk Tulbagh and the Council of Policy issued decrees closing infected business houses, restricting people's movements, and forbidding established funeral practices to try to halt the spread of the disease. This was one of the greatest crises of the mid-eighteenth-century Cape, and displayed its vulnerability as a port town. Nevertheless, it continued to operate as an important site of respite for ill travelers. Its function as an imperial hospital remained a key element of the town throughout the Company period.[24]

Despite climatic differences, what fundamentally separated Cape Town from places like Batavia and Colombo was the absence of a preexisting indigenous urban culture upon which the settlement and its society were built.[25] Unlike in most other Company settlements, Company authorities at the Cape did not have to deal with a recognized indigenous aristocracy and court culture at the apex of complex state structures that competed politically and culturally with the emergence of colonial society within the colony. After the Company claimed sovereignty over the Cape in the late seventeenth century, diplomatic and political relationships with Khoekhoe polities dissolved with the conquest of land and the gradual destruction of these societies after a century of resistance. In contrast to Batavia's dealings with archipelagic societies, the Cape authorities tacitly stopped recognizing the Khoekhoe polities as sovereign entities with their own legal system that had to be taken into consideration. The VOC at the Cape dealt internally with resistance by incorporating the indigenous population in the colony under its criminal jurisdiction. Unofficially, settlers took the law into their own hands through the violent and systematic attack on Khoekhoe settlements as a strategy of land-grabbing and coercing captive labor. The Company rarely punished such acts of aggression upon indigenous people of the region.

---

[23] This epidemic also decimated the Khoekhoe population and was one of the main factors in the decline of the free Khoi polities. Elphick and Malherbe, "The Khoisan to 1828," in Elphick and Giliomee, eds., *Shaping of South African Society*, p. 21.
[24] Russel Viljoen, "Disease and Society: VOC Cape Town, Its People and the Smallpox Epidemics of 1713, 1755 and 1767," *Kleio*, XXVII, 1995, pp. 22–45.
[25] Worden, "Space and Identity," p. 79.

By the late eighteenth century, the spread of the colony's frontiers to the east would result in a different kind of colonial conflict against larger-scale African polities and the free descendants of the Khoekhoe and slaves who had regrouped and settled in the eastern Cape. Clashes with these indigenous polities at the Cape did not generate a constant stream of political prisoners and exiles like those emanating from Batavia, and, to a lesser extent, Colombo. Banishment to foreign colonies was not used as a weapon against the African population by the Cape Company government.

Nevertheless, a survey of the criminal records at the Cape reveals a striking similarity with that of Batavia. Heese's survey of the Cape's criminal records during the eighteenth century gives details of 1,756 cases. Of these, 306 were brought against Europeans, including women, burghers, and Company servants. The sentence of banishment was imposed in 171 of these cases, with eighty-three people being banished directly to Robben Island, including five women. While eight people (including one woman) were banished to the fatherland, only two (a European burgher and a European woman) were banished to Batavia. Mauritius operated as a place of secondary banishment for the Cape, with ten Europeans being banished to that island. Of the Cape residents who were categorized under various ethnicities that are not European, 119 of a total of 850 people were sentenced to banishment. The majority of these were slaves, who comprised 696 cases, with eighty-four being sentenced to banishment and eighty-one of them to Robben Island. Of the indigenous Africans, eighty-four Khoekhoe, seven Bastaard-Hottentots, and one Hottentot-Boesman were convicted of crimes, with eleven Khoekhoe being banished to Robben Island, while five women and four men were banished to the Company's Slave Lodge.

Despite their proportionally small numbers, fifty-five cases were brought against convicts and exiles for secondary convictions while at the Cape. Of these, six Chinese men, one prisoner of war, and one convict were sentenced to further banishment in addition to their original sentences. All but one of them were sent to Robben Island, with the remaining Chinese man banished to beyond the borders of the Company.[26]

Crimes for which people at the Cape were sent into banishment were similar to those determined by the Batavian courts that received the same

---

[26] H. F. Heese, *Reg en Onreg: Kaapse Regspraak in die Agtiende Eeu.* Belville: Insituut vir Historiese Navorsing, Universiteit van Wes-Kaapland, 1994, pp. 122–272. See also, H. F. Heese, "Kriminele Sake: Hofuitsprake aan die Kaap, 1700–1750," *Kronos*, no. 12, 1987, pp. 33–42.

sentence. Typically, Company servants of the lowest ranks were convicted of the usual crimes of assault, desertion, theft, insubordination, and sometimes the more serious crimes of rape, sodomy, manslaughter, and murder. On a late spring evening in 1734, Jan van Rossum, a soldier at the Castle, was at the house of fellow soldier, Rijnier Meijer, in town. He got drunk, started an argument, and was thrown out by his host. This incensed Van Rossum so much that he forced his way back into the house and, wielding a knife that hit a soldier named Joris Harpe, injured the unlucky man in his side. Van Rossum ran to one of the town's many bars, *het laeste Stuijvertje* (roughly translatable as "The Last Ha'penny"), where he fell asleep and was later found and arrested. In his defense, he claimed that he was so drunk he could not remember any of the events that had taken place but was convicted anyway of assault and sentenced to a flogging, banishment, and loss of three months wages.[27]

Company justice punished crimes committed against free inhabitants of the colony with equal severity. When sailor Salomon de Lange of Danzig acted out his self-confessed hostility against the Chinese by breaking and entering into the homes of two Chinese residents of Cape Town, he was arrested and punished severely by being flogged, branded, and sentenced to ten years of hard labor.[28] Chinese people living in Cape Town were often time-expired convicts or people who had been banished to the Cape from Batavia, the latter mostly for having been illegal residents but not having committed any other criminal offense. At the Cape they were ordered to fend for themselves and most often worked as traders, shopkeepers, chandlers, fishermen, craftsmen, or petty merchants who sold provisions to ships from small boats.[29] During the smallpox epidemic of 1755, the government ordered all taverns and eating-houses where the disease was evident to be closed. When four drunken soldiers arrived at the house of Patri, a Chinese man, to eat curry, his wife turned them away because there was smallpox in the house. In retaliation they assaulted Patri and vandalized his house with an axe. Patri sent for the *caffers* who arrested the men. The two main perpetrators received heavy sentences; Philip Leonard Baart of Ossenheijm was flogged and sent to Robben

---

[27] Unless otherwise specified, all cases quoted in this section have been taken from Teun Baartman's database of the Cape criminal records from 1730 to 1750, and I am quoting the criminal roll reference in the Cape archives. The database was commissioned by the Cape Town History Project. CA: CJ16, 58–60.
[28] CA: CJ31, 93–96.
[29] Armstrong, "Chinese at the Cape," p. 31; Melanie Yap and Dianne Leong Man, *Colour, Confusion, and Concessions: The History of the Chinese in South Africa*. Hong Kong: Hong Kong University Press, 1996, p. 8.

Island for five years of hard labor and, Johan Adam Brand of Smalkalden was flogged and banished to an unspecified plan.[30]

The Chinese people at the Cape were a small but visible part of the town's population. Accusations that they were often involved in fencing stolen goods were not without foundation. Otto Mentzel, one of the most observant travelers to the Cape in the eighteenth century, responded directly to this charge, tempering his own criticism of Chinese business practices with the following comment:

> But it is dangerous to generalise, and condemn them all as rogues. Some of them will show more consideration to those who owe them money than Europeans do. I have met people to whom Asiatic dealers have given various commodities such as tea, chinaware, and Eastern fabrics on long credit, even until their return from Holland. On the whole, these Chinese live a humble, quiet and orderly life at the Cape.[31]

Several cases in the criminal record indicate that a few Chinese men were actively encouraging slaves to steal goods that they would then buy from them.[32] One case shows that Chinese men lived close by and socialized with each other. Tiombinko, alias Claas, and Cabeljouw were both convicted of assaulting Touako, who was a tenant of Cabeljouw, after the three men had been drinking together at the home of another Chinese man, Satiako. Tiombinko was sentenced to flogging, branding, and ten years of hard labor, and Cabeljouw to flogging and five years of hard labor.[33] Both served out their whole sentences in the Slave Lodge.[34] Chinese residents at the Cape were always categorized separately from other free blacks at the Cape and, indeed, from other convicts. Whereas most convicts from Asia were categorized as *Indiaanen*, the Chinese were listed separately. As James Armstrong has portrayed, the Chinese comprised a small, distinct, fairly close-knit, and often-prosperous community, evidenced by both their deceased estates and the existence of a Chinese burial ground just outside the boundaries of the town.[35]

As the legal representative of Company justice, the Cape court brooked no challenge to its authority. When the burgher Jacob Taillard of Doornik had a civil case filed against him in court, he lost his temper and verbally

---

[30] CA: CJ37, 83–86.
[31] Mentzel, *Description of the Cape*, p. 150.
[32] CA: CJ14, 51–54; CA: CJ15, 93–95; CA: CJ15, 58–60; CA: CJ31, 99–102; CA: CJ37, 97–99.
[33] CA: CJ17, 53–56.
[34] CA: CJ3188: Tombionko; CA: CJ3188: Cabeljouw.
[35] James Armstrong, "The Estate of a Chinese Woman in the Mid-Eighteenth Century at the Cape of Good Hope," in Worden, ed., *Contingent Lives*, pp. 75–90.

abused the court, accusing it of injustice. The court subsequently ordered Taillard to be arrested, and he was convicted of contempt, earning him the sentence of ten-years hard labor on Robben Island.[36]

Outright brutality against slaves by town burghers could lead to banishment, as was the case with Michel Lourich who was sent back to the fatherland in 1741 as a "useless subject" after having beaten his wife and ordering the beating of his slave Diana, resulting in her death.[37] The Company also took harsh action against burghers who resisted Company *caffers* while they were doing their duty to protect the public peace and order. In early February 1755, the burgher Hendrik Truter cracked his whip in town, a foolhardy action that had been expressly forbidden by the Company only five months earlier. When the Company *caffers* tried to take his whip away from him, he resisted their authority and earned himself an arrest and a fine of twenty-five rixdollars.[38]

Historians of Cape slavery have stressed that the slave society at the Cape resulted in the brutalization of masters and slaves alike, creating an extremely violent and volatile society in which, nonetheless, one found many instances of cooperation and resistance in the Cape underclass.[39] One of the most common forms of resistance by both Company servants and slaves was desertion, and this problem was endemic at the Cape. Similarly, Batavia's criminal records are full of cases in which Company servants and slaves are apprehended for desertion, and undoubtedly many more escaped successfully, prompting the courts to impose harsh sentences on multiple offenders. It was these repeat offenders who were sometimes banished to the Cape.[40]

Opportunities to flee the Cape colony were many, with up to half the 150-plus ships entering Table Bay yearly belonging to foreign nations, many of them short-crewed due to illness and death.[41] Deserters,

---

[36] CA: CJ37, 78–79.
[37] Nigel Worden and Gerald Groenewald, eds., *Trials of Slavery: Selected Documents Concerning Slaves from the Criminal Records of the Council of Justice at the Cape of Good Hope, 1705–1794*, pp. 176–187.
[38] CA: CJ37, 15–16.
[39] Robert Ross, *Cape of Torments: Slavery and Resistance in South Africa*. London: Routledge and Kegan Paul, 1983, pp. 2–10.
[40] Wayne Dooling, "The Castle: Its Place in the History of Cape Town in the VOC Period," in Elizabeth van Heyningen, ed., *Studies in the History of Cape Town*, vol. 7. Cape Town History Project in association with the Center for African Studies. Cape Town: University of Cape Town Press, 1994, pp. 9–31.
[41] Jaap Bruijn calculates that there were 4,730 outgoing and 3,358 homeward-bound ships passing by or through the Cape between 1602 and 1795, with the peak period for shipping between 1720 and 1740. After the establishment of the Cape settlement in 1652 it

particularly Company servants, were therefore often welcomed aboard despite attempts by the Cape authorities to prevent such escapes.[42] The Cape *bandieten rollen* (criminal rolls) listed yearly and by name the many convicts who had escaped and evaded capture.[43] The brutal treatment of common Company servants by those in authority is well illustrated in the story of one failed attempt of desertion. Johannes Winter of Wessel, Pieter Vleeschhouwer of Warneton, and Jacob Boerij of Zurich were all Company soldiers detained in the Castle for a minor case of absenteeism. The three managed to get drunk and decided to run away that night, foolishly jumping over the Castle walls to make their escape. As these walls were at least twenty feet high, the drunken lads hurt themselves when they landed on the ground and were immediately discovered and arrested. The Company court sentenced them to gamble who would live and who would die. Boerij drew the proverbial short straw and was executed, while the other two unfortunate men were banished for life.[44]

Slaves were sentenced to banishment for only minor offenses, but at the Cape they were incarcerated locally, often on Robben Island. Privately owned slaves could also be transferred to the ownership of the Company to defray the legal costs of court cases in which they appeared as the accused.[45] Any slave who committed an act of violence, particularly against his or her master, was dealt with the greatest severity by the courts. Barkat van Timor, slave of the ex-burgher councillor Abraham Cloppenburg, was sentenced to death by the breaking of his limbs for having assaulted his master with a knife and also for having assaulted the *caffers* who tried to arrest him. Barkat had likely been driven to this desperate act by Cloppenburg's own brutal behavior toward his slaves. Previously, Cloppenburg had ordered Barkat to be beaten merely because he was late setting the table for supper. The slave retaliated mostly out of fear and his

---

was the only port in the VOC empire that ships were obliged to stop at between Asia and Europe, partly because the fleets were required to regroup in order to protect themselves from piracy. Jaap R. Bruijn, "Between Batavia and the Cape: Shipping Patterns of the Dutch East India Company," *JSEAS* 11 (2), September 1980, pp. 251–159. For the complete register of Dutch voyages to Asia see J. R. Bruijn, F. S. Gaastra, and I. Schoffer, eds., *Dutch-Asiatic Shipping in the 17th and 18th Centuries*. 3 vols. Rijks geschiedenkundige publicatien, grote serie, nos. 165–167. Den Haag: Martinus Nijhoff, 1979–1987.

[42] Ross, *Cape of Torments*, pp. 74–79.
[43] M. Boucher, "The Cape and Foreign Shipping, 1714–1723," *SAHJ* 6, November 1974, p. 19.
[44] CA: CJ30, 29–30.
[45] M. Boucher, "Cape and Company in the Early Eighteenth Century," *Kleio*, vol. IX, nos. (1& 2), June 1977, p. 62.

attack against his master had not been premeditated. Cloppenburg himself was reprimanded by the court and warned to treat his slaves better.[46] This was no consolation to Bakat, who suffered the kind of slow and painful death that captured the imagination of many travelers to the Cape:

[W]e beheld a horrid spectacle. Upon the sand were erected a number of stakes and gibbets, upon which were the remains of upwards of a dozen malefactors who had been executed at the Cape at different periods. Some were suspended by the feet, decapitated: others were laid across the narrow wheel on which they had been racked, bent double and hanging down on each side; whilst many seemed to preserve, by the attitude in which they were placed, the last writhings of pain and approaching death.[47]

This litany of crime and fear, escape and capture, is a fair summary of the more extreme consequences of slavery and bondage in the Cape.[48] The expansion of the Cape economy under the VOC was predicated on the use of imported, and, by the mid-eighteenth century, increasingly locally born, slave labor which was augmented, particularly in the rural areas, by indigenous indentured labor. The majority of slaves, however, were concentrated in Cape Town, as were most of the convicts who resided either in the town or on Robben Island in Table Bay. The largest concentration of slaves were those owned by the Company, whose Slave Lodge also housed convicts, mostly slaves sentenced locally and prisoners banished from other parts of the Company empire.[49]

The most thorough description of the Slave Lodge was contained in the report given by Slave Lodge superintendent, Christian Gottlob Höhne in June 1793. Of the 592 people listed in the Slave Lodge register, 518 were slaves and 74 were convicts. Of the slaves, fifty-six were children under the age of ten and thirty-six were old or sick and unable to work. There were fifteen slave convicts listed as living on Robben Island (but only four were present), leaving 422 able-bodied adult Company slaves, 316 men, and 100 women. Of the seventy-four convicts, all men, fourteen were incapacitated, leaving sixty able-bodied men. Based on these numbers,

---

[46] CA: CJ26, 14-16.
[47] De Kock, *Those in Bondage*, pp. 165-166.
[48] Robert Shell argues that the incorporation of slaves into the master's household is predicated on gender. Shell, *Children of Bondage*.
[49] Shell, "The Company Slave Lodge," in *Children of Bondage*, pp. 172-205. The most thorough collection of sources on the Slave Lodge is in Robert Shell comp., *From Diaspora to Diorama: The Old Slave Lodge in Cape Town*, CD-ROM, Cape Town: Ancestry24, 2005.

approximately 14 percent of the Company's own bonded labor in 1793 consisted of convicts.

Convicts listed in the Slave Lodge register were assigned to various public duties. Nineteen were *caffers* in Cape Town, whereas no Company slaves had held this post. Eleven were *caffers* in rural towns; two in Graaff-Reinet, six in Stellenbosch, and three in Swellendam. Three convicts were assigned to the Company outpost in Rietvallei. The other convicts were spread around Cape Town in various duties; one at the hospitals one at the dairy, two at the Company's corn warehouse, three each in the government offices and Company wine cellars, eight assigned to the Fiscal's boat, and nine were assigned to the general works. Slaves had an even greater variety of duties around Cape Town, the rural towns, and Company outposts.

During his tenure at the Slave Lodge, Höhne further recommended that unfit convicts be granted permission to live outside the Lodge with "good friends among their free countrymen at the Cape" because they were not dangerous in their incapacitated state and their removal would relieve the Company of the financial burden of supporting them.[50] Although these examples give just a glimpse of the various jobs performed by convicts, they do highlight their usefulness to the Company.

Cape Town was by far the most fluid and cosmopolitan social milieu in the colony. Owing to this, bondage took a form in Cape Town that could not be replicated in the smaller towns and rural areas.[51] The town's position as the center of the garrison, the quartering (or at least, temporary shore-leave) of hundreds of sailors and soldiers in transit between Europe and Asia, and the densest concentration of population, both slave and free, made Cape Town far less of a face-to-face society than the more sparsely populated rural areas. Court records confirm the considerable degree to which the underclass, including common VOC servants, mixed unhindered in town until they fell afoul of the law.[52]

Bandieten and *Bannelingen* at the Cape

Convicts and exiles arriving at the Cape were most often accompanied by some form of documentation that gave their basic biographical details, the

---

[50] CA: C210 [old series] Bijlagen, 1793, folios 539 ff. Reproduced in Shell, *Diaspora to Diorama*, pp. 455–461.
[51] Nigel Worden, *Slavey in Dutch South Africa*, Cambridge, UK: Cambridge University Press, 1985, p. 4.
[52] Ross, *Cape of Torments*. See especially, Chapters 4, 6, and 7.

length of their sentence, and, more rarely, the reason for which they had been banished to Africa. Cape authorities had little room to maneuver in altering banishment, except in cases for which no details were specified, but they still exercised a degree of discretion. Most convicts were sentenced to hard labor, so the Company could assign them where it saw fit. In contrast, high-ranking political exiles often arrived with explicit instructions from Batavia detailing where they should be housed and what monthly allowance they should receive. The Company sometimes treated exiles of noble rank with respect, though they could also banish them to Robben Island where they were treated little better than slaves.

Very rarely, a high-ranking Company official was banished to the Cape for having committed a serious transgression against VOC law. Coenraad Frederik Hofman, a senior merchant at the Company's settlement at Padang on Sumatra's west coast, was sentenced to fifteen years of banishment for illegal trade and arrived at the Cape on the *Kiefhoek* in January 1721. Although no official documents concerning his case accompanied him, it is likely Hofman's case would have been gossiped about by Company personnel. At first, Hofman was not forthcoming in giving his version of the events that surrounded his downfall. Because of his previous rank, Cape authorities used their discretion and decided to allow him to live quietly on one of the outlying farms of the colony.

However, when a copy of his sentence arrived with the next ship, Cape authorities were obliged to rescind this offer and carry out his sentence as detailed in the Batavian criminal records: specifically that he be beaten and placed in chains to labor without pay on the Company works for fifteen years. Although Hofman was temporarily transferred to Robben Island, the Company authorities did not carry out the beating or put the man in chains. Moreover, he was not put to labor and was quietly transferred back to the mainland because by 1726 Hofman was negotiating legal documents with senior burghers at the Cape, and in 1727 he purchased a valuable farm in the outlying area of Wynberg, including fourteen slaves, where he lived quietly until his death in 1734.[53]

Margaret Cairns speculates that Hofman's case would have generated appropriate sympathy from the senior Company officials at the Cape who constantly sought to alleviate the conditions of his exile. There is no suggestion that he was socially ostracized at the Cape. Although little is known of his daily life, he had regular legal dealings with burghers

---

[53] Margaret Cairns, "Coenraad Frederik Hofman, an Exile at the Cape, 1721–1734," *Cabo*, 2(1), February 1978, pp. 7–17.

and Company officials and kept up a regular correspondence with Batavia and Europe. Hofman's harsh sentence for illegal trading would have given senior Company officials pause to reflect upon their own illegal dealings because it was common practice for Company officials to enrich themselves at the expense of Company trade. Occasionally, a senior Company official was prosecuted to prevent these dealings, but these "scapegoats" were usually linked to other political or personal feuds that left particular individuals vulnerable to prosecution by higher-ranking Company officials.[54] Despite the Cape authorities' sympathetic treatment of Hofman, they were powerless to change his status as a convicted criminal. He remained on the criminal rolls until his death, sadly, the year he would have been released from detention and allowed to rejoin his children in Batavia.[55]

Political prisoners from Asia constituted a small but significant group of exiles with high social status sent to the Cape. Batavia set the conditions of exile for political prisoners, and the Cape authorities generally carried out these orders as directed. In some cases, political prisoners were treated according to their rank and provided for by the Company, particularly when their imprisonment was at the behest of an ally or when it was strategically important for the Company to keep the exile "in the wings" for potential repatriation.[56] Occasionally, a political prisoner exiled on behalf of an ally was also a convicted criminal. In this case, the terms of exile were negotiated between the polity and the Company.

A major difference in the experiences of political exiles at the Cape was whether or not they came from a region over which the Company had extended jurisdiction or from a polity with which the Company was engaged in open hostility. In the first case, Batavia exiled high-ranking prisoners from polities under their jurisdiction as "rebels" against the Company. This was the case with Raja Boekit of Padang, who was banished to Robben Island, and with Raden Dule Ganie from Cheribon, who was banished for life to labor on the Company works in 1753. Although Raden Ganie arrived at the Cape with very little documentation about his particular case, he was considered a "rebel," and therefore had been sentenced to exile by Batavia for opposing Company rule.

The broad reach of Company jurisdiction served to extend the network of penal transportation from cases in the immediate vicinity of Batavia to other parts of the island of Java. These farther-flung cases were sometimes difficult to differentiate from cases of political exile. For

[54] Ibid., pp. 10–12.
[55] Ibid., pp. 12–13.
[56] Ibid., chapter 3.

example, between 1745 and 1747 one hundred prisoners were exiled from Cheribon to the Cape; ninety-five indigenous *Indiaanen* (Asian) and five Chinese. Of the ninety-five indigenous Asians, sixty-seven were free Javanese people, possibly the highest influx of Javanese prisoners to the Cape for the entire Company period.[57] Many of these people were sent without accompanying case notes, but in one case thirty Javanese prisoners were condemned to exile "by the princes" to a place of banishment to be chosen by Batavia, and twenty-four of them were sent to the Cape.[58] In another case of twenty-three prisoners sent in 1747, the General Resolutions from Batavia detail that they had been condemned by the Cheribon resident, the highest Company official in that town.[59] The lines between political and penal transportation were blurred by the extension of jurisdiction under Company law that simultaneously recognized indigenous legal authority.

Both penal transportation and political exile were heavily gendered. Women convicts of any ethnicity were rarely sentenced to penal transportation, and there were almost as many women exiled to the Cape in the entourages of political prisoners as the total number of women transported as criminals.[60] Mansell Upham has traced the life and family of the first female convict sent to the Cape, Groote Catrijn, who arrived within the first decade of establishment of the colony. As one of the few marriageable women in the colony she eventually established herself as a free black settler.[61] The criminal rolls show less than twenty women sentenced to penal transportation at the Cape in the mid-eighteenth century, although some had died en route. These female convicts arrived with very few accompanying details about their crimes or whereabouts once at the Cape. At least three of the women were slaves. Tang laij van Bogies was banished for life under suspicion of murder in 1740.[62] Ahora van Batavia was sentenced to ten years banishment in 1739 in a case of theft.[63] In 1735, Boenga van Johoor was sentenced to five years of banishment in addition to her previous sentence for having broken out of her chains in Batavia.[64]

---

[57] CA: CJ. Vonnis 3, Cases 49, 53, 66, 67, and 70.
[58] CA: CJ. Vonnis 3, Case 49c.
[59] CA: CJ. Vonnis 3, Case 70. See General Resolution Castle Batavia, April 21, 1747.
[60] See Chapter 3.
[61] Mansell Upham, "Groote Catrijn: Earliest Recorded Female *Bandiet* at the Cape of Good Hope – A Study In Upward Mobility," *Capensis*, no. 3, September 1997, pp. 8–33.
[62] CA: CJ3188: Tang laij. This could also be Tang kiok, who is categorized as a Chinese female slave convicted on the same day in Batavia.
[63] CA: CJ3188: Ahora van Batavia.   [64] CA: CJ3188: Boenga van Johoor.

Finally, in one of the most enigmatic cases, Ambonia Opdulla, was listed as a "moorin," the ethnic category used in Batavia to denote an Indian-born Muslim woman despite name indicating she may have been from Ambon. She was banished for life in 1737.[65] Unlike most criminals whose names are entered every year with their place of incarceration and added notes about whether they are sick, in hospital, and so on, no further details are given about these women apart from their initial entry onto the criminal roll.

Many of the common Company convicts sent to the Cape were chastened by their experience and were not tempted into further crime or escape. They tried merely to survive and serve out their sentences hoping to live for better times. Jan Schimmel from Arnhem, who had been sentenced to five years banishment in 1740 for attacking a Chinese Batavian with a knife, finally arrived at the Cape in 1742. He duly entered the Cape criminal rolls but no further details were given about his place of residence at the Cape. It is probable that he was on the mainland working on the Company's fortifications for the remaining time of his sentence. Then, in 1745, he was released and probably sent on the next ship back to Batavia.[66] Arij Heijman, who had been one of fourteen soldiers arrested for stealing the Company's wine and engaging in drunken revelry in 1740, was also a prisoner on the mainland at the Cape from 1742 until he served out the remainder of his five-year sentence and was released in 1745, probably traveling back to Batavia on the same fleet as Schimmel.[67]

Jacobus Bunnegam, the carpenter on Onrust Island who had gone on a drunken rage and assaulted a fellow soldier, had been sentenced to banishment for a total of fifteen years in 1734. He arrived at the Cape in 1737 with another twelve years to serve on his sentence. After remaining imprisoned on the mainland for two years, Bunnegam was placed on Robben Island where he remained to serve out his term for another nine years before being released. His name disappeared from the criminal roll with the note that he had been released.[68] Willem Cornelis Butting from Amsterdam had been convicted of disobedience against a superior officer in Batavia in 1731, for which crime the prosecutor recommended banishment to the fatherland. The Company court in Batavia changed his sentence, and Butting was sent to the Cape instead for five years where he labored on Robben Island before being released in 1736 and sent onward to the fatherland on the return fleet.[69]

[65] CA: CJ3188: Ambonia Opdulla.
[67] CA: CJ3188: Arij Heijmand.
[69] CA: CJ3188: Willem Cornelis Butting.
[66] CA: CJ3188: Jan Schimmel.
[68] CA: CJ3188: Jacobus Bunnegam.

It is sometimes impossible to trace the whereabouts of convicts sentenced to the Cape once they arrive, particularly if they do not appear to get into further trouble. Sijbrand Schordijk, quartermaster from The Hague, was sentenced with Arij Heijman, and arrived at the Cape on the ship *Buikesteijn*, but no further information about his incarceration exists in the Cape convict records. Other convicts documented with their sentences, but with no further information concerning their whereabouts at the Cape, include Ephraim Pauluszoon and Jan Dirkszoon Groen, and the Javanese Singa Carta and Raxa Nanga. It is likely that these men were working on the mainland on the Company's public works rather than living on Robben Island where the criminal population was more closely guarded and enumerated.

The Cape criminal rolls give some indication that convicts transported to the Cape had enough freedom of movement in their sentences of hard labor to engage in a variety of nefarious activities. For example, convicts were commonly used as labor in the Company hospital. When Baatjoe van Boegies was physically chastised for not working quickly enough to satisfy the undersuperintendent of the Hospital, Johan Jacob Wieber, Baatjoe took Wieber's knife and stabbed him. For this act, he was given the same punishment as a slave who had committed an offense against his master. His right hand was cut off and he was hanged.[70] Another convict working in the Hospital, Brodjo van Batavia, stabbed a female convict slave, Candace van Boegies, when she refused his advances. He was flogged, branded, and sentenced to fifteen-years hard labor on Robben Island.[71] The Cape court did consider intent in its deliberations. The convict Isak van Java, who lived in the Slave Lodge, was known to have bouts of temporary insanity. When he stabbed another convict during such a period, he was not convicted, but locked up instead in the Company Hospital to see whether he would recover. Several months later he was released under supervision with no further punishment.[72] In two separate instances, four convicts living in the Slave Lodge were caught trying to sell wood they had stolen from the Company stores to people who became suspicious and had them arrested. Their punishments were flogging, branding, and longer terms of hard labor for the Company.[73]

It appears that in some ways Asian convicts sent to the Cape had more opportunity to interact with the town's population than other convicts because many of them were housed in the Slave Lodge and the hospital,

[70] CA: CJ30, 52–54.
[72] CA: CJ27, 77–78.
[71] CA: CJ34, 59–62.
[73] CA: CJ20, 12–14; CA: CJ18, 61–63.

giving them access to other Company slaves, including slave women. Although convicts transported to Cape Town often shared their lives with the Company slaves in town and had similar opportunities and constraints on their relationships, convicts were, paradoxically, valued less highly than slaves. They constituted an unpaid labor force for the Company with no book value, unlike Company slaves who were a financial asset and investment. Therefore, whether a convict lived or died was of little consequence to the Company.

More than any other instance, the failed attempt to build a breakwater at Mouille Point illustrates this logic. James Armstrong has analyzed this episode and argues that Batavia specifically sent higher numbers of convicts than slaves during the mid-1740s to work on this project, and almost all drowned, as strong seas made it impossible to stabilize the breakwater. Armstrong further argues that although this period covered the "Chinese massacre" in Batavia, there was no significant increase in the importation of Chinese convicts to the Cape, which is surprising, given the high numbers who were banished from Batavia in the aftermath of this event.[74]

The Company *Caffers*

The institution of the Company *caffers* most clearly illustrates the complexities and ambiguities of the network of exile and the social inversions it created at the Cape of Good Hope. The Company *caffers* acted as an urban police force and in Cape Town operated under the authority of the Company *Fiscal*, who was the public prosecutor. In smaller urban settlements like Stellenbosch, *caffers* were under the authority of the *landdrost* (magistrate). In general, *caffers* had powers of arrest and summary corporal punishment over anyone in the colony who transgressed Company law. They were used to inflict corporal punishment on privately owned slaves. Upon payment of a small fee, masters could send their slaves to the *caffers* for this specific purpose. The *caffers* also acted as the executioner's assistant, inflicting sentences of torture and execution handed down from the court.[75] They were housed both in the Slave Lodge and in the Naval Storehouse near the Castle.[76] In Cape Town, Asian

---

[74] Armstrong, "Chinese at the Cape," pp. 25–27.
[75] For the fullest treatment of the role of the *caffers* in Cape Town, see Shell, *Children of Bondage*, pp. 188–194.
[76] Mentzel, *Description of the Cape*, p. 108.

Forced Migration and Cape Colonial Society

convicts, including slave convicts, were the main source of the Company *caffers*.[77]

Shell suggests that the *caffers* "were low in the [Slave] Lodge hierarchy, just above the convicts, but they held a quite anomalous position in the colony, somewhat removed from the intramural hierarchy of the Lodge... Although the *caffers* occupied a despised echelon of the slave hierarchy, the Company issued them superior clothing – special police uniforms with waistcoats. They were also the only slaves allowed to bear arms."[78] He compares them with the ancient Greek slave police, the *toxotai*, imported slaves with "no blood ties to the citizenry, which was presumably a safeguard against corruption."[79]

There is ample evidence to suggest the burghers were extremely hostile to this institution, but there is no corresponding evidence that the urban underclass, including slaves, made consistent attempts to ostracize those working as *caffers*.[80] There is also no evidence that other slaves isolated themselves from the *caffers* because of the latter's role in the Cape's disciplinary system. The criminal record indicates enough examples of crimes committed by *caffers* in cooperation with others to argue that their social bonds were not unlike those of other slaves and convicts.[81] For instance, Tagal van Balij, a *caffer* in Cape Town, was arrested for acts of drunken violence after he was denied entry into the house where the slave woman Sanna was living. Presumably, he and Sanna were engaged in some kind of romantic liaison, as he attacked the other house slaves who tried to stop him from forcing his way into the house to see her.[82] Moreover, *caffers* were not immune from the temptations of desertion, as the 1735 case of sheep theft against the Company slave Marre de Kleijne van Madagascar shows. He was persuaded to

---

[77] Shell argues that all *caffers* were "full-breed" and no "mulattos" were *caffers*. I'm not convinced this is the case. The criminal rolls list one Cape-born slave, Valentijn, who was a Company slave sentenced to ten years of hard labor in 1735. In the last year of his sentence he was made a *caffer* and continued in this position for several years after his sentence was completed. This is the rare exception, however. CA: CJ3188: Valentijn from the Cape.

[78] Shell, *Children of Bondage*, pp. 188–190.   [79] Ibid., p. 193.

[80] As early as 1780 the Cape Company officials were recommending that it was undesirable to have Indian convicts serving as *caffers* arrest European burghers and that only European servants of justice should be allowed to do so. *Cape Resolution*, August 12, 1780.

[81] Heese gives eight cases of *caffers* committing crimes at the Cape. *Reg en Onreg*, pp. 162, 177, 178, 213, 240, 243, 252, 262.

[82] CA: CJ34, 49–51.

commit the crime by another deserter, a former *caffer* who had escaped detection.[83]

That many *caffers* were convicts and exiles brings into question their capacity to enforce law and order. It is possible that convicts and exiles accepted assignment as *caffers* in order to be removed from Robben Island, as many of them were, and possibly to increase their chances of being pardoned and sent back home. Panaij van Boegies was a slave of the Malay captain in Batavia before being sentenced in 1730 by the Court of Aldermen to banishment for life in chains with hard labor for his alleged arson. After being transported to the Cape as a convict and toiling on Robben Island for twelve years, he was appointed a *caffer* in Cape Town and transferred to the Slave Lodge, after which he appears only in this capacity in the criminal records, including a case in which he assisted in the capture of a slave who had run *amok*.[84]

While Panaij van Boegies' fate is unknown because he disappears from the archival record, disappointment at the unfulfilled expectation of pardon for services rendered as a *caffer* appears to have been the motive behind another case of amok at the Cape. Soera Brotto, a man of high social rank, was sentenced to indeterminate banishment as a convict from Batavia in 1772.[85] He began his sentence at the Cape in 1781 as a general laborer but was transferred to the status of *caffer* in 1786. When the Cape Governor refused Soera Brotto's request to be repatriated to Batavia, he soon thereafter armed himself with various knives, attacked his European superior officer, and then ran *amok* in town, killing seven men and wounding another ten. Significantly, Soera Brotto did not attack a single woman; his anger was specifically targeted at men. A day later, after having terrorized the whole town, he was eventually arrested by a group of soldiers and taken to the court already dying of a head wound. Soera Brotto, who was too incoherent to confess or answer his charges, was immediately convicted of murder and taken to the place of execution where he was broken on the wheel, and, while still alive, his right hand was cut off and his heart cut out, whereupon he was hit in the face with both hand and heart. He was then decapitated, cut into four pieces, and

---

[83] Gerald Groenewald, "Crime and Company Slaves," In Shell comp., *Diaspora to Diorama*, pp. 444–446.

[84] Gerald Groenewald, "Panaij van Boegies: Slave-Bandiet-Caffer," *Quarterly Bulletin of the National Library of South Africa*, 59(2) 2005, pp. 50–62; Worden and Groenewald, eds., *Trials of Slavery*, pp. 220–221.

[85] Edna Bradlow, "Mental Illness or a Form of Resistance? The Case of Soera Brotto," *Kleio*, 23, 1991, pp. 4–16.

his body parts dragged through town and displayed on poles at prominent street intersections.[86]

Soera Brotto's extreme reaction to the conditions of his incarceration was most likely motivated in part by what he perceived to be his equally extreme fall from status as a convict living in the Slave Lodge at Cape Town. Having fulfilled the Company's request to carry out the duties of a *caffer*, he expected to be pardoned and returned home. When these hopes were dashed, he may have felt he had nothing to live for and in his despair ran *amok*. This is one of the cases in which the contradictions in the original social status of an exile and the conditions of his banishment led to extreme consequences. Cape authorities responded to these problems by doubling the number of European servants of justice in proportion to the number of convicts serving as *caffers*, and by phasing out the use of political prisoners and convicts in favor of Company slaves.[87] There is no evidence that this resolution was enforced because at the end of the Company era there were nineteen *Indiaanen caffers* in Cape Town, still mostly convicts, as opposed to ten Europeans.[88]

Soera Brotto's case can be contrasted with the cases of Said Aloewie and Hadjie Mattaram, who were categorized as *"mahomeden priesters"* (Muslim priests) in Batavia and sentenced to banishment for life in chains in 1744. They arrived at the Cape in 1745 and sent to Robben Island, but they were taken to the mainland later that year and thus must also have been removed from their chains.[89] The exiled Muslims were a special category of prisoners sentenced to what amounts to religious exile. Of these, Shaykh Yusuf was the most prominent, but his case was also clearly one of political exile. In other cases, political motives are not as clearly stated beyond the religious categorization of prisoners. Whether they were sentenced to penal transportation for committing a specific crime, or whether their exile was linked to their religious standing, is not specified. However, because no criminal offense is mentioned, it would appear that they were not common criminals.

Status as a political or religious exile did not rule out being coopted by the colonial state. Said Aloewie, who is now known to Cape Muslims

---

[86] Ibid., pp. 8–12. NA: 10805, September 24–27, 1786.
[87] Cape Resolution of 1786 quoted in Coenraad Beyers, *Die Kaapse Patriotte gedurende die laaste kwart van die agteende eeu en die voortlewing van hul denkbeeld*, Pretoria: J. L. van Schank, 1967, p. 50.
[88] Theal, quoting 1795 report by W. S. van Ryneveld in *Records of the Cape Colony*, vol. 1, p. 244.
[89] CA: CJ3188: Said Aloewie; CA: CJ3188: Hadjie Mattaram.

as Tuan Sayeed Alawie, became a *caffer* in town. Legend has it that he also became a religious leader among the small Muslim community. His *kramat* (tomb) in the Muslim cemetery in town is testament to this status, although little is known about how he conducted this role. The lives of Said Aloewie and Hadjie Mattaram are not well documented in the archives, but Said Aloewie's role as a *caffer* and religious leader shows definitively that *caffers* were not isolated socially in Cape Town, despite their position as the Company's police force. It also reveals the complexity of political allegiance operating within the VOC's imperial network of exile.

Another case in the Cape criminal records attests to these complexities. The convict known as Norman (Tuan Nuruman) sentenced from Batavia in 1770 and housed in the Slave Lodge, although not a *caffer*, was a prominent Muslim leader in Cape Town.[90] He was called a "Muslim priest" by the Company and attracted the attention the Court of Justice during a case of slave desertion in 1786, when it was discovered that one of the deserters had "a small square lead disc, on which were written with a needle some letters, seemingly in Malay," that was an amulet for protection.[91] Tuan Nuruman was brought before the Court of Justice and examined regarding this case but he denied all knowledge of the amulet; however, Cape authorities banished him to Robben Island. Prisoners in another case admitted they were also in possession of "a kind of incense with which to smoke the aforementioned small disc on Fridays, in order to keep the power of the charm."[92]

This example, as well as other examples of charms written in Malay, reveals the circulation of mystical Islam embodied in religious objects and writing considered by adherents to be powerful modes of protection and alternative authority.[93] Although none of the prisoners in this case explicitly stated they were Muslim, they were found using Islamic protective charms, and this constituted in its own right a double threat to the

---

[90] Mansoor Jaffer, ed., *Guide to the Kramats of the Western Cape*, pp. 42–45; Achmat Davids, *The History of the Tana Baru*. Cape Town: Committee for the Preservation of the Tana Baru, 1985.

[91] 1786 Augustus van de Caab et al. in Worden and Groenewald, eds., *Trials of Slavery*, p. 549.

[92] Ibid., p. 548.

[93] In 1800 a Persian Muslim traveler who sojourned at the Cape on the way to London wrote in his travel account that he sold a talisman to obtain money for his stay. Mirza Abu Taleb Khan, *Westward Bound: Travels of Mirza Abu Taleb*. Trans., Charles Stewart, ed., Mushirul Hasan. New Delhi: Oxford University Press, 2005. p. 28.

VOC. The men in this case were cold-blooded murderers, killing women and children in their attempt to rob a farmhouse, and their execution was conducted with the maximum of torture and without the coup de grâce, while their corpses were dismembered and put on the gibbet to rot.[94]

Robben Island as a Place of Banishment

If Cape Town claimed a special position in the Company empire because its peculiar social structure was borne partly from its geographical location, so too did Robben Island. Everyone who viewed or visited the Cape saw Robben Island and must have been aware of its role as a prison. Passing ships were forbidden to visit the island, yet they sometimes surreptitiously and illegally picked up willing convicts to supplement their depleted crews.[95] It is difficult to determine exactly what reputation Robben Island had as a prison in the VOC empire, although some travelers' accounts specifically mention the hardships endured by royal exiles from Asia who had been banished to the Island.

What is clear, however, is that Robben Island became a specific site of banishment from both Batavia and Ceylon. This follows a pattern of prison islands established in the Company's empire. Batavia used the islands of Onrust and Edam just off its coast as prisons and holding stations for prisoners awaiting dispatch to more distant places of exile. Prisoners from Batavia were also exiled to Banda in the Moluccas and from there to the tiny atoll of Rosingain, which appears to have served a function very similar for the Moluccas as Robben Island did for the Cape. In this sense, the Cape and, more particularly, Robben Island, were both considered the "ends of the earth" for the purpose of banishment in the Indian Ocean.

Not all European convicts were willing or able to quietly live out their sentences on Robben Island. Marten de Wilde from Sloteijn had been sentenced to twenty-five years of banishment for stealing gunpowder in Batavia. He arrived at the Cape in 1740 and was sent directly to Robben Island to serve out his punishment. He was recorded in the criminal rolls as resident there for seven years. Hard labor on Robben Island took various forms but primarily consisted of gathering shells for the limekilns. Convicts were periodically taken to the even smaller neighboring

[94] Ibid, pp. 548–555.
[95] Nigel Penn, "Robben Island, 1488–1805," in Deacon, *The Island*, p. 22.

Dassen Island, to collect shells for the same purpose.[96] Dassen Island was more desolate than Robben Island and perhaps this drove Marten de Wilde to desperation, for in 1747 he drowned in the waters off Dassen Island. A notation confirms that his body was actually recovered because if he had disappeared off the island without a trace, he would have been recorded as "escaped."[97]

Hendrik Wessel from Hogenvos, who was co-conspirator with De Wilde in the gunpowder theft and was likewise sentenced to twenty-five years banishment, probably accompanied De Wilde to Robben Island because they both appear on the records at the same time. However, Wessel successfully escaped a year before De Wilde drowned and was never found.[98] Wessel was likely picked up by a passing ship and perhaps it was De Wilde's intention to swim out to one of the ships in Table Bay to seek his own escape. This was a risky endeavor as these waters were known to contain sharks. There are a few cases of convicts sentenced to terms as long as twenty-five years who survived and were released after serving their terms. Few European convicts had their sentences reduced or clemency shown to them during their imprisonment. Not one of these European convicts left a written account of his experience.[99]

Status, Ethnicity, and Transgression on Robben Island

One unique case sheds light on the daily life of those condemned to this prison island in the mid-eighteenth century. Conditions on Robben Island in August 1751 were rough, even by eighteenth-century standards. The flat landscape, dominated by low-lying saltbush scrub, provided no protection from the howling north-westerly winter winds and rain. The

---

[96] Francois Valentijn, *Description of the Cape of Good Hope with the Matters Concerning It. Amsterdam, 1726*, E. H. Raidt, ed. Cape Town: Van Riebeeck Society, 1973, pt. I, pp. 42–45; pt. II, p. 247.

[97] CA: CJ3188: Marten de Wilde.   [98] CA: CJ3188: Hendrik Wessel.

[99] Indeed, it has been extremely difficult for Cape historians to reconstruct the lives of the urban underclasses at the Cape. Both Robert Shell and Antonia Malan have successfully used estate records to trace the material possessions of individuals. See Robert Shell, "The Short Life and Personal Belongings of One Slave: Rangton of Bali, 1672–1720," *Kronos*, no. 18, October 1991, pp. 1–6, and "Rangton van Bali (1673–1720): Roots and Resurrection," *Kronos*, no. 19, November 1992, pp. 167–187. Gerrit Schutte critiqued Shell's article in "Nogmaals Rangton van Bali," *Kronos*, no. 19, November 1992, pp. 161–166, to which Shell's second article listed above was a response. Antonia Malan has attempted to reconstruct the lifestyles of free black women in Cape Town in her article, "Chattels or Colonists? 'Freeblack' Women and their Households," *Kronos*, no. 25, 1988–98, pp. 50–71.

squat overcrowded prison building, known as the *kraal* (corral), was situated next to the Postholder's more spacious house. Both were a slight distance from the soldiers' quarters and the church. Directly in front of the prison was the landing site for the provision boats from the mainland. At some distance were the lime quarries where the prisoners labored and the lighthouse that guided ships through the treacherous waters of the bay into the Cape roadstead.[100]

In that winter of 1751, there were at least forty people living on Robben Island.[101] Prisoners were divided for the purpose of the convict rolls into "European and Asian."[102] Most of the Europeans were company servants sentenced at the Cape, but a significant number had been banished from the far reaches of the Company's empire. Many VOC servants were sentenced to extremely short times of imprisonment on the Island, (six to eighteen months), as punishment for being absent without leave. A smaller number were sentenced to long-term imprisonment, mostly for multiple criminal convictions; a few miscreant burghers shared this fate for having committed serious crimes that fell short of demanding the death penalty.

The convicts designated as *Indiaanen* were a more diverse lot, coming either as criminals from VOC settlements in South and Southeast Asia, or as political and religious exiles from indigenous polities hostile to VOC intervention who attempted dominance in their homelands. *Indiaanen* came to be used as a term for all non-European prisoners, except the Chinese. The ethnic origin of prisoners was defined in the convict roll and the few high-ranking exiles, who often had an independent stipend, were categorized separately at the end of the register, sometimes along with their slaves.

In one sense, the Robben Island prison population in the eighteenth century was far more mobile than has hitherto been recognized, probably because most historians of the Island are more familiar with the long-term imprisonments suffered under apartheid. The transfer of prisoners to work on the VOC public works or reside in the Slave Lodge was routine, as was the hospitalization of sick prisoners on the mainland. There

---

[100] Penn, "Robben Island," pp. 20–23. This description is based on the drawing of Colonel Robert Gordon in 1777.
[101] CA: CJ3188. *The Bandieten Rollen* (1728–1795) stops giving yearly summaries of the numbers of people on Robben Island in 1748. It is difficult to correlate the exact number of residents from the scattered information available.
[102] CA: CJ3188. Chinese convicts were sometimes listed as a separate ethnic category.

was a continual trickle of escapes from both the Island and the mainland; only when dead bodies were recovered was it assumed that such attempts were unsuccessful. In another important sense, high death rates on the Island constantly reminded prisoners that survival was precarious. Nevertheless, repatriation after their sentences had expired, in addition to being pardoned, was by far the most frequent means by which prisoners let the island alive.

In 1750, ten *Indiaanen* prisoners were returned to Batavia on the ships *Naarstig* and *Vrijberg*, and in the summer of 1751, six more sailed to their homelands.[103] Perhaps it was their return that made the following winter even more unbearable than usual for those who remained, for it was during this time that as escape plot began to take place. From at least May onward, the convicts Robo of Bouton and Raja Boukit of Padang had been hatching an escape plan, garnering support from various *Indiaanen* prisoners as they gathered to talk behind the *kraal*. The plan itself was daringly simple, if overly ambitious. The conspirators began stealing and burying knives and weapons. They decided that when the provision boat next arrived from the mainland, they would run *amok*, murder all Europeans on the Island, and steal the soldiers' guns. They intended to temporarily spare the lives of European convict Michiel van Embdneelen and black convict Arend van den Velde, who were to guide them on the captured boat into open waters. After throwing their kidnapped pilots overboard, Raja Boukit would set a course for Batavia and thence sail onward to their homelands.

Of the fifteen prisoners convicted in this case, twelve were identifiably from the eastern Indonesian archipelago. Eight were ethnic Bugis and two were Makassarese from the island of South Sulawesi; two others including Robo of Bouton were from neighboring islands. Raja Boukit, from Padang in the Minangkabau region on West Coast Sumatra, had been convicted of rebellion in Batavia in 1749.[104] Toerbattoe of

---

[103] CA: CJ3188.
[104] NA: VOC: 779. General Resolutions of the Batavia Castle 1748/49. A report from the West Coast of Sumatra details the capture and imprisonment of the regent of Padang, Radja Boekit, for rebellion. He was sentenced to the Cape of Good Hope pending further instructions. Thursday, June 26, 1749. Merle Ricklefs argues that the latter half of the eighteenth century saw VOC positions weakening in the archipelago outside of Java as financial collapse set in. Ricklefs, *History of Modern Indonesia*, p. 105. Nevertheless, attempts at ensuring political control continued in areas like Padang that had been VOC strongholds. See also *Generale Missiven* vol. 11, 1743–1750, p. 790, which documents the arrest and banishment of Radja Boekit.

Mandhaer was possibly from the South Sulawesi region of Mandar.[105] In their confessions, most of the Bugis prisoners admitted that the plan had been hatched when they were talking among themselves in their own language, in which both Raja Boukit and Robo of Bouton could converse.[106] Others who could not understand the conversations taking place were told later of the plan in Malay or Portuguese.[107]

Four Bugis convicts and one from Porttonova had been sentenced to life in chains at the Cape following a conviction of piracy in Batavia in 1748. None of the prisoners involved in the plot had been on Robben Island for more than two years. Robo of Bouton a "free Boutonder," had been sent to the Cape in chains for twenty-five years by the Batavian Council of Aldermen in 1739. This usually indicated that a criminal conviction had been passed. It was due to his second conviction for theft at the Cape that he was sent to Robben Island in 1750.

The Chinese convict, Limoeijko, used as his defense the excuse that he could not understand what was being discussed around him. The Cape Council of Justice convicted Limeoijko of theft in November 1749.[108] As this was a subsequent conviction from that which caused his banishment, he was convicted to labor for life on the Company's general works.[109] Giving his testimony in Malay, Limoeijko said that the Bugis and Portuguese languages were unknown to him. The court believed he didn't know what was happening, despite testimony from others who claimed they were told about the plot in Malay, and he was subsequently returned to Robben Island.

One of the prominent characters in this plot was the "old prince" Daeng Mangenang of Makassar.[110] A member of the noble house of Tanete, he had also been exiled by order of the Governor General and Council of the Indies in 1749 to be held as a prisoner of state until further notice but with an allowance of ten rixdollars a month for his support.[111] In

---

[105] It is extremely difficult to differentiate between places of origin with the same name without further evidence. For a detailed history of South Sulawesi see Andaya, *Arung Palakka*, pp. 1–70.
[106] NA: VOC: CJ10950. Confession of Robo of Bouton.
[107] NA: VOC: CJ10950. Confession of September of Ternate.
[108] Worden and Groenewald, eds., *Trials of Slavery*, pp. 270–276.
[109] Armstrong, "Chinese at the Cape," pp. 21–24.
[110] Spelling of this name varies. I am using the spelling from the Batavian records, Daing Mangenang, as the closest likely transliteration of his name. It was often spelled as Djang Mangenam at the Cape.
[111] NA: VOC: 799. General Resolutions of the Batavia Castle, 1748/49, Saturday, November 22, 1749. Daing Mangenang departed on the ship *Polander* for the Cape on

his testimony the prince declared he was innocent of any participation or knowledge of the plot. He further asserted that he understood neither Bugis nor Malay.[112] This is highly unlikely. Given both his noble status and ethnicity, he was most likely to have been fluent in both languages. Most of the confessants, and more importantly the Postholder, Sergeant Frederick Hofman, specifically said that the old prince was not involved. Under these circumstances it was convenient for the VOC not to pursue the matter further, and he was thus pardoned and sent back to the Island. Daeng Mangenang's position as a prisoner of state made it very difficult for the Cape authorities to execute him without approval from Batavia. Raja Boukit's status as a rebel against the VOC, confirmed again in his leadership of the Robben Island plot, enabled the Cape to take harsh measures against him.

Of the convicts involved in the case, Lodewijk Rets from The Hague, a European VOC servant convicted in Batavia in 1744 to be banished for twenty-five years of hard labor in chains, was the longest serving prisoner.[113] It was Rets's testimony to the Postholder that led to the interrogation of September of Ternate, who, during a beating by the Postholder, confessed about the escape plot. Rets was apparently sharing quarters with the *Swarte Jongens* (black men) and was smarting from the theft of his two knives. Moreover, it was clear that Rets knew what was going on in the *kraal*, as he implicated September of Ternate in this and other thefts. What isn't clear is what language Rets was using to communicate with the other convicts and what else he had overheard.[114] In the end, it was division within the ranks of the co-conspirators that caused their downfall. If September of Ternate had hoped to gain favor with the Postholder by revealing something much more important than his petty larceny, he would soon realize the enormity of his mistake.

September of Ternate arrived on Robben Island earlier in 1751, having been convicted of housebreaking and theft. He shared with Robo of Bouton a conviction for theft at the Cape, leading to imprisonment on

---

November 25, 1749. NA: VOC: 1003. Letters dispatched from Batavia to the Cape of Good Hope. See also Andaya, *Arung Palakka* for details of Tanete's place in South Sulawesi history during the seventeenth century.

[112] Penn, "Robben Island," pp. 29–30. Penn gives a brief but colorful account of this case, abiding by the summary of evidence regarding Daing Manganam.

[113] NA: VOC: 9306. Batavia Criminal Records, 1743; NA: VOC: 9308. Batavia Criminal Records, 1744.

[114] NA: VOC: CJ10950. Testimony of the Robben Island Postholder, Sergeant Frederick Hofman.

Robben Island. Whereas Robo was an exiled convict, September was a slave. Two other slaves, September of Bugis and Jephta of Bugis, had been sent to Robben Island in 1750 and 1749 respectively in cases in which their Cape masters had felt so personally threatened by their presences that they were removed to the Island by the authorities. Had either raised his hand in anger against his master, he would have been liable to have it chopped off before the death penalty was administered. It was not uncommon for masters in the Cape to demand that the VOC remove their recalcitrant slaves from their midst because they were so afraid of them. The three other slaves from South Sulawesi, Pomade of Makassar, Fortuijn of Bugis, and another fellow called Jephta of Bugis, had joined the Robben Island rebellion after having taken part in the attempted slave escape, led by the convict Tallone of Bugis and the slave Jason of Bugis in March, resulting in the execution of the latter two.[115]

It is obvious from these accounts that there was considerable interaction between slaves and convicts in the town. Robo of Bouton was not alone in his conviction for housebreaking and theft; his two accomplices were the Mardijker Leander Coridon and his father, the free-black Coridon of Bengal. Robo, a banished convict from Batavia living in the Slave Lodge, had been ordered to work at the Company's wine warehouse located near the Castle, a ten-minute walk from the Slave Lodge. This job was often reserved for Muslim convict exiles, supposedly to minimize the risk of workers imbibing while on duty because of their religious sanctions against alcohol. It does not seem to have operated as a deterrent for Robo.

One evening, while visiting the home of Coridon the elder, who earned his keep as a fisherman at the Cape, Robo induced his two acquaintances to join him in breaking into the warehouse and stealing some arak and wine to sell in town. Robo must have known Leander from the Slave Lodge where they both lived. However, a month earlier Leander had escaped from the lodge and had been living on Table Mountain, surviving by selling firewood to Chinese residents in the town. On the evening of the first break-in, Leander was visiting his elderly father. Literally and figuratively intoxicated by their successful heist, they were tempted to repeat their daring crime at the same time on three successive evenings. Perhaps their judgment was impaired by sampling their illicit wares, not surprisingly, on the third evening the cellar master, Jan Raak, and four European coopers lay in wait for the thieves, who were

[115] NA: VOC: CA10950.

duly apprehended.[116] It was recorded that both Robo and Leander gave their testimony to the court in Malay, while Coridon gave his in Dutch. The court officials used in this case were obviously conversant in Malay and translated their verbal testimony into Dutch for transcription.

The forays of Robo and his friends into the Company's wine cellars exemplify the mobility of convicts, slaves, and free-blacks in the town. It was apparently impossible to keep track of everyone, even in the Slave Lodge, which was supposedly guarded at night. This security measure was clearly abused because the Cape criminal records are replete with crimes committed by people who should have been locked up at night in the Slave Lodge after the evening roll call. Furthermore, the incidence of "escape" in various forms was endemic. Leander Coridon was a *Mardijker*, by definition a freed slave or person of freed slave descent, yet he confessed to having run away from the Slave Lodge.

This is not unlike the case of the European Company soldier, Lodewijk Rets from Den Haag, one of the informers on Robben Island. Rets had been convicted twice in Batavia of being absent without leave. In being absent without leave once, Rets joined literally hundreds of VOC servants who were caught out of barracks every year in all the Company settlements. His second conviction, for breaking out of his chains and escaping while he was categorized as a *kettingganger* (chain-ganger) toiling in the craftsmen's quarter of Batavia, earned him a sentence of scourging and branding as well as banishment to the Cape for twenty-five years. Rets had been sent to the Cape with one of his fellow chain-gangers, Arnoldus van Zuijlen from Utrecht.[117] Van Zuijlen had managed to escape from Robben Island in 1746 and had not been recaptured.[118]

Presumably he was one of the lucky ones to escape by ship. Although the Company gave relatively short sentences for a first offense of desertion, a second offense was treated very seriously. In this case, the punishment meted out to the unfortunate Company servants was very similar to that of a slave. Rets's case also underlines how close Cape Town's criminal landscape was to that of Batavia and how similar were the crimes committed by Company servants and slaves. Victor de Kock confirms this association by citing a letter by a French-speaking convict, written in Dutch, which was delivered to a member of the Cape Town clergy:

The unhappy European slaves who sigh in their chains assure you of their humble respect. They beg of you to look with compassion on their unfortunate

---

[116] NA: VOC: CA11019.
[117] NA: VOC: 9306. Lodewijk Rets; NA: VOC: 9308. Arnoldus van Zuijlen.
[118] CA: CJ3188. Arnoldus van Zuijlen.

circumstances... for although we have brought punishment on ourselves through our bad behavior, yet we do not deserve eternal condemnation. The misdeeds of which we are guilty consist merely of a form of punishable desertion... Never in Africa has it happened that Europeans had to live in chains for so long a time, nor found themselves mingled with heathens who not only are guilty of the most unprecedented crimes but also are born slaves... it is a shame and a blot on Christians that we should be mixed with them and treated in such a brutal manner... Have mercy on the unhappy European slaves.[119]

Finally, we return to the case of Jephta and Fortuijn of Bugis and Pomade from Makassar. They had taken part in the unsuccessful slave escape and had been sentenced to scourging and branding and to being chained in pairs to labor on the Company's works for fifteen years. Apparently, they were spared the paired chains; as when they were arrested in the Robben Island rebellion, they were not chained together. Their initial crime had taken shape during various discussions at the well behind the Castle where slaves would gather to draw water from the streams that ran down the side of Table Mountain to the sea. Tallone of Boegies, a convict living in the slave lodge, had been working in the wine cellars too, but apparently went occasionally to a pump located behind the Castle where he began organizing his escape plot. He and the slaves who gathered under his leadership planned to run away to the free 'Negro land' in Madagascar. In his confession, Pomade of Makassar, a slave of the soldier Nicolaas van Blerk, admitted that he had known Tallone in Batavia and upon meeting up with him at the Cape had agreed to throw in his lot with his old friend. A commando squad mustered to pursue the runaway slaves apprehended the eleven fugitives not more than a few miles from the town at Jan Biesjes Kraal, just over the Salt River.[120] All testimony was given in Malay and transcribed into Dutch for the court records. It is not clear whether Tallone's band realized that Madagascar was not part of the mainland. Unlike Robo, they had no definite navigational plan to their destination.

Tallone and the slave Jason from Boegies were executed as ringleaders of the group of runaways. The other nine slaves in this case were spared the death penalty, however, all were sentenced to be tied to a pole and scourged on their naked backs. Four were then branded and chained in pairs to work on the Company's public works for fifteen years – three of these men, Jephta and Fortuijn of Bugis and Pomade from Makassar, were

---

[119] De Kock, *Those in Bondage*, pp. 192–193. Although this particular letter was written in 1794, it is representative of the experience of the European convicts of the whole VOC era.
[120] NA: VOC: 10950. Confession of Pomade van Macasser.

in the Robben Island plot. Three others were sentenced to be chained for five years and one for three years before being returned to their masters.

The Prosecutor, Pieter Reede van Oudshoorn, in summarizing his case against the Robben Island prisoners, called them (among other colorful eighteenth-century Dutch curses) "damnable godless creatures intent on the most cruel murder and destruction of human society imaginable."[121] Indeed, the prosecutor left nary a curse unuttered in his condemnation of the men who had dared to threaten the order of Dutch East India Company rule at the Cape. After consideration of the written depositions in the case, the Council of Justice with due ceremony had its sentence delivered in public from the Kat Balcony inside the Castle of Good Hope. The defendants were brought from dungeon cells inside the Castle to hear their fates. All prisoners were then handed at the execution site to their executioners.

The place of execution was a walled compound outside the Castle. The prisoners were marched to the execution place under a guard of armed soldiers in the duly solemn custom of the Court. The first nine prisoners including the two ringleaders, Robo of Bouton and Raja Boukit of Padang, were to be bound to a cross, have their limbs broken, and remain there until they perished. The last six defendants were condemned to undergo the same punishment, but their torture was to be mercifully cut short with the coup de grace. The violence of the sentence matched the fear long held by Cape authorities that they were vulnerable to slave and convict rebellion.

Another traveler to the Cape, Otto Mentzel, gives a detailed description of the process whereby prisoners, witnessed by the public, were bound to a double wooden cross and their limbs broken with a heavy iron club. "In some cases the *coup de grace* is administered by a blow on the chest with the same instrument; if this is not done, the wretched man may be stretched by chains on a wheel, notwithstanding his broken limbs, and linger on in agony until death releases him."[122] After the prisoners were pronounced dead, they were to be rehung outside the place of execution where their bodies were to remain, as it was so poetically termed, "until the air and birds of the heavens shall consume them."[123] When the bodies of the fifteen Robben Island prisoners were taken to the site of execution

---

[121] NA: VOC: CJ10950. Cape Criminal and Judicial Roll and Papers, 1751. Prosecutor's summary by Independent Fiscaal, Pieter Reede van Oudshoorn.
[122] De Kock, *Those in Bondage*, p. 147.
[123] NA: VOC: CA10950. This was a standard legal term for the era.

on the outskirts of town, they joined the rotting corpses of Tallone of Boegies, and Jason of Boegies, who had both been hung in March. Both these elaborate plans of escape and freedom came to an abrupt end at the site of execution.

The overwhelming majority of perpetrators in both cases were ethnic Bugis or Makassarese. These two groups, especially the Bugis, have captured the imagination of Europeans as being particularly dangerous. The English idiom "bogeyman" is a direct descendent of this ethnic stereotyping. In the case of the Robben Island rebellion, the evidence specifies that the perpetrators intended to run amok and kill all the Europeans before escaping.[124] Although this does not follow the definition of an uncontrollable murderous anger, the use of the term compounded the seriousness of their crime in the eyes of the Cape authorities. Under both Company and indigenous Malay law codes, a person running *amok* could legally be killed on the spot.[125]

That the Cape authorities were terrified about the possibility of a Bugis uprising must be seen in terms of the experience of the VOC in the Indies, where they had been involved in wars with and against the Bugis and Makassarese since the late seventeenth century. As a result of the displacement of the South Sulawesi polities, ethnic Bugis and Makassarese slaves became more and more common. Simultaneously, displaced Bugis communities formed in polities around the archipelago, many of whom were involved in mercenary activities.

Robert Ross and Sirtjo Koolhof have solved the mystery of the infamous Bugis slave letter written in 1760 and preserved in the Cape archives. It is telling of research on the VOC that it took a collaborative effort between historians of colonial South Africa and Indonesia to decipher the letter's full meaning. They tell a story of profound fear and mistrust on the part of Cape authorities concerning the Bugis slaves and convicts at the Cape, resulting in the execution of an innocent man who was accused of plotting a Bugis slave conspiracy through a secret message. In fact, the letter was an exhortation for healing.[126] Travelers' accounts in the VOC era abound with frightful tales of the inherent violence of the Bugis people. The European fear of Malays in general and of Bugis in particular

---

[124] Sleigh, *Die Buiteposte*, pp. 389–390.
[125] John C. Spores, *Running Amok: An Historical Enquiry*. Athens: Ohio University Center for International Studies, 1988. Liaw Yock Fang, *Undang-Undang Malaka*. Bibliotecha Indonesica, 13, KITLV. The Hague: Martinus Nijhoff, 1976.
[126] Robert Ross and Sirtjo Koolhoff, "Upas, September, and the Bugis at the Cape of Good Hope: The Context of a Slave's Letter," *Archipel*, 70, 2005, pp. 281–308.

running *amok*, in a homicidal and suicidal murderous rage, supposedly part of their mental composition, resulted in the Cape passing a decree in 1767 banning the importation of male slaves from the Indies, particularly Bugis. However, the order was largely ignored and was issued again in 1787, after Soera Botto's case, revealing that it had not been honored in the first instance.[127] Besides, this order did not affect the importation of transported criminals and political prisoners who continued to be sent to the Cape until the end of the Company era.

Shifting Security Priorities

By the late eighteenth century, the VOC was in dire financial straits, its profitability having been largely drained by the combination of the enormously unprofitable cost of running what had become a territorial empire. Its predicament was caused also by shifts in the commodity markets in Europe that undercut the Company's main source of revenue, competition from other European sea powers for European (particularly the British) markets, and endemic warfare in Europe that would eventually result in the conquest of the United Provinces by revolutionary France. Commissioners Nederburgh and Frykenius who were sent to the Cape by the Seventeen Gentlemen in 1792 and 1793 were ordered to find ways to increase Company revenues and decrease spending at the Cape, an almost impossible task given the declining number of ships stopping there during this time.[128] Cape Company officials were also fearful of imminent invasion and were recalibrating their internal defenses. One of the issues to which they turned their attention was the condition of prisoners on Robben Island. The recommendations of the committee commissioned to investigate this issue describe in clearest detail the Company's perspective of penal and political bondage at the Cape, revealing some of the core issues of governance according to the Company, and of the Cape officials as part of the VOC empire – it is therefore quoted at length[129]:

1. What would be the best use to put the convicts to, at the same time indemnify the Company as much as possible for the expense unavoidably connected with their maintenance?

---

[127] Armstrong and Worden, "The Slaves," p. 117. See also Edna Bradlow, "Mental Illness or a Form of Resistance? The Case of Soera Brotto," *Kleio*, 13, 1991, pp. 4–8.
[128] Gerrit Schutte, "Company and Colonists at the Cape, 1652–1795," in Elphick and Giliomee, *Shaping of South African Society*, p. 314.
[129] CA: LM, vol. 31. Cape Resolution, March 13, 1792, pp. 360–364.

2. Whether besides the work which they might still find to do on Robben Island, they might not likewise be employed in the Capital, and if so, where they should be located?
3. What precautions should be taken that no harm need be feared from them?

In order to reply as fully as possible, the committee deemed it necessary to classify the convicts as follows:

1. Those who must be considered as political prisoners.
2. Those who are Europeans.
3. Slaves and Hottentots banished during the natural term of their lives.
4. Slaves and Hottentots sentenced to hard labor for a term of years.

The first class could not very well be employed on public labor... because to say nothing of the difference which must be maintained between those who have been sent hither for political reasons, who are generally Indian Princes, and Priests, and slaves and Hottentots who have been publicly condemned and punished for crimes, it would in the first place be very dangerous to give these Indian Potentates in their humbled state, an opportunity of having communication with the Eastern slaves... Whilst in the second place should these state prisoners be kept in the Capital, they might... succeed in making their escape with the assistance of others and take refuge among strangers.

Regarding the second class... Should they be transferred to the Cape and be put in irons... it would be directly contrary to the express orders of the High Government of the Indies, which require that no European shall be chained, the object being no doubt that the difference may appear which it is necessary to make in the colony between Europeans and slaves, and the subordination of the latter to the former be maintained as a matter of necessity.

Those of the third and fourth class excepting the halt and the lame, might besides doing work on Robben Island during the summer months, be employed usefully in the capital during the rainy season when there are no ships in the bay and there will be no opportunity of escaping.

The dilemmas posed by this report were not resolved during the Company era. Batavia ordered the Cape Company officials to stop keeping European convicts in chains in 1746. The order was removed in 1761 and apparently imposed again by the early 1790s. Predikant J. P. Surrier petitioned the Cape government on behalf of the European convicts who complained about being treated like slaves. Although the Seventeen Gentlemen sent a commission to assess conditions at the Cape and turned their attention to the prisoners on Robben Island, they did so with larger imperial interests and defenses in mind. The fates of the prisoners themselves were minor considerations. They were motivated by the need to secure Robben Island in case of an invasion. Company officials at the Cape had complained regularly and vociferously against penal transportation and political exile on a regular basis from the inception of the colony to no avail. Asian exiles and convicts on the Cape mainland had close relations with slaves in multiple ways, through daily social contact, shared cultural life, through common acts of resistance, and in the transmission of Islam. Paradoxically, the Company used Asian exiles as *caffers*, the local police and executioners' assistants, who were granted certain privileges in return for upholding the laws that kept them in bondage. This exploitation of exiles by the Cape officials sometimes backfired with disastrous consequences as individuals resisted their fates.

The circuit of exile removed real or potential enemies of the Company from the imperial capital Batavia and from Colombo, but the consequences were less beneficial for the smaller Cape colony. Exiled princes and religious leaders were removed from their former positions of privilege and power, but they circumvented the Company's efforts to neutralize their influence as exiles in a number of ways. The Company sought to isolate potentially dangerous prisoners on Robben Island, but even this was not sufficient to stem individual acts of resistance and an attempted group rebellion. The disruption of status resulting from the circuit of forced migration to the Cape potentially threatened the social order on another level by becoming one of the focal points for settler complaints against Company sovereignty. The growth of the Cape from a refreshment post to a colony both consolidated the site as a Company node and weakened the Company's ultimate control over the colony by multiple challenges to its authority.

Chapter 7 pursues this trajectory by focusing on settler complaints against the Company within the context of the wider imperial web. These challenges were ultimately unsuccessful because colonists underestimated the coherence of the networks of authority that bound the Cape node to the broader interests of the Company as an empire. It was not until the conquest of the Cape by the British that colonists' demands would be met and the condition of prisoners alleviated, ironically, by the disintegration of the Dutch East India Company's imperial web and the incorporation of the Cape as a node in an expanding and reconfigured British imperial web.

7

Disintegrating Imperial Networks

The Dutch East India Company consisted of networks of trade, shipping, information, law, diplomacy, and migration that combined in different ways in each of its nodes to constitute the whole of its imperial web. The Company's empire emanated from a particular conjuncture in state-building in early modern Europe and derived, and to some extent replicated, the split sovereignty of the United Provinces in its governance structure. The specific terms of the VOC charter set forth by the States-General and overseen by the Seventeen Gentlemen in Europe determined the extent of the Company's domain in the Indian Ocean and granted it partial sovereign rights. In this domain, sovereignty was extended through an evolving legal network created with respect to particular conditions at Batavia. Conditions in Batavia, while not identical to conditions in other imperial nodes, therefore disproportionately determined the parameters of a legal template intended to extend as an imperial network across the whole of the Company's web.

In practice Company law, as developed in Batavia, could not be strictly applied in all its factories, settlements, and colonies. Regional circumstances determined the ability of the Company to impose its jurisdiction in any one node and, correspondingly, local laws were passed to accommodate specific conditions regarding particular, but not all, aspects of the Company's legal code.

Nevertheless, Batavia and other parts of Java remained the Company's main actor in determining the principles of the Company's legal system, as Batavia sought to accommodate indigenous populations under its jurisdiction and to negotiate treaties regarding territorial sovereignty with local polities. These principles were to be applied to the fullest extent possible in the rest of the empire. The extension of the Company's legal network was therefore biased (toward central authority and the local conditions in Batavia) and contingent (with respect to their universal applicability) because the conditions of possibility for governance and the rule of law in all of the Company's nodes and networks were fundamentally derived from the priorities of its capital node.

The Company's claim to sovereignty and exclusive legal determination at the Cape, which began as a coastal transoceanic refreshment station, faced unique challenges as it expanded into a land-based colony. The Cape evolved into a settler colony based mainly on slave labor, with an expanding territorial frontier that continued to bring settlers into violent conflict with indigenous Khoekhoe and San people (Khoisan) who were often coerced into bonded labor after the appropriation of their land and resources. The Company's imperial legal system used a forced migration network, including penal transportation and political exile, as a means of social control. This became an added source of tension between the Company and its Cape-based colonists.

The first indication of this tension was during the Van der Stel dispute in the early eighteenth century. This political struggle pitched the governor and his allies, who were accused of manipulating the Company's trade monopolies for their own gain, against Cape colonists who sought access to these markets and who in turn petitioned the Seventeen Gentlemen for redress. Although Van der Stel was censured, the Company's grasp on the economy was not significantly weakened, nor were the settlers' complaints regarding labor and exile addressed. As the eighteenth century wore on, settler families were more likely to have been in the Cape for several generations or to have married into these family networks and to consider the Cape, rather than the United Provinces, their home. Disputes continued to surface between the Company and the colonists that challenged the Company's exclusive right to control the economy and determine the rule of law without their consultation.

The "Barbier Rebellion" in the 1730s centered on the perception of some colonists that they, as loyal subjects of the Company, could appeal directly to the High Government in Batavia and the Seventeen Gentlemen in the United Provinces against the actions of corrupt Cape officials. Similarly to the Van der Stel dispute, the main protagonist in this dispute, Estienne Barbier, was mistaken in his interpretation of the rights of Company subjects and was outmaneuvered by Company officials who had access to communication networks denied to him.

By the 1770s, the major European states and their colonies had become increasingly embroiled in revolutionary politics, and this reverberated at the Cape with the emergence of the Cape Patriots. Politically motivated colonists moved by the republican spirit of the age, the Cape Patriots sought to assert their political rights under Company rule, first by appealing to the Seventeen Gentlemen against the Cape government, and when that proved fruitless, to the States-General against Company rule itself. This was a direct challenge to Company sovereignty, a recognition of the partial nature of that sovereignty, and a signal of an awareness among the settlers of the possibilities of alternative imperial formations. Although their main motivation was economic, the colonists resented that they suffered because of the Company's forced migration network, particularly the circuit of penal transportation and political exile that brought convicts and exiles to the Cape. They also resented their own vulnerability to the possibility of having these punishments applied to them, and this resentment was an important aspect in all internal political disputes between colonists and the Company. In this regard, the Company's network of forced migration had political implications at the Cape that were exceptional in the Company empire, as no other colony manifested internal political disputes on this basis.

This book explores the Company's circuit of penal transportation and political exile from Batavia to the Cape of Good Hope, as only one of the circuits in Company's forced migration network. A similarly close study of the circuit between Ceylon and Batavia, for example, would reveal different aspects and consequences of the broader migration network. At the level of the entire empire, Batavia had a network of forced migration that included political exile and penal transportation encompassing not only the Cape and Ceylon, but also Banda and Ambon and other secondary sites of exile like Robben Island at the Cape or at the Islands of Edam and Onrust in the Batavia roadstead.

Most previous studies of the VOC have focused on the trading and political networks that either concentrate on relationships and mechanisms of exchange or on the extension and negotiation of Company power within limited geographical contexts. Forced migration has been examined within the context of the slave trade and the widespread use of slave labor in various Company nodes, with the resulting literature on Cape slavery being by far the best developed of any on slavery in the VOC empire. This book analyzes forced migration within a spectrum that included the slave trade, penal transportation, and political exile, but focuses more closely on the latter two forms that have received far less attention in the study of the Dutch East India Company. Penal transportation and political exile were part of the legal network through which the VOC extended its economic and political power regionally over indigenous peoples and maintained control over its own civilian subjects and personnel in overseas service. Convicts and exiles in both Batavia and the Cape constituted a small but disproportionately visible part of the Company's labor force, particularly at the Cape, where these prisoners disrupted categories of social distinction at the foundation of colonial society.

Debates over the Cape legal system in the Company period have centered on the institution of slavery. *Networks of Empire* attends to the interconnections between the different legal types of forced migration that together form a complex set of practices of social control by the VOC but simultaneously presented opportunities for resisting this control. Dichotomies of slave and free, Christian and non-Christian, African and colonist, which have characterized many studies of the VOC Cape are made more complex by considering these other forms of bondage. Indeed forced migration in the form of penal transportation cut across the categories of slave and free. Slaves could be banished to the Cape as criminals, while freed convicts were a distinct social presence at the Cape. Muslim political and religious exiles of both noble and common birth occupied another category of bondage and were crucial to the spread of Islam at the Cape. Attention to individual cases of forced migration in this book demonstrates that these social categories of rank, ethnicity, and freedom were much more unstable than has been previously recognized and are therefore in need of revision.

The network of forced migration that brought slaves, convicts, and exiles to the Cape also complicates our understanding of social taxonomies of race. People forcibly migrated to the Cape from Batavia were categorized according to race, religion, and social status, but often these categories differed from those they had previously been assigned in Batavia. The point is that the categorization of people was never fixed; it was negotiated among the legal, political, and social contexts of the Cape and Batavia. Perhaps the most striking example of categorical inversion at the Cape is the case of Asian political and religious exiles and convicts who were specifically chosen by the Company to act as functionaries of the law as police and executioners' assistants. These were the *caffers* who occupied a dual role through their banishment, as simultaneously the victims and the enforcers of Company law.

The existence of European convicts as a category of forced labor at the Cape and Batavia belies the equation of freedom with being European and alters the way in which constructions of race and status have been analyzed in the early colonial contexts of these Company towns.

Glimpses of the criminal record of both towns reveal the degree to which slaves and common Company servants sought to subvert social control in similar ways through desertion and other crimes. At the Cape, the consequences of the network of forced migration played out most significantly in the realm of colonial politics between the free burghers and the Company. This chapter examines these disputes in detail before offering a concluding discussion of the concept of imperial networks as the analytical framework of this book.

The Barbier Rebellion

Tensions between the Company and some frontier settler farmers reached boiling point by the late 1730s in an episode in which a French-born Company sergeant, Estienne Barbier, led a resistance movement against Company authority. This was a small-scale rebellion, yet tacit and instrumental support for the rebels among the frontier farming community allowed Barbier to continue to foment open opposition to the Company until he was captured a year later. As a result, the limitations of the Company's sovereignty and their authority to enforce the rule of law were starkly exposed because Company authorities based in Cape Town were unable to control Barbier without the cooperation of rural free burghers.

Barbier's rebellion coincided with a serious outbreak of organized Khoisan resistance in the Colony's frontier regions. The Company responded to the widely held sympathies for his complaints by offering amnesty to his followers and co-opting them to participate in a militia strike against the Khoisan. The colonists' potential bounty of Khoisan stock and captured Khoisan prisoners for farm labor was an incentive the Company knew would likely result in settler cooperation. Given that the perceived support of the Company for the Khoisan over the colonists was one of the main complaints inspiring Barbier's uprising, this strategy succeeded in undermining the basis of broad settler participation in the rebellion.[1] Even so, despite the Company's having issued rewards for his

---

[1] Gerrit Schutte, "Company and Colonists at the Cape, 1652–1795," in Elphick and Giliomee, *Shaping of South African Society*," pp. 308–309. I think Schutte overplays the cynicism of this offer of amnesty by arguing that the Company organized the commando to distract and placate Barbier's supporters. As Marks points out, the Khoisan raids on the border regions of the colony were becoming increasingly aimed at explicitly expelling the Dutch from the region, while commando retaliation was aimed at capturing Khoekhoe stock. Marks, "Khoisan Resistance," pp. 70–71.

capture, the colonists did not betray Barbier and thus further revealed the limitations of their loyalty to the Company. Estienne Barbier was eventually brought into custody in September 1739 while apparently on his way to Cape Town to surrender. He was convinced he would be pardoned because he sought to expose corrupt local Company officials through his appeals for justice to the High Government in Batavia as the ultimate VOC authority. Barbier's reading of Company legal networks was theoretically correct but politically naive, and he was tried by the Cape Council of Justice and executed as a traitor.

Estienne Barbier, according to Nigel Penn, was "the first genuine southern African (and perhaps even African) social bandit."[2] Penn identifies three elements in the rebellion. "These [rebellions] are the nature of the early-eighteenth-century colonial state; the existence of class struggle in the remote rural areas of the Western Cape; and the pressures and processes behind the expansion of the Cape's frontier."[3] However, Penn's interpretation does identify the imperial dimension of Company law and authority as one of the most important factors in the case. Estienne Barbier rebelled after being convicted of making a false accusation of embezzlement against a high-ranking Company official. Barbier believed he was righteously exposing high-level Company corruption at the Cape, and after his conviction he demanded an appeal to the highest court in the Company empire, the Council of Justice in Batavia. This case, among others, shows that Company servants and colonists at the Cape were aware of the VOC chain of authority and appeals in the legal network and that they claimed the right to justice in this system.

What Barbier did not understand is that by managing access to the Company's communication circuit from the Cape, local officials were able to present their version of accounts to Batavia, thereby prejudicing Barbier's case. It was only after Barbier judged, apparently correctly, that Council of Justice officers at the Cape had falsified court transcripts to make his appeal to Batavia baseless, that he decided to flee into the rural districts. By controlling the production of legal documents and access to official communication circuits, Cape Company authorities had rightly calculated that Batavia would uphold its version of events and support its legal decisions.

---

[2] Nigel Penn, "Estienne Barbier," in *Rogues, Rebels, and Runaways: Eighteenth-Century Cape Characters*. Cape Town: David Philip, 1999, p. 102.
[3] Penn, *Rogues, Rebels and Runaways*, p. 102.

Barbier fled to the outskirts of the settled western Cape regions where poorer settlers were simmering in resentment against the Cape government for restrictions they had imposed on bartering with the Khoisan, the ruinous cost of farm land, and the Cape authorities' protection of the Khoisan over and above their own interests. Throughout the rebellion, Barbier and his followers consistently framed their criticism of the Cape Company government in terms of appealing for justice to Batavia and to the Seventeen Gentlemen as the VOC's supreme authority and imperial representative of the States-General.[4] The Company was not unjust and evil, Barbier claimed; only the government at the Cape was corrupt. After his arrest Barbier again appealed, this time to have his case heard by the Seventeen Gentlemen in the United Provinces. His appeal was denied by Cape authorities who had enough evidence to convict him of armed rebellion and treason.[5]

Estienne Barbier was sentenced on November 12, 1739 to a form of public execution consistent with the manner of the day and reserved for the most heinous crimes. He was bound on a cross. First, his right hand and his head were cut off, his body quartered, his entrails removed and burnt under the scaffolding, and the quarters of his body displayed at four major crossroads of the colony. His severed head and hand were placed on a stake at the farm where he had taken refuge. At least one of his accomplices was banished from the Cape to the fatherland under pain of life imprisonment should he return to the Company's domain. In having faith in the legal system and access to justice through the Company's communication network, Barbier had completely misread how these imperial networks upheld their power in the Company's empire.[6]

Through his protests against the Cape authorities, Barbier had a clear perception of the Company's chain of command. His first legal appeal was to the governor-general and council at Batavia. When that path was blocked by the Cape officials, he demanded appeal directly to the Seventeen Gentlemen. Barbier had been at the Cape only for four years before his first clash with his superiors. Identification of his supporters

---

[4] Ibid., p. 127.
[5] The Barbier rebellion was not an isolated case of popular or local resistance to increasing European domination and consolidation of power in the colonial world. For comparison with the Atlantic world, see Linebaugh and Rediker, *Many-Headed Hydra*.
[6] The monopolization of technologies of discipline in this case was used for the management of empire rather than nation-state. Michel Foucault, *Discipline and Punish: The Birth of the Prison*. Translated by Alan Sheridan. New York: Vintage Books, 1987, pp. 3–72.

and sympathizers is not possible, but it is, nevertheless, probable that his rural support was mostly composed of locally born colonists who did not have the means to access the networks of Company authority. Members of the wealthier rural elite at the Cape had close patronage relations with high-ranking Company officials that garnered them land and resources. The growth of the Cape as a settler colony had resulted in increasing class divisions. As direct access to land title was not available to marginal frontier farmers, who also struggled to gain access to markets, they were increasingly alienated from the center of Company authority at the Castle in Cape Town. The extension of VOC territorial sovereignty at the Cape and the settlers' unauthorized appropriation of land across the colony's frontier meant that the Company's authority and control of its borders in this region were partial at best.

Barbier became the spokesman for these marginalized rural settlers, but he was not a member of their class. He was a town-based Company sergeant with a highly developed sensitivity to VOC justice, and he was outraged at the abuse of rank and privilege he saw at the Cape. Evidently, Barbier sincerely believed he would be able to triumph over the corrupt Cape Company officials and achieve his freedom through appealing to the imperial chain of command. Here, his understanding of the Company's legal system and networks failed him. Because he entered into open and armed rebellion, it was not necessary for Cape authorities to forward his case to Batavia or to the United Provinces before sentencing him to death for treason. Barbier's appeals to the Seventeen Gentlemen were never heard during his lifetime. His brutal execution was a stark warning to others about the consequences of challenging the Company's authority locally at the Cape where VOC officials retained control of the communication circuit to Batavia. The growth of the colony had outpaced the capacity of Company networks in the frontier region, but it did not exceed the authority of the imperial networks that bound the Cape node to the rest of the Company.

The Emergence of the Cape Patriots

The Cape economy grew steadily throughout the Company period and Robert Ross argues that tensions between the colonists and the Company cannot be seen in terms of VOC monopolistic practices hindering the settler development.[7] What changed in the second half of the

---

[7] Robert Ross, "The Cape and the World Economy, 1652–1835," in Elphick and Giliomee, *Shaping of South African Society*, pp. 243–280.

eighteenth century was the focus of the conflicts between the Company and colonists from land-based issues in the Van der Stel and Barbier era toward urban-based commercial disputes. The complaints of the Cape Patriots, an elite political movement, centered on expanding their access to booming markets, particularly trade with foreign ships passing through the Cape. Moreover, more than a century of Company settlement at the Cape had produced a colonial settler population that was entirely localized in their loyalty toward their "home" rather than to the Company's intrinsically imperial interests.

An astute visitor to the Cape during the early 1750s, M. l'Abbe Nicolas Louis de la Caille, recorded his impressions of grievances expressed unofficially by some of the Cape burghers with whom he came into contact. These complaints foreshadowed what later emerged as the major platform of the Cape Patriots from the 1770s onward. The colonists' primary concern was the continued restriction on trade imposed by the Company. They demanded open access to the shipping market and freedom to trade directly with Batavia and the United Provinces. The colonists also objected to the continued use of the Cape as a site of banishment for Asians by the Company courts in Batavia. The *bandieten* (convicts) were perceived as an injurious population and dangerous criminal element in the town. Exiles banished to the Cape and ordered to find their own means of support, or time expired convicts who remained, competed with colonists in some urban small businesses, particularly catering and accommodation.[8] Otto Mentzel, who wrote his *Description of the Cape* in the 1780s, responded to these economic issues in defense of the VOC's authority, arguing that "[t]he colonists cannot object to this practice, without impugning the sovereign powers of the Honourable Company."[9]

The codification of the New Statutes of Batavia in 1766 reiterated the primacy of Batavia in the VOC imperial structure but had no immediate impact on the Cape.[10] The New Statutes of Batavia were primarily concerned with law and governance in Java and did not have direct bearing on the political disputes between the Company and the colonists at the Cape and clearly demonstrates Batavia's priorities in determining Company law. Yet the colonists' complaints were partly couched in terms of the unjust application of Company law at the Cape with specific reference

---

[8] Otto Mentzel, *A Geographical and Topographical Description of the Cape of Good Hope*, pt. 2. Translated from the German by H. J. Mandelbrote. Cape Town: Van Riebeeck Society, 1925, pp. 146–150.

[9] Ibid., p. 150.

[10] J. L. W. Stock, "The New Statutes of India at the Cape," *South African Law Journal*, 32, 1915, pp. 332–333.

to exile. Significantly, they objected to the concentration of legal power in the hands of the Company without sufficient free burgher representation. By the late 1770s, opposition to the Company's autocratic power was being organized more or less openly at the Cape.

Du Toit and Giliomee argue that this structural crisis came to a head in the later eighteenth century.[11] They identify this crisis in terms of the shift from "refreshment station" to colony, and the changing self-identification of colonists toward being "Afrikaners" rather than temporary European colonists. Cape burghers by this time had to apply for naturalization papers to acquire burgher status in the United Provinces. Meanwhile, Cape burghers continued to claim Dutch citizenship rights. These rights were not granted in the VOC charter to people living under Company rule. Nevertheless, the gap was widening between the legal rights of colonial-born and European-based burghers, while simultaneously the Cape burghers were making further demands to the VOC for political representation in matters of colonial governance.[12]

The Cape Patriots were intellectually influenced by revolutionary political events taking place in the United Provinces and in the American colonies. Enlightenment ideas of the rights of free citizens were infused with the Cape burghers' demands for political and economic concessions from the Company. The Cape Patriots were not a revolutionary movement seeking independence for the colony like the colonial Americans. They were challenging instead the Company's right to rule arbitrarily and to deny them their rights as free citizens of the United Provinces. In other words, they challenged the Company's imperial sovereignty.

In making these claims, the Cape Patriots sought direct redress in the United Provinces, bypassing the imperial headquarters at Batavia. Initial burgher requests to the Cape governor to allow a delegation to meet with the Seventeen Gentlemen were refused. The Cape Patriots went ahead and sent an unofficial delegation to the Seventeen Gentlemen in October 1779 who traveled to Europe as private passengers on Company ships.

---

[11] Andre du Toit and Hermann Giliomee, eds., *Afrikaner Political Thought: Analysis and Documents, Volume One: 1780–1850*. Cape Town: David Philip, 1983, pp. 1–4.

[12] Schutte, "Company and Colonists," p. 287. One of the interesting texts by a Cape-born colonist of this era is the thesis presented to the University of Leiden by Gijsbert Hemmy regarding the legality of testimony of Africans, Chinese, other pagans, and Hottentots at the Cape of Good Hope. Hemmy's conclusion was that all the above categories except slaves should be allowed to give testimony in court on the basis of human equality. Gijsbert Hemmy, *De Testimoniis: A Thesis by Gysbert Hemmy on the Testimony of the Chinese, Aethiopians and Other Pagans, 1770*. Edited and translated from the Latin by Margaret Hewett. Cape Town: University of Cape Town, 1998.

The colonists acted with the rather naïve idea that the Seventeen Gentlemen would support them against the patrimonial networks that comprised the Company. The direct appeal to the United Provinces and the Cape Patriots' rejection of the VOC colonial chain of command are not surprising, given that one of colonists' major complaints was that Cape Company officials used their power unjustly to exile their free burgher opponents to Batavia.

The case of Carel Fredrick Buytendagh, who was exiled to Batavia in 1779 because of his political activities, caused outrage among many Cape burghers.[13] Hendrick Swellengrebel was a Cape-born burgher with Dutch regent-class familial ties who had retired to the United Provinces and he outlined the issues in the Buytendagh case. Swellengrebel kept abreast of the Cape Patriot delegation in the United Provinces and informed interested parties in Europe and the Cape through private correspondence. His opinion is interesting for his grasp of the wider imperial dimension of Cape affairs:

> In the matter of Buytendagh my sympathies are on their [the Cape Patriots] side as the most important requisite of freedom is the right to be allowed a fair trial by a competent judge. That was one of the main issues in our revolt against Philip II... Buytendagh was a very bad character, but in that case there was all the more reason to have him judged by the Council of Justice... the Governor-General in Batavia was of the same opinion. The XVII [Seventeen Gentlemen] gave instructions to such effect... It makes no difference that Buytendagh was first taken into the service of the Company. To do this against his will was itself a despotic act. I know that the Company reserves this right, but it should never be exercised as a punishment, but only in times of real need. Moreover, he was a *born* burgher, not a former Company servant [original emphasis]... The burghers in Batavia and in our West-Indian colonies have a greater share in the government, and I cannot see why this should not also be the case at the Cape, where the burghers in my experience are not at all slow-witted.[14]

Swellengrebel's correspondence shows the extent to which knowledge about imperial issues circulated among Dutch elites based in the colonies

---

[13] Resolutien van den Politicquen Raad, Woensdag den 20 Jannuarij, 1779. Reprinted in Kathleen Jeffreys, ed., *Historiese Dokumenten over die Kaap de Goede Hoop. Kaapse Archiefstukken 1779*. Kaapstad: Cape Times Beperkt, 1927, p. 11. This was followed by a request from the Burgher Council and *Heemraden* that burghers should only be exiled to Europe if such a sentence was imposed. March 30, 1779. Jeffreys, ed., *Kaapse Archiefstukken 1779*, pp. 34–35.

[14] Swellengrebel to J. J. le Sueur, September 17, 1780. Quoted in G. J. Schutte, ed., *Briefwisseling van Hendrik Swellengrebel Jr. oor Kaapse Sake 1778–1792*. With English translation by A. J. Böeseken. Kaapstad: Van Riebeeck-Vereniging. Tweede Reeks Nr. 13, 1982, pp. 338–339.

and in the Netherlands.[15] Close patrimonial ties between these elites facilitated their communication network through private correspondence, an avenue Barbier attempted to access to save himself. The imperial dimension of these political issues was not lost on the Cape burghers and was directly addressed in the Burgher Petition submitted to the Seventeen Gentlemen.

Furthermore [Your Honours are requested] to prohibit anyone born at the Cape or any free burgher who has faithfully served out his contract with the honourable Company from being pressed into the service of the honourable Company once again, or being sent as a sailor from the Cape to Batavia, as this is in conflict with the civil law... But [it is requested] that a citizen who has earned this [deportation] in terms of the law should be sent directly to the fatherland though only after... permission has been obtained from the burgher councils.[16]

Although the demands of the burghers were primarily localized, there was a fundamental imperial dimension to their complaint that the Company used its legal network against them. A particular target for burgher complaints was the presence of convicts and exiles in the towns. Article 25 of the petition requested: "No Chinese, Javanese, or convicts belonging to Robben Island should be allowed to open shops or trade and lead astray slaves by encouraging thievery."[17] Another issue repeated throughout their petition was their demand not to be arrested by the soldiers and *caffers,* but only by fellow burghers.[18] The Cape Patriots also sought clarification on the rule of law at the Cape:

Furthermore Your Honours are requested with great urgency to determine according to exactly which general laws those at the Cape are in future to be governed, whether according to the written statutes of India or according to the Placaat [decrees] of the honourable States-general of these countries [i.e. the United Provinces]... [and] also to see that Burgher councils... are given instructions in terms of which they can act and that authentic copies be made available to them of all individual placaats, or statues and resolutions which are effective in the Cape and concern the burghers... so that neither the fiscal nor the landdrost will in future be able to demand arbitrary fines... and the inhabitants in this

---

[15] For comparative dimension of the circulation of knowledge within imperial realms see C. R. L. James, *The Black Jacobins; Toussaint L'Ouverture and the San Domingo Revolution*, 2nd ed. Rev. New York: Vintage Books, 1963.

[16] "Second and Concluding Parts of the Burgher Petition of 9 October 1779," translated from "Kaapsche Geschillen" (Amsterdam, 1785) in the Cape Archives, C742. Reproduced in Du Toit and Giliomee, *Afrikaner Political Thought*, p. 255.

[17] Coenraad Beyers, *Die Kaapse Patriotte gedurende die laaste kwart van die agteende eeu en die voortlewing van hul denkbeelde*. Pretoria: J. L. van Schank Beperk, 1967, p. 57.

[18] Ibid., Point 4, pp. 254–255.

way might no longer be kept in ignorance as to the laws of the country and the respective orders of the honourable Company.[19]

The Cape Patriots did not remain unified as a political movement, but they continued to submit petitions while their representatives were in Europe. They found supporters among the Dutch Patriot movement, but, ultimately, the Cape burghers were representatives of their own local colonial interests and were not an offshoot of any other European or colonial revolutionary movement. They did not call for independence, like the American colonists; they wanted the support of the fatherland against the Company.

An anonymous Cape Patriot pamphlet entitled *Dutch Africa* published in Leiden in 1783, expanded further on the movement's political ideas:

> Europe has almost no arbitrary despots any longer, as almost all its peoples have gradually been enlightened as to the rights which whey are granted by nature... One forgives the tyrannous despots of the east for ruling their people with an iron rod... But can one forgive the rulers of Europe for tyrannizing those of their subjects who have left their fatherland and settled in remote countries, distant from their sovereignty?... But it is only too true, however, that almost all the settlers in Asia, Africa and America are oppressed, vexed and mistreated. It is only too certain that these victims of arbitrary rule complain most bitterly of the oppression under which they suffer... This is particularly and most obviously the case with the valuable settlement of the Cape of Good Hope. The officials of the Dutch East India Company have for many years permitted themselves conduct which has become intolerable....[20]

The pamphlet goes on to describe the era of Van Riebeeck as a "golden age" in which "one had nothing to fear from the officials of the Company," particularly "of being taken away by violence, or being unexpectedly removed from the heart of their families and sent, as they are today, to Batavia or any other possession of the Company in the East Indies." The burghers presented themselves as having their sovereign rights infringed upon by Company officials who must be "forbidden from having any citizen or settler arrested by the Bailiff accompanied by the black constabulary [*caffers*] in his house or on the street or anywhere else."[21]

---

[19] Ibid., Point 7, p. 255.
[20] B. J. Artoys, *Dutch Africa; Or an Historical and Political Description of the Original Condition of the Settlement at the Cape of Good Hope, Compared with the Present Condition of This Settlement*, 1783. Translated and reprinted in Du Toit and Giliomee, *Afrikaner Political Thought*, pp. 256–257.
[21] Du Toit and Giliomee, *Afrikaner Political Thought*, pp. 258–261.

The most hated Company official at the Cape, *Fiscal* W. C. Boers scoffed: "One would be greatly mistaken if one were to draw a comparison between the inhabitants of a colony such as this and the privileged citizens of our large cities in the Republic."[22] Boers, who had arrested and exiled the Cape burgher Buytendagh to Batavia, was well protected by his patrimonial network. His uncle was the advocate-general of the VOC, the most powerful person running the Company's daily affairs in Europe, and an official with close ties to the Seventeen Gentlemen. The Company upheld the authority of its colonial officials and its own imperial sovereignty against burgher demands that it largely ignored.

In 1782 the Cape governor, Van Plettenberg, was finally asked by the Seventeen Gentlemen to respond to the burgher complaints, which he did by basically dismissing their validity. The Cape Patriots then appealed directly to the States-General in December 1784, which was at that time under the power of the Dutch Patriots. When the regent elites who supported the *stadhouder* against the republican Patriots regained control of the States-General, the Cape Patriots realized their political position had weakened.[23] The Seventeen Gentlemen and the States-General backed the Company's argument against the colonists and their movement forced no real change. The Seventeen Gentlemen referred the petitioners to the general *plakaat* (ordinance) of VOC governance that reinforced the primacy of the Governor-General and the Council of Policy in Batavia. They made a token concession by ordering that convicts assigned to Robben Island not be allowed to live on the mainland.[24]

By the later days of VOC rule at the Cape, the Patriots had not only lost ground in the United Provinces but the threat of war also was looming over them at the Cape as the English East India Company gained power in the Indian Ocean at the Company's expense. The VOC was by this time mired in a financial crisis in the United Provinces that had significantly undermined its own independent operation as the States-General intervened to stabilize the republic's finances. Commissioners-General Nederburgh and Frykenius, who were sent out to assess the position of the Cape in 1792 and 1793, further precipitated the local economic crisis by imposing spending cuts and new taxes. They had also been ordered

---

[22] W. C. Boers, 1785, quoted in Schutte, "Company and Colonists," p. 287.
[23] Simon Schama, *Patriots and Liberators: Revolution in the Netherlands 1780–1813*. New York: Vintage Books, 1992.
[24] Beyers, *Die Kaapse Patriotte*, p. 74.

to investigate individual cases of convicts and exiles at the Cape but did nothing to improve the general situation.[25] People living in bondage at the Cape were not a priority in terms of the Company's imperial interests.

From Dutch East India Company Empire to British Empire

With revolution and war in Europe and increasing challenges in the colonies, the Company was so weakened it could not protect its imperial nodes or its ships from British conquest. This further corroded the imperial networks crucial for the VOC's existence and precipitated the disintegration of the Company's empire. The Cape was conquered by the British in September 1795, ending nearly a century and a half of Company rule. As one of their first acts of conquest, the English demanded that Cape government officials swear an oath of allegiance to His Britannic Majesty, George III.[26] The transfer of sovereignty of the Cape node from the VOC to the British empire prompted some of the clearest expositions of Company law, as the new imperial overlords sought to reconcile their concepts of law and governance with those of the Cape governing elite.

The British were at pains not to destabilize the foundation of the rule of law in this valuable new imperial node. They did not, therefore, undermine the authority of the colonial elite but instead tried to fold them into their own institutions of governance. In response to questions about the use of torture and the punishment of black people and slaves, the Cape Council of Justice replied that the basis of criminal jurisprudence was not the distinction between slave and free but rather the distinctions of rank and the nature of the crime, which was consistent with the laws of the United Provinces where there was no slavery[27] and on "the statutes which have been successively issued in the Dutch Indies, relative to slaves, and are observed here."[28] The new British government at the Cape did not disturb the status quo regarding slavery at the Cape, nor did it fundamentally change the legal system except with regard to the transfer of sovereignty to Britain, although they did outlaw the use of judicial torture in accordance with their own legal system. The stability of the colony at

---

[25] A. J. Böeseken, *Die Nederlandse Kommissarisse en de 18de eeuse sameleving aan die Kaap*. Archives Yearbook of the South African Library, vol. 1. Cape Town: South African Library, 1944, Chapter 5.
[26] George McCall Theal, ed., *Records of the Cape Colony*, vol. 1. Cape Town and London: Government Printers, 1905, p. 298.
[27] Ibid., pp. 298–303.   [28] Ibid., p. 304.

the Cape was not dependent upon the Company's imperial networks, and the maintenance of order by the British facilitated its transformation into a node in the usurping British imperial web.

The VOC network of exile ended with the first British conquest.[29] The British were fully enmeshed in their own network of forced migration, including the early decades of the largest circuit of penal transportation from Europe, the foundation of penal colonies in Australia. As a British imperial node, the Cape was absorbed into these new British networks. The first British ruler at the Cape, Major-General James Henry Craig, held a court martial at the Castle of Good Hope on October 24, 1796, convicting the soldier Charles Melon of counterfeiting and sentencing him to hang. In accordance with contemporary British legal practices, the death sentence was commuted to transportation to New South Wales where he would serve fourteen years as a convict. Melon traveled on the ship *Ganges* to Port Jackson in New South Wales "there to be delivered over to the orders of the Governor in the same manner as other convicts in similar circumstances."[30] Within a few months, a Scots Brigade private, John Richards, was found guilty of murder and sentenced to hang. He was later granted a stay of execution on condition of his penal transportation to "His Majesty's settlement in New South Wales for the term of his natural life."[31] Thus did the Cape enter a new imperial web and correspondingly a new network of forced migration.

The circuit of political exile operated by the Dutch East India Company had been fundamentally tied into indigenous politics as Batavia sought to pursue Company interests in the core region of Java. The political implications of this circuit of exile outlived the Company empire. Individual cases of exile could reverberate across the breadth of the entire Indian Ocean and echo over temporal distances of many decades and generations. In 1813, while Java was under temporary British rule, three great-grandsons of Chakaraningrat IV, King of Madura, who was banished to the Cape of Good Hope in the 1740s, attempted to claim the throne of Madura by appealing to the British on the basis that "one's enemies' enemies are one's friends." The princes argued eloquently:

We cannot refrain from entertaining a confident hope that on the demise of the King who now rules, one of us may be seated on the vacant throne to which

---

[29] In 1802 when the Cape was returned to Dutch control under the Peace of Armiens, there was no resumption of the network of exile that had existed under the VOC.

[30] S. D. Naude, ed., *Kaapse Plakaatboek*, vol. 5 (1795–1803). Parrow: Cape Times Ltd, 1950, pp. 69–70.

[31] Ibid., p. 70.

we have a lawful right. We look forward to this as an act of retribution justice. The Dutch are the ancient enemies of the English; the Dutch deprived us of our birthright, it is in the power of the English to restore it to us... We further humbly hope... the Ruler of India [i.e. the British monarch]... condescend to succor men of rank reduced to poverty through the machinations of the Dutch (who are the ever-bitter foes of the English who know not what it is to love Justice and good order and who do not respect the rights of Rulers or of Kingdoms).[32]

The princes argued that the current king was not the legitimate heir and had been installed by the VOC to further its own political power in Madura. They pledged allegiance to the British Crown and appealed for support in their claim. Despite the princes' astute appeal to imperial politics, the British declined their request, preferring the status quo in Madura.

Nevertheless, official British imperial correspondence concerning this matter demonstrates that the claim was taken seriously. The VOC's network of exile influenced archipelagic politics long after the Dutch East India Company and its empire had ceased to exist and its remnants were incorporated into a new empire controlled by the Dutch state. Meanwhile, the Cape of Good Hope was permanently integrated into the British imperial web in 1806. At this time, the British were on the brink of banning the slave trade in its empire and thus the Cape's new imperial network of forced migration had changed fundamentally.

Networks of Empire

The process of ending the Company's rule at the Cape began with the first British conquest in 1795 and took nearly twenty years to complete. It is fitting, therefore, to conclude with the transfer of the Cape of Good Hope from the Dutch to the British and to trace, within this transition, the subsequent incorporation of the Dutch East India Company's network of forced migration into the British imperial web. The aspect of primary concern to this book is that the Dutch and British continued bartering particular nodes and networks in the Indian Ocean grid to achieve continuity of rule at the Cape and regional consolidation within their respective empires. There are, however, inherent limitations as to what can be said about this process, short of considering it within the history of the impact and aftermath of the French Revolution and Napoleonic era on the reconfiguration of European imperial aspirations during these decades. A brief

---

[32] ANRI: Madura: 6b. Letter translated and copied to G. A. Addison Esq. Assistant Secretary to the Governor of Java, Stamford Raffles, May 14, 1814.

outline of political events that directly relate to the transformation of the Dutch empire during this period will, nevertheless, suffice to provide sufficient context for considering the state of VOC nodes and networks of forced migration between 1795 and 1814, when the Dutch formally ceded the Cape of Good Hope to the British.

The 1790s was a decade of political upheaval in Europe and this was particularly the case in the Netherlands. The Batavian Republic was declared in 1795 when the Dutch *Stadhouder*, William V, fled and took refuge in England. This new republic centralized the state and ended the split sovereignty of the United Provinces. In 1798, the Batavian Republic absorbed what remained of the quasi-independent empire of the Dutch East India Company into its newly formed governance structure a year before it dissolved the bankrupt Company in 1799. The Batavian Republic thereupon laid claim to parts of the Company's former empire, including the Cape of Good Hope.

Subsequently, the Cape was returned to Dutch rule in 1803 under the Treaty of Amiens that established an alliance between the British and Dutch states. This alliance collapsed in 1806 when Napoleon appointed his brother, Louis Bonaparte, to be monarch of the new Kingdom of Holland. In response to the French having installed one of their own in the Netherlands, the English reoccupied the Cape to prevent the spread of French influence in the Indian Ocean and Asia and to secure the English East India Company's imperial web. Despite British success at the Cape, their sovereignty was not finally and formally recognized until the London Convention was negotiated and agreed upon in August 1814 by the Dutch provisional government under Prince William VI and George III in Great Britain. This occurred seven months before the full restoration of the Dutch monarchy as the United Kingdom of the Netherlands.[33]

The London Convention encompassed the colonies of the Dutch and the British in the Atlantic and Indian Oceans and involved the direct transfer of several imperial nodes between the two empires. Owing to events in Europe, and especially to the consolidation of the Dutch state, the principles according to which the Dutch bartered with the British differed from those by which the British bartered with the Dutch. In

---

[33] William Freund, "The Cape under the transitional governments, 1795–1814," in Elphick and Giliomee, eds., *Shaping of South African Society*, pp. 324–351. Edward Hertslet, *The Map of Europe by Treaty; Showing the various political and territorial changes which have taken place since the general peace of 1814* (originally published 1875). London: Gregg International, 1969, pp. 42–47.

looking closely at this exchange and what it signals about Dutch and British imperial aspirations going forward, one gains insight into the changing dynamics of the Indian Ocean grid, in the widest scope; and, in the narrowest scope, into the lives of people at the Cape and across the newly configured imperial grid who remained subject to forced migration, not the least of whom were supposedly freed slaves.

In the Indian Ocean, the British agreed to cede the island of Banca on the Straits of Malacca near south Sumatra "in exchange for the [Dutch] settlement of Cochin and its dependencies on the coast of Malabar."[34] The Dutch thereby severed ties to the Company's former Indian nodes and sub-circuits in this region to consolidate its imperial networks in the core region of the Indies archipelago. They furthermore agreed to stop Dutch slaving vessels on the coast of Africa from using British colonial ports, while gaining assurances from the English that their other ships would be allowed access to the Cape of Good Hope on equal terms. Further pledges were exchanged regarding the rights of Dutch subjects living in its former possessions to live and trade under the same laws as British subjects, with their property and personal rights fully protected.

Thus the London Convention, or Anglo-Dutch Treaty of 1814 as it is also known, demonstrates that the partial sovereignty embedded within specific imperial networks could be reapportioned across imperial webs by severing rights over some networks and allowing the continuity of others. For instance, the Dutch state negotiated continued access to the Cape as a refreshment stop for its ships, even though the British now governed at the Cape of Good Hope. The Dutch transportation network that had relied on the Cape for its transoceanic shipping was therefore not fundamentally disrupted by the Dutch loss of sovereignty at its former Cape node.

Looking at how these and other respective nodes, networks, and circuits of the British and Dutch empires were bartered during the transitional decades at the Cape also points to the difference between a new Dutch empire incorporated directly into the state and a former one that functioned as a semiautonomous merchant empire. The imperial domain of the Dutch East India Company was determined by a charter granted by the States-General and its exercise of sovereignty was partial. Dutch conquest of the nodes and networks of other European powers in the Indian Ocean grid was also limited by European politics. Within these

---

[34] Hertslet, *Map of Europe*, p. 43.

constraints, however, the Company operated with a large measure of self-determination in its imperial web as well as independently from the other Dutch-chartered merchant empire, the Dutch West India Company, operating in the Atlantic Ocean for part of the seventeenth century before it was incorporated into the United Provinces. The VOC maintained a large degree of imperial autonomy until its gradual demise in the last decades of the eighteenth century. Once the terms of barter were inscribed in the Anglo-Dutch treaty, the Dutch and the British began the important process of consolidating their new and remaining nodes and networks into their respective core regions. The process of consolidation was, in itself, important for how new state-based empires functioned and exercised their sovereignty.

Over the previous century and a half, the Dutch East India Company had created its own institutions of law and governance and its own imperial networks (including law, diplomacy, trade, communication, and migration), through which it had exercised partial sovereignty according to conditions within individual nodes. The interests of the Company and the Dutch state were inextricably linked, but not necessarily identical, and the VOC pursued its own self-interest as much as possible. However, while the Company had exercised partial sovereignty within its own imperial web until its demise, including the right to sign treaties with indigenous powers in its charter domain in the name of the States-General, the Dutch state controlled foreign policy within the European arena, which, in turn, determined Company interactions with European traders, companies, and merchant empires in the Indian Ocean. Once the Company's empire was fully incorporated into the Dutch state, its partial sovereignty was dissolved. From this point forward, state and colonial interests were unified in the same system of law and government.

Under the Dutch East India Company, the network of forced migration was largely an internal imperial matter with little effective oversight or control by the Dutch state. The slave trade, penal transportation, and political exile constituted a network that connected VOC imperial nodes to one another and to the capital at Batavia. The empire's only links to the Dutch state with respect to its network of forced migration was through the banishment of Europeans to the fatherland and through appeal to the States-General made by settlers and Company servants when they felt the justice system of the Company had failed them, although these appeals were unsuccessful. The Company used its network of forced migration to facilitate the movement of slaves, convicts, and exiles among its imperial nodes, primarily to supply labor. The Dutch state had no control over the slave trade, penal transportation or political exile in the Company domain, and penal transportation was intended to both punish crimes and deter others by moving convicts for incarceration to one of several imperial nodes. The slave trade was by far the largest, most important, and extensive circuit in the network of forced migration because slave labor was crucial to most of the Company nodes. Political exile was intended to further the political aims of the Company. Both penal transportation and political exile were supposed to facilitate political control in the empire, but these forms of forced migration had varied and often negative effects on the nodes that received convicts and exiles.

Forced migration constituted part of the peopling of empire and helps explain how VOC settlements evolved as colonial societies; however, the implications of the Company's forced migration network differed according to place. At the Cape, it fundamentally shaped the contours of colonial society through its dependence on slave labor and the influence of political exiles in the transmission of Islam to the region. Furthermore, the presence on the one hand of European convicts condemned to public labor alongside slaves, and, on the other, of the privileged treatment of some high-ranking Asian political exiles as well as the degradation of others, challenged social hierarchies at the Cape. This challenge to existing hierarchies is clearly demonstrated by exiles who were appointed Company *caffers* with powers of arrest and chastisement over free burghers. The Company's strategy of social control, as well as its laws that allowed the forcible reenlistment into the Company and banishment of free burghers, became rallying points for protests against VOC governance at the Cape. After the Company period, forced migration in the reformulated Dutch empire was more closely tied to the state and joined the Atlantic Ocean and Indian Ocean colonial domains into one network. For instance, Javanese criminals convicted to penal transportation could now be sent to the Dutch colony Surinam in South America. In the Netherlands East Indies, political prisoners were more often banished to other islands in the archipelago, as was the case in the Java War of 1825 to 1830 that resulted in the exile of Prince Diponegoro from Java to Manado in North Sulawesi.

The transitional period at the Cape, from the end of Company rule to the beginning of permanent British rule, corresponded with the end of the global British slave trade, and the Anglo-Dutch treaties ended Dutch participation in the transoceanic slave trade of Africans. Under the state-controlled Dutch colonial empire, the network of penal transportation and political exile shifted geographical orientation, but these circuits of forced migration were not dismantled entirely.

During the first and second periods of British rule at the Cape, institutional continuities in law and governance and in circuits of trade and transportation not only endured in this imperial node but also were expanded through the British transformation of colonial sovereignty. The extension of multiple networks in the Company's imperial web had created the conditions for the evolution of the Cape node from refreshment post to colony, while simultaneously creating a settler population whose primary interest was the stability of their colonial homeland and not the continuity of Dutch sovereignty. There was, accordingly, an alignment of interests and a relatively high degree of cooperation between Cape colonial elites and British colonial officials regarding governance of the colony and the uninterrupted stability of the rule of law. The British supported slavery and control over labor, including indigenous Khoisan labor, but dismantled the oceanic slave trade.

The Cape was brought into the British empire during the period in which the British state began to enforce the end of the slave trade and, eventually, of slavery. The British therefore intervened fundamentally in the former Company circuit of forced migration that comprised part of the southwest Indian Ocean slave trade. Perhaps the most dramatic transformation in the transition from Dutch to British rule was that the Cape, instead of being a receiving node of slaves through this circuit of the slave trade, became the headquarters of the British naval fleet that intervened to stop the slave trade along the entire East African coast.

Paradoxically, British anti-slave trade expeditions produced a new source of bonded labor in the form of "Liberated Africans" who were brought to the Cape and forced to work under multiyear contracts, instead of being repatriated to their homelands as free people. The British anti-slave trade network encompassed the entire African coastline and was divided into Atlantic and Indian Ocean circuits of British Navy patrols. The so-called liberated Africans removed from slaving vessels by the British Navy then entered into a network of migration that traversed British imperial nodes. Those sent to Sierra Leone in West Africa were free to settle in the territory. Other British colonies in the Atlantic and Indian Oceans received liberated Africans as a new source of bonded labor throughout the nineteenth century, despite the emancipation of slaves in the British empire in 1834.[35]

---

[35] Christopher Saunders, "'Free, Yet Slaves': Prize Negroes at the Cape Revisited," in Nigel Worden and Clifton Crais, eds., *Breaking the Chains: Slavery and Its Legacy in the Nineteenth-Century Cape Colony*. Johannesburg: Witwatersrand University Press, 1994, pp. 99–116.

The imposition of British imperial ideology regarding slavery did not necessarily correspond with the perceived interests or beliefs of colonists in the empire. Nevertheless, the British state fully exercised its sovereign right to determine law in its imperial domain. Although the literature on the British slave trade and emancipation is massive, additional research on migration networks in the British empire would reveal the variety of experiences of people whose statuses changed from formal slavery and temporary bondage to freedom during this long transitional period.

This book has analyzed the multiple networks of trade, law, administration, exchange, and migration that constituted Dutch imperial sovereignty through the two centuries from the beginning of the seventeenth to the early nineteenth century. It has demonstrated how and why individual networks are grafted, reorientated, transformed, strengthened, weakened, or severed and what each of these changes implied for the development of colonial society at the Cape of Good Hope. This analysis has thereby escaped the teleology of the "rise and fall" of empire by considering change and continuity within a specific imperial web and, to a limited degree in this chapter, through the transfer of sovereignty from one to another imperial web. In examining the evolution of Company sovereignty, with Batavia as imperial capital and the Cape as crucial refreshment settlement, this book has created a connective narrative of one particular circuit of forced migration without losing sight of its broader imperial context. In so doing, *Networks of Empire* implicitly suggests that similar attention to other nodes and relational circuits are possible and that, when considered together, these multiple yet partial views, open for consideration the further dynamic working of the nodes, networks, circuits, and sub-circuits that together constitute an imperial web.

The opportunities of this analytical framework therefore include the ability to readily shift the analysis from the spatial to the temporal level over an entire imperial era, to close descriptions of time and space within one locality, and, closer still, to narrate the trajectory of the life of one individual and the links and relationships among individual lives. The archival evidence for forced migration in the Company's empire, particularly the slave trade, is fragmentary at best. Drawing together evidence of a single circuit along a single network of forced migration allows one to envisage the operation of the whole network and its variations over time and space in the absence of ideal source material. Writing a history of the Batavia-Cape circuit of forced migration through penal transportation and political exile has involved piecing together disparate and fragmentary pieces of evidence, particularly from the criminal and diplomatic records housed in three different archives on three different continents, each of which document different aspects and localities of the Company's empire. Rarely can individuals be traced across these archives, and piecing together at least part of their lives, as determined by the network of forced migration, constitutes an advance in colonial historiography.

The limitations of this book include, largely for the sake of brevity and the nature of archival evidence, its partial attention to free migration and the slave trade. Archival sources for free migration circuits outside Company personnel records could probably be fruitful and there are quite a few personal accounts of life on board Company ships and within the empire. In the case of the slave trade, archival evidence is very scattered and incomplete in the Company records. It is also rare to be able to trace the life of an individual slave within this circuit of forced migration, which imposes constraints on this kind of biographical archival project.

Networks of Empire attends most closely to the lesser-known aspects of forced migration: political exile and penal transportation. Its concentration on individual convicts and exiles was achieved at the expense of a fuller picture of the entire spectrum of bondage. This choice was deliberate because a focus on convicts and exiles disrupts an analysis of colonial society through the binary of freedom and slavery. Moreover, the literature on imperial networks tends to focus on colonial officials because their footprints in the archives are much deeper, and it is possible to trace individual career patterns across multiple imperial sites. The innovative literature on the "middle passages" of slavery and on "coerced and free migration" has enabled comparative perspectives across empires and forms of forced migration. Historians engaged in these projects have benefited immensely from collaborative projects, resulting in edited collections that bring together case studies that allow explicit comparisons to emerge from their juxtaposition.[36]

This book extends the existing literature by thinking comparatively about the spectrum of bondage within a single imperial network of forced migration and thereby argues that slavery, penal transportation, and political exile have a shared history. Bringing these forms of forced

---

[36] David Eltis, "Introduction," in David Eltis, ed., *Coerced and Free Migration: Global Perspectives*. Stanford: Stanford University Press, 2002, pp. 1–31; Emma Christopher, Cassandra Pybus, and Markus Rediker, eds., *Many Middle Passages: Forced Migration in the Making of the Modern World*, Los Angeles and Berkeley: University of California Press, 2007.

migration together in a single study contributes to a fuller understanding of bondage at an imperial and an individual level. As Cooper and Stoler have asserted "[t]he current weight given to the transnational movements of the postmodern moment contrast such a moment to the accepted fixity of colonial history within national boundaries. But it is colonial and postcolonial historiography rather than colonial history that has constructed those self-contained units and invested in that story... there are clearly other circuits of movement and axes of mobility to explore."[37]

The framework used in this book – of nodes, networks, circuits, and sub-circuits of partial sovereignty constituting an imperial web that operates within a chartered domain that is embedded within a geographical grid composed of indigenous polities and other European imperial webs – offers new prospects for further research that do not require a focus on the network of forced migration. Most importantly, this explanatory model promises to yield new questions about the workings of empire. *Networks of Empire* has argued that forced migration, as practiced by the Dutch East India Company in the seventeenth and eighteenth centuries, constitutes one of the "circuits of movement" within the study of empire and opens out to an examination of other networks within the broader dynamics of particular imperial grids. This book thereby brings the histories and historiographies of nations as diverse as Indonesia and South Africa into the same field of vision. It is fitting that the national mottos of both Indonesia – bhinneka tunggal ika – and South Africa – !ke e:/xarra//ke – translate into the phrase that best describes the Dutch East India Company "unity in diversity."

---

[37] Ann Laura Stoler and Frederick Cooper, "Between Metropole and Colony: Rethinking a Research Agenda," in Cooper and Stoler, eds., *Tensions of Empire*, p. 27.

Bibliography

Archival Sources

Arsip Nasional Republik Indonesia (ANRI) – Jakarta, Indonesia

Ambon, vol. 788.
Banten, vol. 73.Batavia, vol. 179.
Buitenland, vols. 193.
Cheribon, vol. 38.
Commisse tot secrete zaken, vol. 4352.
Dag Registier vanhet Casteel Batavia, 1682.
Djokjakarta, vol. 20.
General Resolutien van het Casteel Batavia, vols. 662–817, 1666–1755.
Justitie, vols. 1–31, 1642–1855.
Madura, vol. 6.
Raad van Justitie, vols. 3–18, 1704–1859.
Secrete Resolutien, vols. 840–847, 1645–1781.
Sumenap, vol. 16
Ternate, vol. 158.

Cape Town Archive Repository (CA) – Cape Town, South Africa

A1657, M. K. Jeffreys Collection, vols. 20–398.
AG, Attorneys General: Diverse stukken, vols. 68–71, 1661–1827.
CJ, Court of Justice: Convict Rolls, vol. 3188, 1728–1795.
CJ, Court of Justice: Criminele Stukken, vols. 335–339, 1730–1733.
CJ, Court of Justice: Criminele Stukken, vol. 677, 1751.
CJ, Court of Justice: Criminele Stukken, vol. 3219, 1751.
CJ, Court of Justice: Index to Court Cases, vols. 12–40, 1730–1758.
CJ, Court of Justice: List of Convicts Sent to Robben Island, vol. 3189, 1758–1802.
CJ, Court of Justice: List of Exiles Sent Back to India After the Expiration of Their Sentences, vol. 3190, 1750–1781.

CJ, Court of Justice: Miscellaneous List of Sentences, vol. 3192, 1790–1827.
CJ, Court of Justice: Notebooks. Convicts, vol. 3186, 1722–1757.
CJ, Court of Justice: Notebooks. Convicts, vol. 3187, 1786.
CJ, Court of Justice: Sentences Not Executed, vol. 3191, 1750–1781.
CJ, Court of Justice: Vonnissen der Persone de welke zoo van Batavia als Ceijlon Herwaarts gesonden zijn, vols. 2562–2568, 1722–1789.
CP, Politieke Raad: Inkomende Briewe, vols. 362–366. 1698–1699.
CP, Politieke Raad: Gemengde stukken betreffende Bannelinge van Batavia, vol. 798.
LM, Leibbrandt Manuscripts, vols. 30–38, no dates.

Nationaal Archief (NA) – The Hague, The Netherlands

Geschillen tussen de Hoge Regering en de Raad van Justitie in Batavia, vol. 11197, 1779.
Kopieboeken van uitgaande secrete missiven van Gouverneur-Generaal en Raden aan de Buitenkantoren, vols. 7652–7655, 1783–1789.
Kopie-civiele en-criminele rollen van de Raad van Justitie van Kaap de Goede Hoop, vols. 10948–10950, 1749–1751.
Kopie-criminele en civiele processstukken van de Raad van Justitie in Batavia, vols. 9350–9432. 1729–1751.
Kopie-criminele processtukken van de Raad van Justitie van Kaap de Goede Hoop, vol. 11019, 1750.
Kopie-criminele rollen van de Raad van Justitie in Batavia, vols. 9294–9331, 1728–1780.
Kopie-criminele sententiën van de Raad van Justitite in Batavia, vols. 9350–9432, 1728–1751.
Kopie-generale land- en zeemonsterrollen van de VOC-dienaren in de vestigingen en op de schepen in Indië. Met inhougsopgaven van de opgenomen kantoren en/of schepen, vol. 5168, 1720; vol. 5173, 1725; vols. 5178–5198, 1730–5198; vol. 5203, 1755; vol. 5208, 1760; vol. 5213, 1765; vol. 5218, 1770; vol. 5223, 1775; vols. 5228–5229, 1780–1781; vol. 5233, 1785; vol. 5238, 1790.
Kopie-missiven en-rapporten ingekomen bij Gouverneur-Generaal en Raden uit Java's Oostkust, vols. 7882–7886, 1784–1789.
Kopie missiven van de Raad van Justitie in Batavia aan de Heren XVII en de kamer Amsterdam, vols. 9221–9222, 1719–1734.
Kopie-secrete missiven en rapporten ingekomen bij Gouverneur-Generaal en Raden uit Malakka, vols. 8667–8668, 1768–1787.
Kopie-secrete resoluties betreffende de opstand van de Chinezen, vol. 781, 1751.
Kopie-uitgaande stukken van Gouverneur-Generaal en Raden, vols. 7642–7647, 1784–1788.
Overgekomen brieven en papieren uit Kaap de Goede Hoop en Mauritius aan de Heren XVII en de kamer Amsterdam, vol. 4181, 1750; vol. 4318, 1785.
Register op de Brieven van de Vergadering van Zeventien, vols. 345–349, 1613–1776.
Verdragen met Aziatische vorsten, vols. 11195–11196, 1684–1742.

Bibliography

Unpublished Primary Sources

Baartman, Teun. *Cape Town Criminal Records*, 1730–1759. 4 vols. Cape Town History Project, University of Cape Town.
Shell, Robert. Census of the Dutch East India Company Slaves in the Lodge, 1693, 1714, 1727.
———. Lijste der Maccasareschen Princen en Groten en dieselven dienaren, 1686.
University of Cape Town. African Studies Library. McMillan Collection. Sheikh Yusuf.

Published Bibliographies

Ebing, Ewald, and Youetta de Jager, comps. *Batavia-Jakarta, 1600–2000: A Bibliography*. KITLV Bibliographic Series, no. 23. Leiden: KITLV, 2000.
Haron, Muhammed, comp. *Muslims in South Africa: An Annotated Bibliography*. Cape Town: South African Library, 1997.
Meilink-Roelofsz, M. A. P., Remco Raben, and H. Spikerman, eds. *De archieven van de Verenigde Oostindische Compagnie (1602–1795)*. Algemeen Rijksarchief, Eerste Afdeeling. 'sGravenhage: Sdu Uitgeverij, 1992.
Shell, Robert C-H, Sandra Rowoldt Shell, and Mogamat Kamedien, comps. *Bibliographies of Bondage: Select Bibliographies of South African Slavery and Abolition*. Princeton: Markus Wiener Publishers, 2008.

Published Primary Sources

Böeseken, A. J., ed. *Belangrike Kaapse Dokument. Memoriën en Instructiën*, 1657–1699. 2 vols. Cape Town: South African State Archives, 1966–1967.
———. *Memoriën en Instructiën, Deel I: 1657–1699*. Suid-Africaanse Argiefstukke. Belangrike Kaapse Dokument. Kaapstad, 1966.
———, ed. *Die Nederlandse Kommissarisse en de 18de eeuse sameleving aan die Kaap*. Archives Yearbook of the South African Library, vol. 1. Cape Town: South African Library, 1944.
———, ed. *Uit die Raad van Justisie, 1652–1672*. Pretoria: Die Staatsdrukker, 1986.
Böeseken, A. J., and J. C. de Wet, eds. *Resolusies van die Politikie Raad, 1651–1743*. 9 vols. Cape Town and Pretoria: Kantoor van die Hoofargivaris, 1957–1984.
Bruijn, J. R., F. S. Gaastra, and I. Schoffer, eds. *Dutch-Asiatic Shipping in the 17th and 18th Centuries*. 3 vols. Rijks geschiedenkundige publicatien, grote serie, nos. 165–167. Den Haag: Martinus Nijhoff, 1979–1987.
Coolhaas, W. P. and J. van Goor, eds. *Generale Missiven van Gouverneurs-Generaal en Raden aan Heren XVII der Verenigde Oostindische Compagnie*. Rijks geschiedkundige publicatiën, grote series nos. 104, 112, 125, 134, 150, 159, 164, 193, and 205. 9 vols. 'sGravenhage, 1960–1988.

De Jonge, J. K. and M. L. van Deventer eds. *De Opkomst van het Nederlandsch Gezag in Oost-Indië. Verzameling van onuitgegeven stukken uit het Oud-Koloniaal Archief*. 13 vols. 'sGravenhage: Martinus Nijhoff; Amsterdam: Frederick Muller, 1862–1909.

Grotius, Hugo. *The Freedom of the Seas: Or the Right Which Belongs to the Dutch to Take Part in the East Indian Trade*. Translated with a revision of the Latin text of 1633 by Ralph van Deman Magiffin. Edited with an introduction by James Brown Scott. New York: Oxford University Press, 1916.

Heeres, J. E., and F. W. Stapel, eds. *Corpus Diplomaticum Neerlando-Indicum. Versameling van politieke contracten en verdere vedagen door de Nederlanders in het Oosten gesloten*. Bijdragen tot de Taal-, Land-, en Volkenkunde. 57, 87, 91, 93, 96. 'sGravenhage, 1907–1955.

Hemmy, Gysbert. *De Testimoniis: A Thesis by Gysbert Hemmy on the Testimony of the Chinese, Aethiopians and Other Pagans, 1770*. Edited and translated from the Latin by Margaret Hewett. Cape Town: University of Cape Town, 1998.

———. *Oratio Lattina de Promontorio Bonae Spei 1767*. Translated and edited by K. D. White. Cape Town: South African Public Library, 1971.

Jeffreys, Kathleen M., ed. *Historiese Dokumenten over the Kaap de Goede Hoop. Kaapse Archiefstukken 1779*. Kaapstad: Cape Times Beperkt, 1927.

———, ed. *Kaapse Archiefstukken 1778–1783*. 8 vols. Cape Town: Cape Times; Pretoria: Staatsdrukker, 1926–1938.

———, ed. *The Memorandum of Commissary J A de Mist. Containing Recommendations for the Form and Administration of the Government at the Cape of Good Hope, 1802*. Cape Town: Van Riebeeck Society, 1920.

Jeffreys, Kathleen M, S. D. Naude, and P. J. Venter, eds. *Kaapse Plakkaatboek, 1653–1806*. 6 vols. Kaapstad: Cape Times Limited, 1944–1951.

Khan, Mirza Abu Taleb. *Westward Bound: Travels of Mirza Abu Taleb*. Trans. Charles Stewart, ed. and intro. Mushirul Hasan. New Delhi: Oxford University Press, 2005.

Leibbrantdt, H. C. V., ed. *Precis of the Archives of the Cape of Good Hope. The Defense of Willem Adriaan van der Stel*. Cape Town: Government Printers, 1897.

———, ed. *Precis of the Archives of the Cape of Good Hope. Letters and Documents Received, 1649–1662. Part II*. Cape Town: W. A. Richards & Sons, Government Printers, 1896.

———, ed. *Rambles through the Archives of the Colony of the Cape of Good Hope 1688–1700*. Cape Town: J. C. Juta, 1887.

———, ed. *Requesten (Memorials), 1715–1806*. 5 vols. Cape Town: Government Printers and South African Library, 1905–1989.

Mentzel, Otto. *A Geographical and Topographical Description of the Cape of Good Hope*. Translated from the German by H. J. Mandelbrote. Cape Town: Van Riebeeck Society, 1925.

Moodie, Donald, ed. *The Record, Book One: Or a Series of Official Papers Relative to the Condition and Treatment of the Native Tribes of South Africa*. A photostatic reprint of the original published in 1838. Amsterdam and Cape Town: A. A. Balkema, 1960.

Raffles, Thomas Stamford. *A History of Java*. 2 vols. With an introduction by John Bastin. Kuala Lumpur: Oxford University Press, 1965.

Raven-Hart, R., ed. and trans. *Cape of Good Hope 1652–1702. The First Fifty Years of Dutch Colonisation as Seen by Callers*. 2 vols. Cape Town: A. A. Balkema, 1971.

Schoonveld-Oosterling, J. E., ed. *Generale Missiven van Gouverneurs-Generaal en Raden aan Heren XVII der Verenigde Oostindische Compagnie*. Deel XI: 1743–1750. Den Haag: Instituut voor Nederlandse Geschiedenis, 1997.

Schutte, Gerrit ed., *Briefwisseling van Hendrik Swellengrebel Jr. oor Kaapse Sake, 1778–1792*. With English translation by A. J. Böeseken. Kaapstad: Van Riebeeck-Vereniging, 1982.

———, ed. *Hendrik Cloete, "Groot Constantia" and the VOC 1778–1799*. Documents from the Swellengrebel Archive. With English translation by N. O. van Gylswyk and D. Sleigh. Van Riebeeck Society, 2nd ser., no. 34. Cape Town: Van Riebeeck Society, 2003.

Sparrman, Anders. *A Voyage to the Cape of Good Hope, 1772–1776*. Edited by V. S. Forbes. 2 vols. Cape Town: Van Riebeeck Society, 1975–1977.

Tas, Adam. *The Diary of Adam Tas, 1705–1706*. Fouché, Leo, ed., A. J. Böeseken, rev., and J. Smuts, trans. Van Riebeeck Society, 2nd ser., no. 1. Cape Town: Van Riebeeck Society, 1970.

Theal, George McCall, ed. *Abstract of the Debates and Resolutions of the Council of Policy at the Cape from 1651–1687*. Cape Town: Saul Solomon and Company Printers, 1881.

Theal, George McCall, ed. *Records of the Cape Colony*. 36 vols. Cape Town and London: Government Printers, 1905.

Thunberg, Carl Peter. *Travels at the Cape of Good Hope, 1772–1775*. Edited by V. S. Forbes. 2nd ser., no. 17. Cape Town: Van Riebeeck Society, 1986.

Transcription Project (TEPC), *CJ Series: Documents Regarding Convicts and Exiles*, TANP (Towards a New Age of Partnership) www.tanap.net/content/activities/documents.

Valentijn, François. *Description of the Cape of Good Hope with the Matters Concerning It, Amsterdam 1726*. Pt 1. Edited and annotated by Edith Hildegard Raidt. 2nd ser., no. 2. Cape Town: Van Riebeeck Society, 1971.

Van Dam, Pieter. *Beschrijvinge van de Oostindische Compagnie*. 7 vols. Edited by F. W. Stapel and C. W. Th van Boetzelaer. Rijks gescheidenkundige publicatien, grote series, nos. 63, 68, 74, 76, 83, 87, 96. s'Gravenhage: Martinus Nijhoff, 1927–1954.

Van Der Chijs, J. A. ed., *Realia. Register op de generale resolutiën van het Kasteel Batavia, 1632–1805*. 3 vols. Leiden: Gualth Kolff; Den Haag: Martinus Nijhoff; Batavia: W. Bruining, 1882–1885.

Van Der Chijs, J. A., comp *Nederlandsch-Indisch Plakaatboek, 1602–1811*. 17 vols. Batavia: Landsdrukkerij; 'sHage: Martinus Nijhoff, 1885–1900.

Van Riebeeck, Jan. *Journal of Jan van Riebeeck*. 3 vols. Thom, H. B., ed. and trans. Published by the Van Riebeeck Society. Cape Town and Amsterdam: A. A. Balkema, 1952.

Worden, Nigel, and Gerald Groenewald, eds. *Trials of Slavery: Selected Documents Concerning Slaves from the Criminal Records of the Council of Justice*

at the Cape of Good Hope, 1705–1794. Van Riebeeck Society for the Publication of South African Historical Documents. 2nd ser., no. 36. Cape Town: Van Riebeeck Society 2005.
Cape Times, November 21, 1997.
Impact International 24(6), 1994.
Kompas (Jakarta) November 10, 1995.

Select Secondary Sources

Abdullah, Taufik. *Sejarah lokal di Indonesia Kumpulan Tulisan.* Yogjakarta: Gadjah Mada Universitas, 1985.
Abeyesekere, Susan. *Jakarta: A History.* Singapore: Oxford University Press, 1987.
Abu-Lughod, Janet. *Before European Hegemony: The World System, A.D. 1250–1350.* New York: Oxford University Press, 1989.
Adams, Julia. "The Familial State: Elite Family Practices and State-Making in the Early Modern Netherlands." *Theory and Society,* 23(4), August 1994, pp. 505–539.
———. *The Familial State: Ruling Families and Merchant Capitalism in Early Modern Europe.* Ithaca, NY: Cornell University Press, 2005.
———. "Principals and Agents, Colonialists and Company Men: The Decay of Colonial Control in the Dutch East Indies." *American Sociological Review,* 61, February 1996, pp. 12–28.
———. "Trading States, Trading Places: The Role of Patrimonialism in Early Modern Dutch Development." *Comparative Studies in Society and History,* 36(2), 1994, pp. 319–355.
Adas, Michael, ed. *Technology and European Overseas Enterprise: Diffusion, Adaption and Adoption.* Hampshire: Variorum, 1996.
Alders, Lucas. "Internasionale Rechtspraak Tussen Indonesische Rijken en de VOC tot 1700." Unpublished PhD diss., Katholieke Universiteit te Nijmegen, 1955.
Alexandrowicz, C. H. *An Introduction to the History of the Law of Nations in the East Indies (16th, 17th and 18th Centuries).* Oxford: Clarendon Press, 1967.
Allen, Richard. *Slaves, Freedmen, and Indentured Laborers in Colonial Mauritius.* Cambridge: Cambridge University Press, 1999.
Alpers, Edward, Gwyn Campbell, and Michael Salman, eds. *Resisting Bondage in Indian Ocean Africa and Asia.* London: Routledge, 2007.
———, eds. *Slavery and Resistance in Africa and Asia.* London: Routledge, 2005.
Andaya, Barbara Watson. *To Live as Brothers: Southeast Sumatra in the Seventeenth and Eighteenth Centuries.* Honolulu: University of Hawaii Press, 1993.
Andaya, Leonard. *The Heritage of Arung Palaka: A History of South Sulawesi (Celebes) in the Seventeenth Century.* Verhandelingen KITLV, no. 91. The Hague: Martinus Nijhoff, 1981.

———. "Treaty Conceptions and Misconceptions: A Case Study from South Sulawesi." *Bijdragen KI*, 134(2–3), 1978, pp. 275–295.

———. *The World of the Muluku: Eastern Indonesia in the Early Modern Period*. Honolulu: University of Hawaii Press, 1993.

Andrade, Tonio. *How Taiwan Became Chinese: Dutch Spanish and Han Colonization in the Seventeenth Century*. New York: Columbia University Press, 2006.

Andearson, Clare. *Convicts in the Indian Ocean: Transportation from South Asia to Mauritius, 1851–53*. Houndsmill, Hamps. and London: Macmillan Press; New York: St. Martin's Press, 2000.

Anonymous. *Memperingati 300 Tahun pendaraan Syekh Yusuf di Afrika Selatan: Katalog Naskah Tentang Syekh Yusuf*. Ujung Pandang, Indonesia: Universitas Hassanudin, 1994.

Armstrong, James. "The Chinese at the Cape in the Dutch East India Company Period." Unpublished paper presented at the UNESCO Slave Route Project Conference, Robben Island, Cape Town, 1997.

Axelson, Eric. *Portuguese in South-East Africa, 1600–1700*. Johannesburg: Witwatersrand University Press, 1969.

Azra, Azyumardi. *The Origins of Islamic Reformism in Southeast Asia: Networks of Malay-Indonesian and Middle Eastern Ulama in the Seventeenth and Eighteenth Centuries*. Honolulu: University of Hawaii Press; Crows Nest, NSW: Allen and Unwin, 2004.

Ball, John. *Indonesian Legal History*. Sydney: Oughtershaw Press, 1982.

Barend-van Haeften, Marijke. *Oost-Indië gespiegeld: Nicholaas de Graaff, een schrijvend chirurgijn in dienst van de VOC*. Zutphen: Walburg Pers, 1992.

Barnard, Timothy P., ed., *Contesting Malayness: Malay Identity across Boundaries*. Singapore: Singapore University Press, 2004.

Bayly, C. A. *Empire and Information: Intelligence Gathering and Social Communication in India, 1780–1870*. Cambridge: Cambridge University Press, 1996.

Bentley, Jerry, Renate Bridenthal, and Kären Wigen, eds. *Seascapes: Maritime Histories, Littoral Cultures, and Transoceanic Exchanges*. Honolulu: University of Hawaii Press, 2007.

Benton, Lauren. *Law and Colonial Cultures: Legal Regimes in World History, 1400–1900*. Cambridge: Cambridge University Press, 2002.

Beyers, Coenraad. *Die Kaapse Patriotte gedurende die laaste kwart van die agteende eeu en die voortlewing van hul denkbeelde*. Pretoria: J. L. van Schank Beperk, 1967.

Bialuschewski, Arne. "Pirates, Slavers, and the Indigenous Population in Madagascar, c 1690–1715." *International Journal of African Historical Studies*, 38(3), 2005, pp. 401–425.

Biewenga, Ad. *De Kaap de Goede Hoop: een Nederlandse vestingskolonie, 1680–1730*. Amsterdam: Prometheus/Bert Bakker, 1999.

Bilby, Kenneth. "Swearing by the Past, Swearing to the Future: Sacred Oaths, Alliances, and Treaties among the Guianese and Jamaican Maroons." *Ethnohistory*, 44(4), Fall 1997, pp. 655–689.

Blackburn, Robin. *The Making of New World Slavery: From the Baroque to the Modern, 1492–1800*. New York: Verso Books, 1997.

Blussé, Leonard. *Bitter Bonds: A Colonial Divorce Drama of the Seventeenth Century*. Princeton, NJ: Markus Wiener, 2002. Originally published in Dutch as *Bitters bruid: een koloniaal huwelijksdrama in de Gouden Eeuw*. Amsterdam: Balans, 1998.

———. "Four Hundred Years On: The Public Commemoration of the Founding of the VOC in 2002." *Itinerario*, 27(1), 2003, pp. 79–92.

———. *Strange Company: Chinese Settlers, Mestizo Women and the Dutch in VOC Batavia*. Dordrecht, Holland: Foris Publications, 1986.

Blussé, Leonard, and Femme Gaastra. *Companies and Trade*. The Hague: Martinus Nijhoff, 1981.

Böeseken, A. J. *Jan van Riebeeck en Sy Gesin*. Kaapstad: Tafelberg, 1974.

———. *Simon van der Stel en Sy Kinders*. Kaapstad: Nasou Beperk, 1984.

———. *Slaves and Free Blacks at the Cape, 1658–1700*. Kaapstad: Tafelberg Pers, 1977.

———. "Die Verhouding tussen Blank en Nie-Blank in Suid-Afrika aan die hand van die Vroegste Dokumente." *South African Historical Journal*, 2, November 1970 pp. 3–18.

Botha, C. G. *Cape Archives and Records*. Collected Works, vol. 3. Cape Town: C. Struik, 1962.

———. *General History and Social Life of the Cape of Good Hope: Collected Works*, vol. 1. Cape Town: C. Struik, 1962.

———. *History of Law, Medicine, and Place Names in the Cape of Good Hope*. Collected Works, vol. 2. Cape Town: C. Struik, 1962.

Boucher, Maurice. "Cape and Company in the Early Eighteenth Century." *Kleio*, 9(1–2), June 1977 pp. 57–69.

———. "The Cape and Foreign Shipping, 1714–1723." *South African Historical Journal*, No. 6, November 1974, pp. 3–29.

———. *The Cape of Good Hope and Foreign Contacts, 1735–1755*. Pretoria: University of South Africa, 1985.

Boxer, Charles R. *Dutch Merchants and Mariners in Asia, 1602–1795*. London: Vaorium Reprints, 1988.

———. *The Dutch Seaborne Empire, 1600–1800*. London: Penguin Books, 1965.

Bradlow, Edna. "Mental Illness or a Form of Resistance? The Case of Soera Brotto." *Kleio*, 23, 1991, pp. 4–16.

Bradlow, Frank, and Margaret Cairns. *The Early Cape Muslims: A Study of Their Mosques, Genealogy and Origins*. Cape Town: A. A. Balkema, 1978.

Bradlow, M. Adil. "Imperialism, State Formation, and the Establishment of a Muslim Community at the Cape of Good Hope, 1770–1840: A Study in Urban Resistance." Unpublished MA thesis, University of Cape Town, 1988.

Bredekamp, Henry C. "'Tot Afschrikt van Anfre': Die VOC-Regstelsel en geweld ten opsigte van die Khoisan aan die Kaap, 1677–1705." *Kronos*, 12, 1987, pp. 8–32.

Broeze, Frank, ed. *Brides of the Sea: Port Cities of Asia from the 16th to the 20th Centuries*. Honolulu: University of Hawaii Press, 1989.

Broeze, Frank, ed. *Gateways of Asia: Port Cities of Asia in the 13th to the 20th Centuries*. London and New York: Columbia University Press, 1997.

Bruijn, Jaap R. "Between Batavia and the Cape: Shipping Patterns of the Dutch East India Company." *Journal of Southeast Asian Studies*, 11(2), September 1980, pp. 251–265.

Burman, Jose. *The Saldanha Bay Story*. Cape Town: Human and Rousseau, 1974.

Burton, Antoinette, ed. *After the Imperial Turn: Thinking with and through the Nation*. Durham, NC: Duke University Press, 2003.

Cairns, Margaret. "Coenraad Frederik Hofman, An Exile at the Cape, 1721–1734." *Cabo*, 2(1), February 1978, pp. 7–17.

Campbell, Gwynn, ed. *The Structure of Slavery in Indian Ocean Africa and Asia*. London and Portland, OR: Frank Cass, 2004.

Cense, A. A. "De verering van Sjaich Yusuf in Zuid-Celebes." In *Bingkisan Budi: een bundle opstelen aan Dr Philippus Samuel von Ronkel door vrienden en leerlingen aangeboden op zijn tachtigste verjaardag 1 Augustus 1950*. Leiden: A. W. Sitjhoff, 1950.

Chandler, David, et al. *In Search of Southeast Asia: A Modern History*. Edited by Joel Steinberg. Rev. ed. Honolulu: University of Hawaii Press, 1987.

Chanock, Martin. *Law, Custom, and Social Order: The Colonial Experience in Malawi and Zimbabwe*. Cambridge: Cambridge University Press, 1985.

Chaudhuri, K. N. *Asia before Europe: Economy and Civilization of the Indian Ocean from the Rise of Islam to 1750*. Cambridge: Cambridge University Press, 1990.

Christopher, Emma. *Slave Ship Sailors and Their Captive Cargoes, 1730–1807*. New York: Cambridge University Press, 2006.

Christopher, Emma, Cassandra Pybus, and Markus Rediker, eds. *Many Middle Passages: Forced Migration and the Making of the Modern World*. Los Angeles and Berkeley: University of California Press, 2007.

Coates, Timothy J. *Convicts and Orphans: Forced and State-Sponsored Colonizers in the Portuguese Empire, 1550–1755*. Stanford, CA: Stanford University Press, 2001.

Cohen, Robin. *Global Diasporas: An Introduction*. Seattle: University of Washington Press, 1997.

Coldham, Peter Wilson. *Emigrants in Chains: A Social History of Forced Emigration to the Americas of Felons, Destitute Children, Political and Religious Non-Conformists, Vagabonds, Beggars and Other Undesirables, 1607–1776*. Surrey: Genealogical Publishing Company, 1992.

Cook, Scott. "Imperial Diasporas." In *Colonial Encounters in the Age of High Imperialism*. New York: HarperCollins, 1996.

Cooper, Frederick, and Ann Laura Stoler, eds. *Tensions of Empire: Colonial Cultures in a Bourgeois World*. Berkeley, Los Angeles, and London: University of California Press, 1997.

Cummings, William. "'Only One People but Two Rulers': Hiding the Past in Seventeenth-Century Makasarese Chronicles." *Bijdragen tot de Taal-, Land- en Volkenkunde (BKI)*, 155(1), 1999, pp. 97–120.

———. *Making Blood White: Historical Transformations in Early Modern Makassar*. Honolulu: University of Hawaii Press, 2002.

Curtin, Philip. *Cross-Cultural Trade in World History*. Cambridge: Cambridge University Press, 1984.

Da Costa, Yusuf, and Achmat Davids. *Pages from Cape Muslim History*. Pietermaritzburg: Shuter and Shooter, 1994.

Dangor, Suleman. *Shaykh Yusuf*. Mobeni: Iqra Research Committee, 1982.

Davids, Achmat. *The History of the Tana Baru*. Cape Town: Committee for the Preservation of the Tana Baru, 1985.

———. "The Kramat at Zandvleit – Sheikh Yusuf of Macassar." Unpublished manuscript, no date.

———. *The Mosques of the Bo-Kaap*. Athlone: South African Institute of Arabic and Islamic Studies, 1980.

Day, Clive. *The Policy and Administration of the Dutch in Java*. New York: Macmillan, 1904.

Day, Tony. "The Drama of Bangun Tapa's Exile in Ambon: the Poetry of Kingship in Surakarta, 1830–58." In L. Gesick ed., *Centers, Symbols and Hierarchies*. New Haven: Yale University Southeast Asia Series (Monograph Series No. 26) 1983, pp. 148–151.

———. "Ties That (Un)Bind: Families and States in Premodern Southeast Asia." *Journal of Southeast Asian Studies (JSEAS)*, 55(2), May 1996, pp. 384–489.

Deacon, Harriet, ed. *The Island: A History of Robben Island, 1488–1990*. Cape Town: Mayibuye Books and David Philip, 1996.

De Graaf, H. J. *Geschiedenis van Indonesië*. 'sGravenhage and Bandung: W. van Hoeve, 1949.

De Haan, F. W. *Oud Batavia*. 3 Deel. Batavia: G. Kolff & Co., 1922.

———. *Priangan: De Preanger-Regenschappen onder het Nederlandsch Bestuur tot 1811*. 4 vols. Batavia: G. Kolff & Co.; 'sGravenhage: Martinus Nijhoff, 1910.

De Kiewiet, C. W. *A History of South Africa: Social and Economic*. London: Oxford University Press, 1941.

De Kock, Victor. *Those in Bondage: An Account of the Life of the Slave at the Cape in the Days of the Dutch East India Company*. Pretoria: Union Booksellers, 1963.

De Korte, J. P. *De jaarlijke financiele verantwoording in de Verenigde Oostindische Compagnie*. Leiden: Het Nederlandsch Economisch-Historisch Archief, no. 17, 1984.

Dirks, Nicholas, ed. *Colonialism and Culture*. Ann Arbor: University of Michigan Press, 1992.

Dooling, Wayne. "The Castle: Its Place in the History of Cape Town in the VOC Period." In Elizabeth van Heyningen, ed., *Studies in the History of Cape Town*, vol. 7. Cape Town History Project in association with the Center for African Studies. Cape Town: University of Cape Town Press, 1994. pp. 9–31.

———. "'The Good Opinion of Others': Law, Slavery and Community in the Cape Colony, c. 1760–1830." In Nigel Worden and Clifton Crais, eds., *Breaking the Chains: Slavery and Its Legacy in the Nineteenth-Century Cape Colony*. Johannesburg: Witwatersrand University Press, 1994, pp. 25–44.

———. *Law and Community in a Slave Society: Stellenbosch District, South Africa, c.1760–1820*. Communication no. 23. Cape Town: Centre for African Studies, University of Cape Town, 1992.

Drakard, Jane. *A Malay Frontier: Unity and Disunity in a Sumatran Kingdom.* Ithaca, NY: Studies on Southeast Asia, Southeast Asia Program, Cornell University, 1990.
Drewes, G. W. J. "Sech Joessoep Makasar." *Djawa,* 6(2), 1926, pp. 83–88.
Duffield, Ian, and James Bradley, eds. *Representing Convicts: New Perspectives on Convict Forced Labour Migration.* London: Leicester University Press, 1997.
Du Plessis, I. D. *The Cape Malays.* Cape Town: Maskew Miller Longman, 1941.
Du Toit, Andre, and Hermann Giliomee. *Afrikaner Political Thought: Analysis and Documents, Volume One: 1780–1850.* Cape Town: David Philip, 1983.
Edwards, Charles S. *Hugo Grotius: The Miracle of Holland: A Study in Political and Legal Thought.* Chicago: Nelson-Hall, 1981.
Elphick, Richard. *Kraal and Castle: Khoikhoi and the Founding of White South Africa.* New Haven: Yale University Press, 1977.
Elphick, Richard, and Hermann Giliomee, eds. *Shaping of South African Society, 1652–1840,* 2nd ed. Cape Town: Maskew Miller Longman, 1989.
Eltis, David, ed., *Coerced and Free Migration: Global Perspectives.* Stanford, CA: Stanford University Press, 2002.
Emmer, P. C. *The Dutch Slave Trade, 1500–1800.* Translated by Chris Emery. New York and Oxford: Berghahn Books, 2006.
Emmer, P. C., and M. Mörner, eds. *European Expansion and Migration: Essays on the International Migration from Africa, Asia, and Europe.* New York: Berg Press, 1992.
Engerman, Stanley, ed. *Terms of Labor: Slavery, Serfdom, and Free Labor.* Stanford: Stanford University Press, 1999.
Evans, Grant. "Between the Global and the Local There Are Regions, Cultural Areas, and National States: A Review Article." *Journal of Southeast Asian Studies,* 33(1), February 2002, pp. 147–162.
Fine, Hilton Basil. "The Administration of Criminal Justice at the Cape of Good Hope 1795–1828." Unpublished PhD diss., University of Cape Town, 1991.
Florida, Nancy. *Writing the Past, Inscribing the Future: History as Prophecy in Colonial Java.* Durham, NC: Duke University Press, 1995.
Foucault, Michel. *Discipline and Punish: The Birth of the Prison.* Translated by Alan Sheridan. New York: Vintage Books, 1987.
Furnivall, J. S. *Netherlands India: A Study of Plural Economy.* Cambridge: Cambridge University Press, 1939.
Gaastra, Femme S. *Bewind en Beleid bij de VOC. De financiële en commerciële politiek van de bewindhebbers, 1672–1702.* Zutphen, Netherlands: Walburg Pers, 1989.
———. *De geschiedenis van de VOC.* 2nd ed. Zutphen, Neterlands.: Walburg Pers, 1991.
———. *The Dutch East India Company: Expansion and Decline.* Zutphen, Netherlands: Walburg Pers, 2003.
———. "The Independent Fiscaals of the VOC, 1689–1719." In Centre for the History of European Expansion, Rijksuniversiteit Leiden, *All of One Company: The VOC in Biographical Perspective.* Utrecht, Netherlands: Hes uitgevers, 1986, pp. 92–107.

———. "The Organization of the VOC." In Meilink-Roelofsz, Raben, Spikerman. *De archieven van de Verenigde Oostindische Compagnie (1602-1795)*. Algemeen Rijksarchief, Eerste Afdeeling's Gravenhage: Sdu Uitgeverij, 1992, pp. 11-29.

Gepken-Jager, Ella, Gerard van Solinge, and Levinus Timmerman, eds. *VOC 1602-2002: 400 Years of Company Law*. Nijmegen, Netherlands: Kluwer Legal Publishers, 2005.

Gesick, Lorraine, ed. *Centers, Symbols, and Hierarchies: Essays on the Classical States of Southeast Asia*. New Haven: Yale University Southeast Asia Series, 1983.

Goslinga, Cornelis. *A Short History of the Netherlands Antilles and Surinam*. The Hague: Martinus Nijhoff, 1979.

Gould, Eliga. "Zones of Law, Zones of Violence: The Legal Geography of the British Atlantic c 1772." *William and Mary Quarterly*, 60, July 2003, pp. 471-510.

Greene, Jack P. *Peripheries and Center: Constitutional Development in the Extended Polities of the British Empire and the United States, 1607-1788*. Athens, GA: University of Georgia Press, 1986.

Groenewald, Gerald. "The Culture and Economy of Taverns, Inns, and Lodging Houses in Dutch Cape Town, 1652-1795." PhD diss., University of Cape Town, forthcoming.

———. "Panaij van Boegies: Slave-Bandiet-Caffer." *Quarterly Bulletin of the National Library of South Africa*, 59(2), 2005, pp. 50-62.

Gyory, Joanna, et al. "The Agulhas Current" and "The Benguela Current" at http://www.oceancurrents.rsmas.miami.edu. Accessed on July 26, 2007.

Hahlo, H. R., and E. Kahn. *The South African Legal System and Its Background*. Cape Town: Juta, 1968.

Hall, Catherine, ed. *Cultures of Empire, a Reader: Colonizers in Britain and the Empire in the Nineteenth and Twentieth Centuries*. Manchester: Manchester University Press, 2000.

Hall, Richard. *Empires of the Monsoon: A History of the Indian Ocean and Its Invaders*. New York: HarperCollins, 1998.

Hamid, Abu. *Syekh Yusuf Makassar: Alim, Sufi, Author, Hero*. Ujung Pandang, Indonesia: University of Hasanuddin, 1994. Published in Indonesian as *Syekh Yusuf: Seorang Ulama, Sufi dan Pejuang*. Jakarta: Yayasan Obor Indonesia, 1994.

Hamilton, Caroline, Verne Harris, and Graeme Reid, eds. *Refiguring the Archive*. Cape Town: David Philip; Dordrecht: Kluwer Academic Publishers, 2002.

Hancock, David. "The British Atlantic World: Co-ordination, Complexity, and the Emergence of an Atlantic Market Economy, 1651-1815." *Itinerario*, 2, 1999, pp. 1-20.

Hanna, Willard A. *Indonesian Banda: Colonialism and Its Aftermath in the Nutmeg Islands*. Philadelphia: Institute for the Study of Human Issues, 1978.

Hattingh, J. L. "Grondbesit in die Tafelvallei. Deel 1: De Eksperiment: Vryswartes as Grondeienaars, 1652-1710." *Kronos*, 10, 1985, pp. 32-48.

Heese, H. F. *Groep sonder Grense: Die rol en status van de gemengde bevolking ann die Kaap, 1652-1795*. Belville: Wes Kaaplandse Instituut vir Historiese Navorsing, 1984.

———. "Kriminele Sake: Hofuitsprake aan die Kaap, 1700–1750." *Kronos*, 12, 1987, pp. 33–42.

———. *Reg en Onreg: Kaapse Regspraak in die Agtiende Eeu*. Belville: Insituut vir Historiese Navorsing, Universiteit van Wes-Kaapland, 1994.

Hertlet, Edward. *The Map of Europe by Treaty; Showing the various political and territorial changes which have taken place since the general peace of 1814* (originally published 1875). London: Gregg International, 1969.

Hoadley, Mason C. *Selective Judicial Competence: The Cirebon-Priangan Legal Administration, 1680–1792*. Ithaca, NY: Cornell University Southeast Asia Program, 1994.

Hoffman, J. E. "Early Policies in the Malacca Jurisdiction of the United East India Company: The Malay Peninsula and Netherlands East Indies Attachment." *Journal of Southeast Asian Studies*, 3(1), March 1972, pp. 1–38.

Holleman, J. F., ed. *Van Vollenhoven on Indonesian Adat Law: Selections from Het Adatrecht van Nederlandsch-Indië (Volume I, 1918; Volume II, 1931)*. The Hague: Martinus Nijhoff, 1981.

Hooker, M. B. *A Concise Legal History of South-East Asia*. Oxford: Clarendon Press, 1978.

Huusainmiya, B. A. *Orang Rejimen: The Malays of the Ceylon Rifle Regiment*. Bangi, Malaysia: Penerbit Universiti Kebangsaan Malaysia, 1990.

Huussen, A. H. "De rechtspraak in strafzaken voor het Hof van Holland in het eerste kwart van de achittiende eeuw." *Holland: Regionaalhistorischtijdschrift*, 8(3), 1976, pp. 116–139.

Israel, Jonathan I. *Dutch Primacy in World Trade, 1585–1740*. Oxford: Clarendon Press, 1989.

Jacobs, Els M. *Merchant in Asia: The Trade of the Dutch East India Company during the Eighteenth Century*. Leiden: CNWS Publications, 2006. Originally published in Dutch as *Koopman in Azië: De handel van de Verenigde Oost-Indische Compagnie tijdens de 18de eeuw*. Zutphen, Netherlands: Walburg Pers, 2000.

Jaffer, Mansoor, ed. *Guide to the Kramats of the Western Cape*. Cape Town: Cape Mazaar (Kramat) Society, 1996.

James, C. R. L. *The Black Jacobins: Toussaint L'Ouverture and the San Domingo Revolution*, 2nd ed. New York: Vintage Books, 1963.

Jeffreys, K. M. "The Malay Tombs of the Holy Circle." Pts. 1–6. *Cape Naturalist*, 1(1), November 1934, pp. 15–17; 1(2), July 1935, pp. 40–43; 1(3), July 1936, pp. 89–92; 1(4), April 1937, pp. 118–121; 1(5), June 1938, pp. 157–163; 1(6), June 1939, pp. 195–199.

Jeppie, Shamil. "Historical Process and the Construction of Subjects: I D du Plessis and the Reinvention of the 'Malay.'" Unpublished BA Honors thesis, University of Cape Town, 1987.

———. "Politics and Identities in South Africa: Reflections on the 1994 Tricentenary Celebration of Islam in South Africa." Unpublished paper presented to the American Council for the Study of Islamic Societies, Villanova University, April 20–22, 1995.

Johns, A. H. "From Coastal Settlement to Islamic School and City: Islamization in Sumatra, the Malay Peninsula, and Java." *Hamard Islamicus*, 4(4), Winter 1981, pp. 3–28.

———. "Sufism as a Category in Indonesian Literature and History." *Journal of Southeast Asian History*, 2(2), July 1961, pp. 10–23.

Kalff, S. *De Slavernij in Oost-Indie*. Barn, Netherlands: Hollandia-drukkerij, 1920.

Kathirithamby-Wells, J. and John Villiers, eds. *The Southeast Asian Port and Polity: Rise and Demise*. Singapore: Singapore University Press, 1990.

Kelly, David, and Anthony Reid, eds. *Asian Freedoms: The Idea of Freedom in East and Southeast Asia*. Cambridge: Cambridge University Press, 1998.

Klerk de Rues, G. C. "Geschichtlicher Uberblick der Administrativen, Rechtlichen und Finanziellen Entwicklung der Niederlandisch-Ostindischen Compagnie." In *Verhandelingen van het Bataviaasch Genootschap van Kunsten en Wetenschappen, deel XLVII, 3e stuk*. Batavia: Albrecht en Rusche; 'sHage: Martinus Nijhoff, 1894.

Knaap, Gerrit. "The Demography of Ambon in the Seventeenth Century: Evidence from Colonial Proto-Censuses." *Journal Southeast Asian Studies*, 26(2), September 1995, pp. 227–241.

Knaap, Gerrit and Ger Teitler, *De Verinigde Oost-indische Compagnie tussen oorlog en diplomatie*. Leiden: KITLV, 2002.

Knox-Johnston, Robin. *The Cape of Good Hope: A Maritime History*. London: Hodder and Stoughton, 1989.

Kumar, Ann. *Java and Modern Europe: Ambiguous Encounters*. Richmond, UK: Curzon Press, 1997.

———. "Javanese Historiography in and of the 'Colonial Period': A Case Study." In Anthony Reid and David Marr eds., *Perceptions of the Past in Southeast Asia*. Singapore: Published for the Asian Studies Association of Australia by Heinemann Educational Books (Asia) 1979, pp. 187–206.

———. *Surapati: Man and Legend. A Study of Three Babad Traditions*. Center of Oriental Studies, Oriental Monograph Series, no. 20. Australian National University. Leiden: E. J. Brill, 1976.

La Bree, Jacobus. *De Rechterlijke Organisatie en Rechtsbedeling te Batavia in de XVIIe Eeuw*. Rotterdam and 'sGravenhage: Nijgh & Van Ditmar. 1951.

Lambert, David, and Alan Lester. "Introduction: Imperial Spaces, Imperial Subjects." In David Lambert and Alan Lester, eds., *Colonial Lives across the British Empire: Imperial Careering in the Long Nineteenth Century*. Cambridge: Cambridge University Press, 2006, pp. 1–31.

Lasker, Bruno. *Human Bondage in Southeast Asia*. Chapel Hill, NC: University of North Carolina Press, 1950.

Lekkerkerker, C. "De Baliërs van Batavia." *De Indische Gids*, 1918, pp. 1–23.

Lequin, Frank. "Het personeel van de Verenigde Oost-Indische Compagnie in Azië in de achttiende eeuw, meet in het bijzonder in de vesting Bengalen." Unpublished PdD thesis, University of Leiden, 1982.

Lester, Alan. *Imperial Networks: Creating Identities in Nineteenth-Century South Africa and Britain*. London and New York: Routledge, 2001.

Leupe, P. A. "Letter Transport Overland to the Indies by the East India Company in the Seventeenth Century." In M. P. P. Meilink-Roelofsz, M. E. Van Opstall and G. J. Schutte eds., *Dutch Authors on Asian History*. A selection of Dutch historiography on the Verenigde Oostindische Compagnie. Dordrecht, Holland: Foris Publications, 1988, pp. 77–90.

Lev, Daniel S. "Colonial Law and the Genesis of the Indonesian State." *Indonesia*, no. 40, 1980, pp. 57–74.
Lewis, Dianne. *Jan Compagnie in the Straits of Malacca, 1641–1795*. Athens, OH: Ohio University Center for International Studies, 1995.
Lewis, Martin W., and Kären E. Wigen. *The Myth of Continents: A Critique of Metageographies*. Berkeley, Los Angeles, and London: University of California Press, 1997.
Liaw, Yock Fang. *Undang-Undang Malaka*. Bibliotecha Indonesica 13, KITLV. The Hague: Martinus Nijhoff, 1976.
Liebenberg, Helena. "Introduction to the documents of the Court of Justice at the Cape of Good Hope Regarding Convicts and Exiles." TECP Project CJ 3186, 1722, 96/97.
Linder, Adolphe. *The Swiss at the Cape of Good Hope, 1652–1971*. Basel: Basel Afrika Bibliographien, 1997.
Linebaugh, Peter, and Marcus Rediker. *The Many-Headed Hydra: Sailors, Slaves, Commoners, and the Hidden History of the Revolutionary Atlantic*. Boston: Beacon Press, 2000.
Malan, Antonia. "Chattels or Colonists?: 'Free Black' Women and Their Households." *Kronos*, 25, 1998–99, pp. 50–71.
Malherbe, V. C. *Krotoa, called "Eva": a woman between*. Communications no. 19. Cape Town: Centre for African Studies, University of Cape Town, 1990.
Marks, Shula. "Khoisan Resistance to the Dutch in the Seventeenth and Eighteenth Centuries." *Journal of African History*, 13(1), 1972, pp. 55–80.
Mason, John. "A Faith for Ourselves: Slavery, Sufism, and Conversion to Islam at the Cape." *South African Historical Journal*, 46, 2002, pp. 3–24.
Matheson, Virginia. "Strategies of Survival: The Malay Royal Line of Lingga-Riau." *Journal of Southeast Asian Studies*, 17(1), March 1986, pp. 5–38.
Matthes, B. F. "'Boegineesche en Makassarsche Legenden." *Bijdragen tot de Taal-, Land-, en Volkenkunde*, 14, 1885.
Mayson, John Schoffield. *The Malays of Capetown*. Originally published in 1861. Cape Town: Africana Connoisseurs Press, 1963.
Mazlish, Bruce, and Ralph Buultjens, eds. *Conceptualizing Global History*, Boulder, CO: Westview Press, 1997.
Mbeki, Thabo. "Reply by the President of South Africa, Thabo Mbeki, to the Toast Remarks by His Excellency, the President of the Republic of Indonesia, Dr Susilo Bambang Yudhoyono, at the State Banquet, Istana Negara, Jakarta." April 19, 2005, http://www.info.gov.za/speeches/2005/05042008451004.htm.
McNeill, J. R., and William H. McNeill. *The Human Web: A Bird's Eye View of World History*. New York: W. W. Norton, 2003.
McVay, Pamela Anne. "'I Am the Devil's Own': Crime, Class and Identity in the Seventeenth Century Dutch East Indies." Unpublished PhD diss., University of Illinois at Urbana-Champaign, 1995.
Meilink-Roelofsz, M. A. P., M. E. van Opstall, and G. J. Schutte, eds. *Dutch Authors on Asian History*. Dordrecht, Holland: Foris Publications, 1988.
Metcalf, Thomas R. *Imperial Connections: India in the Indian Ocean Arena, 1860–1920*. Berkeley, Los Angeles, London: University of California Press, 2007.

Miller, Joseph C. *Way of Death: Merchant Capitalism and the Angolan Slave Trade, 1730–1830*. Madison: University of Wisconsin Press, 1988.

Milone, Pauline. "'Queen City of the East': The Metamorphosis of a Colonial Capital." Unpublished PhD diss., University of California, Berkeley, 1966.

Mitchell, Laura. *Belongings: Property, Family and Identity in Colonial South Africa; An Exploration of Frontiers, 1725–c 1830*. New York: Columbia University Press, 2008.

Moree, P. J. *A Concise History of Dutch Mauritius, 1598–1710*. London: Columbia University Press, 1998.

Nagtegaal, Luc. *Riding the Dutch Tiger: The Dutch East India Company and the Northeast Coast of Java, 1680–1743*. Verhandelingen KITLV, no. 171. Leiden: KITLV Press, 1996.

Nas, Peter J. M., ed. *The Indonesian City: Studies in Urban Development and Planning*. Verhandelingen KITLV, no. 117. Dordrecht, Holland: Foris Publications, 1986.

Newton-King, Susan. "Company Castle and Control: The Social, Moral, and Emotional World of Servants and Slaves of the Dutch East India Company in Seventeenth and Eighteenth Century Cape Town." National Research Foundation, South Africa, 2002.

———. "For the Love of Adam: Two Sodomy Trials at the Cape of Good Hope." *Kronos*, 28, 2002, pp. 21–42.

———. *Masters and Servants on the Cape Eastern Frontier, 1760–1803*. Cambridge: Cambridge University Press, 1999.

Nicholas, Stephen, ed. *Convict Workers: Reinterpreting Australia's Past*. Cambridge: Cambridge University Press, 1988.

Niemeijer, Hendrik. *Batavia: Een koloniale samenleving in de 17de eeuw*. Amersfoort, Netherlands: Uitjgeverij Balans, 2005.

———. "A Feigned Peace? Maritime Power and Ritual Diplomacy in the Relations between the Sultanate of Ternate and the Dutch East India Company (VOC), 1700–1750." Paper presented at the Association of Asian Studies Annual Conference, San Diego, March 2000.

———. "De Geveinsde vrede: Eer, protocol en diplomatie in de machetsverhouding tussen de Verenigde Oost-Indische Compagnie en Ternate omstreeks 1750." In Gerrit Knaap and Ger Teitler, eds., *De Verenigde Oost-Indische Compagnie Tussen Oorlog en Diplomatie*. Verhandelingen van het KITLV 197. Leiden: KITLV Uitgeverij, 2002, pp. 309–336.

Oostindie, Gert, ed. *Fifty Years Later: Antislavery, Capitalism and Modernity in the Dutch Orbit*. Leiden: KITLV Press, 1995.

Opper, Edward. "Dutch East India Company Artisans in the Early Eighteenth Century." Unpublished PhD diss., Indiana University, 1975.

Pearson, Michael. "Littoral Society: The Case for the Coast." *Great Circle*, 7, 1985, pp. 1–8.

Pierce, Steven, and Anupama Rao, eds. *Discipline and the Other Body: Correction, Corporeality, Colonialism*. Durham, NC: Duke University Press, 2006.

Pemberton, John. *On the Subject of "Java."* Ithaca, NY: Cornell University Press, 1994.

Penn, Nigel. "Daily Life in Eighteenth Century Cape Town." *Cabo*, 4(1), 1986, pp. 4–8.

———. *The Forgotten Frontier: Colonist and Khoikhoi on the Cape's Northern Frontier in the 18th Century.* Athens, OH: Ohio University Press, 2005.

———. "Robben Island, 1488–1805." In Deacon, *The Island.* Cape Town: Mayibuye Books and David Philip, 1996, pp. 1–14.

———. *Rogues, Rebels, and Runaways: Eighteenth-Century Cape Characters.* Cape Town: David Philip, 1999.

Perlas, Christian. "Religion, Tradition, and the Dynamics of Islamization in South Sulawesi." *Archipel*, 29, 1985, pp. 107–135.

Picard, Hyman. *Masters of the Castle: A Portrait Gallery of the Dutch Commanders and Governors of the Cape of Good Hope.* Cape Town: C. Struik Pty, 1972.

Pike, Ruth. *Penal Servitude in Early Modern Spain.* Madison: University of Wisconsin Press, 1983.

Postma, Johannes M. *The Dutch in the Atlantic Slave Trade, 1600–1815.* New York: Cambridge University Press, 1990.

Prakash, Om. *The Dutch East India Company and the Economy of Bengal, 1630–1720.* Princeton, NJ: Princeton University Press, 1985.

Raben, Remco. "Batavia and Colombo: The Ethnic and Spatial Order of Two Colonial Cities." Unpublished PhD diss., University of Leiden, 1996.

Reid, Anthony. *An Indonesian Frontier: Acehnese and Other Histories of Sumatra.* Leiden: KITLV Press, 2005.

———. "The Islamization of Southeast Asia." In Mohanned A. Bakar, A. Kaur, and A. Z. Gazali, eds. *Historia: Essays in Commemoration of the 25th Anniversary of the Department of History, University of Malaysia.* Kuala Lumpur: Malaysian Historical Society, 1984, pp. 13–33.

———, ed. *Slavery, Bondage, and Dependency in Southeast Asia.* St. Lucia: University of Queensland Press, 1983.

———. *Southeast Asia in the Age of Commerce.* Vol. 1: *The Lands Below the Winds.* New Haven, CT: Yale University Press, 1988.

———. *Southeast Asia in the Age of Commerce, 1450–1680.* Vol. 2, *Expansion and Crisis.* New Haven, CT: Yale University Press, 1993.

———, ed. *Southeast Asia in the Early Modern Era: Trade, Power, and Belief.* Ithaca, NY and London: Cornell University Press, 1993.

Reid, Anthony, and David Marr, eds. *Perceptions of the Past in Southeast Asia.* Singapore: Heinemann Educational Books, 1979.

Remmelink, Willem. *The Chinese War and the Collapse of the Javanese State, 1725–1743.* Verhandelingen KITLV, no. 162. Leiden: KITLV Press, 1994.

Resink, G. J. "The Significance of the History of International Law in Indonesia." In Soedjatmoko, Mohammad Ali, G. J. Resink and G. McT. Kahin, eds., *An Introduction to Indonesian Historiography.* Ithaca, NY: Cornell University Press, 1993, pp. 359–379.

Ricklefs, M. C. *A History of Modern Indonesia since c 1300,* 2nd ed. Stanford, CA: Stanford University Press, 1993.

———. *Jogjakarta under Sultan Mangkumbumi, 1749–1972: A History of the Division of Java.* London: Oxford University Press, 1974.

———. *Modern Javanese Historical Tradition: A Study of an Original Kartasuran Chronicle and Related Materials.* London: School of Oriental and African Studies, 1978.

———. *Mystic Synthesis in Java: A History of Islamization from the Fourteenth to the Early Nineteenth Centuries*. Norwalk, CT: East Bridge, 2006.

———. *The Seen and Unseen Worlds in Java, 1726–1749: History Literature and Islam in the Court of Pakubuwana II*. Honolulu: Allen and Unwin and the University of Hawaii Press, 1998.

———. "Unity and Disunity in Javanese Political and Religious Thought of the Eighteenth Century." *Modern Asian Studies*, 26(4), 1992, pp. 663–678.

———. *War, Culture, and Economy in Java, 1677–1726: Asian and European Imperialism in the Early Kartasura Period*. Sydney: Asian Studies Association of Australia in association with Allen & Unwin, 1993.

Riddell, Peter. *Islam and the Malay-Indonesian World: Transmission and Responses*. Honolulu: University of Hawaii Press, 2001.

Rochlin, S. A. "A Forgotten Name for the Cape Malays." *Bantu Studies*, 8(1), March 1934, pp. 95–97.

Ross, Robert. *Beyond the Pale: Essays on the History of Colonial South Africa*. Johannesburg: Witwatersrand University Press, 1994.

———. *Cape of Torments: Slavery and Resistance in South Africa*. London: Routledge and Kegan Paul, 1983.

———. *A Concise History of South Africa*. Cambridge: Cambridge University Press, 1999.

———, ed. "The Dutch on the Swahili Coast, 1776–1778: Two Slaving Journals, *International Journal of African Historical Studies*. Pt. 1. 19, 2, 1986, pp. 3057–360. Pt 2. 19, 3, 1986, pp. 479–506.

———. *Status and Respectability in the Cape Colony, 1750–1870: A Tragedy of Manners*. Cambridge: Cambridge University Press, 1999.

Ross, Robert, and Sirtjo Koolhoff. "Upas, September, and the Bugis at the Cape of Good Hope: The Context of a Slave's Letter." *Archipel*, 70, 2005, pp. 281–308.

Ross, Robert, and Gerard Telkamp, eds. *Colonial Cities: Essays on Urbanism in a Colonial Context*. Dordrecht, Netherlands: Martinus Nijhoff for Leiden University Press, 1985.

Saunders, Christopher C. "'Free, yet slaves:' Prize Negroes at the Cape Revisited." In Worden and Crais, *Breaking the Chains*. pp. 99–116.

Scarr, Deryck. *Slaving and Slavery in the Indian Ocean*. Basingstoke and London: Macmillan Press; New York: St. Martin's Press, 1998.

Schaap, Dirk. *Onrust: Het Nederlandse duivelseiland*. Utrecht, Netherlands: A W Bruna Uitgevers, 2002.

Schama, Simon. *The Embarrassment of Riches: An Interpretation of Dutch Culture in the Golden Age*. New York: Vintage Books, 1997.

———. *Patriots and Liberators: Revolution in the Netherlands, 1780–1813*. New York: Vintage Books, 1992.

Schiller, A. "Conflict of Laws in Indonesia." *Far Eastern Quarterly*, 2(1), November 1942, pp. 31–47.

Schoeman, Karel. *Armosyn van die Kaap: Voorspel tot Vesting, 1415–1651*, 2nd ed. Kaapstad: Human and Rousseau, 2005.

———. *Early Slavery at the Cape of Good Hope, 1652–1717*. Pretoria: Protea Book House, 2007.

———. *Kinders van die Kompagnie: Kaapse lewens uit die sewentiende eeu.* Pretoria: Protea Boekhuis, 2006.
Schutte, Gerrit. "Between Amsterdam and Batavia: Cape Society and the Calvinist Church under the Dutch East India Company." *Kronos*, 25, 1998–99, pp. 17–50.
———. "'Johannes Henricus Redelinghuys. Een revolutionair Kapenaar.'" *South African Historical Journal*, 3, November 1971, pp. 49–62.
———. "Nogmaals Rangton van Bali." *Kronos*, 19, 1992, pp. 161–166.
Seed, Patricia. *Ceremonies of Possession in Europe's Conquest of the New World, 1492–1640.* Cambridge: Cambridge University Press, 1995.
Seeman, U. A. *Fortifications of the Cape Peninsula, 1647–1829.* Cape Town: Castle Military Museum, 1997.
Shell, Robert C.-H. *Children of Bondage: A Social History of the Slave Society at the Cape of Good Hope, 1652–1838.* Johannesburg: Witwatersrand University Press, 1994.
———, ed. *From Diaspora to Diorama.* Cape Town: Ancestry 24, 2003.
———. "Islam in South Africa, 1652–1997." Paper presented to the Van Leer Institute, Jerusalem, revised January 8, 1998.
———. "The March of the Mardijckers: The Toleration of Islam at the Cape, 1633–1861." *Kronos*, 2, 1995, pp. 3–20.
———. "Rangton van Bali (1673–1720): Roots and Resurrection." *Kronos*, 19, 1992, pp. 167–187.
———. "The Short Life and Personal Belongings of One Slave: Rangton of Bali, 1672–1720." *Kronos*, 18, 1991, pp. 1–6.
Sleigh, Dan. *Die Buiteposte: VOC-buiteposte onder Kaapse bestuur 1652–1795.* Pretoria: Haum, 1993.
———. *Jan Compagnie: The World of the Dutch East India Company.* Cape Town: Tafelberg, 1980.
———. *Islands: A Novel.* Translated from the Afrikaans by André Brink. London: Secker and Warburg, 2004.
Slot, B. J., M. C. J. C. van Hoof, and F. Lequin. "Notes on the Use of the VOC Archives." In Meilink-Roelofsz et al., *De archieven van de VOC*, pp. 47–70.
Sonius, H. W. J. "Introduction." In J. F. Holleman ed. *Van Vollenhoven on Indonesian Adat Law.* The Hague: Martinus Nijhoff, 1981, pp. 33–58.
Spilhaus, M. W. *Company's Men.* Cape Town: John Malherbe Pty., 1973.
Spooner, Frank. "Batavia 1673–1790: A City of Colonial Growth and Migration." In Ira Glazier and Luigi de Rosa, eds., *Migration across Time and Nations: Population Mobility in Historical Context.* New York: Holmes and Meier, 1986, pp. 30–57.
Spores, John C. *Running Amok: An Historical Enquiry.* Athens: Ohio University Center for International Studies, 1988.
Stapel, F. W. "Bijdragen tot de Geschiedenis der Rechtspraak bij de Vereenigde Oostindische Compagnie." *Bijdragen tot de Taal-, Land- en Volkenkunde van Nederlandsch-Indië*: pt. 1, 89, 1932, pp. 41–74; pt. 2, 89, 1932, pp. 297–313; pt. 3, 90, 1933, pp. 89–139.
Stock, J. L. W. "The New Statutes of India at the Cape." *South African Law Journal*, 32, 1915, pp. 332–333.

Stoler, Ann Laura and Frederick Cooper. "Between Metropole and Colony: Rethinking a Research Agenda." In Frederick Cooper and Ann Laura Stoler, eds., *Tensions of Empire: Colonial Cultures in a Bourgeois World*. Berkeley: University of California Press, 1997, pp. 1–56.

Sunstein, Cass R. "Unity and Plurality: The Case of Compulsory Oaths." *Yale Journal of Law and the Humanities*, 2, 1993, pp. 107–111.

Sutherland, Heather. "Ethnicity, Wealth, and Power in Colonial Makassar: A Historiographical Reconsideration." In Peter J. M. Nas ed. *The Indonesian City. Studies in Urban development and planning*. Dordrecht Cinnaminson. Foris Publications, 1986, pp. 37–55.

———. "The Historiography of Slavery in Indonesia." Unpublished paper, Kuala Lumpur, 1980.

———. "Performing Persona: Identity in VOC Makassar." In Worden, *Contingent Lives*, pp. 345–370.

Tagliocozzo, Eric. "Trade, Production and Incorporation: The Indian Ocean in Flux, 1600–1900." *Itinerario*, 1, 2002, pp. 75–106.

TANAP: "Towards a New Age of Partnership," http://www.tanap.net.

Taylor, Jean Gelman. *The Social World of Batavia: European and Eurasian in Dutch Asia*. Madison: University of Wisconsin Press, 1983.

Tayob, Abdulkader. *Islam in South Africa: Mosques, Imams, and Sermons*. Gainesville: University of Florida Press, 1999.

Teelock, Vijayalakshmi. *Mauritian History: From Its Beginnings to Modern Times*. Moka, Mauritius: Mahatma Gandhi Institute. 2001.

Theal, George McCall. *History of South Africa before 1975*. Originally published in 1922. Cape Town: C. Struik, 1964.

Thomson, Janice E. *Mercenaries, Pirates, and Sovereigns: State-Building and Extraterritorial Violence in Early Modern Europe*. Princeton, NJ: Princeton University Press, 1994.

Thornton, John. *Africa and Africans in the Making of the Atlantic World, 1400–1800*, 2nd ed. Cambridge: Cambridge University Press, 1998.

Tyler, James Ednell. *Oaths: Their Origin, Nature, and History*. London: John W. Parker, 1834.

Upham, Mansell. "Groote Catrijn: Earliest Recorded Female *Bandiet* at the Cape of Good Hope – A Study in Upward Mobility." *Capensis*, no. 3, September 1997, pp. 8–33.

Van Dijk, C. "Java, Indonesia, and Southeast Asia: How Important Is the Java Sea?" In V. Houben and H. Maier, eds., *Looking in Odd Mirrors: The Java Sea*. Semaians 5. Leiden: Rijksuniversiteit te Leiden, 1992.

Van de Vrugt, Marijke. *De Criminele Ordonnantiën van 1570: Enkele beschouwingen over de eerste strafrecht codificatie in de Nederlanden*. Zutphen: Walburg Pers, 1978.

Van Duin, Pieter and Robert Ross. *The Economy of the Cape Colony in the Eighteenth Century*. Leiden: Intercontinenta 7, 1987.

Van Hear, Nicholas. *New Diasporas: The Mass Exodus, Dispersal and Regrouping of Migrant Communities*. London: University College London Press, 1998.

Van Ittersum, Martine Julia. *Profit and Principle: Hugo Grotius, Natural Rights Theories and the Rise of Dutch Power in the East Indies, 1595–1615*. Leiden: Brill, 2006.

Van Kan, J. "De Bataviasche Statuten en de Buitencomptoiren." *Bijdragen tot de Taal-, Land- en Volkenkunde*, 100, 1941, pp. 255–282.
Van Klaveren, J. J. *The Dutch Colonial System in the East Indies*. The Hague: Martinus Nijhoff, 1953.
Van Rheede Van Der Kloot, M. A. *De Gouverneurs-Generaal en Commissarissen-Generaal van Nederlandsch-Indië, 1610–1888*. 'sGravenhage: W. P. van Stockum & Zoon, 1891.
Van Till, Margreet. "Social Care in Eighteenth Century Batavia: The Poor House, 1725–1750." *Itinerario*, 19(1), 1995, pp. 18–31.
Vaughan, Megan. *Creating the Creole Island: Slavery in Eighteenth-Century Mauritius*. Durham, NC: Duke University Press, 2005.
Viljoen, Russel. "Disease and Society: VOC Cape Town, Its People and the Smallpox Epidemics of 1713, 1755 and 1767." *Kleio*, 27, 1995, pp. 22–45.
Vink, Markus. "'The World's Oldest Trade': Dutch Slavery and Slave Trade in the Indian Ocean in the Seventeenth Century." *Journal of World History*, 14(2), 2003, pp. 131–177.
Visagie, G. G. *Regspleging en Reg aan die Kaap van 1652–1806*. Kaapstad: Juta, 1969.
Vos, Reinout. *Gentle Janus, Merchant Prince. The VOC and the Tightrope of Diplomacy in the Malay World, 1704–1800*. Translated by Beverly Jackson. Verhandelingen KITLV, no. 157. Leiden: KITLV Press, 1993.
Wang, Gungwu, ed. *Global History and Migrations*. Boulder, CO: Westview Press, 1997.
Ward, Kerry. "'The Bounds of Bondage': Forced Migration from Batavia to the Cape of Good Hope in the Dutch East India Company (VOC) Era, c. 1652–1795." Unpublished PhD diss., University of Michigan, 2002.
———. "Castles in the Dutch East India Company's Indian Ocean Empire." Paper presented at the World Archaeological Congress, Cape Town, South Africa, January 1999.
———. "'Crimes and Misdemeanors': Forced Migration and Forced Labor in the Dutch East India Company Empire." Unpublished paper presented at the African Studies Association Conference, Chicago, October 29 to November 1, 1998.
———. "'Tavern of the Seas?' The Cape of Good Hope as an Oceanic Crossroads during the Seventeenth and Eighteenth Centuries." In Jerry H. Bentley, Renate Bridenthal and Kären Wigen eds. *Seascapes: Maritime Histories, Littoral Cultures, and Transoceanic Exchanges*. Honolulu: University of Hawaii Press, 2007, pp. 137–52.
Waterhouse, Gilbert, ed. *Simon van der Stel's Journal of His Expedition to Namaqualand, 1685–1686*. London: Longmans Green, 1932.
Welch, Sidney. *Portuguese and Dutch in South Africa, 1641–1806*. Cape Town and Johannesburg: Juta Press, 1951.
Westra, Piet, and James C. Armstrong. *Slave Trade with Madagascar: The Journals of the Cape Slaver Leijdsman, 1715*. Cape Town: Africana Publishers, 2006.
Winius, George, and Markus Vink. *The Merchant-Warrior Pacified: The VOC (The Dutch East India Company) and Its Changing Political Economy in India*. Delhi, India: Oxford University Press, 1994.

Worden, Nigel. "Cape Town and Port Louis in the Eighteenth Century." In Gwyn Campbell, ed., *The Indian Ocean Rim: Southern Africa and Regional Co-operation*. London: Routledge-Curzon, 2003, pp. 42–53.

———, ed. *Contingent Lives: Social Identity and Material Culture in the VOC World*. Cape Town: Department of Historical Studies, University of Cape Town, 2007.

———. *Slavery in Dutch South Africa*. Cambridge: Cambridge University Press, 1985.

———. "Space and Identity in VOC Cape Town." *Kronos*, 25, 1998–99, pp. 72–87.Worden, Nigel and Clifton Crais eds. *Breaking the Chains: Slavery and its legacy in the nineteenth century Cape Colony*. Johannesburg: Witwatersrand University Press, 1994.

Worden, Nigel, Elizabeth van Heyningen, and Vivian Bickford-Smith. *Cape Town: The Making of a City*. Cape Town: David Philip, 1998.

Yang, Anand. "Indian Convict Workers in Southeast Asia in the Late Eighteenth and Early Nineteenth Centuries." *Journal of World History*, 14(2), 2003, pp. 179–208.

Yap, Melanie, and Dianne Leong Man. *Colour, Confusion and Concessions: The History of the Chinese in South Africa*. Hong Kong: Hong Kong University Press, 1996.

Zimba, Benigna, Edward Alpers, and Allen Isaacman, eds. *Slave Routes and Oral Tradition in Southeastern Africa*. Maputo, Mozambique: Filsom Entertainment, 2005.

Index

Abdul Basir, 211–12
Abdul Fathi, Abdul Fattah, Sultan, Ageng Tirtayasa, *see* Ageng, Sultan; Surya, Pangeran
absence without permission, 112
African slave trade, 13
Afrikaners, 39, 292
Ageng, Sultan, 201, 203, 204–5
Ahora van Batavia, 261
Al-Palimbani, 229
Amangkurat III, 190, 212, 217
Amangkurat IV, 92, 216, 219
Ambon, 71, 75, 285
American colonies, 30
amulat (*jimat*), 229, 268
Anglo-Dutch Treaty, *see* London Convention
Angola, 128
apartheid regime, 4, 25, 26
archival sources, 27–28
arms, provision of, 175
arson, 141
Arung Palakka (Bugis leader), 195, 196, 197, 203, 206–7
Asian convicts, 241, 263–4, 265
Asian exiles, 45, 241, 244, 286
Asian imperial web, 57
Asian migrant populations, 50, 143–4
Asian political prisoners, 260
Asian sailors, 34
assault, 105, 113, 120, 137, 253
Aurangzeb (Moghul emperor), 206
Australia
   British convicts in, 13, 46
   penal colonies, 30, 298

Autshumao (Goringhaicona leader), 2, 129, 137, 140

babads, see epic poems
Bailiff (*baljuw*), 69, 102
Banca, Island of, 301
Banda archipelago, 39, 71, 75, 139, 285
banishment, 110, 117, 118, 122, 123, 154, 252
Banten, 66, 67, 196, 201
Barbier, Estienne, 284, 287–90
Barbier Rebellion, 284, 287–90
barter trade, 129
Batavia, 5, 43, 45, 55, 56, 66, 67, 154, 184, 283
   administration of justice, 68–70
   Chinese residents, 73, 73n53
   Council of the Indies, 16–17
   decline, 98–101
   displays of wealth, 101, 101n45
   "Golden Age," 93
   law and governance, 85–86
   population, 95–98
   "Queen of the East," 67, 90–95, 102
   status and crime, 86–90
Batavia Castle, 187, 188
Batavian courts, 102–16
Batavian Republic, 15, 54, 300
Batavia-to-Cape Circuit, 56–57, 192, 236, 285
Bax, Joan, 160
Bengal coast, 61
bigamy, 115–16, 115–16n92
Bitter, Johan, 89
Boenga van Johoor, 261
Boers, W. C., *Fiscal*, 296

331

Bonaparte, Louis, 300
bondage, 5, 82
  in Cape Town, 258
  social landscape, 243–4
bonded labor, 81, 284
  "Liberated Africans," 304
branding, 120
Britain
  forced migration, 36–37
  legal practices, 298
British antislave trade network, 46, 63, 304
British East India Company, 30
British empire, 297–9
British sovereignty, 46, 297–9
Brotto, Soera, 266–7
brutality against slaves, 255
buccaneers, 175
Bugis,
  allies, 195
  Kingdom of Bone, 196
  slave letter, 279–80
Bunnegan, Jacobus, 262
Burgher Petition, 294–5
burgher status, application for, 292
Buytendagh, Carel Fredrick, 293

Caabse Vlek (Cape hamlet/village), 131–46, 148
caffers (executioner's assistants), 45, 102, 123, 244, 258
  of Company, 264–9, 286
Cakraningrat IV (Raden Djoerit), 220, 222–3
Cape, *see* Cape of Good Hope
Cape Cauldron, 127
Cape Court, 254–5
Cape Islam, 222–30
Cape Island (*Pulo Kap*), 193
Cape Malays, 25–26
Cape of Good Hope, 5, 10–11, 44, 71, 284
  from Dutch to British, 299–307, 304
  economy, 241, 257
  penal colony, 132
  prisoners from Batavia, 71, 179
  refreshment post, 63
  ships before VOC settlement, 128–31
  site of exile, 190–194
  slave society, 132
  strategic site, 127–8
  trading post, 63

Cape of Storms, 130
Cape of Patriots, 284–5, 290–7
  Dutch Africa pamphlet, 295
Cape Town, 239
  de Indische Zeeherberg, 175–6
  transoceanic port city, 169–75
capital punishment, 38
Castle of Good Hope, 156, 249–50
Catholic Church, 36
Catrijn, Groote, 144, 261
"Ceremonies of possession," 173–4
Ceylon (modern Sri Lanka), 32, 60, 61, 193
  and Batavia circuit, 285
  site of exile, 124
chain gangers (*kettinggangers*), 82, 118, 276
Chainouqua Khoekhoe, 160, 164
Chakaraningrat IV (King of Madura), 298–9
chattel slavery, 3, 74
China, 62
Chinese, 73, 73n53, 249, 253
  empire, 187
  immigrants, 99–101
  junk trade, 96, 100–101
  labor, 142, 142n33
  massacre, 22, 85–86, 92–93, 98–101, 221–2
  men, 152
  migrants, 143–4, 245
  sailors, 34
  trading network, 14, 196
  uprising, 62, 111
Christian identity, 19
Christianity, 21, 25, 40, 243
Church institutions, 88
civil cases, 17, 17n21
civil law, 97, 102
Cnoll, Pieter, 89
Cochoqua Khoekhoe (Saldanhars), 137, 141, 160
Coen, Jan Pieterszoon, 19, 55, 67
Coesoemas, Radinmas Tintas
Colombo, 5, 32, 45, 60–61, 71, 154
colonial archives, 27, 27n42
colonial law, 53
colonial society at the Cape, 242–4
colonists, self-identification of, 292, 292n12

Index

Company, *see also* under Dutch East India Company
  from charter to empire, 55–57
  claims in settlements 58
  control at the Cape, 152–8
  elites, 89, 89n10, 185
  geographical extent, 189, 189n24
  law and indigenous law, 74–77
  law at the Cape, 291–2
  legal code, 283
  personnel, 77–81
  ships and employees, 50
compounds (*kampung*), 96
Concordancy Principle, 71
concubines, 39
Conflict of Laws, theory, 71–72, 102n47, 102–3
contracts, 180–185
convicted criminals, 29
convicts (*bandieten*), 11, 20, 29–30, 37, 51, 80
  Batavia to the Cape, 245–8
  in the Cape, 258–64, 285
  as labor, 118, 144, 148, 150
  Slave Lodge, register, 258
copper, 137, 165
  illegal trade in, 88
copper-tipped canes, 163–4
Coree (Goringhaiqua), 129–30
Coromandel coast, 61
corporal punishment, 112, 113, 123
corporate slave ownership, 43, 53
Corpus Diplomaticum (treaty records), 140, 181, 181n4, 182–3, 189–90
corruption, 99, 112, 166, 288
cottons and silks, 61–62
Council of Aldermen (Batavia), 69
Council of Justice (Batavia), 69–70, 69–70n44, 71, 97, 103–4, 115, 121, 155
  criminal records, 85
Council of Policy, 246
Council of the Indies (*Raad van Indië*), 57, 58, 182
Court of Aldermen (Batavia), 69, 69n43, 93, 97, 102
Court of Justice, 17, 158, 158n74, 297
  Batavia, 69, 69n44, 70
court politics, 187–94
Craig, James Henry (Major-General), 298
Creole population, 39–40

Creolization of Cape slaves, 146
crime, 88, 105–9, 137
  and punishment at the Cape, 248–58
  punishment for, 44, 97, 109–16
criminal laws, 50–51, 97, 102
criminal records, 287
  at the Cape, 252, 263
  of the City of Batavia, 90–95
  of the Company, 88–90
criminal rolls, 263
culture of legality, 180–185

Dackkgy (alias Cuyper) (Khoekhoe leader), 159
Dassen Island, 270
death penalty, 53, 69, 70, 117, 123, 163
debt
  bondage, 144
  slavery, 3, 37
de Chavonnes, Maurice Pasques, 65, 214, 215, 245
de la Caille, M. l'Abbe Nicolas Louis, 291
de Mauregnault, Johan (*Fiscal* of Colombo), 111
Denuraga, Patih, 219–20
desertion, 44, 104–5, 112–13, 117, 136, 137, 253
Deshima Island, 152
Dipanagara, Pangeran, 215–17, 223, 231, 235
Dipanegoro, Pangeran, 303
diplomacy, protocols of, 23
diplomatic relations, 189–90
directors, 58
district supervisors (*Wijkmeesters*), 69
Djoerit, Raden, *see* Cakraningrat, IV
Dohra (Chainouqua leader), 160, 164
Doman (alias Anthony) (Goringhaiqua leader), 140–141
Drakenstein, 157
drunkenness, 119
Dutch citizen rights, 292
Dutch East India Company 1, 1n1, 5, *see also* under Company
  Batavia as capital, 85–86
  British conquest, 297–9
  charter domain (*octrooigebied*), 49
  legal system and rule of law, 18–25
  split sovereignties, 14–17
Dutch National Archive, 28, 28n44
Dutch Patriots, 295, 296

334 Index

Dutch Reformed Church, 36, 102
Dutch West India Company, 302

East African slave trade, 11
ebony, 146
Edam, Island of, 100, 213, 285
Edict of Nantes, 38
elite
   Batavian, 101, 101n45
   indigenous familial bonds, 185, 210
empire
   and nation, historiographies of, 25–29
   peopling of, 43
English East India Company, 129, 296, 300
epic poems (*babads*), 192n31, 192–4
   Babad Tanah Jawa, 192
   Surakarta Major *Babad*, 216
escape, attempted, 114
ethnic boundaries, 242
ethnic categorization, 22, 43–44, 91, 95, 95n25, 97, 286
ethnic separation, 91–92
"Eurasian" colonial population, 40
European civilian subjects, 50
European colonialism, 53
European colonists, 292
European convicts, 74, 241, 286
execution
   by firing squad, 112
   by hanging, 109–10
   sites in Cape Town, 239, 240
exile, 23, 23n19
   circuit of, 194
   protocols of, 187–94
   as punishment, 71
   sites of, 190–1
   as tool of empire, 185–7
   VOC network, 298
exiles (*bannelingen*), 11, 20, 51, 144, 148
   Batavia to the Cape, 245–8
   at the Cape, 258–64, 285, 286

factory head (*Opperhoofd*), 58
farming, 149
fears of slave attack, 123
female European convicts, 150
First Javanese War of Succession, 212
First Khoekhoe-Dutch War, 141, 158
Fiscal 70, 264
Fontaine, Jan de la, 219
forced labor, 81, 144

forced migration, 5, 12–13, 18, 30, 44, 45, 50, 124
   Batavia-to-Cape Circuit, 56–57
   British, 298
   Cape government's response, 244–8
   Cape of Good Hope, 128, 132, 240, 241
   Java-Makassar-Cape, 194–9
   network, 74, 284, 285
   Mauritius, 64
forcible reenlistment, 154, 154n68
foreign traders, 75
Formosa (Taiwan), 62, 164
fortifications, 148
France
   free and forced migration, 13
   migrant refugees, 38
Franschhoek, 157
free and forced migration, 13
free black population, 167, 249, 249n18
free burghers, 19–20, 39, 149, 153, 167, 187
   reenlistment, for 154
free indigenes, 121–2
free settlers, 156, 157
French Huguenots, 157
French Revolution, 54, 299

Gede, King Kiai, 190
gender relations, 92
General Instructions, 145
General Land and Sea Muster Rolls, 77–79
gendered forced migration, 36
gendered penal transportation, 261–2
gendered political exile, 261
George III, 297, 300
Gogosoa (Goringhaiqua leader), 139, 141
Gonnema (Cochoqua leader), 160
Gorachoqua (Peninsular) Khoekhoe, 130, 135, 139, 158
Goringhaiqua Khoekhoe, 135
Goringhaicona Khoekhoe (Watermen/Strandlopers), 130, 141, 158
governance and forced migration, 63–64
government and judicial structures, 69–70, 69n41
governors, 58

Haji, Sultan ('Abd al-Qahhar), 204
Hamengkubauwana I, Sultan (Jogykarta), 224

hanging, 120
hard labor, 113, 115, 117, 120, 241
Hasanuddin Tumenanga ri
    Balla'pangkana, Sultan, 203
Heemraden (Council), 157
Heijman, Arij, 263
Heren XVII, see Seventeen Gentlemen,
Herport, Albrecht, 130-1
High Government (Batavia), 17, 57, 65
Hindu-Buddhist traditions, 235
Hofman, Coenraad Frederik, 259-60
homelands, 4
homosexual activity, punishment for, 34, 113
Höhne, Christian Gottlob, 257
Hooreman, Director General, 224
hostage-taking, 139, 188
Huguenot refugees, 38, 38n64
humiliation as punishment, 117
Hüsing, Henning, 166

Iberian wars, 35
identity, legally assigned, 51, 76
illegal residency, 111
illegal trading, 111, 259
illness in settlements, 79, 136-7
imperial elite, 87-90
imperial law, 17-18, 24
imperial migration, 33
imperial networks, definition of, 6-14
imperial sovereignty, 43
incapacitation and incarceration, 88-81
incarceration,
    of prisoners, 80
    sites, 154-5
indentured servitude, 37
Independent *Fiscal*, office of, 165-6
India, 35
Indiaanen (Asian prisoners), 261, 272-3
Indian Ocean
    indigenous trading networks, 60
    slave trade, 81-83
Indian subcontinent, 59
indigenous courts, 188
indigenous hostages, 139-40
indigenous law, 43, 74, 75
indigenous populations, 33, 50, 145
indigenous slaves, 43, 122
indigenous trading networks, 171, 171n119
indigenous women, 40

Indonesia, 1, 2, 3, 4, 184, 241
insubordination, 122-3, 253
inter-Asian trade, 59
intermarriage, 186
international diplomacy, 187-8
international law, 140
intra-Asian trade, 61-62, 96
Irish exiles, 37
Islam, 45, 179, 243
    exile at the Cape, 231-7
    pilgrimage networks, 235
    religious objects, 268-9
    spread of, at the Cape, 20, 191, 231, 286
Islamic education, 234-5
Islamic heritage, 3
Islamic networks, 24-25
Islamic rebellion, 180
Islamic religious dissidents, 230
Islamic scholars, 191

Jambi kingdom, 185
Jambi regalia, 190
Japan, 62
Java, 1, 5, 55, 66, 67, 182, 184, 186, 283
Java-Makassar-Cape nexus, 194-9
Javanese Islamic mysticism, 235
Javanese law, codification, of, 76-77
Javanese politics, 45, 222-30
Javanese royalty at the Cape, 212-22
Javanese state, 193
Java War, 303
Jawi alim, *see* Shaykh Yusuf
Jayakarta (renamed), *see* Batavia
judicial administration, 70
jurisdiction of Company, 260-1
justice, administration of, 68, 68n40

Kaerang Abdul Jallil, Sultan of Goa, 206
Kartasura, 190, 215
Khoekhoe, 129-31, 137-8, 155, 249
    accultured into European society, 162, 162n91
    law at the Cape, 18, 138, 284
    peace treaty, 160
    polities, 44-45, 127-8, 251
Khoisan (San), 242, 284
    resistance, 287-8
knowledge networks, 64
kramats (tombs), 232
Kreti, Raden Mas, 224-8, *see also* Mascaretti, Raden

Krotoa (alias Eva) (Cochoqua) 141–2, 142n32

labor, 142–3, 244–5
  convicts, 30
  force, 148
  shortages, 80
  slaves, 81–83
Lambengi, Karaeng, 197
land
  grants, 156–7
  occupation, 158
Landdrost (magistrate), 157, 264
land-grabbing, 251
Laws of Nations, 138, 161
Laws of Nature, 161
leadership categories, 58
legal identities,
  definition of, 17–25
  of individuals, 12–13, 18–20, 23–24
legal institutions, extension of, 157
legal system, 43, 50, 86–90, 152, 283–4
littoral societies, 171, 172
livestock, 129, 137
  theft, 163
local administrator/bailiff (*landdrost*), 69
London Convention, 300–301

Madagascar, 11, 30, 146, 151, 173
madrasah (religious school), 231, 232
Maetsucyker, Joan, 196, 196n45
Makassar, 1, 32, 185, 196, 200, 200n67
  Ujung Pandung, renamed Fort Rotterdam, 195–6
Makassarese exiles, 195, 195n43
Makassarese politics, 45
Malabar coast, 61
malaria, 79–80, 95
Malay seafarers, 3
Mandela, Nelson, 1, 3
Mangale, Daeng, 164–5, 198, 199, 203–4
Mangenang, Daeng, 273–4
Mania, Bappa, 103
Mankunegara I, 224, 225, 228
Mankunegara, Pangeran Azia, 219–20, 224, 225, 229
manslaughter, 105, 113, 253
manumitted slaves, descendants of, 72

maps, 48, 84, 126, 178, 238
marginalized farming clans, 157
maritime migrations, 33
marriage bonds, 184–5
Mascaretti, Raden (Raden Mas Kreti), 224–9
Matoedje, Daeng, 197–8
Mauritius, 11, 62, 63–64, 71, 146, 147, 150, 151, 154, 172, 173
Mbeki, Thabo, 2, 3
merchant(s),
  elite families, 52
  trading ventures, 37
Mexico, 35
migrant refugees, 38
migration
  free and forced, 25, 149–52
  networks, 12
  peopling of empire, 29–41
military court, 155
military engagement (Red Sea circuit), 60
mineral resources, 165
Mocha, 59
Moghul empire, 60, 187
Moluccas, 32, 59, 66, 75, 196
monopoly contracts, 58
mosques, 232
Mossel, Jacob, 76
Mozambique, 128, 134, 151, 172
Muda, Iskander (Sultan of Aceh), 4, 4n2
Muhammad Yusuf al-Maqassari, *see* Shaykh Yusuf
murder 103, 105, 111–12, 121, 253
Muslim
  Cape population, 227
  exiles, 45, 232–4, 275, 286
  history, 226
  Indian-born women, 262
mutiny, 34–35, 137

Namaqualand, 164
Napoleonic era, 299
Nassau Castle, 75
Netherlands, 52
  Houses of Correction, 38
  political upheaval, 300
network, concept of, 41–42
networks of empire, 299–307

New South Wales, 298
New Statutes of Batavia, 291–2
Norman (Tuan Nuruman), 268
Nuruddin, Shaykh 201

oaths
  of allegiance and office 180
  of loyalty 182
oil works 247, 247n247
Onrust, 285
Opdulla, Ambonia, 262
opium trade in Bengal, 88–89
orphans, migration of, 36
Osingkhimma (Goringhaiqua leader), 139, 158, 159
Ottoman empire, 187
outposts (*buiteposte*), 148, 246–7
overseers (*knechten*), 19

Pakubuwana I (Susuhunan), 190, 212, 215, 216, 224
Pakubuwana II (Susuhunan), 92, 220
Pakubawana III (Susuhunan), 219, 224, 228
Palembang kingdom, 185
Panembahan Erucakra, *see* Dipanagara, Pangeran
Pannabahan, Bantenese Prince, 103
pastoral farming, 157
pastoralism, 166
patrimonial principles, 16
patrimonial regent elites, 52
patrimonial ties, 294
penal colonies, 298
penal settlement, 150
penal transportation, 5, 18, 22, 29, 36, 37, 45, 46, 110, 124, 154
  Batavia, 71, 74, 85, 116–24
  British, 298
  Cape, 241, 242, 284, 285
  Mauritius, 64
  to settlement nodes, 51
  VOC network, 124–6
performative practice, 180–5
permanent residence, 149
Persia, 59, 60
Peru, 35
pilgrimage networks, 235
piracy, 122, 174–5, 273
plantation owners, 39
political banishment, 51

political exile, 5, 18, 45, 46, 74, 85, 124, 179, 188–9
  Cape, 241, 242, 284, 285, 286
  Makassar, 195
political prisoners, 37, 260
  defined as "Muslim," 231–2
political protests, 46
Portuguese
  empire, 35, 36, 128
  imperial nodes, 53
  trading posts, 60
power of pardon, 69
Principles of Jurisprudence (Batavia), 70–74
prisoners
  of state, 51
  of war, 51
privateering, 132
profiteering, 88
prostitutes, 19, 36
Protestant Huguenots, 38
public international law, 23
Pulo Kap (Cape Colony), 188, 193
Purbaya, Pangeran, 215, 217

Qadiriyyah Sufi order, 232

race
  and colonial migration, 33
  social taxonomies, 286
Raja of Tambora, 211
rape, 253
rattan cane, 164
refreshment posts, 133–4, 134n11, 134n12
religious beliefs, 20–21, 35–36, 243
religious boundaries, 242
religious categories, 43–44
religious exile, 242, 286
repatriation of royal exiles, 199, 199n65
residency permit system, 99
Resident (title), 58
resistance
  acts of, 46
  suicidal rage (*amok*), 247–8
Resolution of the Council of Policy, 158
revenge and reparations, 140, 140n26
Reynst, Governor-General, 87
Ribbe, Jan Coenraat, 113

Rifaiyyah Sufi order, 233
Rio de la Goa, 71, 147, 154, 173
Robben Island, 11, 44, 80, 130, 139–40, 150, 154, 195
  Batavia circuit, 285
  lime quarries, 247, 271
  place of banishment, 269–70
  postal exchange spot, 129
  prison for criminals, 244
  site of banishment, 241
  status, ethnicity, and transgression, 270–80
Roepa, Care, 197
royal family links, 197n49
royal regalia, 189, 190
rule
  by conquest, 58
  of law, 18, 152
rural settlers, 290

Said, Mas, *see* Mankunegara I
sailing community networks, 34
sailor(s), 32–33, 87
salaries of Company servants, 78
Saldanha Bay, 148, 174
  oil works, 247
Saloringpasar (Raden Surykasuma), 213–15, 217, 218, 219, 221
Schagen, Nicolaes, 88–89
Schimmel, Jan, 262
Schordijk, Sijbrand, 263
scurvy, 131
Second Javanese War of Succession, 92, 216
Second Khoekhoe-Dutch War, 160
security priorities, shifting, 280–2
Selong, *see* Ceylon
semibonded labor, 157
separate development ideology, 4
settlers
  elites, 157
  families, at the Cape, 284
  and indigenous populations, 33
Seventeen Gentlemen, 16–17, 54, 57, 61, 64–65, 135, 137, 165, 166, 245, 283
  authority, 289
  categories of claims, 58
  General Orders, 58
  record keeping, 77
sex crimes, 113

shipping
  network, 169
  seasonal nature of, 169
ships, 255–56n41
  desertion, 255–6
  fleet of to Cape, 135–7
  discipline, 135–6
ship's crews, composition of, 170
silk trading, private, 132
Simons, Cornelis Johan, 168
Siva-Buddhist mysticism, 216, 235
skilled artisans, 119
Slave Lodge (Cape), 19, 148, 257, 257–8
slavery, 11, 51
  code, 51
  institution of, 286
  labor, 73–74, 145, 285
  laws, 21
  prosecution of, 114
  resistance, 247–8
  trade, 5, 18, 45, 46, 51, 85, 242
slaving expeditions, 151
smallpox epidemics, 251, 253–4
social groupings, 249
sodomy, 113, 137, 253
soldiers, 87
soul sellers (*Zielverkoopers*), 19
South Africa
  commemoration of VOC, 25
  Nationalist Party, 25
  presidents of, 3
South Asia, 60, 60n23
South China Sea, 59
Southeast Asia,
  elites, 189
  envoys, 187
  succession disputes, 184
  treaties and tributary relationships, 181, 181n5
Southwest Indian Ocean Sub-Circuit, 146–8
sovereignty, 77, 180, 283–4
  limitations of, 134–5
  new concept, 54–55, 163
  transfer to Britain, 297–8
Sparrman, Anders, 240
Speelman, Cornelis, 195, 205
spice, 139
  cinnamon, 60
  cloves, 67, 75
  islands, 35, 66–67, 196

mace, 139
market, 59
nutmeg, 67, 75, 139
trade, 32
Stadhouder (Vice-regent/Prince), 182
States-General (VOC), 49, 51, 51n3, 54, 181, 283, 289
status
  boundaries, 242
  and the law, 89
Statutes of Batavia, 43, 67, 67n36, 70–74, 137, 145, 152, 151n61
Stellenbosch, 157, 215
St. Helena Bay, 148, 172, 247
stock theft, 139, 161, 161n87
Straits of Malacca, 59
subalterns, 119–20
subsistence, living at the Cape 138, 138n21
Sufi orders, 234, 235
sugar
  collapse of industry, 98
  plantations, 63, 98
  production, 62
Suharto, General 1, 3
suicide, 162
Sultanate of Banten (Java), 66, 67
Sultanate of Malacca, 59
Sumatra, 185
sumptuary laws, 86
Surapati, 193, 194, 194n40, 205
  babads (epic poems), 193–4, 205
Surya, Pangeran (Crown Prince), 201
Swellengrebel, Hendrick, 293–4
Synod of Dort, 21

Table Bay, 169
Tang laij van Bogies, 261
Tas, Adam, 166, 166n105
tavern of the seas (Cape), 131, 175–7
taxes, 153
territorial nodes, 57–64
territorial sovereignty, 163
textile production, 61
Thedens, Johannes, 103
theft, 113, 114, 120, 137, 253
Third Javanese War of Succession, 92
titles in settlements, 58
tobacco, 137
trade, 25, 31
  by treaties, 58

networks, 57–64
through conquest, 50
trading
  currency (VOC), 52–53, 52–53n8
  posts, 33
transoceanic perspective, 172, 172n121
transportation networks, 128
travel, unauthorized, 122
treaties, 180–1, 283
Treaty of Amiens, 300
Treaty of Bungaya, 195, 196
Treaty of Giyanti, 92
tropical diseases, 250–1
Tulbagh, Rijk (Cape governor), 224, 225, 251
Tuwan Seh, *see under* Shaykh Yusuf, 194, 200

unfree labor, 145
Union of Utrecht, 51
United Kingdom of the Netherlands, 300
United Provinces, 14–15, 49, 53, 57, 181, 184, 185
  split sovereignty, 283
urban-based commercial disputes, 291
urban underclasses, 270, 270n99

Valckenier, Adriaan, 22, 111
Van Balij, Carangassan, 103
Van der Stel, Adrien, 63, 147
Van der Stel, Simon, 25, 63, 147, 155, 163, 164, 167, 194, 199
  dispute, 164–8, 284
Van der Stel, Willem Adriaan, 66, 164, 207
Van Diemen, Antonia, 132, 186
Van Goens, Rijkloff Jr., 61, 155, 195, 204
Van Goens, Rijkloff Sr., 60–61
Van Hoorn, Joan, 186
Van Imhoff, Gustav Willem Baron, 111
Van Meerhoff, Pieter, 142
Van Nijenroode, Cornelia, 89–90
Van Overbeke, Arnout, 159
Van Plettenberg, Cape governor, 296
Van Quaalbergen, Cornelis, 59
Van Reede van Mijdrecht tot Drakenstein, Hendrik Adriaan, 88, 155, 165, 199
Van Riebeeck, Abraham, 187
Van Riebeeck, Jan, 63, 131–2, 135–7, 143, 145, 147, 154, 156, 156n71, 186, 245
Van Riebeeck, Johanna-Maria, 186

Van Suijlen, Arnoldus, 112–13
Van Swol, Christoffel, 215
Veldcornets (district constables), 157
victualling stations, 173
VOC (*Verenigde Oostindische Compagnie*), *see also* under Dutch East India Company
  categorization of people, 90–92
  Charter, 42–43, 51–55, 68, 283
  communication and administration, 64n31, 64–66
  Enkhuizen Chamber, 224
  government and law structures, 66–70
  imperial power, 55, 55n13
  slavery, 81–83
VOC-Khoekhoe relations, 158–64

Wagenaer, Zacharias, 142, 147
Walling, Christoffel, 215
war, right to wage, 53
wealth, divisions of, 165
West India Company, 21–22

whipping (punishment), 112–13, 115
William V (Dutch *Stadhouder*), 300
William VI, Prince, 300
wine production, 131, 165
Wirjakusuma (son of Raden Mas Kreti), 228–30
women
  convicts, 261
  and exile, 211
  slaves, 19, 149, 242, 264
women's prison (*Spinhuis*), 150

Yudhoyono, Susilo Bambang, 2, 3
Yusuf, Shaykh (Tajul Khalwati), 1, 2, 3, 4, 23, 45, 194, 199–212
  students, 202, 202n75
  religious writings, 200, 200n68, 200n70

Zamorin of Malabar, 62
Zheng Chenggong, 62
Zwaardecroon, Hendrick, 190, 217